TERENCE DAVIES
SCREENPLAYS

Distant Voices, Still Lives (1988): Terence Davies on set. (BFI National Archive)

TERENCE DAVIES SCREENPLAYS

VOLUME I: AUTOBIOGRAPHY AND BIOGRAPHY

Edited by James Dowling

THE BRITISH FILM INSTITUTE
Bloomsbury Publishing Plc
50 Bedford Square, London, WC1B 3DP, UK
1359 Broadway, New York, NY 10018, USA
29 Earlsfort Terrace, Dublin 2, Ireland

BLOOMSBURY is a trademark of Bloomsbury Publishing plc

First published in Great Britain 2025 by Bloomsbury
on behalf of the
British Film Institute
21 Stephen Street, London W1T 1LN
www.bfi.org.uk

The BFI is a cultural charity, a National Lottery distributor, and the UK's lead organisation for film and the moving image. We believe society needs stories. Film, television and the moving image bring them to life, helping us to connect and understand each other better. We share the stories of yesterday, search for the stories of today, and shape the stories of tomorrow.

Copyright © Foreword Ben Roberts 2025; © Preface James Dowling 2025; © Introduction Lillian Crawford 2025; © Interview, pp. 41–50 © Guardian News and Media, 2025.
Copyright © Individual screenplays The Terence Davies Estate 1976, 1980, 1983, 1988, 1992, 2008, 2016, 2021

The authors have asserted their right under the Copyright, Designs and Patents Act, 1988, to be identified as author of this work.

Cover design: Louise Dugdale
Cover image: *Distant Voices, Still Lives* (1988) Courtesy BFI/CHANNEL FOUR FILMS/Z.D.F. Ronald Grant/Mary Evans

All rights reserved. No part of this publication may be: i) reproduced or transmitted in any form, electronic or mechanical, including photocopying, recording or by means of any information storage or retrieval system without prior permission in writing from the publishers; or ii) used or reproduced in any way for the training, development or operation of artificial intelligence (AI) technologies, including generative AI technologies. The rights holders expressly reserve this publication from the text and data mining exception as per Article 4(3) of the Digital Single Market Directive (EU) 2019/790

Bloomsbury Publishing Plc does not have any control over, or responsibility for, any third-party websites referred to or in this book. All internet addresses given in this book were correct at the time of going to press. The author and publisher regret any inconvenience caused if addresses have changed or sites have ceased to exist, but can accept no responsibility for any such changes.

For product safety related questions contact productsafety@bloomsbury.com.

A catalogue record for this book is available from the British Library.

ISBN: HB: 9781350559455
      PB: 9781350559448
      ePDF: 9781350559479
      eBook: 9781350559462

Designed and typeset by Tom Cabot/Ketchup
Printed and bound in Great Britain by Bell and Bain Ltd, Glasgow

To find out more about our authors and books visit www.bloomsbury.com and sign up for our newsletters.

ACKNOWLEDGEMENTS

Heartfelt thanks to Jason Wood, Ben Roberts and the British Film Institute for their generous support of this publication.

Interview with Terence Davies by Jason Wood from *The Guardian*, 28th October 2008. Reproduced by kind permission of and © Guardian News and Media, 2025.

Quotations from 'Burnt Norton' and 'East Coker' by T. S. Eliot from *Collected Poems 1909–1962*, © T. S. Eliot, 1963 (London: Faber & Faber, 2002) reproduced by kind permission of Faber & Faber Ltd and HarperCollins Publishers.

CONTENTS

Foreword by Ben Roberts 7
Editor's Preface by James Dowling 11
Introduction by Lillian Crawford 15
Interview with Terence Davies by Jason Wood 49

THE SCREENPLAYS

AUTOBIOGRAPHY

The Terence Davies Trilogy
    Part I: *Children* (1976) 63
    Part II: *Madonna and Child* (1980) 89
    Part III: *Death and Transfiguration* (1983) 109

Distant Voices, Still Lives (1988) 133

The Long Day Closes (1992) 195

Of Time and the City (2008) 247

BIOGRAPHY – THE POETS

A Quiet Passion (2016) (Emily Dickinson) 279

Benediction (2021) (Siegfried Sassoon) 381

The Contributors 512

FOREWORD

Ben Roberts

I was introduced to Terence Davies in 1992, aged 17, while watching Barry Norman's *Film* programme on BBC One. It was always scheduled at an unreasonably late hour, so I would set the video to record it, as they usually showed an early preview or trailer of a major new film.

This episode featured a report from the set of a new British film called *The Long Day Closes* – the location was the Tatler News Theatre in Liverpool – where the director and his crew were shooting a scene featuring the lead character, a young boy called Bud, at the movies. The item featured another more unusual shot being set up: a line of apples on strings dropping into frame in front of Bud's happy face.

I was intrigued. Like Bud, I spent my spare time at the local Odeon – and as soon as could, I would get a job as an usher in my local multiplex which came with the perk of free entry to screenings. But I had no experience of impressionistic cinema to this point. The cinemas in Coventry screened mostly new films from Hollywood, the films were diverting and exciting, but straightforward, nothing you would consider artistic. The nearest I had gotten to art cinema was David Lynch's *Twin Peaks*, which had screened on BBC2 – I had been obsessed not just with the plotlines but the mood that Lynch had created.

While David Lynch played with dreams, Terence Davies was recreating memories. There was a nostalgic glow to the photography, and the director talked about his film and his characters in an intensely personal way that was unlike other filmmakers I'd seen on TV or read about in mainstream film magazines. On another level, I recognised *myself* in both the boy, Bud, and the filmmaker. I didn't yet identify as gay, but there was something queer and coded that struck a chord.

Opposite: *The Long Day Closes* (1992): Leigh McCormack as Bud. (BFI National Archive)

It wouldn't be true to say that I searched down Terence Davies' films with zeal. In 1993, in Coventry, it wasn't easy to access film. Besides, this was also only his second feature film, and I realise now that he only made three more films – *The Neon Bible* (1995), *The House of Mirth* (2000), and *Of Time and the City* (2008) – before I met him in a professional capacity on *The Deep Blue Sea* (2011).

★ ★ ★

My first meeting with Terence Davies didn't go as I had hoped, but how I could have predicted.

It was 2011, and I was running a young film sales company called Protagonist Pictures. Putting together the money for an independent film is like completing a jigsaw puzzle, and my job was to find film projects – often still at script stage – and sell the rights country-by-country to international film distributors for an upfront advance against the proceeds.

These deals provided critical income or security to the film's financiers and lenders. Much of this business takes place in markets (trade fairs) that run alongside major international festivals in Berlin, Cannes, and Toronto. It can be a desperate by-whatever-means-necessary business, and one that you tend to protect the filmmaker from experiencing. Terence had enjoyed a career resurgence with his archival documentary film *Of Time and the City* and his new project – an adaptation of Terence Rattigan's *The Deep Blue Sea* – had been financed by Film4 and the BFI. Although my company was part-owned by Film4's parent Channel 4, we had to pitch to win Film4 projects and I leapt at the chance to work on one of his films.

We won the rights to represent the film, and we were getting ready to launch international sales for it in Berlin in February. The film was in post-production so we had access to images, and one of our most important jobs was to produce a poster. I was pleased with the design, a simple shot of lead actors Rachel Weisz and Tom Hiddleston at a window, untreated and presented with a simple title style.

We met Terence at the offices of the film's UK distributor Artificial Eye to show him the artwork. He hated it, specifically the title treatment which he found so completely wrong that he turned red with anger and raged to the point of tears. The meeting was over, and a near 20-year build up to this meeting with one of my heroes collapsed in less than five minutes.

I learned several things. That every detail mattered to Terence, and of course I was stupid not to realise that he would consider a title font to be fundamental. I also learnt that Terence operated across a broad emotional range – we would go on to have friendlier meetings.

★ ★ ★

Not long after the release of *The Deep Blue Sea*, I left Protagonist for a job at the BFI, to manage the BFI's National Lottery investments in film development and production.

The BFI had taken over the functions of the recently abolished UK Film Council and resumed a film funding role that dated back to the 1960s. The BFI had a long history with Terence. He left Coventry School of Drama in 1971 when the BFI gave him a grant to produce his first short film, *Children* and in 1983 supported the concluding film in his trilogy, *Death and Transfiguration*. The BFI Production Board later co-financed *Distant Voices, Still Lives* in 1998 and *The Long Day Closes* in 1992.

For Terence, money and the gatekeepers of money were a source of endless frustration. In 2014, his latest film – a long-gestating adaptation of Lewis Grassic Gibbon's *Sunset Song* – was teetering near to collapse, and under pressure we increased our BFI grant to ensure the film made it into production in New Zealand (which was doubling for Scotland in order to access a local tax credit).

By the time of *Sunset Song*'s world première at the Toronto International Film Festival, Terence and I had formed an amicable relationship. I was deeply respectful of him as a filmmaker, and he was thankful for the renewed support of the BFI, which he still considered to be a paternalistic commissioning institution even though things were now quite different. I was sat next to Terence at a celebratory lunch in a Chinese restaurant the day after the film's première. We talked about what he planned to do next. He said that he had a number of films he wanted to make, but it would depend where he could get the money. It was the centenary of WWI, and I said that I thought he would make a fantastic film about the great war poets, Siegfried Sassoon and Wilfred Owen. The poetry, the melancholy, the devastation and loss of the war. I didn't say it, but I had also been thinking he should make a film that dealt more overtly with gay romantic love and sex. I felt that other than his early autobiographical films, this was a missing piece of his work, despite his trying to get several more explicitly gay films made.

In a moment he was reciting Wilfred Owen's 'Dulce et Decorum Est' in its entirety to the tables of festival guests.

Within a year he had delivered a draft of *Benediction*. I reminded him several times that the BFI no longer commissioned work as the Production Board once did, that his producers would have to apply to us for money and there was no guarantee that he would get it. However, he continued to treat the project as an assignment from the BFI, even though he was customarily dismissive of script notes. Ultimately, we did support the film into production and whilst there was no expectation of its being Terence's last feature, I felt the parallels in Siegfried Sassoon looking back on his life with a combination of nostalgia and sadness.

I'm grateful that the film gave me an opportunity to interview Terence about his career onstage at the BFI, and when the film premièred at the BFI London Film Festival he was glowing from the response. I watched Mike Leigh give him a great hug, and he was surrounded by devotees in the corridors outside NFT1.

★ ★ ★

I didn't have the chance to see him again before he passed away. I had a call from his producer to tell me he was terminally ill, and suggest that perhaps I might have the chance to make it down to the house to visit. We both felt he would appreciate a visit from the Director of the BFI, to honour his career and pay him due respect, but sadly he died sooner than we expected.

I remember Terence as someone who was tortured by the challenges of making his films, by finding the money, and by all the projects he didn't get to realise (he dreamt of making Sondheim's *Follies*), but he remained uncompromising and each of his films contain extraordinary moments of cinema.

A true hero of mine, and what an honour it was to know him and support his work.

PREFACE

James Dowling

'If you bring forth what is within you, what you bring forth will save you. If you do not bring forth what is within you, what you do not bring forth will destroy you.'

The Gospel, according to Thomas

This quotation appears on the first page of James Hollis's book about mid-life crisis, *The Middle Passage: From Misery to Meaning* (1993) which I found on Terence's bookshelves shortly after his death in October 2023. The hand-written inscription on the inside page indicates that the slim volume was a gift (or a never returned borrow) from his friend, the actor Jane Lapotaire, in October 1993. It is well thumbed, has many corners of pages turned down and is annotated throughout with asterisks and Terence's characteristically neat under-linings in blue ink. The book poses the question: 'Who am I apart from my history?' It is tempting to surmise that the book offered a meaningful framework for introspection for Terence at this time in his life, aged 48, poised between the release of *The Long Day Closes* in 1992 and *The Neon Bible* in 1994. For extra vivid emphasis, the quotation stands out on the page in bright pink highlighter pen, perhaps suggesting Terence's acknowledgement of its critical relevance to the links between his own journey of self-exploration and his creative mission. The quotation serves as a perfect summary of his internal battles, creative processes, and the themes that play out within the screenplays included in these two volumes.

Terence was a filmmaker who, by his own admission, stood apart from mainstream cinema. His films, deeply personal and introspective, explore themes of longing, faith, and identity that make them both intimate and universal. Born in Liverpool in 1945, Terence was shaped by a working-class Catholic upbringing, a violent and abusive father, and the awakening of his identity as a gay man in a society that offered little acceptance for such selfhood. These formative experiences influenced his work profoundly, reverberating within him throughout his entire life.

Terence was one of the most singular and poetic voices in cinema. His films – achingly lyrical, exquisitely crafted – stand as testament to the power of cinema to capture memory, time, and the ineffable beauty of everyday life. To read his screenplays is to experience the depth of his artistry on the page: the careful rhythm of his dialogue, the precision of his imagery, the echoes of music and silence that shape his worlds. As we mark what would have been his 80th birthday in 2025, it is fitting that his collected screenplays are being published, offering audiences, filmmakers, and scholars a new way to engage with his legacy.

Terence once said, 'Art doesn't change anything, except the way we look at things'. His films – and these screenplays – do precisely that. They offer us a new way of seeing, hearing, feeling, and remembering. They allow us to glimpse the world through his eyes, and in doing so, perhaps come to understand our own memories, our own longings, just a little more clearly.

For many, Terence's work is synonymous with nostalgia, but his films do not simply yearn for the past – they interrogate it with honesty, battle with its ghosts, and uncover both its beauty and its pains. In Terence's films, as in his life, memory is never just a source of comfort, it is something to be wrestled with, something that shapes identity and lingers across time. Even in the closing days of his life, Terence returned to the bittersweet memories of his childhood to ask: 'What was the point of all that pain?'

2025 will be a pivotal moment for the continued and evolving appreciation of Terence's work and its enduring influence. In addition to this collection, his novel *Hallelujah Now* (1984) will be republished, accompanied by a selection of his poetry. The year also sees the establishment of the Terence Davies Archive at Edge Hill University, a significant step in preserving and deepening our understanding of his artistic contributions. Meanwhile, a major retrospective mounted by the British Film Institute (BFI) will showcase his films to audiences both familiar and new.

EDITOR'S PREFACE

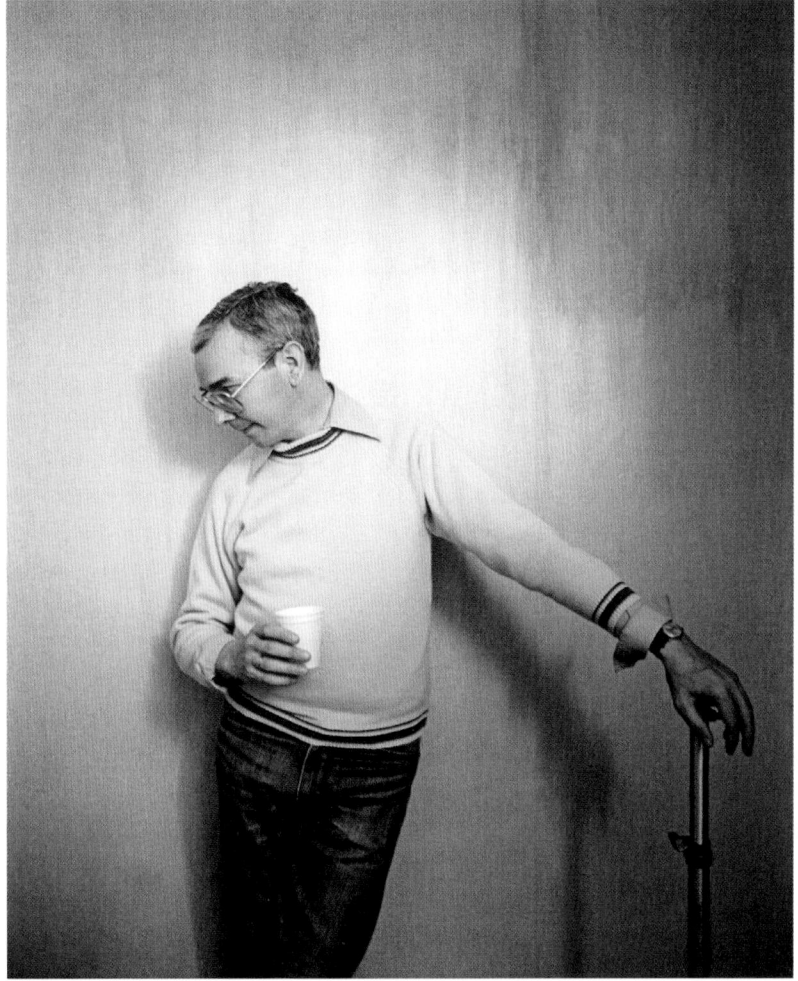

Terence Davies on the set of *Distant Voices, Still Lives* (1988). (BFI National Archive)

These projects together will help shape the narratives around Terence's work for generations to come, further solidifying his place as one of world cinema's most important filmmakers.

The screenplays included in these volumes represent Terence's cinematic output – those projects that evolved from the spark of an initial idea to a fully formed script that then made it through the labyrinth of funding rounds and production development to become what we now know as the

Terence Davies canon. Yet Terence leaves behind an extensive archive of scripts that did not reach the screen, as well as novellas and short stories that were never published, and boxes of poetry that, as yet, remain unread. This extensive body of work reveals a literary mind that was never still, ceaselessly working, remembering, dreaming, and re-imagining. It is now the work of the Terence Davies Estate over the years to come to bring this unseen material into the public consciousness. By doing so, I hope we can provide further fresh insights that will not only enrich our understanding of Terence's cinematic vision but will also reveal new dimensions of his voice beyond the screen.

In bringing together these screenplays I am indebted to a dedicated team of Terence film fans who have made this project possible: Rebecca Barden at Bloomsbury; Tom Cabot at Ketchup Productions; and Dan Copley and Sophie Smith at the Terence Davies Archive at Edge Hill University. My thanks also to the BFI for providing access to film stills and behind the scenes photos; to Ben Roberts and Lillian Crawford for their newly written essays; and, to Jason Wood for his interview with Terence for *The Guardian*. I am also deeply grateful to the many producers of Terence's films for allowing the publication of the text of the screenplays. And to John Taylor, Terence's long-standing manager, colleague, and friend, and co-representative with me of the Terence Davies Estate – thanks for always being there through this journey.

THE POETRY OF THE ORDINARY

Lillian Crawford

Footfalls echo in the memory
Down the passage which we did not take
Towards the door we never opened
Into the rose-garden. My words echo
Thus, in your mind.
                But to what purpose
Disturbing the dust on a bowl of rose-leaves
I do not know.
            Other echoes
Inhabit the garden. Shall we follow?[1]

      'Burnt Norton', T. S. Eliot, 1936

And now the purple dusk of twilight time
Steals across the meadows of my heart
High up in the sky, the little stars climb
Always reminding me that we're apart
You wandered down the lane and far away
Leaving me a song that will not die
Love is now the stardust of yesterday
The music of the years gone by[2]

   'Stardust', Mitchell Parish (lyrics), 1929

Terence Davies does not describe the opening titles of *The Long Day Closes* in his script. Cast and crew are listed in ornate serifs the colour of yellowed parchment. The names hang adjacent to a silver bowl of roses, several petals having fallen, sepia-toned against what appears to be the stripped wall of a derelict building. Davies does not use them, but no doubt the words of T. S. Eliot in 'Burnt Norton', the first of the *Four Quartets*, inspired the tableau. Poetry that Davies carried with him, revisiting them regularly since he heard Alec Guinness recite them on BBC Radio 3 in 1972. The music, the minuet from Boccherini's *String Quintet in E*, calls to mind Guinness in another guise – as Professor Marcus in the 1955 Ealing Studios black comedy, *The Ladykillers*.

'Mrs Wilberforce? I understand that you have rooms to let.'[3]

The ominous words echo in the abandoned hallway of the house on Kensington Street, Liverpool where Davies grew up. While in *The*

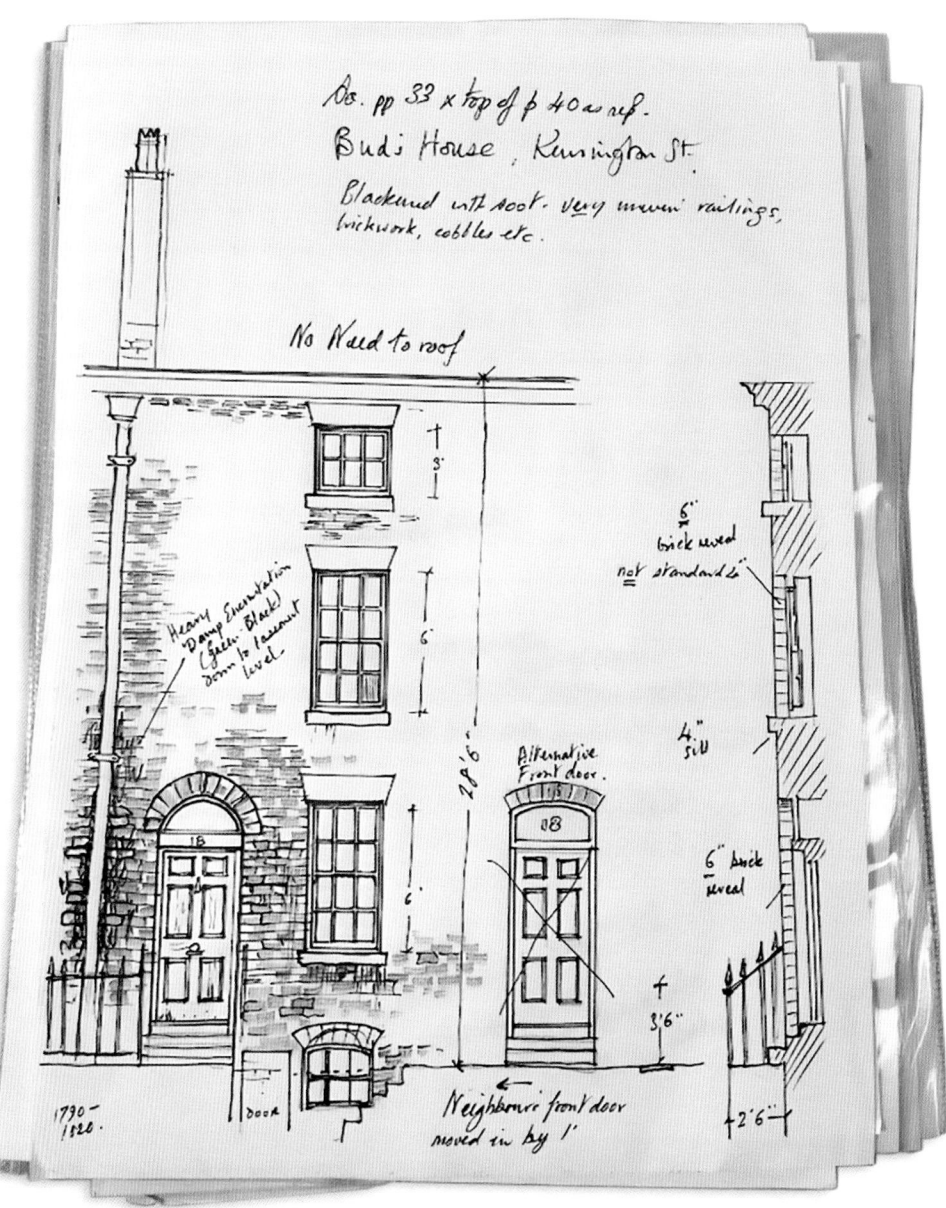

The Long Day Closes (1992): Early set designs for Kensington Street by Christopher Hobbs.
(© The Terence Davies Estate, held by the Terence Davies Archive at Edge Hill University)

INTRODUCTION: THE POETRY OF THE ORDINARY

Ladykillers, which Davies saw aged ten, Mrs Wilberforce's house appears at the end of a well-maintained cul-de-sac, William Rose's description in the shooting script differs:

> Directly below is Mum's two-storey Victorian house. Neighbouring buildings have suffered bomb damage and are uninhabited and Mum's house has clearly been damaged, because its walls on one side are supported by massive wooden struts. It looks lopsided, and yet its roofs and chimneys have such character that the cottage itself has a comic charm.[4]

Louisa Alexandra Wilberforce – a rather regal, political name for one addressed simply as 'Mum'. She is a bastion of a bygone Britain, sheltered from the hellfire of the Luftwaffe while all around her has been destroyed. As the camera at the opening of *The Long Day Closes* moves through Kensington Street in the pouring rain, Mrs Wilberforce has long since passed. She remains as a memory, an echo, just as other voices appear.

> 'A tap, Gossage, I said a tap – you're not introducing a film.'[5]

Margaret Rutherford, staunchly defiant of ever being seen as a little old lady like Mrs Wilberforce, in 1950's *The Happiest Days of Your Life*. While the Rank gong signals black-and-white British esotericism, the 20th Century-Fox fanfare heralds a colourful, epic American picture – a tattered poster for 1953's *The Robe* appears, the first film released in CinemaScope: 'the audience gasped. I can hear it. No one had ever seen a screen that wide.'[6]

> Between joy and consolation,
> no easy path ... some flights of fancy,
> some colour, (glorious old Hollywood),
> small comic England (black and white).[7]

The rain is continuous. Nat King Cole sings 'Stardust'. A magic wand is waved, Davies takes our hand, and leads us over the threshold and into the past.

Houses Live and Die

'We love the place we hate, then hate the place we love. We leave the place we love, then spend a lifetime trying to regain it.'[8] These words from *Of Time and the City* give meaning to the opening of *The Long Day Closes* – it is an acknowledgement that while the past can be resurrected through art, this cannot be achieved in reality. An edition of *The South Bank Show* focusing on Davies was recorded in 1992 in anticipation of the Cannes premiere of *The Long Day Closes*. It begins with narrated documentary footage, a precursor to the feature-length video essay *Of Time and the City* released in 2008, which echoed his earlier words:

> The house stood about here. So many houses, so many names. Names which will mean nothing to you, gentle viewer, but for me are part of the very fabric of my life [...] all, all are gone. The old familiar faces.[9]

In 'East Coker', the second of the *Four Quartets*, Eliot writes that 'Houses live and die'.[10] The poem appears in *Of Time and the City*, which in its most

The Long Day Closes (1992): Helen (Ayse Owens) and Bud (Leigh McCormack).
(The Terence Davies Estate)

INTRODUCTION: THE POETRY OF THE ORDINARY

Distant Voices, Still Lives (1988): Mother (Freda Dowie), Tony (Dean Williams), Eileen (Angela Walsh) and Maisie (Lorraine Ashbourne). (BFI National Archive)

affecting montage shows houses being knocked down and new roads and tower blocks appearing in their place soundtracked by Peggy Lee singing 'The Folks Who Live on the Hill'. 'In my beginning is my end', Davies recites from Eliot. Looking at the Liverpool of today superimposed over the Liverpool of yesterday, he sighs: 'And now I am an alien in my own land.'[11]

> There is a time for the evening under starlight,
> A time for the evening under lamplight
> (The evening with the photograph album).[12]

Images recur throughout Davies's films. A character framed by a window as they look out. Couples and families gathered as if being photographed. Snapshots, tableaux, arranged neatly but perhaps out of order. Was the wedding then, or did it happen later? Davies's scripts read in this way– fragments put to paper, and then rearranged in the edit to create a flow. Not to impose narrative, for to do so would be to create a doctored impression of the past, but to return to memory as it was lived. In *The Long Day Closes*, Bud sits on the stairs, watching the front door. It slides away to reveal a table laid for Christmas in the street, snow falling. Reality

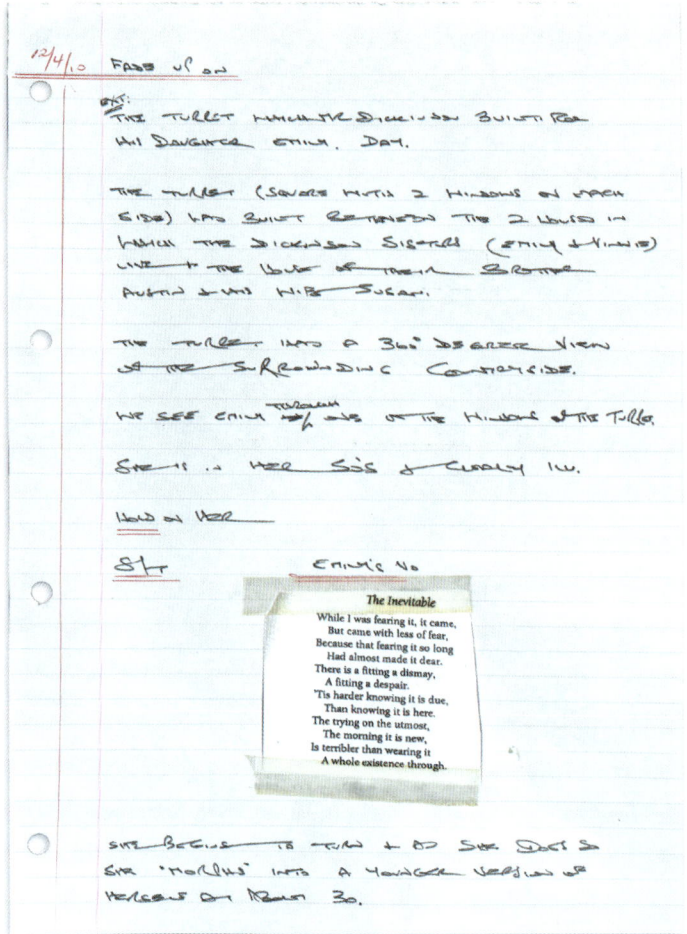

A Quiet Passion (2016): Original opening scene in first draft. (© The Terence Davies Estate, held by the Terence Davies Archive at Edge Hill University)

gives way to fantasy. We project onto photographs the stories and lives of the people in them – in *A Quiet Passion*, Emily Dickinson and her family morph into their older selves before our eyes while posing for their daguerreotypes to be taken as the camera tracks towards them. The tiny image of Emily, aged 17, is pointed out in Davies's script to be the only known picture of her to exist. Davies's imagination conjures the rest.

What appears small or insignificant to other filmmakers has great significance to Davies. On *The South Bank Show*, Davies told Melvyn

INTRODUCTION: THE POETRY OF THE ORDINARY

Bragg that he was interested in 'the poetry of the ordinary'. Most people do not experience Hollywood car chases or mass murder, but what is enormous is instead marriage, birth, death, moving house – 'We all share that.'[13] Emily expresses this sentiment in *A Quiet Passion*: 'give me something pressed from truth and that is poetry.'[14] From the stairs, upon which Bud conjures his family's Christmas in *The Long Day Closes*, Davies could see the rug on the hallway floor – a pattern which transformed throughout the year depending on the light coming through the glass of the door. '*Hold on floor*' reads the script, but the shot holds for what feels like forever, as the orchestral rhapsody *A Shropshire Lad* by George Butterworth is heard.[15] Poetry out of carpet – Davies recites A. E. Houseman in *Of Time and the City*:

> That is the land of lost content,
> I see it shining plain,
> The happy highways where I went
> And cannot come again.[16]

In his note at the beginning of the script for *Distant Voices, Still Lives*, Davies wrote, 'As in painting, the drama lies not so much in the bowl of fruit or the vase of flowers but the ways in which these objects are perceived – in effect, stasis as drama.'[17] What may read as incidental detail in the script becomes in front of Davies's camera the centre of the universe. It is a purer way to live to seek poetry in the ordinary. It is evident in the cadences and rhythms of the Shipping Forecast, which began the schedule of broadcasting each day on the BBC Home Service. It is the first sound we hear in *Distant Voices*: 'Faroes, Cromarty, Forth, Tyne …'[18] Mother opens the door to get the milk. Then she calls up the stairs to her children to 'get your skates on!' It is a choreographed routine, replete with British colloquialism, harked back to in *Benediction* when Siegfried Sassoon says to his wife, Hester, 'Come on! You'll have to get your skates on and I'll have to get my glad rags out of mothballs.'[19] Siegfried laughs at the description of Eliot as, 'Poor old Tom who sits there ironically analysing an empty sardine tin.'[20] Variations on a theme.

'As soon as you hear the delivery of announcers at the BBC in the 50s, you're put back to the 50s [sic]. It's like smell.'[21] Perhaps the best way to define Davies's mode of reminiscence is not in the crumbs of a madeleine, but another Proustian morsel. In 'On Reading', Proust recalls the days spent in childhood with a favourite book. It is not necessarily the contents of the book that one remembers, but the associated comings and goings of life experienced while reading the book:

> if, today, we happen to leaf through the pages of these books of the past, it is only because they are the sole calendars we have left of those bygone days, and we turn their pages in the hope of seeing reflected there the houses and lakes which are no more.[22]

This memory archaeology drives Davies's autobiographical films. They came from more than a reason, 'a deep *need* to do so in order to come to terms with my family's history and suffering, to make sense of the past and to explore my own personal terrors, both mental and spiritual.'[23] *Death and Transfiguration*, the final part of Davies's *Trilogy*, is autobiographical in so far as it is a forward projection of fear – the imagined death of the mother, and his own lonely passing. Layers of memory bubble up and clash together without the softer ebb and flow of *Distant Voices, Still Lives* or *The Long Day Closes* – pub songs and Christmas carols overlap, ending with the sound of the elderly Robert Tucker's Cheyne–Stokes breathing brought to rest by his mother singing 'If You Were the Only Boy in the World'. If when I die my whole life will flash before my eyes, what is it that I will see?

Davies's scripts are episodic, sometimes consisting of isolated scenes only a few lines long, others several pages rich with dialogue and description. Reading them alongside the films has one flicking the pages forwards and backwards as the scenes seldom play out in the written chronology. The collage brings 'order to the chaos of life', to help make sense of it.[24] To put the childhood book back on the shelf, and allow it to gather dust.

The Images Must Live

In the introduction to *A Modest Pageant*, the published version of his first five screenplays, Davies explained his writing process with remarkable clarity and methodology. He made notes for between ten and twelve months, including certain sequences which appeared fully formed in his imagination.

INTRODUCTION: THE POETRY OF THE ORDINARY

Children (1976): Terence Davies on set. (BFI National Archive)

This formed a narrative, chiselled down into the first draft: 'In this draft every track, pan, dissolve, piece of music and every bit of dialogue appears.' Left to percolate for four to six weeks, Davies then wrote a second, final, draft which became the shooting script ('I *never* do a storyboard'). From this process, Davies could hold the entire film in his mind.[25]

There is no budgetary consideration in the script, and even with his smaller budgets his vision was realised in the finished film. Some of the music Davies wanted to use in *Children* proved too costly, replacing Shostakovich's eighth symphony with an original cor anglais piece for the scene in which Tucker and his mother ride a bus, and omitting Peggy Lee's 'The Folks Who Live on the Hill'. The film was produced in 1976 for only £8,500, awarded by the British Film Institute (BFI) Production Board on the proviso that Davies directed it himself. Each film welcomed a larger budget than the last, completing *Madonna and Child* as his student project at the National Film School in London in 1980, and

INTRODUCTION: THE POETRY OF THE ORDINARY

Death and Transfiguration in 1983 with financing from the BFI and the Greater London Arts Association. Davies found that the value of outlining every detail in his scripts was to allow money to be allocated precisely, without the risk of overspending or missing deadlines.

Detail also afforded Davies creative control. When producers complained about a scene, he could say it was in the script they approved, and therefore that is what they got. No doubt it is Davies's own frustrations with attempts to alter his visual poetry which is channelled by Emily when she argues with Samuel Bowles about the editing of her writing in *A Quiet Passion*. Bowles explains, 'I was merely trying to make your meaning clearer to my readers.' To which Emily responds, 'Clarity is one thing sir. Obviousness quite another. The only person qualified to interfere with a poet's work is the poet herself. From anyone else it feels like an attack.'[26] The script was tightly guarded. Actors only received their copy a fortnight before shooting, instructed to read it twice – once for sense, once for character. Rehearsal was brief, between 15 and 20 minutes, and each scene was captured in fewer than ten takes, preferably fewer than five. This is not to say that Davies was entirely dictatorial in his approach – some things happen in the moment, or change in the process of filming. 'I do believe in collaboration, but the film *must* have a central vision and that vision must be the director's.'[27]

Some of the most beautiful moments in Davies's films could not be planned. In the script for *Children*, Davies describes a montage of shots to create Tucker's perspective of his father's funeral. In the film, as the coffin is taken out, Tucker stands in the door of the house with his mother. The hearse is stationary in the foreground, and as the coffin slides across the frame, it appears to erase the mourners watching as the house opposite appears reflected in the now-dark window. It is a visual effect difficult to describe – Davies reflected that while writing, 'what you don't see in your mind is it happened to be a bright day, there's reflections in the hearse from the windows opposite, and of course it makes it seem completely out of time and surreal'.[28] This unpredictable nature of the footage meant that Davies never referred back to the script during the edit. 'The images *must* live, the images must *reveal* the story.'[29] It is a compilation process based on instinct, musicality, and sensibility.

Opposite: *Children* (1976): Tucker (Phillip Mawdsley) and Mother (Val Lilley) in mourning.

Modes That Seemed Cacophonous And Queer

'Any real piece of cinema tells you the story by what it reveals and the juxtaposition of images, and the ambiguities which arise between those juxtapositions.'[30] This, to Davies, is what disambiguates television or theatre from cinema – everything is subtext. Meaning is contained not in words but in reference and associated imagery. Some of those references have held a legacy, for example any fan of British cinema will instantly connect Boccherini to *The Ladykillers* in the opening credits. But even that has a sell-by date, a time when context or explanation will be required. *O tempora, o mores!* Things come and go, sometimes seeming dated, at others enjoying a revival. Davies's films shift in meaning, and their relationship to the present, each time they are screened. Time past and time future.

Davies's films are not, however, nostalgia pieces. There is fondness, even yearning for the world of yesterday, but it is melancholic. The joy and lightness of popular music is frequently played over disturbing images, creating a frisson which at times can be totally overwhelming. In *Distant Voices*, after smiling pub patrons sing 'If You Knew Suzie', there is a cut to Tony holding Eileen as she cries and says she wants her Dad. 'In the Bleak Mid-winter', the Holst setting of Christina Rossetti's 'A Christmas Carol', comes in as the camera tracks into the darkness of the street, moving into a church as the family light candles before arriving at Father decorating a small Christmas tree. There are subtle differences in the description of the

Distant Voices, Still Lives (1988): Tony (Dean Williams) and Rose (Antonia Mallen).

INTRODUCTION: THE POETRY OF THE ORDINARY

Terence Davies, in playful mood on the set of *Distant Voices, Still Lives* (1988).

sequence in the script compared to the finished film – mostly Davies has stripped back the layers to something simpler, such as here removing the children reciting a prayer in voiceover. The contrast comes at the end of the sequence, when silence falls and the Father pulls off the tablecloth with the Christmas dinner in a fury and yells at Mother to clean it up. The serenity of the carol is broken by the sudden violence, an act which Davies's father performed every Christmas.

By contrast to the organic flow of the carol sequence, *Still Lives* features a carefully choreographed use of the title song from the 1955 film *Love Is a Many-Splendored Thing*. This is CinemaScope, Deluxe Color, Jennifer Jones, William Holden… Davies discovered his paradise at the movies when his sister took him to see *Singin' in the Rain* in 1952. Umbrellas in the rain appear frequently in Davies's filmography; here the camera opens on a canopy of umbrellas outside the Gaumont Cinema, as the song pulls the camera inside towards Maisie and Eileen 'weeping profusely'. Then two men crash through a glass roof in slow motion as the song continues.

Real-life tragedy depicted with all the sensationalism of Hollywood melodrama. As Maisie runs down the hospital corridor, we hear her say, 'When he dies and she ran up that hill – I thought I was going to cry my eyes out.'[31] Memories, music, and movies merge in the mind.

Davies gives levity to light entertainment, lending it a camp sensibility. On *The South Bank Show* Davies said, 'I desperately wanted to be Doris Day, and still do.' 'Do you practise?' replied Bragg. 'Well, only at home with the windows closed!' Cut to Day's smiling face filling the frame, zooming out to reveal Davies lip syncing to 'I'm Not at All in Love' from 1957's *The Pajama Game*.[32] It is a startlingly extroverted moment for Davies. While his double, Bud, in *The Long Day Closes* spends much of the film observing others, there is a moment when he performs 'A Couple of Swells' from 1948's *Easter Parade* with Helen in front of their family and friends. It is a repressed camp at odds with the apparent bleakness of Davies's cinema. Davies's reverence for Day is aligned with his all-consuming love for his mother in the opening sequence of *Death and Transfiguration*, describing in great detail in the script a montage of Tucker's mother's funeral. In the original draft, the sequence is jarringly set to 'The Surrey with the Fringe on Top' from *Oklahoma!*, but in the final film it is soundtracked by Day singing 'It All Depends on You'. The tension between Day's romantic strains and the black-and-white images of the coffin captures the melancholy of grief, of happy memory converging with tragic ending.

The most powerful transformation of kitsch into art comes near the end of *The Long Day Closes*. Bud watches his siblings ride away on bicycles as he begins to swing on an iron railing over the staircase descending from the street to the basement. Shot directly overhead, the voice of Debbie Reynolds emerges singing 'Tammy', the theme from her 1957 picture *Tammy and the Bachelor*, saccharine and cutesy:

> I hear the cottonwoods whisperin' above
> Tammy, Tammy, Tammy's in love
> The old hootie owl hootie-hoo's to the dove
> Tammy, Tammy, Tammy's in love[33]

The camera tracks left, dissolving to the cinema filled with cigarette smoke caught in the white projector beam; to the church during Mass; to Bud's classroom as the children stand and move out in regimentation.

INTRODUCTION: THE POETRY OF THE ORDINARY

Three worlds, all alike, pointing towards some great teacher. It is blasphemous, and it is honest. Davies could have played a hymn or a symphony over these images, but it was 'Tammy' which pierced his heart.

'There is a school of thought that regards musical theatre as a second rate means of expression.'[34] So says Siegfried to Ivor Novello in *Benediction*, but Davies holds no such snobbery. As Bentham wrote, push-pin is as good as poetry. Davies makes no delineation between high and low art, treating the Hollywood musical or the pub song with equal reverence to the symphonies Sibelius or Mahler. There is a shift towards an increased use of classical music, however, in Davies's later films – in *Of Time and the City* he explains:

> After the rise of rock and roll, my interest in popular music waned and as it declined, my love of classical music increased, Sibelius, Shostakovich, and my beloved Bruckner. Then in my overwrought adolescent state of mind, I discovered Mahler, and responded completely to his every overwrought note.[35]

Each film is constructed like a symphony. There are movements, with their own refrain, and leitmotifs which emerge, disappear, and later return. 'Notes and chords on their own don't mean anything. They only mean something when you juxtapose them with something else.'[36] There is beauty in dissonance – *Benediction* opens with the riot-inspiring *Le Sacre du printemps* by Stravinsky described by Sassoon in 'Concert Interpretation' as having 'modes that seemed cacophonous and queer', but then:

> Bassoons begin… Sonority envelopes
> Our auditory innocence; and brings
> To me, I must admit, some drift of things
> Omnific, seminal, and adolescent…[37]

That dissonance is seminal in Davies's imagination. Sometimes Davies allows his symphonies to reach resolution – *Of Time and the City* ends with the earth-shattering climax of Mahler's 'Resurrection', mirroring the ending of his poetic interludes in *The South Bank Show* which features the staggered concluding chords of Sibelius's fifth. Siegfried is permitted emotional release at the end of *Benediction*, sobbing on a bench for several minutes as *Fantasia on a Theme of Thomas Tallis* by Vaughan Williams plays. By contrast Emily's death at the close of *A Quiet Passion* merits something altogether dissatisfying – Charles Ives's *The Unanswered Question*, a piece which depicts 'Fighting Answers' growing frustrated and dissonant until they give up. In the script Davies had intended to use Randall Thompson's *Alleluia*, a work for unaccompanied SATB chorus which is not jubilant but rather tragic, taking as inspiration Job's plight: 'The Lord gave and the Lord has taken away. Blessed be the name of the Lord' (Job 1:21).

Davies used 96-frame dissolves, which last for four seconds, to allow the last image to linger over the next. He was inspired by Leonard Bernstein discussing the adagietto from Mahler's fifth symphony, which eventually moves from minor to major: 'we have an inner harmonic so when it comes, you melt because it's what you have been waiting for.'[38]

It was a *man!*

> There's a man goin' 'round takin' names
> He taking my father's name
> And he left my heart in vain[39]

A family portrait. 'I wish me Dad was here', Eileen says to Tony. Pan to Maisie (voiceover): 'I don't. He was a bastard and I bleedin' hated him.' Maisie asks Father if she can go to the dance. '*Cut to shot of* FATHER *from* MAISIE'*s point of view. He picks up a yard brush and turns on her in a fury*'. Cut to Father with the broom as it rises and falls.[40] We never see the actual impact, but it is felt. The art of suggestion; tell, do not show; 'I don't want to watch violence. I had enough of that in my childhood.'[41] *Distant Voices, Still Lives* is constructed through memory by proxy, of stories Davies learned second-hand from his mother, his two eldest sisters, and his brother: 'They talked about my father and the way he had treated them, and their telling of it was so vivid to me that their memories became mine.'[42]

Davies's memory of his father is depicted in *Children*, which invites us to feel horror and joy at the abuser's demise. It took two years for him to die of stomach cancer. Morphine was not given to him until he next needed it, therefore before each injection Davies recalled the man screaming like an animal. The death is not depicted so explicitly in *Distant Voices*; rather it is the silent event which occurs between that first film and its sequel, *Still Lives*. While the two films were released as a single feature, they were written and shot as separate films, two years apart. *Still Lives* is bookended by the birth of Maisie's first child and Tony's wedding, as the memories drift in and out between an extended trip to the pub. Father is never mentioned.

Nor is he mentioned in *The Long Day Closes*. One sequence recalls his presence, in which Bud has a nightmare and two large hands grab his head in bed, waking and screaming, 'It was a man! It was a *man!*'[43] Davies was terrified while his father was alive, with a lingering impact on his ability to discern tension between people: 'I always say: if I've upset you, just come out with it. If you cold-shoulder me, I instantly see him sitting in the corner of the parlour and I'm a seven-year-old again.'[44] There are echoes of Davies's father in *A Quiet Passion* and *Benediction*. A strange, oneiric sequence in the former sees Emily reciting, 'He will mount the stairs at midnight…' as the silhouetted figure of a man moves upstairs to her – it is perhaps a desired lover, 'No ordinary bridegroom he', but the darkness of the man enshrouds him with fear.[45] More explicit trauma plagues Siegfried, visualising a war hospital in his bedroom at Ottoline Morrell's home, and hearing the shell-shocked nightmares of other soldiers at Craiglockhart. 'Why do all the worst terrors come at night?' he asks Dr. Rivers. 'The dark is, I think, like the unconscious… waiting all day so that it can steal over you in the dark.'[46]

Love of and for the mother / Darker pleasures

> Things are mending now
> I see a rainbow blending now
> We'll have a happy ending now
> Taking a chance on love[47]

Ella Fitzgerald's voice plays over one of Davies's most haunting tableaux. 'Why did you marry him, Mam?' 'He was nice, he was a good dancer.'

Close-up of MOTHER'*s face, side view. It is almost unrecognisable – like a boxer's after a particularly vicious fight. She is trying not to cry but clearly every movement is agony. She is polishing the sideboard. Blood trickles down from her nose and mouth and drips on to the sideboard. Pan down to top of sideboard. Blood drips on the surface and* MOTHER *continues slowly to rub the polish and the blood into the surface of the wood.*[48]

It is the most harrowing direction in Davies's scripts – one which horrifies in its attention to detail in writing as much as the image in the film. Davies wrote that *The Long Day Closes* is about 'the all-pervasive, all-enduring power of the love of and for the mother', although this characterises his entire filmography.[49] At the start of *Madonna and Child*, Tucker is sat on a ferry remembering making his mother a cup of tea and taking it to her in bed. The film is constructed as a series of almost wordless snapshots, moving between being at home, and the surreptitious behaviour of queerness. 'But soon darker pleasures. At fifteen, I saw Dirk Bogarde in *Victim*, and discovered something entirely different.'[50]

Madonna and Child frequently cuts away right before and after the moment of touch or intimacy between men. The erotic sequences occur surrounded by enveloping blackness, out of space and time. It is both fantasy and nightmare, where Tucker projects his desires. The elusiveness of sexuality in the film struck Alexander Mackendrick, director of Davies's beloved *The Ladykillers*, who was teaching at the National Film School during Davies's second year. After a screening Mackendrick was asked if it was a gay movie, to which he replied, 'Not at the moment!'[51] Desire is steeped in Catholic guilt – in 2011 Davies reflected, 'Being gay has ruined my life. I hate it. I'll go to my grave hating it.'[52] The tension between the Church and homosexuality is most explicitly staged in a sequence in which the camera moves past the first six Stations of the Cross inside an empty church, while in voiceover Tucker asks to have his genitals tattooed on the phone. Comparison is drawn between Christ's suffering and its masochism with that of queer gratification.

The conversation is extended in Davies's novel *Hallelujah Now*, first published in 1984, revealing that Tucker wants the word 'FUCK' written down the back of his penis and a Swastika on each testicle. Like his scripts, the novel offsets this with a quotation from the Song of Solomon: '*Let him kiss me with the kisses of his mouth,/For thy love is better than wine.*'[53]

The novel is structured, like the *Trilogy*, in three parts: 'Songs for Dead Children', 'Letters to a Friend', and 'The Walk to the Paradise Garden'. In the letters from Robert Tucker's lover, St John, there are strains of romance and promise to be together, which contrast greatly to Robert's narration, which describes the man as physically repulsive and abusive: 'The rest is pain, the rest is ultimate humiliation. And after the panting of his thrusting, grotesque body – the silence drenched in sin.'[54]

Davies attempted a relationship with a woman in 1977 when it was still believed that 'homosexuals' could find the right person and be happy. 'We both knew what the truth was, and it sadly ended.'[55] *Benediction* explores the possibility of feigning heterosexuality through Siegfried's marriage to Hester, and the ultimate sense of dissatisfaction he feels. Yet in the film married life appears no better than Siegfried's years of gay abandon. His relationship with Ivor is depicted in similar terms to the fraught relationship between Robert and St John in *Hallelujah Now*, hanging on despite his apparent distaste for the other man. Davies tried in his early adulthood to go on the gay scene for a couple of months and found that he could not stand 'the sexual venality and the narcissism'.[56] The similarly slimy Stephen Tennant morphs into his older self at a dressing table towards the end of *Benediction*; in the script, as the camera tracks in on him, his self-admiration dissolves into photographs of facially disfigured WWI soldiers. The final sequence is subtler, but equally brimming with disgust.

The Church gave Davies no comfort in his sexuality. 'I felt then that if I prayed and was really good, God would make me like everybody else. Those years when I prayed until my knees bled were awful'[57] Bud's sexual awakening occurs in *The Long Day Closes* when he looks out a window at the appropriately named Smitten's Garage and sees a muscular labourer building a wall. In one of Davies's most complex sequences, which took nine hours to set up and shoot, the camera begins on the right hand of Christ being nailed to the Cross before dollying up and over the body, obscured in darkness like the erotic scenes in the *Trilogy*. The Christ looks at the camera and lets out '*a terrifying human bark*' which sounds like Bud's name. It is the bricklayer from the earlier scene, the ultimate blasphemy, sexual desire for the Messiah. 'Film as an expression of guilt, film as confession'.[58]

Emily Dickinson's sexuality has long been the subject of speculation, especially her relationship with Susan Gilbert; however, it is very subtly played in *A Quiet Passion*. Susan tells Emily that such thoughts of men 'turned me to stone', describing sex with her husband as doing her 'duty'. After Emily says that she has been 'deprived of a... particular... kind of love', Susan observes, 'But in matters of the soul you are rigorous.' 'Rigour is no substitute for happiness', comes the reply of Emily/Terence.[59]

> We outgrow love like other things
> And put it in the drawer,
> 'Till it an antique fashion shows
> Like costumes grandsires wore.[60]

Poems are my solace

Davies was drawn to Sassoon as a subject in *Benediction* initially by his conversion to Catholicism in later life in search of redemption. Perhaps it was the guilt of surviving WWI while others including Rupert Brooke and Wilfred Owen had not. Their deaths gave those poets a legacy and reverence which had been denied of him. It is a sin that Davies confessed to experiencing himself – he had wished that he might win a major prize for his filmmaking, being 'as vain as anybody else', but of course was hateful of pride and arrogance.[61] At the end of the film, George says to his father, 'Most people live for the moment – you live for eternity'. Siegfried compares himself to Eliot, naturally, who had received the Order of Merit and the Nobel Prize. There is a self-awareness to such conversations, as if Davies is having them with himself. 'Why do you hate the modern world father?' 'Because it's younger than I am'.[62]

Emily has a similar conversation with Reverend Wandsworth in *A Quiet Passion*. Like Siegfried, she talks of the possibility of posthumous posterity, although she finds that 'as comfortless as God'. She wrestles with herself – 'But ah, to be wracked by success!'[63] Davies expressed great empathy with this sentiment, his heart going out to Dickinson for not being celebrated in her lifetime, just as it does to Bruckner. Davies identified deeply with Dickinson, more so than Sassoon. 'Poems are my solace for the eternity which surrounds us all', Emily says quietly.[64] Davies's final film, *Passing Time*, is a reading of one of his own poems, written after the death of his sister, Maisie. After mourning her loss, the poem ends with tender resolution:

INTRODUCTION: THE POETRY OF THE ORDINARY

> But echoes of your lovely self
> Will bear us through life's cruel stream
> And if I am to join you there
> Oh what joy your face will bring![65]

Solace in the act of remembering. 'This is my letter to the World / That never wrote to Me –'.[66] Bud looks out of the window at a world which does not understand him. But he too does not understand the world, especially not now, as an adult, returning there to this now-alien land. The end of the script is written out as a poem, directions of imagery intersecting the verses of Arthur Sullivan's setting of Henry Fothergill Chorley's 'The Long Day Closes'. Imagery, like the opening titles, which comes again from Eliot.

The lighted windows dim	And they were behind us, reflected in the pool.
Are fading slowly.	Then a cloud passed, and the pool was empty.
The fire that was so trim	Go, said the bird, for the leaves were full of children,
Now quivers lowly.	Hidden excitedly, containing laughter.
	Go, go, go, said the bird: human kind
Go to the dreamless bed	Cannot bear very much reality.
Where grief reposes;	Time past and time future
Thy book of toil is read,	What might have been and what has been
The long day closes.[67]	Point to one end, which is always present.[68]

(The radio waves are heard from deep space. Fade to black.)

NOTES

1. 'Burnt Norton', in T. S. Eliot, *Collected Poems 1909–1962* (London: Faber and Faber, 2002), p. 177.
2. 'Stardust' (1929), music by Hoagy Carmichael with lyrics by Mitchell Parish, performed by Nat King Cole (1957).
3. Quoted in *The Long Day Closes*, see p. 189, this volume.
4. BFI National Archive, Special Collections, SCR-11052, William Rose, '*The Ladykillers* – Annotated shooting script' (8 April 1955), p. 1.
5. Quoted in *The Long Day Closes*, see p. 189, this volume.
6. Davies interviewed by Sam Wigley, 'Terence Davies on *Distant Voices, Still Lives*, 30 years later', BFI Online (2018). <www.bfi.org.uk/interviews/terence-davies-distant-voices-still-lives-30-years>.
7. *Of Time and the City*, see p. 249, this volume.
8. *Of Time and the City*, see p. 242, this volume.
9. Davies on *The South Bank Show*, London Weekend Television (tx. 5 April 1992).
10. 'East Coker', in Eliot, *Collected Poems 1909–1962* (2002), p. 184.
11. *Of Time and the City*, see p. 265, this volume.
12. 'East Coker', in Eliot, *Collected Poems 1909–1962* (2002), p. 191.
13. *The South Bank Show* (1992), see Note 9.
14. *A Quiet Passion*, see p. 324, this volume.
15. *The Long Day Closes*, see p. 201, this volume.
16. Excerpt from A. E. Houseman, 'A Shropshire Lad', quoted by Davies in *Of Time and the City*, see p. 241, this volume.
17. 'Introduction to *Still Lives*', Terence Davies, *A Modest Pageant* (London: Faber and Faber, 1992), p.103.
18. *Distant Voices*, see p. 128, this volume.
19. *Benediction*, see p. 475, this volume.
20. *Benediction*, see p. 475, this volume.
21. BFI Online (2018). "Terence Davies on *Distant Voices, Still Lives*, 30 years later", interview with Sam Wigley. <www.bfi.org.uk/interviews/terence-davies-distant-voices-still-lives-30-years>.
22. Marcel Proust, 'On Reading'. Translator's preface to *Sesame and Lilies* in Marcel Proust and John Ruskin, *On Reading*, trans. Damion Searls (London: Hesperus Press, 2011), p. 4.
23. 'Author's Introduction', Terence Davies, *A Modest Pageant* (London: Faber and Faber, 1992), p. ix.
24. 'Author's Introduction', Terence Davies, *A Modest Pageant* (London: Faber and Faber, 1992), p. xi.
25. 'Author's Introduction', Terence Davies, *A Modest Pageant* (London: Faber and Faber, 1992), p. x.
26. *A Quiet Passion*, see p. 343, this volume.
27. 'Author's Introduction', Terence Davies, *A Modest Pageant* (London: Faber and Faber, 1992), p. xii.
28. Filmed interview with Davies by Geoff Andrew (2008). <www.youtube.com/watch?v=4JeVDkO4Wnw>.
29. 'Author's Introduction', Terence Davies, *A Modest Pageant* (London: Faber and Faber, 1992), p. xii.
30. *The South Bank Show* (1992), see Note 9.
31. *Still Lives*, see p. 178, this volume.
32. *The South Bank Show* (1992), see Note 9.
33. 'Tammy' (1957), music by Jay Livingston with lyrics by Ray Evans, performed by Debbie Reynolds.
34. *Benediction*, see p. 447, this volume.
35. *Of Time and the City*, see p. 257, this volume.
36. Davies quoted in Wendy Everett, *Terence Davies* (Manchester: Manchester University Press, 2004), p. 204.
37. Siegfried Sassoon, 'Concert Interpretation', quoted in *Benediction*, see p. xxx, this volume.
38. *The South Bank Show* (1992), see Note 9.
39. 'There's A Man Goin' Round Takin' Names', spiritual, performed by Jessye Norman (1979).
40. *Distant Voices*, see p. 131, this volume.

INTRODUCTION: THE POETRY OF THE ORDINARY

41. Davies interviewed in Michael Koresky, *Terence Davies* (Chicago: University of Illinois Press, 2014), p. 127.
42. 'Author's Introduction', Terence Davies, *A Modest Pageant* (London: Faber and Faber, 1992), p. xi.
43. *The Long Day Closes*, see p. 201, this volume.
44. Davies interviewed by Ryan Gilbey, '"I wish I was very good-looking and very stupid": Terence Davies on sex, death and *Benediction*', The Guardian Online (2022). <www.theguardian.com/film/2022/may/20/terence-davies-on-sex-death-and-benediction-siegfried-sassoon>.
45. *A Quiet Passion*, see p. 347, this volume.
46. *Benediction*, see p. 424, this volume.
47. 'Taking A Chance on Love' (1940), music by Vernon Duke with lyrics by John La Touche and Ted Fetter, performed by Ella Fitzgerald.
48. *Distant Voices*, see p. 141, this volume.
49. 'Author's Introduction', Terence Davies, *A Modest Pageant* (London: Faber and Faber, 1992), p. xi.
50. *Of Time and the City*, see p. 247, this volume.
51. *The South Bank Show* (1992), see Note 9.
52. Davies interviewed by Donald Clarke, 'Being Gay Has Ruined My Life (Interview with Terence Davies), *The Irish Times* (25 November 2011). <www.irishtimes.com/culture/film/being-gay-has-ruined-my-life-1.16328>.
53. Terence Davies, *Hallelujah Now* (London: Penguin, 1993), p. 68.
54. Ibid., p. 39.
55. The *Guardian Online* (2022), see Note 44.
56. Ibid.
57. Davies interviewed by Leonard Quart, 'Remembering Liverpool: An Interview with Terence Davies', *Cineaste*, Vol. 34, No. 2 (Spring, 2009). <www.cineaste.com/spring2009/terence-davies-interview>.
58. 'Author's Introduction', Terence Davies, *A Modest Pageant* (London: Faber and Faber, 1992), p. ix.
59. *A Quiet Passion*, see p. 319, this volume.
60. Emily Dickinson, 'We outgrow love like other things', quoted in *A Quiet Passion*, see p. 330, this volume.
61. BFI Online (2018), see Note 21.
62. *Benediction*, see p. 495, this volume.
63. *A Quiet Passion*, see p. 327, this volume.
64. *A Quiet Passion*, see p. 283, this volume.
65. Terence Davies, 'Passing Time' (2023), music by Florencia Di Concilio.
66. Emily Dickinson, 'This is my letter to the World', quoted in *A Quiet Passion*, see p. 370, this volume.
67. 'The Long Day Closes' (1868), music by Arthur Sullivan and lyrics by Henry Fothergill Chorley, performed by Pro Cantione Antiqua.
68. 'Burnt Norton', in Eliot, *Collected Poems 1909–1962* (2002), p. 178.

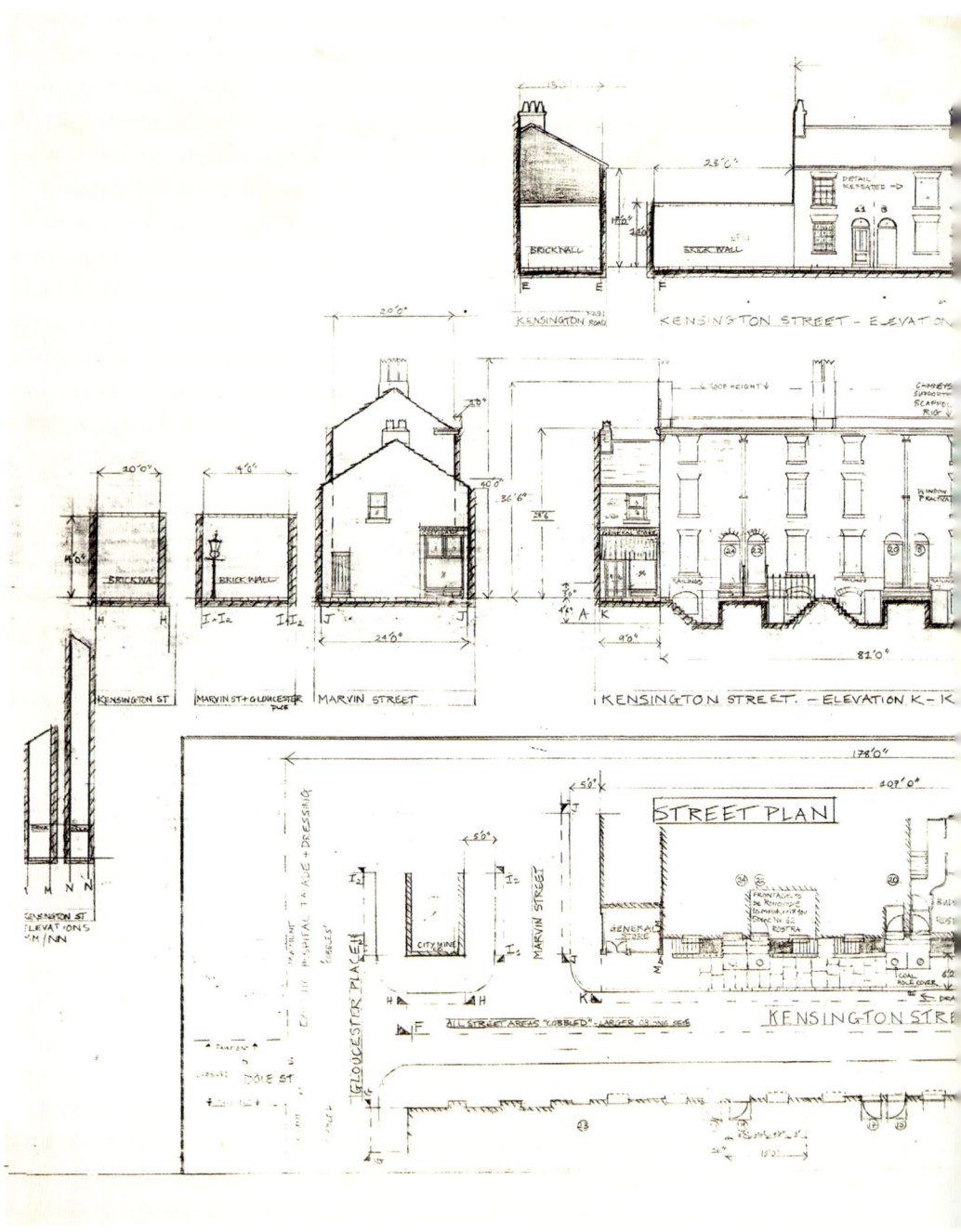

The Long Day Closes (1992): plans for the Kensington Street set, dated 11 January 1991. Designer: Christopher Hobbs. (© The Terence Davies Estate, held by the Terence Davies Archive at Edge Hill University)

ARCHIVAL

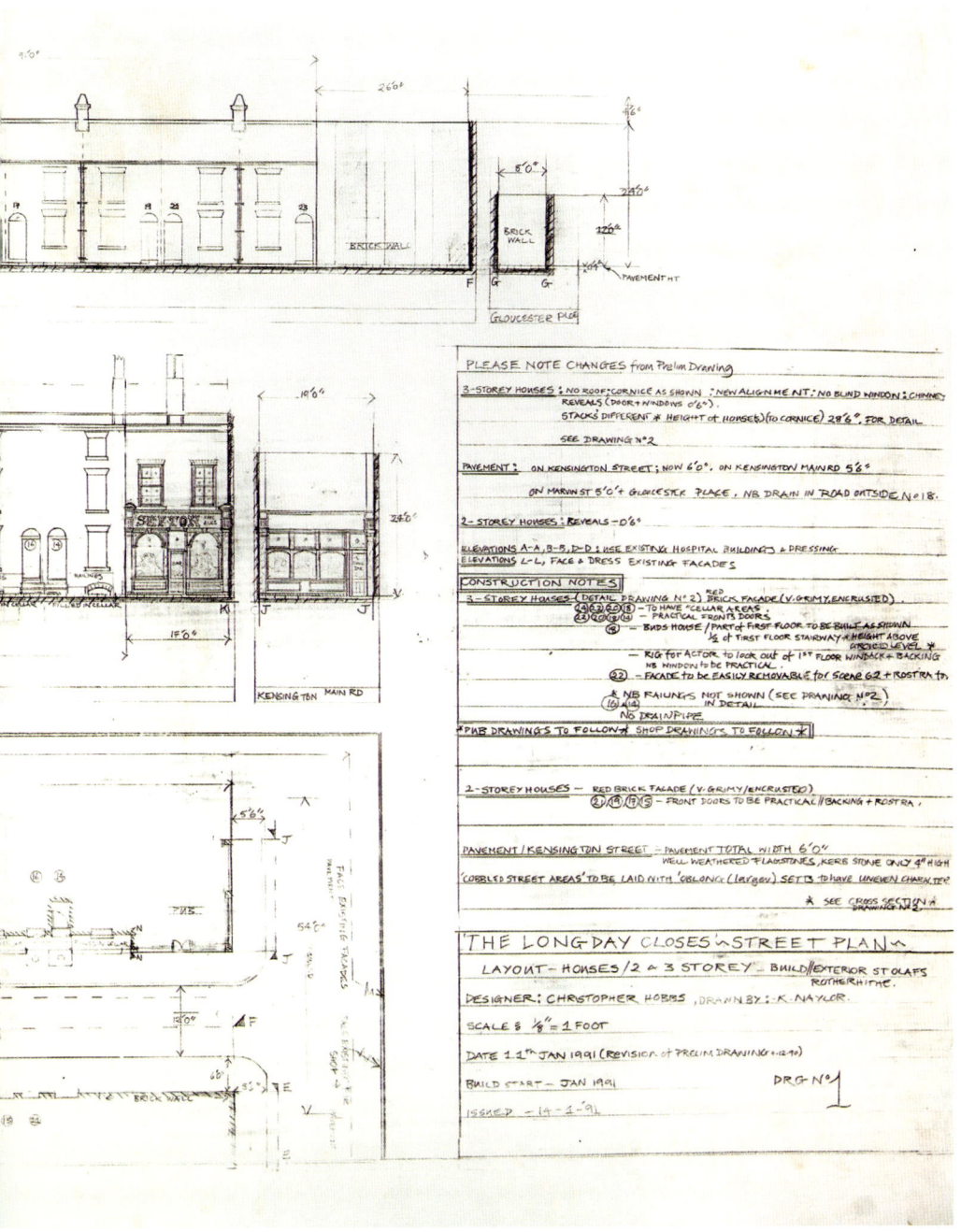

Madonna and Child (1980): First draft. (BFI National Archive)

13.

MANS VOICE OVER :— (CONTINUED)
helluva fuckin' time......I've got a tattoo on me own chopper and it took me three days to get it on.......
.....besides it hurts like fuck.......

TUCKERS VOICE OVER :— (Very desperate) Will you do it?

MANS VOICE OVER :— (Bending a <u>little</u> further) Apart from the time it takes its gotta be as hard as a biscuit.......you'll be wankin' off by the minutes........

A very long pause.

TUCKERS VOICE OVER :— (Almost to himself) Please say you'll do it.
<u>Please!</u>

A complete silence.

MANS VOICE OVER :— (Matter-of-fact)......what d'you want on it anyway?

TUCKERS VOICE OVER :— (Reviving a little, a ray of hope but still very nervous) I want 'fuck' down the back of my cock in big black letters and a swastika on each of my balls......

Silence.

(Pleading) Will you do it?

SILENCE.

DISSOLVE TO:—

Madonna and Child (1980): Second draft – note dialogue cut from the tattooist voiceover. (BFI National Archive)

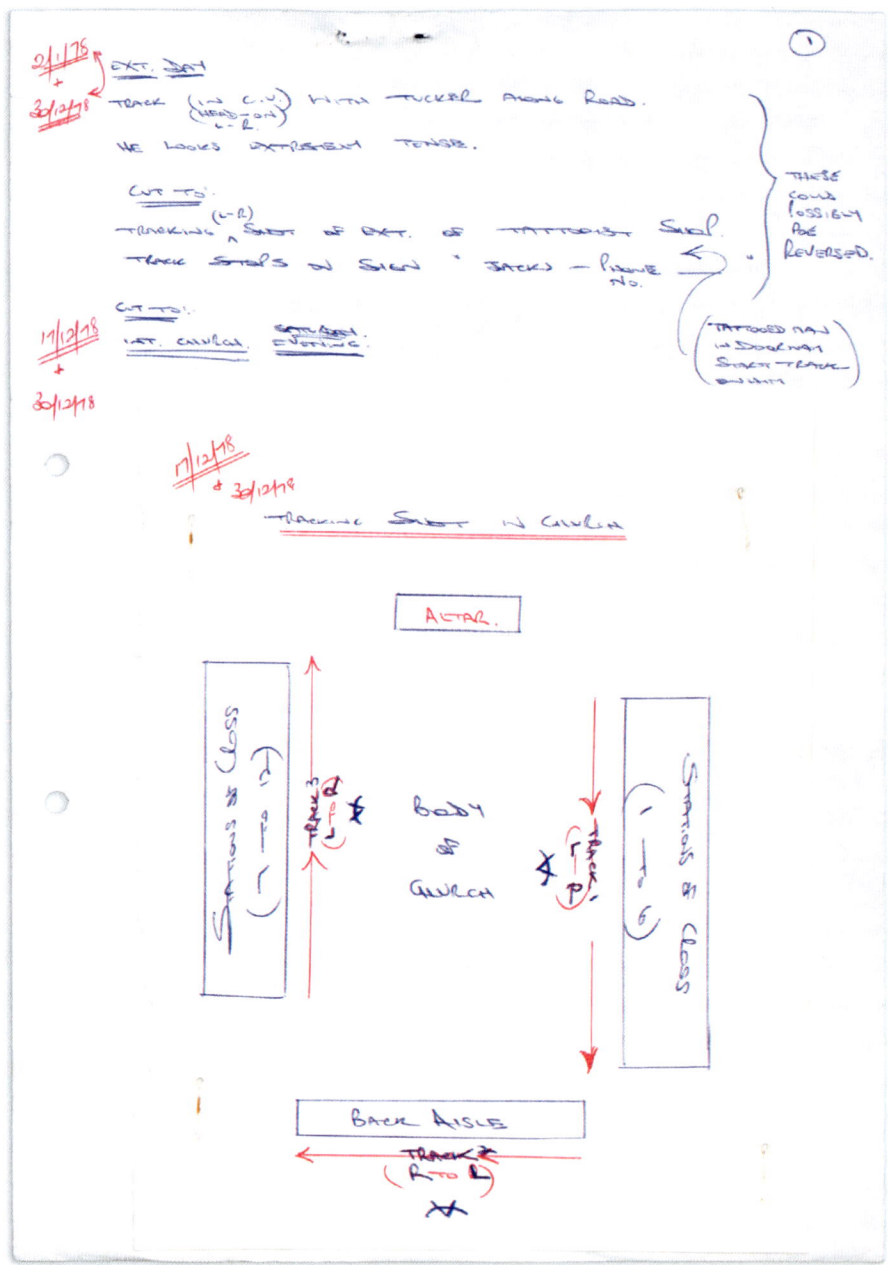

Madonna and Child (1980): First draft – diagram showing the camera movements for the Stations of the Cross/tattooist sequence. (BFI National Archive)

""DEATH AND TRANSFIGURATION""

BY
TERENCE DAVIES

TREATMENT:-

Part 1 ("CHILDREN") and Part Two ("MADONNA AND CHILD") examined the causes and effects of certain problems (ie Religion, violence, sexuality and death) on the main character, Tucker.

Part Three ("DEATH AND TRANSFIGURATION") will attempt to sythesize these problems and to resolve them.

They will be seen through a mosaic of memories as Tucker tries to come to terms with both them and his own mortality. Mortality and Catholicism will be juxtaposed and ultimately he will have to choose between his indoctrinated faith and the beleive in something more amorphous – like returning, metaphorically to the void, ~~his mother~~. His past life – particularly his early childhood, will be seen to hold the key to this dilemma and it will be epitomised by the Christmas period of The Nativity, The School Play, the whole Christmas myth, and it will be seen as a watershed for his beleif in Catholicism – the last time that, for him, it was both 'pure' and 'supportive' and the absolute joy that this brought. Sexuality will be dealth with by trying to juxtapose his aged body with that of the grotesque versions of manhood seen in Parts One and Two.

This all sounds terribly solemn doesn't it?
So I intend to have some jokes. Honest!
As you will see from the opening pages the humour tends to irony, if not black comedy and it is this ironical element which I intend to run through and under the entire film.

Death and Transfiguration (1983): a treatment. (BFI National Archive)

Distant Voices, Still Lives (1988): First draft. (BFI National Archive)

EXTRAS LIST

- SCENE 9 PAGE 6 := • As many as we can afford.
- SCENE 25 PAGE 11 :=)
-         26   12 :=) • As arranged 11 soldiers.
- SCENE 30 PAGE 12 := • NO neighbours.
- SCENE 38 PAGE 14/15:= • Eileen, Dave followed by Mother, Maisie,
  - Tony, Granny, Auntie Nell, Monica, Red.
  - No other wedding guests.
  - Six neighbours.
- SCENE 39 PAGE 15:= • Eileen, Dave, Mother, Tony, Maisie, Red,
  - Monica, Granny, Auntie Nell (6)
- SCENE 40 PAGE 15 := • Mum, Dave, Maise, Red, Monica, Gran, Auntie Nell
  • plus five (6) weddings guests. Dependant on Pub
- SCENE 43 PAGE 17 := • Two - a man and a woman.
- SCENE 56 PAGE 23)
-   "   57 "   24) := • Five(5) might not be needed but just a safety measure.
- SCENE 69 PAGE 29 := • Mother, Monica, Red, Eileen, Tony, Maisie
  • plus 6 wedding guests.
- SCENE 74 PAGE 31 := • As many as we can afford + McKee school
  • peaople. 20+ KIDS.
- SCENE 81 PAGE 33 := •   - ditto -
- SCENE 78 PAGE 32)
-   "   79 "   33) := • SOME extras in b'ground
- SCENE 103 PAGE 40 := • 6 popde in parlour.
- SCENE 105 PAGE 41 := • Couple in hall
- SCENE 108 PAGE 43 := • 3 people in hall
- SCENE 110 PAGE 44 := • 5 people in parlour.
- SCENE 111 PAGE 45 := • 4 men at door. 6 people in parlour.
- SCENE 120 PAGE 48 := • As many w as we can afford.
- SCENE 126 PAGE 52 := • 4 people at door. 6 people in parlour.

Distant Voices, Still Lives (1988): Extras list. (BFI National Archive)

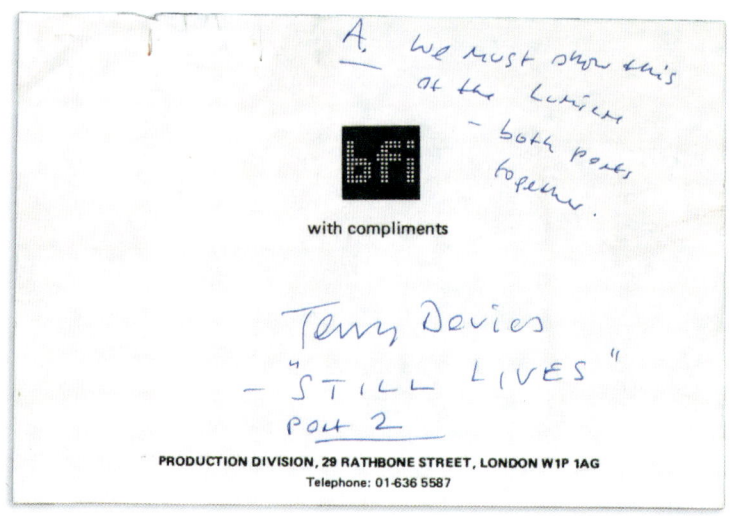

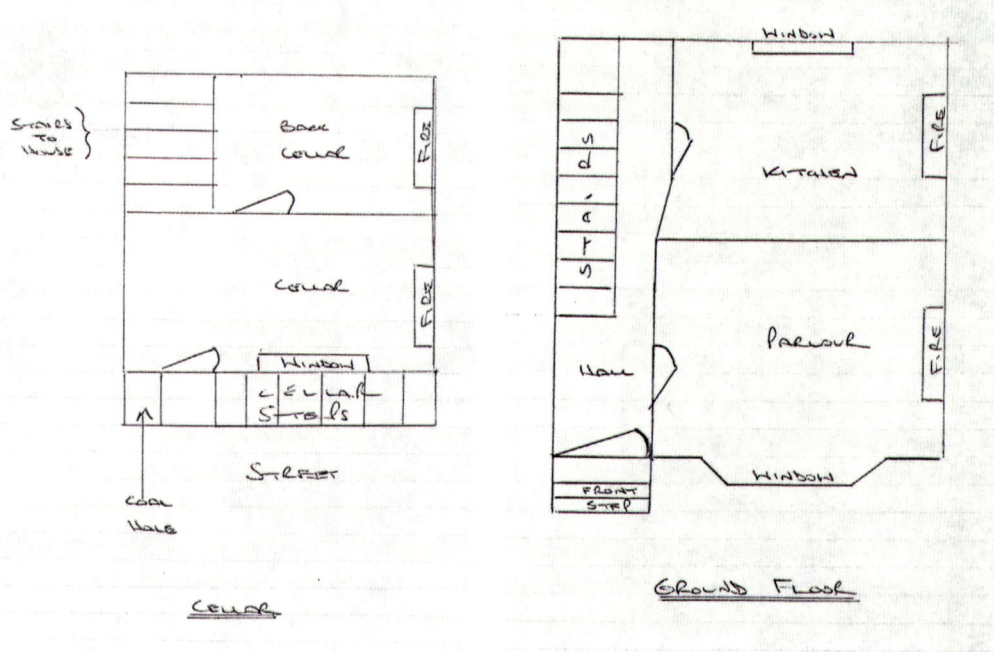

Distant Voices, Still Lives (1988): **(top)** A memorandum, included with the typed script of *Still Lives*, highlighting the BFI decision to screen *Distant Voices* and *Still Lives* together; **(above)** Drawings of the house layout in *Distant Voices* in the second draft script. (BFI National Archive)

Benediction (2021): First draft – notes towards second draft (© The Terence Davies Estate, held by the Terence Davies Archive at Edge Hill University)

Distant Voices, Still Lives (1988): Terence Davies on set. (BFI National Archive)

INTERVIEW WITH TERENCE DAVIES

Jason Wood

[Originally published in *The Guardian*, 28 October 2008.]

Jason Wood: I was in *Of Time and the City*'s screening at Cannes and the reaction was astonishing. The positive response seemed to take you entirely by surprise.

Terence Davies: I never expect it because I had had it beaten out of me as a child; I never think anyone will like what I do. I'm always terrified they won't like it and of course you always count the people who leave. They are on your death list. The people who stayed, stayed because they wanted to. You see it in a different way with an audience. And when it's over it's such a relief. It's such a struggle. I never expected that reaction. I truly never.

I have no illusions about my work but I must add I have no illusions about anybody else's either. I am very strict with myself and I think, 'no, that could have been improved', 'why didn't I put a little bit more then? Why didn't we come out then?' It was what I thought was right at the time and you have to stand by that. And if it completely fails you have got to say, 'But that is what I meant at the time.'

There's a line by Vaughan Williams, I think it's on his Sixth Symphony, when he says, 'I don't know whether I like it but it is what I meant.' And that's a wonderful thing to say upon your own work. Sometimes you don't know whether you like it or not but you think what gave me great joy, more than anything else, is that people from all over the world responded to it.

I've just come back from Poland where they put a retrospective on and they were turning people away. I never thought that would happen in my life, ever. And that it is in a foreign country. You change in some peculiar way. I'm still going through that change and I am still stunned by what happened.

JW: Peter Bradshaw's review in the *Guardian* suggested that the film should play for eternity in cinemas. As the Cannes applause rang out it was as if a weight had been lifted from your shoulders.

TD: I was relieved. People see me as a pessimist and I've been in a cinema where there were literally three people watching the film. So I know what that's like and it does crush you. You shouldn't expect people to go and see the film just because you happen to think they should.

And the other thing I keep in my mind too is my great love is Bruckner. The music is utterly sublime. In 1866 he conducted the Fourth Symphony or the Fifth, I can never remember. And when he finished there were more people in the orchestra than there were in the audience. And a 16-year-old Mahler was there and he went up to the composer and said 'Herr Bruckner, this is wonderful music.' And Bruckner, with tears in his eyes, said 'Yes, but nobody wants to hear it.' And he went on to write another five symphonies. If Bruckner can do it, there really is no excuse is there?

JW: The film is structured so as to resemble the fragmented nature of memory. Was the fact that you hadn't made a documentary before an advantage in terms of not having to be linear or objective? In this way *Of Time and the City* reminded me of Guy Maddin's recent *My Winnipeg*.

TD: A lot of people have mentioned to me that the Maddin film is very good. I had some tussles because of my approach. I said to the editor, who was terrific, that we cut it like it is fiction. I was clear right from the start in all the funding documents that it would be subjective. Some things did cause problems. I was told that I hadn't sufficiently contextualised the Korean war. Well, that's nonsense, of course I have. If you want me to say why it is there three times so Joe Schmo from Kokomo understands it, I'm not prepared to do that. It is a subjective essay. Over this I wouldn't budge.

But when it is subjective and when it is about emotional memory as well, moving from one memory to another, it can be very difficult for other people to get it. There was a point where I thought it's just not going to work, it's not seamless. Too many holes. If it's not seamless I can tell. When people identify a problem in fiction it is never there. It is usually never there but that is what you think it is. It's got to be seamless but it has also got to be true to what I remembered and that is a real problem for some people.

JW: You talk about memory and the way the film is structured; the collages you create between image and sound are another way of invoking memory. You do this with the football results and the way they are read out. Are words and sounds as important as images?

TD: Oh God, yes! We remember hourly probably more in sound than any other sense. The only other sense the cinema can't use is smell. If I smell cut grass I am immediately back in my primary school, with a little strip we were not allowed to cross. It is instantaneous. So I think I've got a very good emotional memory, not just of what was seen, but what was heard. At age 10, nobody talks to you so you listen all the time. So these football results at a quarter to five on a Saturday were huge. I didn't know what they meant as I didn't like sport. Like a mantra, like the one I used in the beginning of *Distant Voices, Still Lives* of the shipping forecast. I had no idea what it meant but it was like a magical mantra, like God speaking. It was fabulous. Silence as well. On Sundays there were times when you were on your own and you would listen to the silence. An absence of sound can be very provocative, especially on a Sunday afternoon when there's nothing to do and nowhere to go. And you felt that this would go on forever.

I think my ear is very acute and my emotional memory is the same because those things are visceral. And I think if those things are true people will recognise them as true, even if they are highly artificial. If it is true I think people recognise it even if they are not cine-literate. And if it is false they can tell. And you can't explain it. You just feel it. That's of huge importance in art, particularly music. Even more so in the cinema. First two or three bars and you are going to believe it or not. It's instantaneous.

JW: The music, for me, was revelatory. The slum clearance was particularly harsh but you cut it to the most transcendental and uplifting music. Was the intention to provide a counterpoint?

TD: Of course. Music as a counterpoint is always much more interesting. I always feel music and image instinctively. I don't have to think about it. It tells me. There are templates. My favourite writer is Chekhov, the dialogue most of all. I think that the play *Uncle Vanya* is one of the greatest achievements in art. But what he does at the end of *Vanya*, I can't even read the play without weeping. Vanya's life has been destroyed. He realises all the years he has strived for have been for nothing. And the last line is, 'Oh my child, there is such a weight on my heart. If you only knew much how my heart aches.' And his niece says two and a half pages about hope. And you know that that hope is going to be crushed when she gets to 40. And you cannot watch the end of that play. You just weep. Even in a bad production. What he shows you is the result of complete disillusionment. It's so simple but Chekhov, what a genius! If you can do that with images and music there is something so sublime about it.

Going back to Bruckner, in the Seventh Symphony there's this long, long tune. It really is heartbreaking. Then it stops. And there is this pause. And then just the violins and this echo. My God! You've waited for this resolution but it is not a resolution, it is just an echo of what is to come 40 minutes later. I love that. And when I see it in films it thrills me. *The Robe*, which is one of the first films in CinemaScope, has got this wonderful score by Alfred Newman. And there is one exquisite scene where Richard Burton is saying goodbye to Jean Simmons and he's getting on this boat. Obviously it is in the studio. But he gets on the boat and the boat just drifts away in this fog and you just hear this main tune. And it's exquisite because it is perfect for what it is showing. And there's this rising score from Jerome Moross in *The Big Country* and I get so thrilled by it.

JW: The film shows you a Liverpool beyond The Beatles and football, which is what people tend to think about when they think about the city. Your narration is very significant. It lends character because it is so impassioned.

TD: What was odd was that I was writing this commentary as I was doing it and recording it as a rough guide. We got someone to do part of the narration but it just didn't work and the producers said, 'No, you must do it.' I was worried that when you hear your own voice it can sound a bit like the Queen Mother after she died. I said, 'Are you sure?'

We recorded it in a day. I do feel impassioned about it. One thing I did notice was my breath control is such that I would become terribly asthmatic. I'm very conscious of that. It's strange because you can't hear yourself and it is always a shock to hear yourself. Do I really sound like that? All my films have strong Liverpool accents. It always makes me feel a bit embarrassed because I wonder where it came from? At one point they asked me to put in how I lost my accent and I said, 'You can't be serious? You really can't be serious? I'm not doing that.' I was worried and I was staying with my sister Maisie and I said, 'When did I lose my accent?' and she said, 'You never had one.' What was wonderful is that part of the narration would come when I would see something that I thought was odd. I've got to put that in. I've got to say something there – something's that elliptical. And sometimes you don't know where it has come from. I don't know why you see three images and you think, 'I've got to say that.' But I was writing it as I was doing it and that was incredibly exciting I must say.

JW: You express great anger at the treatment of the working classes. I sense that the Liverpool we have today is still suffering because of those policies of destroying communities and shunting them out to the outskirts of the city. Liverpool is a cash rich city but it is a city where investment has been at the cost of its soul.

TD: But the tragedy was that we who were living in those slums at the time thought this was the New Jerusalem, we really did. And they were Jerry built, badly designed and they were slums again in waiting. And that is what they became within five years. The tragedy was that no one had enough sense, or perhaps courage, and certainly enough money to say, 'Some of this stock is OK. We'll move you out, renovate it, then move you back in.' Once you destroy a community you never get it back. Alas it was a betrayal that was done with the very best of intentions. That's even harder in a way to accept.

Once that's gone what do you replace it with? And this is not only true of Liverpool but also true of this country. You replace it with finality, and you make finality a virtue. And that is what is really shocking. That's almost worse morally than what happened in the slum cases.

Thatcher did a lot of damage to the psyche of this country. What are you going to go back to, 19th-century capitalism? Where people live in their own sewage? Because that is what will happen. Is that what we want? In New York they had people living in cellars, in the dark. Do we want to go back to that? Of course we don't.

JW: What do you think of the Liverpool of today? It must be a million miles away from the one you grew up in?

TD: It is not the city I grew up in. Everywhere I knew is gone. Within walking distance of my house there were eight cinemas. That was without the eight there were in town. All gone now apart from one left in London Road and Fact, which is a modern cinema. All the places I knew and all the places associated with my childhood are just gone and that is very hard to bear. Going back to Liverpool it was very hard to see that and not feel something very profound had been lost. I'm not saying we should go back to the old days, and the Liverpool of today is in many ways more sophisticated, but I do think that we've lost something. This doesn't apply solely to Liverpool but to England as a whole. Maybe the thing that we have lost at the expense of this newfound sophistication is a certain innocence.

JW: There are themes such as cinema as a means of escape, Catholicism, sexuality and loss that recur throughout your features – certainly your early narrative features. And you have mentioned your reluctance to make another Liverpool film because you had done that. Was making this film a cathartic or painful experience?

TD: It certainly wasn't cathartic because none of the films have provided that. They were just soddened with this real sense of loss. Why does one need to suffer spiritually or physically? Why does anyone need to suffer? It throws up inside you profound questions about the nature of being human. I suppose with every film I wanted to go back, in some way, to that period when I was incredibly happy. My father died when I was seven, and the four years between primary and secondary school I was ecstatically happy. I was literally sick with happiness. I took in movies for the first time. The first film I took in was *Singing in the Rain*. What an impact! It can't get much better than that. Just the house became alive. It became one of those houses that drew people to it. Because my father wouldn't allow any visitors at all. He was very, very psychotic. So it was like I was trying to get back to those four years where I was truly happy. Before the onset of sexuality, which has ruined my life.

All the men were really big in my family and I was very weedy. And I wasn't aggressive and had lost my accent. I was really brought up by and with women. Incredibly loving, warm, happiness you never thought existed. And then you have to go to secondary school and your paradise is shattered. The constant terror of God's wrath. Which I still have in me although I've not been a practising Catholic for 41 years. But still within me. I examine my conscience every day. I can't help but do it. I examine my motives all the time. Why did you do that? You shouldn't have said that. You shouldn't feel envious because he is better looking than you. When men are good looking I am terribly envious of them. That has to be controlled because I say horrible things to myself and I'm still ashamed of it.

JW: I suffer from hair envy, Terence. When I see people with hair I think 'You lucky bugger!'

TD: Are you a Catholic?

JW: No, I'm an atheist.

TD: Immediately my other response is that you shouldn't be doing this. This is envy – simply because they are better looking than you. And that constant tyranny, because it is a tyranny, of a conscience that is very rigorous and very Catholic. When I first went to confession and my schoolmates said they made things up I was really shocked. I said, 'How can you do that? God will know.' And any tiny little infringement of it I would say to the priest on a Saturday. 'This is what I did.' It's still very much there. I don't think I will ever come to a catharsis. I wish I could. Quite honestly I am getting fed up with the struggle.

JW: Did this provide a step closer to closure or is it just an ongoing journey?

TD: I think it will go on till I die really. Which is a pretty depressing prospect.

JW: I want to go back, momentarily, to that moment in Cannes, with the applause ringing in your ears. And I want to counterpoint this with the fairly appalling treatment you have suffered at the hands of the British film industry. For all of the great films you have made you've been dealt a pretty shabby hand I think in recent years. Is there a sense of victory and vindication with this film in the face of all this, particularly the UK Film Council's apathy towards you as a film-maker?

TD: I was relieved. Because being out of work for eight years does something to you. I came back and got great support from Lenny Crooks at the film council, who is a terrific lad and who loves film. I do want Lenny's support put on record. But right now I need two hundred and twenty thousand to close finance on my next project, a romantic comedy. No one will put it up. Potentially it could not get made. You come back to that, particularly from Poland recently, and any kind of sense of worth is destroyed again. Having to start all over again. Re-inventing the wheel, going round knocking on doors and saying are you interested and everyone says, 'We would like to see another Terence Davies film but not with my money.' That is what is in essence has been said. So not just the spiritual struggle, which I'll have for the rest of my life, but the struggle forward which is becoming very hard to find a reason to carry on sometimes. I get very low and think is it worth the struggle and at the lowest the answer comes back: 'No, it isn't.'

That line from *A Man For All Seasons*, 'Most people would have fallen asleep at the sermon on the mount,' and you think, 'How many people out there have heard one note of Bruckner and couldn't care less?' You can struggle when you are 20, 30 or 40. I'm 63 this year. I'm not a kid anymore. It gets harder by the day.

JW: The reviews that you are getting for *Of Time and the City* must surely give you encouragement and the strength to carry on?

TD: It fills me with terror. I don't like being me you see. That's a struggle each day. I know it sounds almost banal but it is true. You know when you go into a shop and it has this overhead lighting and you catch yourself in the mirror and you think, 'God, aren't you ugly? And it's that. I just feel frightened because I think there is some awful disaster in store for me.

JW: There is a nice symmetry in that *Of Time and the City* will be released by the British Film Institute, who were involved in your Trilogy and *Distant Voices, Still Lives*. This must also provide you with sustenance.

TD: I'm very, very grateful towards those people and to you for saying nice things about me and my work. And those things I treasure. I'm as vain as anyone else. I like my vanity and ego rubbed occasionally. But in my heart of hearts it's as if someone else made them. And if I do watch them, and I rarely do, I think: 'Was that me?' I know that sounds strange but that is what I feel. And I think it is because I had my self-esteem battered out of me at such a young age. And you can't even get it through validation of your work.

Once it is gone it is gone forever. The struggle is to keep from despair and there have been occasions when I thought I would die from sheer despair. I hadn't the strength to go on. But then something happens and you think it is worthwhile. The light will fall in a certain way. Or someone will say something or do something really nice and something glows. Because I am not happy being me, these things affect you.

JW: You have spoken of your admiration for Humphrey Jennings and especially Listen To Britain. You also intimated that these portraits of British life could only be made by British directors.

TD: There are films that can only be made in a specific country but that have a wider meaning. I think that's true of any art form. In connection to *Of Time and the City* I think only someone who was raised in Liverpool can do it. It might have been someone else, not me. It's just my particular take on that particular city. I know there is a great pride from people who come from there. And I think at best we are rather unusual. Terrific sense of humour, particularly the women; all northern women have got that sense of humour. People are very sharp. Although this incident happened in America it did remind me of the kind of sharpness that you have in Liverpool. I was there, giving a lecture. It was quite cool and I had this Harvard T-shirt on. I walked down this street and a tramp asked me if I could give him some loose change, he wanted to go to Yale. Isn't that great? It is the sort of remark that had me thinking: 'That's the sort of remark you would get in Liverpool.' I love that. I love that sharpness, that wit. They are still very warm. But this society is changing and once you lose your sense of humour, you might as well be dead. All the people in the world who have created the most evil are those with no sense of humour. They're always trouble.

JW: Though a good number of those that go to see *Of Time and The City* will be enticed by your previous work it will also attract audiences unfamiliar with your previous films. What would you hope that these people take away from it?

TD: I just hope they will be able to respond to the fact it came from my heart. I try to do that with every film. It is very hurtful when someone rejects that because you are very vulnerable. I hope they will respond to its truth. What I've certainly found since it was shown all over the world is that it triggers memories of their own lives which is remarkable. I never thought that would happen. But to remember and not feel like me and be melancholy about it, but remember and be joyful about it.

Christina Rossetti said it I think when she wrote, 'If after you forget and cannot remember, do not grieve, for if the darkness and corruption are the vestige of the thought that once I had, better by far you should forget and smile.'

That you should remember and be sad is not what I want.

THE SCREENPLAYS

Above: Terence Davies with Leigh McCormack (Bud), on the set of *The Long Day Closes* (1992).
Opposite: *Distant Voices, Still Lives* (1988): on-set Polaroids. (© The Terence Davies Estate)

AUTOBIOGRAPHY

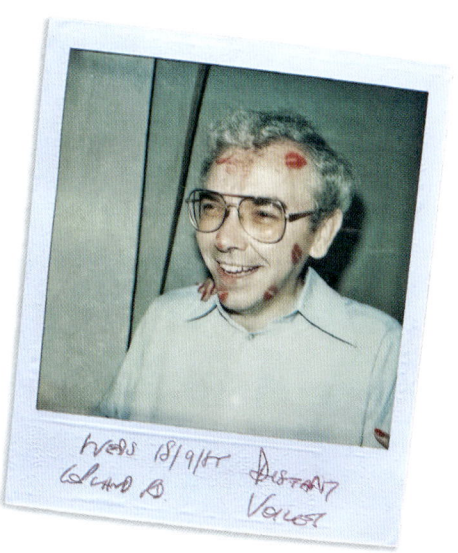

"CHILDREN"

SHOWINGS:- November 1976   NFT 2
            27/7/77   NFT 2
            11/3/78   RIVERSIDE STUDIOS
            5/4/78   NFT 1
                            ICA

FESTIVALS:- 10/11/76   The 12th. Chicago International
                            Film Festival (USA)
            29/1/77   The Tours Film Festival (France)
            14/10/77   The Mannheim Film Festival (Germany)

            (AT THE MOMENT IT HAS BEEN ACCEPTED FOR PRE-SELECTION
            BY MELBOURNE AND SYDNEY FILM FESTIVALS - AUSTRALIA)

AWARDS:-   The Bronze Hugo (The 12th. Chicago International
                            Film Festival)

SALES:-   June 1977 WTTW TV (CHICAGO)
            February 1978 WEST GERMAN TV
            (AT THE MOMENT IT IS BEING CONSIDERED FOR PURCHASE
            BY BBC TV)

                                            T. DAVIES,
                                            172 Camden Street,
                                            LONDON NW1 9PT.
                                            01-267-1061

Children (1976): Shooting script, title page/cover sheet. (BFI National Archive)

TRILOGY: PART I
CHILDREN (1976)

Children (1976): Mother (Valerie Lilley) and Tucker (Phillip Mawdsley).

Cast and crew of *Children* include:

TUCKER (as a boy)	Phillip Mawdsley
FATHER	Nick Stringer
MOTHER	Valerie Lilley
TUCKER (at twenty-four)	Robin Hooper
BULLY	Colin Hignett
BULLY	Robin Bowen
FIRST TEACHER	Harry Wright
SECOND TEACHER	Philip Joseph
MAN IN SHOWER	Trevor Eve
NEIGHBOUR	Linda Beckett
DOCTOR	Bill Maxwell
NURSE	Elizabeth Estensen
MAN IN BEDROOM	Malcolm Hughes
NEIGHBOUR	Katherine Fahey
NEIGHBOUR	Marjorie Rowlandson
Soloist	Ann Kiesler
Cor Anglais soloist	Stella Dickinson

Lyrics to 'The Ballad of Barbara Allen' from the play *Dark of the Moon* are used by kind permission of the author Howard Richardson.

Written and Directed by	Terence Davies
Executive Production Supervisor	Geoffrey Evans
Production	Peter Shannon
Production Assistant	Rick Thomas
Cameraman	William Diver
Assistant Cameraman	Chris Evans
Assistant Director	Dave Wheeler
Continuity	Anna Maysoon Pachachi
Sound Recordist	Digby Rumsey
Editors	Digby Rumsey, Sarah Ellis

A British Film Institute Production, 1976.

LIVERPOOL IN THE LATE 1950s

Fade up on a high shot of a school yard. The main school block is to right of camera and a high wall runs around, from left of camera, to join the building, making a rough triangle. The whole place is an ageing piece of rambling, Edwardian Catholicism.
Cut to a group of five boys consisting of four surrounding a fifth. They stand in the bicycle shed in a semi-circle around TUCKER, *the fifth boy. They are all fifteen.*
Cut to shot of four boys as seen from TUCKER's *point of view. Pan along group.*
BEDSON: Hey ... who's a fruit then? ... hey?
CODLING: It's Al Capone, isn't it?
   (*General laughter.*)
MCCABE: Your name's Al Capone, isn't it?
WOODS: Al Capone!
   (*They snigger.*
   Cut to TUCKER. *He just stares at them.*
   Cut back to shot of the four of them. Their fists shoot out in uniform order from left to right, then back again.
   Cut to TUCKER. *He makes no attempt to stop the flurry of blows which catch him in the mouth and chest.*)
TUCKER: (*Thinking*) I won't cry ... I won't!
   (*Cut to a long shot of the group as they shove and push* TUCKER *around. Cut to a mouth with a whistle in it. Whistle blows once then after a pause blows again.*
   Cut back to high shot of yard. All activity stops.
   Cut to group. They all exchange frightened looks.)
BEDSON: (*Whispering*) If you snitch we'll get you tonight.
   (TUCKER *just looks at them.*)
TUCKER'S VOICE: (*Thinking*) I won't cry ... won't ...
   (*The whistle blows a third time and they begin to form six lines – each line representing a classroom. The group goes into the first line. Slowly* TUCKER *also goes into this line.*
   Cut back to high shot. The six lines standing still and the TEACHER *walking a little distance from them, the whistle still in his mouth.*)
TEACHER: Right ... left wheel ... (*blows whistle.*)
   (*The first line turns into the building. He does this for each line.*)

65

Fade up on a bare classroom on the second floor. There are ten boys scattered about the desks. In one corner BEDSON, CODLING, MCCABE *and* WOODS *all whispering to one another. At a desk by the window is* TUCKER. *All the boys are just in their underpants. At the top of the room two blackboards have been placed together to form a screen, behind which is a* DOCTOR.

Cut to shot of the group whispering and sniggering. Cut to TUCKER.

TUCKER'S VOICE: (*Thinking*) I'm too skinny. I want to get dressed.

(*Cut back to group.*)

BEDSON: (*The words arising out of all the whispering*) … Mister Universe …

(*Furious sniggering.*

Cut to a shot of room.)

TUCKER: (*Voice over*) Mam … I want to get dressed, Mam.

DOCTOR: (*Voice over*) Bedson.

(BEDSON *gets up and goes behind the blackboards.*

Cut to blackboard. Just his legs showing.

A pause.

A cough is heard.

Cut to shot of BEDSON*'s friends exchanging looks and grinning slyly.*

BEDSON *comes out from behind the blackboards and goes to the opposite end of the room where all the clothes are lying in piles. As he passes his friends he grins in a quite revolting way.*

Cut to TUCKER.)

TUCKER: (*Voice over*) Not me! Not me!

DOCTOR: (*Voice over*) Tucker!

(TUCKER *looks across at* CODLING, MCCABE *and* WOODS.

They whisper furiously.)

CODLING: Mister Universe.

(*Suppressed giggling.*

TUCKER *get up and goes behind the screen, and the* DOCTOR *starts his examination of him.*)

DOCTOR: Cough.

(*Cut to* TUCKER*'s face. He closes his eyes, then coughs.*

A single giggle is heard.

TUCKER *and* DOCTOR *exchange looks.*)

DOCTOR: (*Smiling*) Well go on … you can get dressed now.

TUCKER: Thank you, Doctor.

(*Cut to long shot of room.*

TUCKER *goes to his pile of clothes and gets dressed.*)
DOCTOR'S VOICE: Codling.
>   (*Cut to the door leading from the classroom.* TUCKER *comes out. As he closes the door he looks up and gives a little start.*
>   *Cut to* BEDSON *lounging at the top of the stairs.*
>   *Absolute silence.*
>   *They eye one another.* BEDSON *uneasily sadistic,* TUCKER *icily contemptuous.*
>   BEDSON *suddenly pushes* TUCKER, *then follows this with a series of pushes. Pause. Silence.*
>   *Cut to* BEDSON *now unsure what to do.*
>   *Cut to* TUCKER *looking at him with a look which drips with hate. A lull.*
>   *Quite suddenly* BEDSON *lashes out, catching* TUCKER *just below the throat. This blow seems to break the spell.*
>   TUCKER *falls on him in a paroxysm of pent up rage and years of hate. These blows send* BEDSON *reeling down the stairs, but* TUCKER *doesn't stop raining blow after blow on him. During the fight one of* TUCKER's *shoes comes off. He picks this up and begins hitting* BEDSON *with the heel of it.*)

HEADMASTER: (*Voice over*) You two boys – stop that!
>   (*He comes into shot and separates them.*)

HEADMASTER: Who *started* this, *mm?*
>   (*Silence.*) I suppose you're very proud of yourselves.
>   (*Silence.*)
>   I'm very surprised at you, Tucker … very surprised. What have you to say for yourselves?

BEDSON: Nothing, sir.
>   (TUCKER *still does not say anything.*)

HEADMASTER: Both of you come with me. (*Turns and walks away.*)

BEDSON: (*In a whisper*) We'll get you tonight! We'll get you!
>   (*They follow the* HEADMASTER.)
>   (*Mix to study. The* HEADMASTER *picks up a cane and flexes it. Cut to corridor outside.*)

BEDSON: I'm going to get you ton–

HEADMASTER: (*Voice over*) Bedson!
>   (BEDSON *halts at the door, rubs his hands, then blows into them and goes in. Cut to inside study.*)

Come on –
(BEDSON *gingerly half-extends his hand. The* HEADMASTER *makes a strike but* BEDSON *pulls his hand away. This is repeated twice. After each miss the* HEADMASTER *becomes more niggled. Eventually he grabs* BEDSON's *wrist and brings the cane sharply down twice on* BEDSON's *hand,* BEDSON *squeals.*

Cut to TUCKER. *The two strokes are heard. After a pause* BEDSON *comes out blowing into his hand.*)

BEDSON: Just wait till tonight.

HEADMASTER: (*Voice over*) Tucker!

(*Cut to* HEADMASTER, TUCKER *enters the study. He extends his hand and receives two strokes, then turns and goes to the door.*)

HEADMASTER: Tucker …

TUCKER: Yes sir?

HEADMASTER: Aren't you forgetting something?

TUCKER: Sir?

HEADMASTER: (*Shaking his head*) Your shoe, boy … put your shoe on.

(TUCKER *realizes that he's still holding his shoe and attempts to put it on.*)

Not here, boy. Outside.

TUCKER: Yes sir.

HEADMASTER: Yes sir.

TUCKER: Thank you sir.

(*Cut to outside study.* TUCKER *comes out and puts his shoe on, then walks down the corridor.*)

(*Mix to a long rectangular classroom. The* TEACHER *sits at a large table at the head of eight, long, depressing rows of desks.*

Cut to long shot of TUCKER *coming in the door,* TUCKER *makes the long journey to his desk at the top of the first row of desks. Some boys look round at him while the others remain absorbed in their lesson.*)

TEACHER: All right, all right … you've seen Tucker before.

(*They resume their work.*

Cut to TUCKER *at his desk. He gets out his exercise book and a textbook of English grammar. He rises and attempts to go to the* TEACHER.)

TEACHER: It's 'Subject and Predicate', lad.

TUCKER: Thank you sir. (*Begins to look for the appropriate chapter.*)

TEACHER: (*Irritated*) Page twenty-five, lad. Page twenty-five.

TUCKER: Thank you sir. (*Sits back down.*)

(*After finding the page he begins the lesson.*
Fade.
Fade up on a wall-clock showing 3.45 p.m.
Cut to high shot of classroom with the TEACHER *walking up and down the aisles.*
Cut to TUCKER. *He looks up at the clock.*
Cut to BEDSON. *He is deep in his work.*
Cut back to TUCKER.)

BEDSON: (*Voice over*) We'll get you tonight.

(*Cut to clock. It shows 3.50 p.m.*
Cut to TUCKER.
A hand slaps him on the top of the head and he starts.)

TEACHER: I won't forget to tell you when it's time to stop, lad.

TUCKER: Yes sir.

TEACHER: (*Mimicking*) Yes sir.

(*Cut back to high shot of classroom.*
TEACHER *continues his walking up and down the aisles. He stops at one desk and looks over a boy's shoulder.*)

No, that's not the predicate lad.

(*The boy crosses something out and writes.*)

Neither is that.

(*The boy sits there, at a loss what to do. The* TEACHER *walks away, to the top of the class.*)

All right, all right, that's it.

(*They stop.*)

Put your things away.

(*They do so noisily.*)

QUIETLY! Barnes, collect the exercise books.

(*A boy gets up and quickly gathers up the exercise books.*
Cut to TUCKER. *He looks at the clock. It shows 3.56 p.m.*
Cut to long shot of room.
BARNES *puts the books on the* TEACHER'S *desk and resumes his seat.*)

TEACHER: Right.

(*They all stand and join their hands to pray.*
As the prayers proceed the TEACHER *continues walking up and down the aisles and as they finish he is back at the top of the classroom.*)

ALL: (*Making the sign of the cross*) In the name of the Father and of the Son and of the Holy Ghost. Amen.
Our Father who art in Heaven Hallowed be thy name, Thy Kingdom come, Thy will be done on earth as it is in Heaven … Give us this day our daily bread and forgive us our trespasses as we forgive them that trespass against us … and lead us not into temptation but deliver us from evil. Amen.

Hail, Mary, full of grace! The Lord is with thee: blessed art thou amongst women, and blessed is the fruit of thy womb, Jesus. Holy Mary, Mother of God, pray for us sinners, now and at the hour of our death. Amen.

Jesus Mary and Joseph I give you my body and blood.
Jesus Mary and Joseph I give you my heart and my soul.
Jesus Mary and Joseph assist me in my last agony.
May I say when I am dying 'Jesus mercy – Mary help'.
In the name of the Father and of the Son and of the Holy Ghost. Amen.
(*They all make the sign of the cross.*)

TEACHER: Right, get into line.
(*They all step into their respective aisles.*)
Turn.
(*They do so, so that* TUCKER *is now last in the first line and* BEDSON *is first in his, the third line. The door of the classroom now faces the boy. Cut to* TUCKER. *He looks at* BEDSON.
Cut to BEDSON. *He glances over his shoulder at* TUCKER.)

TEACHER: Eyes front there, boy. Or would you like to lead them out?
(*No reply.*)
Well, go on, lad … what would you say?

BEDSON: (*In what he thinks is a posh accent*) Let's go into the school yard.
(*Tittering.*)

TEACHER: (*Smiling*) Any more of that and you'll get a kick up the backside … or should I say the arse?
(*Roars of laughter from the boys to think that the* TEACHER *would use such a daring word.*)
Goodnight boys.

BOYS: Goodnight sir.

TEACHER: Off you go.
>   (TUCKER'S *line moves off.*)
>   Quietly.
>   (*As* TUCKER *draws level with* BEDSON *they exchange looks.*
>   *Pan with* TUCKER *as he leaves the classroom darting looks over his shoulder.*
>   *Cut to second line moving off.* BEDSON *impatient.*
>   *Cut to school entrance. Boys spill out.* TUCKER *runs through them and up the street opposite at top speed. Shot of him running to the top of the street.*
>   *Cut back to school entrance,* BEDSON *and his three friends come flying out.*)

BEDSON: There he is! There!
>   (*They begin to run after* TUCKER *at top speed.*
>   *Cut to* TUCKER. *Pan with him as he runs frantically along the street.*
>   *Cut back to shot of* BEDSON *and* FRIENDS – *head on* – *gasping as they run.*
>   *Cut back to close-up of* TUCKER. *He looks back over his shoulder and sees that they are too far behind to catch him. He smiles and begins to pant but runs all the harder.*
>   *Cut to very high shot of* TUCKER *being chased by* BEDSON *and Co. They are now mere dots.* TUCKER *turns sharp right, darts across a road and runs down the street where he lives. The pursuers also turn sharp right and cross the road but when they reach the street they stop.*
>   *Cut to* TUCKER *getting to his front door. Gasping and panting but smiling and safe.*
>   *Cut to group at top of the street. They gasp for breath and glare after* TUCKER.
>   *Cut back to* TUCKER, *still recovering.*)

TUCKER: (*Voice over*) Safe till Monday.
>   (*Shot of group walking slowly away as seen from* TUCKER'S *point of view.*)

Cut to interior of a DOCTOR'*s surgery.*
Morning. Present day.
Surgery is half empty. Pan camera around room.
Some people read, others stare or look around disinterestedly. Continue pan until camera frames TUCKER'*S face. He is now twenty-four.*

The odd cough is heard. Then silence.
A pause.
A buzzer rings and one of the patients gets up and goes through to the DOCTOR*'s office.*
Cut back to close-up of TUCKER. *He sits staring into space. Track in on him.*
Cut to swimming baths, TUCKER *– then fourteen – is seen coming out of a cubicle and into showers which are packed with other boys.*
Cut back to surgery, TUCKER *in big close-up.*
TUCKER'S VOICE: (*Reading a poster*) Say yes to health, say no to smoking.
   (*Cut back to swimming-bath showers. Two men come into showers.*
   Cut to close-up of TUCKER *at the back of the shower looking at one of the men.*
   Cut back to surgery, TUCKER *staring intently straight ahead.*
   Shouts of boys in swimming baths are heard echoing.
   Cut back to showers, TUCKER *still looking at one of the men.*
   This man has a well-developed physique.
   Cut back to TUCKER *in surgery.*
   Cut back to man washing himself.
   Cut to TUCKER *at the back of the shower. Boys' voices echoing loudly as they splash about in the water.*
   Cut to man. Smiling to himself he finishes washing and then puts his hand down inside the front of his briefs.
   Cut to TUCKER *at the back of the shower.*)
A BOY'S VOICE: (*In a whisper*) Look at his muscles!
   (*Cut back to* TUCKER *at the back of showers staring in fascinated horror at the man.*
   Cut back to TUCKER *in surgery. His eye closing in horror. Shouts echoing.*
   Buzzer goes, TUCKER *gets up and goes through to* DOCTOR*'s office.*
   Cut to DOCTOR*'s office*
   TUCKER *comes in and sits down.*)
DOCTOR: (*Without looking up*) Hello, Robbie.
TUCKER: Hello, Doctor.
   (*Pause.*)
DOCTOR: And how are we today?
TUCKER: Fine, Doctor.
DOCTOR: Back to work, d'you think?
TUCKER: Oh yes. I'm feeling much better.

And I'd rather be at work anyway.

DOCTOR: And d'you like your work, son?

TUCKER: Yes, Doctor. Very much. It's easy and they're a smashing crowd.

DOCTOR: So you'd like to turn in on Monday.

TUCKER: Please, Doctor.

DOCTOR: Good boy, Robbie.

(*Silence as* DOCTOR *writes out signing-off note.*

Cut to TUCKER. *Zoom in on him.*

Cut to his bedroom. He is standing in front of the wardrobe mirror dressed entirely in leather.)

DOCTOR: (*Voice over*) Mother keeping well, son?

(*Cut back to* TUCKER *staring straight ahead.*)

TUCKER: What?

DOCTOR: Your mother, son. Is she keeping well?

TUCKER: Oh ... yea ... you know my mother. Never ails.

Strong as a horse.

DOCTOR: (*Handing him a prescription and note*) Well, stay off for the rest of the week and go in on Monday. I've given you some more tablets for the depression.

TUCKER: Thank you, Doctor.

(*An awkward silence.*)

DOCTOR: Still no interest in girls yet, Robbie?

(TUCKER *shakes his head.*

A Pause.)

Well, that may come, son ... that may come.

(TUCKER *stands up.*)

Good-bye. And don't worry, son.

TUCKER: (*Smiling*) Goodbye. And thank you, Doctor.

DOCTOR: Bye, son. Bye, Robbie.

(TUCKER *goes out.*

Cut to street. He stands and looks at the traffic droning by.

Cut to shot of traffic. A bus comes by and there are some children gathered at one of the windows. They look out at TUCKER. *One of the kids points in* TUCKER'S *direction and says something, and the group laugh.*

Cut to TUCKER.)

TUCKER: (*Voice over*) They're laughing at me. (*Flatly.*)

(*Shot of* TUCKER *walking towards bus stop.*)

All dead ... all dead ...
(*Cut to* TUCKER *at fourteen. Outside his house panting for breath.*)
Safe till Monday.
(*Cut to shot of group walking slowly away from the top of the street as seen from* TUCKER'S *point of view.*
Cut to TUCKER *going into house.*
Cut to a curtain – in place of a door – hanging in front of doorway of parlour. Terrible groaning is heard.
TUCKER *stands looking at the curtain. Voices are indistinctly heard. The groans become more and more terrible.*
TUCKER *pulls back the curtain.*
Cut to close-up of TUCKER *staring in horror into the room.*
Cut to shot (*over* TUCKER'S *shoulder*) *of room.*
TUCKER'S FATHER – *wearing only longjohns* – *is rolling on the floor screaming in pain.*
A NURSE *is trying to get him on to a bed which is pushed up in a corner of this small room. She eventually gets him on to the bed.*
Cut back to close-up of TUCKER. *Unable to take his eyes off the scene.*
Cut to shot of his FATHER *on the bed. He just keeps moaning and moaning. The* NURSE *stands over him and lifts him so that he is kneeling on the bed on all fours. She undoes his underwear and pulls it down revealing* FATHER'S *bare buttocks. She injects him with morphia.*
Cut to TUCKER *both horrified and fascinated. A squeal is heard from his* FATHER.)

FATHER: (*Voice over*) You hurt me! You bleedin' hurt me!
(*Cut to* FATHER *struggling into bed. As he settles down he sees* TUCKER.)
FATHER: How long has he been there? GET OUT!
NURSE: He'll see worse.
(*Cut to long shot* – FATHER'S *point of view* – *of* TUCKER. *He lets the curtain fall.*
Cut to hall, TUCKER *just stands there, staring at the curtain, absolutely shocked.*
FATHER'S *and* NURSE'S *voices are heard arguing.*
MOTHER *comes down the hall carrying two cups of tea.*)
MOTHER: (*Embarrassed*) Hello, son.
(TUCKER *just looks at her then runs upstairs,* MOTHER *looks up after him, pauses, then goes into the parlour.*

Cut to bedroom, TUCKER *comes running in sobbing and throws himself on to the bed, face down.*)

TUCKER: (*Through his sobs with the utmost force*) Die you bastard! DIE!

(*Cut back to bus stop. Bus arrives and* TUCKER *gets on. The bus moves off. Cut to interior of bus. One of the seats upstairs,* TUCKER *is paying his fare. Sitting at the window he looks out.*

Pan with him – from the outside of the bus.

The bus stops at traffic lights.

Zoom in on TUCKER.

Cut to TUCKER *– at fourteen – with his* MOTHER *at bus stop. He looks at her. They both smile.*

Cut to close-up of MOTHER. *Her face is taut, worried.*

Fade in introduction to Peggy Lee's record 'The Folks Who Live on the Hill'.

The bus arrives. They both get on.)

TUCKER: Can we go upstairs, Mam?

MOTHER: If you like, son

(*Cut to upstairs. They take their seat,* TUCKER *by the window and* MOTHER *on the outside,* TUCKER *looks out of window and* MOTHER *takes out her handkerchief and blows her nose.*

Cut to outside of bus. Shot of TUCKER *and* MOTHER *looking out of the window.*)

Soundtrack: 'The Folks Who Live on the Hill'.

(*Cut to interior of bus. Silence except for conductor collecting fares.*)

MOTHER: (*To conductor*) Nine and a scholar please.

TUCKER: Look, there's our street, Mam.

(*Cut to outside of bus. Continue panning with bus and* TUCKER*'s face. Cut to interior of bus.*

MOTHER *looks away from the window and at the other passengers. On the verge of tears, her spirit is utterly broken.*)

FATHER: (*Voice over*) There's an 'A' on the ceiling Nellie … There's a bleedin' 'A'!

(*She closes her eyes. She begins to cry but tries not to let anyone see her. Her sobs become louder. Her sobs now being noticed by the other passengers,* TUCKER *turns around and looks at her then sinks back into his seat.*)

TUCKER: (*Voice over*) Don't cry, Mam … Mam … don't cry … please …

WOMAN PASSENGER: What's the matter, love?
    (MOTHER *shakes her head but continues crying.*)
    What's the matter, love?
    (MOTHER *just shakes her head.*
    Cut back to TUCKER *on the bus alone.*
    Rain begins to fall against the window.
    Cut to exterior of bus disappearing into rain.)
TUCKER: (*Voice over, as a boy*) Mam, I know what that says now …
MOTHER: (*Voice over*) Do you, lad?
TUCKER: (*Voice over*) Yes. It says 'Ophthalmic Optician'.
MOTHER: (*Voice over*) You're a good reader, aren't you, lad?

Mix to bus stopping. TUCKER *as an adult gets off and walks into a small block of flats which are nearby.*
Mix to one of the landings in this block, TUCKER *walks into shot. He opens his front door and goes in.*
Mix to interior of flat. The living room.
The front door is heard closing.
TUCKER: (*Voice over*) Mum? Are you in, Mum?
    (*Silence.*
    He enters the living room. Poking the fire he sits down without taking off his overcoat.)
MAN: (*Voice over*) But I like you in leather …
TUCKER: (*Voice over*) I feel stupid … I just feel soft …
    (*Cut to a low-angled shot, side view, of* TUCKER *in his leather gear.*
    A MAN *sits up and coming into shot puts one hand on* TUCKER'S *buttocks and pulls* TUCKER'S *fly down with the other.*
    Cut to close-up of TUCKER.)
MAN: (*Voice over*) Come on baby … come on …
TUCKER: (*Voice over, exultant, suppressed*) Jesus! … oh JESUS!

    Cut to TUCKER *in living room.*
TUCKER: God … God …
    (*From outside laughter is heard. It quickly dies away.*
    Silence.
    Cut to high shot of room, TUCKER *pokes the fire.*)

TRILOGY I: CHILDREN

Cut to close-up of fire being poked. Pause. Then pull camera back to reveal TUCKER'S FATHER *poking the fire.*
TUCKER – *as a boy of fourteen – is sitting with his* MOTHER *on the far side of the small room.*
Silence.
TUCKER – *exhausted – tries desperately to keep from falling asleep.*
Cut to FATHER'S *face.*
Cut to TUCKER, *more and more exhausted.*
Cut to MOTHER.

MOTHER: (*Mouthing to* TUCKER) Don't go to bed … don't go to bed …
(*Cut to shot of trio looking at the fire.*
FATHER *coughs.*)

FATHER: Time for bed … You'd better get upstairs …
(TUCKER *and* MOTHER *exchange looks,* TUCKER *gets up and goes out.*
MOTHER *looks after him then lowers her head.*
FATHER *starts poking the fire again.*
Cut to TUCKER *in bedroom. He sits on the bed, listening.*
Silence.
Cut to parlour. Silence.)

FATHER: (*Quietly*) Where is he, eh? Your fancy man … where is he? … where's Arthur?
(*Pause. His voice becoming louder and louder.*) Did he have it off with you when I was in the army …? How many times eh Nell? How many bleedin' times!
After church on Sundays …? When I'm out with the cart?
Does Peter get some too!
(*In a fury he gets up and, grabbing her hair, pulls her head back.*) Has that bastard been here too? Has he!
(MOTHER – *not retaliating – just cowers.*
Cut to TUCKER *on his bed.*
Slaps are heard.)

FATHER: (*Voice over*) You bleeding cow! You cow!
MOTHER: (*Voice over*) TOMMY! OH TOM!
(*Cut to* FATHER *hitting* MOTHER.
Cut to TUCKER *on his bed.*
Cut to man in showers washing himself.
Cut to FATHER *raining blow after blow on* MOTHER.)

Cut to man's hand going down the front of his briefs.

Cut to TUCKER *on bed. Hands over his ears, his head buried in the pillow, trying not to hear the commotion in the parlour.*
Cut to parlour, MOTHER *on the floor, crying.*
FATHER: (*Sitting looking into the fire*) Shut up! Shut up!
    (MOTHER *tries to stifle sobs.*)
    Bleedin' shut up Nell.
    (MOTHER *gets up from the floor and sits down. She wipes blood off her face. Silence.*
    Cut to TUCKER *lying down on the bed listening intently.*
    Vaguely, voices are heard. Then footsteps. MOTHER *comes into the room. She goes and sits by* TUCKER.
    They simply look at one another.
    After a pause. She starts to undress TUCKER *and put him to bed.*
    When he is finally tucked in she begins to sing him a lullaby.)
TUCKER: Mam ... oh Mam ...
MOTHER: 'So close your eyes my little drummer boy ... And say
    goodnight to all your friends and foes.'

Cut to present day. TUCKER *poking fire.*
He gets up and goes into the kitchen. He makes himself a pot of tea and some jam and bread. As he does so:
TUCKER: (*Voice over*) How long have you been doing this?
WOMAN: (*Voice over*) The tea and sympathy?
TUCKER: (*Voice over*) Yes.
WOMAN: (*Voice over*) Oh, for years. Since you were a kid.
TUCKER: (*Voice over*) Why?
WOMAN: (*Voice over*) I like to interfere.
TUCKER: (*Voice over*) Oh, stay on the right side, sister.
WOMAN: (*Voice over*) And which side is that?
    (*Pause.*)
TUCKER: (*Voice over*) No one makes bread and jam like you, Astyk.
WOMAN: (*Voice over*) Flatterer! It's the trees that are green y'know, not me.
    (*Pause.*) What's up, lad? (*Pause.*) Eat your bread, drink your tea.
TUCKER: (*Voice over*) You always say that. Remember the first time
    I came in?

WOMAN: (*Voice over*) Yes … and you said, 'Oh Astyk I think you're a bleeder'.
   (*Both laugh.*)
TUCKER: (*Voice over*) I thought it was a compliment.
   (*Their laughter fades.*
   TUCKER *is now sitting down, sipping tea.*)
TUCKER: Astyk died. Had a heart attack on a dance floor. Oh … poor Astyk. (*He finishes his snack and goes upstairs.*)

Cut to bedroom. He takes off his overcoat and puts it in the wardrobe-cum-cupboard. The back of the closet door is completely covered with wrestling photos taken during bouts. He runs his hand over them. Camera pans down these photos. They are of the more violent American kind.
As the camera pans down the photos, superimpose shouting.
Frame a still of a wrestler's contorted face.
The shouting gets louder.
'Un-freeze' this still and pull camera back.
A wrestling bout in progress. One wrestler in a 'Boston crab'.
Cut to close-up of TUCKER, *at fourteen, sitting in one of the ringside seats, wide-eyed at the bout.*
Audience roaring.
Cut to close-up of wrestler in Boston crab. His face is almost unrecognisable as he squeals in pain.
Cut to second wrestler as he applies pressure to the hold.
Cut to TUCKER. *He is almost exultant.*
Crowd roaring, louder and louder.
Cut to close-up of first wrestler's contorted face.
Crowd roaring.
Cut to close-up of second wrestler as he piles the pressure on.
Cut to TUCKER, *almost ecstatic.*
Cut to shot of ring.
FIRST WRESTLER: Yes! Yes!
   (*Roaring.*)
   (*Second wrestler releases hold. General applause.*
   Cut to TUCKER *exhausted. People begin to get up and go.* TUCKER *just sits there.*)
ANNOUNCER: And now ladies and gentlemen your appreciation for the loser.

(*Tepid applause.*
Second wrestler gets down from the ring and is immediately surrounded by schoolboys, TUCKER *lurks in the aisle. As the* WRESTLER *makes his way past* TUCKER, TUCKER *stealthily touches his thigh.*)

Cut back to TUCKER's *bedroom. He stands staring at the photos. He then goes out of the room. Mix to living room.* TUCKER *by the fire.*
TUCKER: (*Voice over*) Work on Monday ... God, what for? ... what do you do with time? ... work on Monday ... If I say it long enough p'raps it'll mean something ... God ... God ... there are times – there are times when I desperately want to feel 'content'... 'contentment'... like the cow in the field, like the zombie on the bed... work on Monday ... work... time... work and time ... what have they replaced? I'M SUFFOCATING TO DEATH! ... OH GOD! I need something to believe in again ... work on Monday ... oh God ... oh Mam ... Mam ... Mummy ...

CHILDREN'S VOICES: I believe in God the Father, Almighty, Creator of Heaven and earth, and in Jesus Christ, His only son, Our Lord.
(*Cut to children spilling out of primary school gates. Fade voices.*)
TUCKER: (*Voice over, superimposed*) I was happy then Mummy ...
I was happy ...
(*Mix to a school backyard. Children – all about eleven – march four abreast towards the camera. They are wearing fancy dress. Cut to a high shot of school yard. Children marking time in front of a window.
Cut to window.
A semi-circle of parents around the window. They applaud.
Under the window a small school choir. Through the open window a teacher plays the piano.
Cut back to high shot of school yard.
The choir begins to sing but their singing is indistinguishable.
Zoom slowly in on the choir.
As the camera gets nearer to it the singing becomes audible.
Everything else is still.*)
TUCKER: (*Voice over*) Way down upon the Swannee River ...
CHOIR: (*Singing*) 'Way down upon the Swannee River,
Far far away, There's where my heart is yearning ever,

There's where the old folk stay.
All up and down the old plantation,
Sadly I roam,
Oh darkies how my heart grows weary,
Far from the old folks at home.'
(*Cut back to* TUCKER *in living room.*)
TUCKER: (*In tears*) Miss Delaney! Miss Delaney!
(*A single note of a piano is heard being struck.*)
WOMAN: (*Voice over*) (*Singing note*) Mmmmm …
CHILDREN: (*Voice over*) (*Singing note*) Mmmmm …
(*This is repeated twice.*)
WOMAN: (*Voice over*) The old folks at home.
CHILDREN: (*Voice over*) (*Singing*) 'Way down upon the Swannee River,
Far far away,
There's where my heart is yearning ever,
There's where the old folks stay.'
(*Fade voices.*)
TUCKER: (*Voice over*) And 'Whistling Rufus The One Man Band'.
(*Silence.*)
Negro Spirituals … Miss Delaney liked negro spirituals …
and Stephen Foster …
(*Almost reverie.*)
Jeffrey Whitby's eyelashes … Swing low – sweet Cha-r-i-ot …
(*Cut back to* TUCKER.)
TUCKER: Bang! Bang! You're dead.

Cut to high shot of small parlour room. FATHER *is on the bed and the room is filled with people standing around it.*
FATHER: (*His voice barely audible*) I can see angels at the foot
of the bed, Nell …
(*A* PRIEST *leans over him murmuring extreme unction.*
GRANDMOTHER *looks at* MOTHER *and shakes her head.*
MOTHER'S *face crumbles into tears.*
Cut to TUCKER. *He is transfixed by the body of his* FATHER *on the bed.*)
A VOICE: Death … death.
(*Cut to high shot of the room directly over the bed.*
The PRIEST *finishes the last sacraments and straightens up.*

The room is very still, very bright, very hot.)
PRIEST: God rest his soul.
GRAN: He's gone ... My Tommy's gone ...
> (MOTHER *is convulsed in sobs.*
> *Zoom slowly in on the corpse of the* FATHER *and his long, rigid features.*
> *Cut back to* TUCKER.)

A VOICE: He's stiff!
> (*Cut back to high shot of the bed.*
> *Continue slow zoom in on* FATHER.
> *Cut to* TUCKER.)

A VOICE: That smell ... it's him that's smelling.
> (*Cut back to high shot of bed.*
> *Continue zoom, until* FATHER's *face is framed.* GRAN *places pennies on* FATHER's *eyes.*
> *Cut to side view of* FATHER's *head.*
> *Cut to* TUCKER. *His jaws are being forced together seemingly by their own volition. He holds his head and begins to rock to and fro faster and faster. A sound like that of an animal is heard coming through his clenched teeth.*)

TUCKER: NNNNNNNNNN! NNNNNNNNNN!
> (*He rushes from the parlour.*
> *Cut to doorstep,* TUCKER *comes flying out and sinks down on the doorstep. Pause.*)

TUCKER: The bastard's dead ... we're free, Mam ...

Zoom in on his hunched figure on the doorstep. When he is framed in close up, hold, then freeze, then blur vision.

Clear vision, TUCKER *is still sitting on doorstep but now he holds a loaf. It is two days later, early evening.*

TUCKER: (*Voice over*) I'm frightened to go in ... past the parlour ...
> I'm scared ...
> (*Cut to high shot of parlour.*
> FATHER *lies in coffin. The rest of the room is filled with flowers from floor to ceiling.*
> *Cut back to* TUCKER *on doorstep.*
> *Pull camera back to reveal two women peering down at him.*)

FIRST WOMAN: Is your mam in, lad?

TUCKER: Yes, Mrs May.
SECOND WOMAN: Can you tell her – we've come to see your dad.
　(TUCKER *just sits there.*)
FIRST WOMAN: Go on lad. Go on.
TUCKER: I'm scared, Mrs May. I'm scared.
　(*She puts her arm around him.*)
FIRST WOMAN: What of, lad?
TUCKER: I'm too scared to go past the parlour.
SECOND WOMAN: Well, your Dad can't hurt you now, son.
FIRST WOMAN: The dead can't bite.
TUCKER: (*In a paroxysm*) I'm scared, Mrs May! I'M SCARED!
FIRST WOMAN: Well you run in and tell your mam we're here …
　We'll watch you.
　(TUCKER *stands up, waits for a minute, then rushes in.*
　The two women look after him. The FIRST WOMAN *shakes her head and tuts.*)

Mix to high shot of parlour. The two women stand looking into the coffin. Silence.
FIRST WOMAN: Well he won't feel any more pain now, Nellie …
God help him.
　(MOTHER *nods. Silence.*)
SECOND WOMAN: I liked Tommy. He always let on when you passed.
　(*Pause. Then the women start looking at the wreaths and reading the condolence cards attached to them.*)
MOTHER: (*After a long silence*) Thanks for the wreath … it was lovely.
FIRST WOMAN: We wanted to.
　(*Pause.*)
SECOND WOMAN: It was the least we could do.
　(*A long silence as the three of them stare into the coffin.*)
FIRST WOMAN: Well, Nellie, we'd better be going.
MOTHER: Thanks for coming.
SECOND WOMAN: T'ra Nell.
　(*All three leave the room.*
　Superimpose FIRST WOMAN*'s voice as camera lingers in high shot of room.*)
FIRST WOMAN's voice: I liked Tommy … I knew him well.

Mix to MOTHER's *bedroom in total darkness. It's about 2 a.m. the following morning. It is a large, sparse room. It contains a double bed in which the* MOTHER *is asleep.*
Cut to TUCKER's *bedroom. A single bed in which* TUCKER *lies.*
Cut to TUCKER. *He is awake.*
He lies perfectly still listening hard.
Slowly he comes into a sitting position.
Silence.
He listens hard.
A long pause.
Silence.
He gets up and waits.
Absolute silence.
Slowly he leaves the bedroom on tiptoe, goes to the head of the stairs and looks down.
TUCKER: (*In a hushed whisper*) Mam!
    (*Nothing.*)
    (*Hushed whisper*) Mam!
    (*Nothing.*)
Cut to bottom of stairs, TUCKER's *face is framed at the top of them. To the right of camera, light is seen under the kitchen door.*
Cut to inside the kitchen.
Several people sit drinking tea in absolute silence.
Cut back to the bottom of the stairs.
TUCKER *gingerly makes his way down them. He slowly goes to the kitchen door and listens.*
Silence.
Very slowly he makes his way along the hall to the parlour and stands in front of the curtain.
For a while he stands there unable to pluck up enough courage to lift the curtain.
Slowly he pulls the curtain up. He steps inside.
Mix to shot of parlour now lit only by candles. Mid-high shot from sideboard end.
TUCKER *comes and stands at right of frame.*
Stillness.

Mix to close-up of TUCKER *rivetted by the coffin.*
Mix to coffin.
Mix to flowers.
Mix to shot of parlour.
Cut to TUCKER *through candles' flame walking towards the coffin.*
Cut to coffin, TUCKER *walking towards it.*
Cut to flowers.
Cut to TUCKER *walking towards coffin as seen from coffin's point of view.*
Cut to coffin with FATHER*'s face showing,* TUCKER *left of scene.*
TUCKER, *now terrified, rushes from the room.*
Cut to the hall, TUCKER *running upstairs.*
Cut to bedroom, TUCKER *comes flying in and throws himself on the bed.*
Blur vision.
Clear vision: bedroom the next morning, TUCKER *sits on the bed dressed in his funeral clothes.*
Pause.
He lifts his arms to his face and sniffs the material. He then lifts the corner of his jacket and sniffs that. He goes to the window. Mix to shot of the street as seen from TUCKER*'s point of view. Neighbours throng around the front door and the four funeral cars. The undertakers' men are loading the wreaths on to the hearse.*
Mix to the parlour. They are screwing the coffin lid down.
Mix to the bedroom, TUCKER *looks at the floor. Superimposed the squealing of cats. A child's voice is heard: 'Don't kill them ... don't kill the kittens.' Shot of* FATHER *kneeling on the bedroom floor dropping kittens into a bucket of water. They squeal, they struggle: they drown, then float around in the water dead.*
Cut back to TUCKER. *He hides his face in the curtains.*
Mix to shot of hall. The mourners – all in black – leave the kitchen. The group is headed by TUCKER *and* MOTHER.
Zoom or track back from this group as they come down the hall. The coffin is loaded into the hearse. At the head of the group of mourners, TUCKER *comes out. He stops and looks down into the street.*
Cut to street and cortège as seen from TUCKER*'s point of view.*
All eyes seem to be on him.
Pan camera around their faces full circle and finish with close-up of TUCKER*'s profile.*

A slight pause, TUCKER *quite suddenly bursts out into a single laugh.*
Mix to long shot of cortège. All get into the cars and the cortège moves off.
Mix to graveside. A man with a shovel full of dirt offers it to each mourner, MOTHER *first, then* TUCKER *and so on. They throw their handfuls of soil into the grave. Mix to* MOTHER*'s face.*)

MOTHER: (*Voice over*) Oh love … oh love.

(*Silence.*

Mix to TUCKER*'s face.*

Cut to him lying in his bedroom, his hands over his ears trying to blot out MOTHER*'s screams of 'Oh Tommy … Tom …'*

Cut to wrestling ring. A wrestler's contorted face.

Cut to man in showers.

Cut to TUCKER; *present day, in living room, closing his eyes.*

Cut to other man pulling his fly down.

Cut to graveside.)

TUCKER: (*Voice over*) Bastards! Bastards!

(*Silence. All look into the grave.* MOTHER *still crying.*

Cut back to living room, TUCKER *present day.*)

TUCKER: Dad … Dad … please say that you love me, Dad …

(*Cut back to graveside. They stand looking into the grave.*

Mix to parlour.

Cut back to graveside.

They stand looking into grave.)

Mix to parlour. They have returned from the cemetery, MOTHER *sits there in an armchair – frozen, expressionless,* TUCKER *looks at her. Then he goes to her and begins to stroke her hair. She just sits there and stares ahead. Silence. As he continues to gently stroke her hair, she takes his other hand in hers.*

Mix to kitchen, TUCKER *stands by the window looking out.*

Mix to outside shot of TUCKER *looking through window.*

Mix back to Tucker inside. Silence.

Mix back to outside shot of TUCKER *looking through window. Hold. Then begin to zoom very slowly away and fade in 'The Ballad of Barbara Allen' being sung by the unaccompanied voice of a girl.*

BALLAD: 'A witch-boy from the mountain came,

  A-pining to be human,
  For he had seen the fairest girl …
  A girl named Barbara Allen.'
  Mix back to TUCKER *in kitchen.*
  Silence.
TUCKER: (*Near to tears*) Oh Dad … Dad!
  (*Mix back outside to shot of* TUCKER. *Continue to zoom away.*)
BALLAD: 'O Conjur Man, O conjur man,
  Please do this thing I'm wanting,
  Please change me to a human man,
  For Barbara I'd be courting.'
  (*Mix back inside to* TUCKER.
  This time the ballad is heard inside kitchen, TUCKER *is crying.*)
BALLAD: 'Oh you can be a man, a man,
  If Barbara will not grieve you,
  If she be faithful for a year,
  Your eagle he will leave you.'
  (*Mix back to outside shot of* TUCKER.
  Continue zooming slowly away until his face and the window and the house become smaller and smaller.)
BALLAD: 'O Barbara will you marry me
  And will you leave me never
  Oh yes my love I'll marry you
  And live with you for ever.'

37 INTERIOR. CANTEEN. DAY.

LONG SHOT of TUCKER at centre canteen table eating his sandwiches and surrounded by his colleagues at other tables.

He is seen across the billiard table at which three men are playing.

Very slowly TRACK and ZOOM in on TUCKER.

INTERCOM:- Call for Mr. Maxwell........telephone call for Mr. Maxwell.......

CONTINUE TRACK and ZOOM

1ST. MAN :- (As 2nd Man sinks a ball) Wonderful fucking shot!

2ND. MAN :- Oh fuck!

3RD. MAN :- Fucking great stuff!

NOT YET DONE

37 MAN :- (At one of the tables behind TUCKER) I got some conti-board and woodstained it.......then I varnished the hardboard.......I'm bloody made-up with them shelves........

TRACK and ZOOM stops.

TUCKER is in CLOSE UP (SIDE WAYS ON).

He has stopped eating his sandwiches.

INTERCOM:- (Annoyed) Calling Mr. Maxwell!......telephone call for Mr. Maxwell!

TUCKER turns and looks at the men who are playing billiards. (Right at camera)

It is a look which drips with a mixture of loathing, anger and longing.

His eyes fill with tears.

CUT TO:-

NOT YET DONE

Madonna and Child (1980): Shooting script. (BFI National Archive)

TRILOGY: PART II
MADONNA AND CHILD (1980)

Madonna and Child (1980): Tucker (Terry O'Sullivan) and Mother (Sheila Raynor).

Cast and crew of *Madonna and Child* include:

TUCKER (middle-aged)	Terry O'Sullivan
MOTHER	Sheila Raynor
TATTOOIST	Paul Barber
PRIEST	John Meynall
MAN IN CLUB	Brian Ward
TATTOOED MAN	Dave Cooper
SECOND MAN	Mark Walton
MAN IN TOILET	Mal Jefferson
WOMAN IN OFFICE	Lovette Edwards
WOMAN IN OFFICE	Rita Thatchery
MAN IN OFFICE	Eddie Ross
Written and Directed by	Terence Davies
Production	Mike Maloney
Cameraman	William Diver
Assistant Cameraman	Sergio Leon
Assistant Director	Kees Ryninks
Continuity	Victoria McBain
Sound Recordist	Antoinette de Bromhead
Grip	Tim Rolt
Editor	Mick Audsley
Dubbing Editor	Geoff Hogg

A National Film School Production, 1980.

LIVERPOOL: THE PRESENT

Fade up on

EXT. PIER HEAD. LIVERPOOL. DAY

It is early morning, and cold. Close-up of a seagull wheeling in the sky above the River Mersey.
Pan with it, following its flight.
Dissolve to other angles of the bird in close-up and medium close-up.
Over this, a CHILDREN'S CHOIR *singing – echoing and distant – :*

CHOIR: 'Hail Queen of Heaven, the ocean star,
        Guide of the wanderer here below,
        Thrown on life's search we claim thy care,
        Save us from peril and from woe.
        Virgin most pure, Star of the sea,
        Pray for the wanderer, pray for me.'

Then a series of pans and dissolves as camera follows other birds in flight, wheeling in the sky and dipping over the river.
Dissolve to high shot of the river, looking out towards the sea.
Pan to the Birkenhead ferry at berth or about to dock.
Cut to:

INT. BUS COMPLEX. PIER HEAD

TUCKER *in medium close-up coming down through the first bus tunnel going towards the pier head. He is in sharp focus but the background/surround is blurred.*
Cut to mid-shot of TUCKER *walking down second bus tunnel on his way to pier gangway.*
Cut to bottom of pier gangway, TUCKER *walks down.*
Cut to:

EXT. LANDING STAGE. PIER HEAD

TUCKER *comes towards the Wallasey ferry berth and waits.*
Cut to TUCKER'S *point of view of Birkenhead ferry. The boat moves away from the landing stage. We watch it drift to mid-river. The Wallasey ferry is also mid-river getting closer quickly, about to dock. Cut to* TUCKER *in medium*

close-up. He looks cold and tired. He yawns. Then his face settles back into impassivity. He seems near to tears.
Cut to Wallasey ferry docking and passengers disembarking.
A ferryman goes by.
Cut to side-view of TUCKER in close-up. He follows the ferryman as he walks across and looks out to sea.
Cut to shot of the ferryman. He takes a drag on his cigarette then flicks it into the river. His arm is noticeably tattooed.
Cut to:

INT. BEDROOM. NIGHT

Close-up of a man. He is naked to the waist. He smiles then turns his head to the right and looks down. The camera slowly travels from his face down over his heavily tattooed chest and arm until it frames his hand. Camera stops. The man lifts his forefinger and TUCKER's head comes into frame.
He is smiling. He looks up. He licks the man's forefinger then, taking the entire finger into his mouth, he sucks it.
Cut to:

INT. FERRY. DAY

TUCKER gets up from the seat and goes to the gangway in order to disembark.
Cut to TUCKER in medium close-up. Liverpool receding further and further away in the background.
Cut to close-up of TUCKER (Back view) waiting to disembark. Wallasey pier getting closer and closer.
Cut to:

EXT. WALLASEY LANDING-STAGE

The gangplank comes crashing down, TUCKER disembarks.
Cut to long shot from top of gangway, TUCKER walks up. He gets to the pay booth and pays.
Cut to:

EXT. WALLASEY FERRY BUILDING BUS DEPOT

TUCKER comes out of the entrance. Pan with him.
Cut to TUCKER walking down by the side of the bus depot building.
A single stroke on a kettledrum is heard.

Cut to:

INT. BACK OFFICE. LATER THAT MORNING

Side view of TUCKER *in close-up. He is absorbed in his work. Silence except for someone's continual coughing and wheezing. Distant phones ringing. Office sounds – dull and far away. Track around desks in medium shot. At the first desk – a man thirty-six, balding. He is working. Continue track. At the second desk – a woman twenty-six. As she works she sucks a sweet. Continue track. At the third desk – a woman, late fifties. She is coughing/wheezing continually. Stop track when she is framed. She takes a drag on her cigarette then stubs it out.*

WOMAN: (*Without looking up and in between coughs*) Did you go anywhere at the weekend?

Cut to:

INT. TUCKER'S BEDROOM. NIGHT

Low angle shot of TUCKER's *feet going into cowboy boots.*
Cut to TUCKER's *thighs. He is squeezing into very light jeans, cut to* TUCKER *putting on a polo-necked sweater then a leather bomber jacket. All this business is done in the dark and very carefully so that no one will hear.*

Cut to:

INT. MOTHER'S BEDROOM. NIGHT

Shot of MOTHER *in bed, asleep.*

Cut to:

INT. LANDING CONNECTING THE TWO BEDROOMS. NIGHT

Low angle shot of TUCKER's *feet coming through his bedroom door. Pan with him to the head of the stairs. He treads very carefully so that he will make no noise.*

Cut to:

INT. BOTTOM OF THE STAIRS. NIGHT

TUCKER *stands at the top of the stairs perfectly still. Silence. He steps forward. A creak is heard.*
Cut to TUCKER *at the top of the stairs in close-up. He freezes and listens. Silence. Long pause. He leans towards* MOTHER's *bedroom door.*

TUCKER: (*In a hoarse whisper*) Mam… Mam …
Cut to:

INT. MOTHER'S BEDROOM. NIGHT

MOTHER *moves in her sleep, sighs, then blinks half-awake but she is still very drowsy.*
Cut to:

INT. LANDING. NIGHT

TUCKER *in close-up. Dead silence. Pause.*
Cut to low angle shot of TUCKER*'s feet. He treads very gingerly on to the first stair.*
Cut to:

INT. MOTHER'S BEDROOM. NIGHT

MOTHER *stirs and murmurs something in her sleep. Still very sleepy she gradually blinks awake and listens.*
Cut to:

INT. HALL. NIGHT

TUCKER *– seen from the bottom of the stairs – he descends very slowly and quietly.*
Cut to:

INT. MOTHER'S BEDROOM. NIGHT

MOTHER *leans up on one elbow – listening intently.*
Cut to:

INT. HALL. NIGHT

TUCKER *reaches the hallway and goes quietly to the front door. Pan with him. He begins – very slowly and gingerly – to take off the alarm bell chain.*
Cut to TUCKER *in close-up. He bends down and begins to draw the bolt back from the bottom of the front door. It squeaks loudly. He stops and listens. Dead silence.*
Cut to:

INT. MOTHER'S BEDROOM. NIGHT

MOTHER *in close-up. She is straining every nerve listening. Dead silence.*
Cut to:

TRILOGY II: MADONNA AND CHILD

INT. HALL. NIGHT

TUCKER *at the front door. He slides the bolt back. Then quietly opens the front door and goes out.*
Cut to:

EXT. FLAT'S LANDING. NIGHT

TUCKER *comes out of the flat. He closes the front door very quietly and with equal care comes through the gate, making sure that he leaves it open.*
Cut to:

INT. MOTHER'S BEDROOM. NIGHT

MOTHER *in bed. Pause. Then she eases herself back against the pillows. She is wide awake. Her eyes wide – she is near to tears.*
Cut to:

EXT. FLAT'S LANDING. NIGHT

Shot of TUCKER. *He smirks to himself, then walks down the landing feeling his crutch.*
Cut to:

INT. BACK OFFICE. DAY

WOMAN: (*Repeating the question*) Did you?
    (*Cut to* TUCKER *in close-up. He looks surprised. Pause.*)
TUCKER: (*Nervous, hesitatingly*) … No …
    (*He continues working but is obviously very disturbed.*
    Hold this shot for a long time.
    Dissolve to tracking shot around desks. Feet in medium close-up. At the first desk – the man's feet. His left foot on the ground his right foot on its tip. Continue track. At the second desk – the woman's feet. Her legs crossed. Continue track. At the third desk – the woman's feet. Her legs crossed behind her. Dissolve to close-up of woman's mouth at third desk. She is coughing through her clenched fist. Track around desks. Close-up of woman at second desk. She is sucking a sweet. Continue track. Close-up of man at first desk. He is sucking his teeth. Continue track until TUCKER *is framed in close-up. Track stops. Silence,* TUCKER *looks at them in utter disbelief.*
    Cut to:)

EXT. STREET. DAY

Shot of the black stones of a wall. Track slowly left to right. A man is seen standing in a doorway. He is looking down the street to his left. He takes a drag on his cigarette. He is very heavily tattooed on the chest and arms. Continue track until shop window is framed. Stop track. The window is covered with designs for tattoos and reads: 'JACKS – TATTOO ARTIST' (and telephone number).
Cut to:

EXT. STREET. DAY

TUCKER *in close-up. Track with him as he walks past tattoo shop. He looks extremely tense.*
Cut to:

INT. CHURCH. EVENING

Three tracking shots over which there are continuous voice overs. Track one: the camera tracks from left to right along the side aisle over the first six Stations of the Cross. Over this, dialling/ringing/and pips heard. Money being put into a phone box. Pause.
MAN: (*Voice over*) (*Short, sharp*) Jacks!
TUCKER: (*Voice over*) (*Extremely nervous*) Is that the tattooists?
MAN: (*Voice over*) Yer …
   (*A long pause.*)
TUCKER: (*Voice over*) (*Almost choked with nerves*) I … er … I want my bollocks tattooed …
MAN: (*Voice over*) (*Decisively*) I won't touch a prick for less than twenty notes …
   (*Pause.*)
TUCKER: (*Voice over*) (*Desperate*) Will you do it?
   (*Slight pause.*)
MAN: (*Voice over*) (*Bending very slightly*) It takes a helluva fuckin' time … I've got a tattoo on me own chopper and it took me three days to get it on … besides it hurts like fuck …
TUCKER: (*Voice over*) (*Very desperate*) Will you do it?
MAN: (*Voice over*) (*Bending a little further*) Apart from the time it takes, its gotta be as hard as a biscuit … you'll be wankin' off by the minute …

(*A very long pause.*)
TUCKER: (*Voice over*) (*Almost to himself*) Please say you'll do it. *Please!*
(*A complete silence.*)
MAN: (*Voice over*) (*Matter-of-fact*) … what d'you want on it anyway?
TUCKER: (*Voice over*) (*Reviving a little, a ray of hope but still very nervous*) I want 'fuck' down the back of my cock in big black letters and a swastika on each of my balls …
(*Silence.*)
(*Pleading.*) Will you do it?
(*Silence.
Dissolve to track two: the camera tracks from right to left along the back aisle looking down towards the high altar.*)
MAN: (*Voice over*) (*Uncertainly*) Well … I mean … you might have a dose. I do it for you then three weeks later I'm scratchin' the bollocks off meself …
(*Dissolve to track three: the camera tracks from left to right over the last six Stations of the Cross.*)
TUCKER: (*Voice over*) (*Quickly*) You won't get a dose off me.
MAN: (*Voice over*) (*Snapping back*) Yer – that's what they all say when they come in here – and a lotta guys want their bollocks tattooed …
TUCKER: (*Voice over*) (*Trying to resolve the situation*) Will you do it for me?
MAN: (*Voice over*) (*Still annoyed*) It's no skin off my fuckin' nose … but it'll cost yer … if I hold a prick in me hand I want payin' – thirty notes – no messin'!
(TUCKER *does not answer. An anguished silence.*)
TUCKER: (*Voice over*) (*Trance-like*) When can I come round?
MAN: (*Voice over*) (*Perfunctory*) No – I won't touch a prick for less than fifty.
(*And the line goes dead.
End of track.*)
Cut to:

INT. CHURCH. EVENING

Side view of MOTHER'S *hands in close-up clasped – praying. She holds rosary beads.*
Cut to Side view of MOTHER *and* TUCKER *in two-shots kneeling in confessional pews,* MOTHER *crosses herself and moves to sit back in pew.*

Cut to Medium close-up of MOTHER *and* TUCKER *in two-shots.* MOTHER *sitting in pew.* TUCKER *still kneeling. He is praying, although his prayer is inaudible. Pietà in background. He finishes praying and moves back and sits in pew beside* MOTHER.
Cut to close shot of them both sitting in pew. Pietà in background. Silence.
Cut to side view of MOTHER *and* TUCKER *sitting outside confessional box. A penitent comes out and* TUCKER *gets up and enters confessional box.*
Cut to:

INT. CONFESSIONAL BOX

Blackness. Silence. Pause, TUCKER *is seen kneeling down at the grille. He is just discernible in the darkness. He makes the sign of the cross.*

TUCKER: (*As he does so*) In the name of the Father, and of the Son, and of the Holy Ghost. Amen.

(*The* PRIEST *momentarily lifts the curtain behind the grille then drops it back again.*)

Bless me Father, for I have sinned.

PRIEST'S VOICE: (*Barely audible*) May the Lord be in your heart and on your lips, that you may, with truth and humility, confess all your sins, in the name of the Father, and of the Son, and of the Holy Ghost. Amen.

TUCKER: I confess to Almighty God, to Blessed Mary, ever Virgin, to Blessed Michael the Archangel, to Blessed John the Baptist, to the holy apostles Peter and Paul, and to all the saints, that I have sinned exceedingly, in thought, word, and deed, through my fault, through my fault, through my most grievous fault. Pray, father, give me your blessing. It is three weeks since my last confession and I accuse myself of missing Mass on Sundays through my own fault – three times, taking God's holy name in vain – many times, being disobedient – four times, being proud-twice …

(TUCKER'S VOICE *begins to fade. Pan away from him, from left to right, to blackness.*)

Coveting my neighbour's goods – three times …

(*His voice now completely gone. Pan ends. Blackness.*)

Oh, you've got a fucking gorgeous arse!

(*Cut to:*)

INT. BEDROOM. NIGHT

Pan from right to left, to medium close-up of TUCKER. *He sits on a bed. On the extreme left of frame a man stands – back to camera – facing* TUCKER. *The man is visible only from the waist to the knees. He begins to unbuckle his belt and jeans.*

When he has unbuckled the belt and undone the top of his jeans he stops. A pause, TUCKER *then pulls the man's jeans slowly down and he is naked underneath them. A pause,* TUCKER *looks up at the man then directly at the man's crotch,* TUCKER *then opens his mouth very wide. As camera tracks from right to left behind the man so that his buttocks entirely fill the frame. Slight pause. Then* TUCKER'*s hands come into shot being placed on the man's buttocks,* TUCKER'*s hands clutch at man's buttocks once – then twice. Cut to:*

INT. CONFESSIONAL BOX

Blackness. Pan right to left until TUCKER *is framed. He is still kneeling at the grille.*

TUCKER: (*Fade up his voice*) … dishonouring my parents – many times, despairing – many times, borne hatred – three times. (*Long pause.*) That is all I can remember, father.

(*The* PRIEST *raises the curtain.*)

PRIEST: (*From behind the grille*) Is there anything else you wish to confess, my son?

(*Cut to close-up of* TUCKER *seen from the* PRIEST'S *point of view through the grille.*)

TUCKER: (*Wanting desperately to speak but unable to do so. Shakes his head*) No Father …

(*Curtain is dropped.*

Cut to shot of TUCKER *kneeling at grille.*)

(*With no conviction, almost despair*) For these and all other sins that have escaped my memory, I am heartily sorry, humbly ask pardon from God, and penance and absolution from you Father.

(*The words of absolution are spoken by the* PRIEST.)

PRIEST: (*Voice over, ending*) … and for your penance say three Hail Mary's, two Our Fathers and one Glory Be. God bless you, my son.

TUCKER: Thank you Father.

(*He just kneels there in the darkness.*

Cut to:)

EXT. ALLEY, NIGHT

TUCKER – *in medium long shot – is seen coming down an alley and stopping at a door. He knocks.*
Cut to TUCKER *in close-up at the door. It has a grille in it. Getting no reply he knocks again. A small door behind the grille slips back.*
YOUNG MAN: (*From behind the grille throughout*) Yer?
TUCKER: (*Trying to sound very masculine*) Are you open yet pal?
YOUNG MAN: (*Suspiciously*) This is a gay club.
TUCKER: Yes, I know.
YOUNG MAN: I haven't seen you here before.
TUCKER: I came here about two years ago.
YOUNG MAN: Who with?
TUCKER: A mate.
YOUNG MAN: (*Not convinced*) Oh.
   (*He snaps the grille-door shut.*
   Cut to:)

INT. CHURCH. EVENING

Close up of crucifix on the high altar.
Cut to TUCKER *kneeling at altar rails saying his penance. His prayers peter out and he looks at the cross. Pause. He closes his eyes in horror, covering his face with his hands.*
TUCKER: Say but the word, and my soul shall be healed.
   (*A single stroke on a kettledrum is heard.*
   Cut to:)

INT. BACK OFFICE. DAY

General shot of the four desks. Silence. Then a siren is heard and everyone gets up and exits. It is lunchtime.
Cut to:

INT. CANTEEN. DAY

Long shot of TUCKER *at centre canteen table eating his sandwiches and surrounded by his colleagues at other tables. He is seen across the billiard table at which three men are playing. Very slowly track and zoom in on* TUCKER.

INTERCOM: Call for Mr Maxwell ... telephone call for Mr Maxwell ...
(*Continue track and zoom.*)
FIRST MAN: (As SECOND MAN *sinks a ball*) Wonderful fucking shot!
SECOND MAN: Oh fuck!
THIRD MAN: Fucking great stuff!
MAN: (*At one of the tables behind* TUCKER) I got some conti-board and woodstained it... then I varnished the hardboard ... I'm bloody made-up with them shelves ...
(*Track and zoom stops. Side view of* TUCKER *in close-up.*
He has stopped eating his sandwiches.)
INTERCOM: (*Annoyed*) Calling Mr Maxwell! ... telephone call for Mr Maxwell!
(TUCKER *turns and looks at the men who are playing billiards, right at camera. It is a look which drips with a mixture of loathing, anger and longing. His eyes fill with tears.*
Cut to:)

EXT. STREET, NIGHT

Low angle shot of TUCKER's *feet. He is wearing cowboy boots and walking along pavement. Track with him.*
Cut to:

INT. TOILETS. NIGHT

Silence except for dripping water. Semi-darkness. Low-angled shot of TUCKER's *feet coming into toilets. Track with him as he goes to one of the urinals and stands there. Hold. Then track slowly along to next but one urinal and frame a man's feet.*
Cut to close-up of TUCKER. *He is looking down. Pause. He then looks right towards man. Cut to close-up of man at other urinal. He is also looking down.* TUCKER *coughs, and the man looks left towards him. Pause. Then the man passes his tongue nervously across his lips.*
Cut to long shot of TUCKER *and man standing perfectly still at their respective urinals, their backs to camera. Silence. A long pause. Then* TUCKER *moves to urinal next to man. A long pause. Then simultaneously their hands reach towards one another.*
Cut to:

INT. FILING AND RECORDS OFFICE. DAY

Immediately after lunch. Rows and rows of files are stacked, TUCKER *comes swiftly in and bangs the doors shut as if in an absolute fury and walks to the files. He gets a file down and begins to go through it.*
Track slowly in on him. As we get closer he stops reading and stares at the papers, then looks up. He begins to cry. TUCKER *now in close-up. He is sobbing. His crying reaches a climax then begins to subside. Track back from him to mid-shot. He stops crying. He wipes his eyes and blows his nose.*
Cut to:

INT. BOARDROOM. DAY

Late afternoon. Long shot of TUCKER *from the end of the board table.*
He looks towards us.
Cut to long shot of man from TUCKER'S *point of view at other end of table speaking into the telephone, although what he is saying can only be faintly heard.*
Cut to side or back view of TUCKER *in close-up. He is looking towards us.*
Pause. He sighs, then looks out of the window.
Cut to:

INT. DAY

TUCKER *is seen coming slowly down the corridor outside the boardroom.*
Pan with him as he turns into reception. He goes upstairs.
Cut to:

INT. GENERAL OFFICE. LATE AFTERNOON

Mid-shot of TUCKER *coming through the door. He is seen through the glass panelled inner office. Pan with him.* TUCKER *goes to a desk in the outer office and begins to go through the day book.*
Man at desk in inner office looks around then taps on the glass partition and beckons TUCKER *in.*
Cut to:

INT. BACK OFFICE. LATE AFTERNOON

Pan around office. All the desks are empty and cleared. Frame TUCKER *in close-up. He is still at his desk. He bangs a filing cabinet shut and then tidies his desk. He finishes tidying up then rubs his face with his hands. Then he stares straight ahead. It is a look of weariness, mingled with despair.*

Cut to:

EXT. STREET. LATE AFTERNOON

Shot of TUCKER *as he walks over the first iron bridge in Birkenhead.*

VOICE OVERS: Good night June …
    Good night Lynn …
    Nigh-night Chris …
    Night …

Cut to TUCKER *walking down a street in Birkenhead with Victorian lamp-standards along it.*
Cut to TUCKER *walking across second iron bridge in Birkenhead.*
Cut to:

INT./EXT. FERRY BUILDING/BUS DEPOT. WALLASEY. LATE AFTERNOON

TUCKER *walks down the gangway towards ferry berth.*
Cut to mid-shot of TUCKER *from behind looking towards Liverpool waiting for the ferry to dock. From the same angle ferry docks and* TUCKER *boards.*
Cut to mid-shot of TUCKER *from behind at gangway on ferry looking towards Liverpool, waiting for ferry to dock. Ferry docks,* TUCKER *disembarks.*
Cut to:

EXT. STREET. LATE AFTERNOON

Bus stops and TUCKER *gets off and walks across waste ground towards flats. Pan with him.*
Cut to long shots of blocks of flats.
MOTHER: (*Voice over*) I've done a bit of sausage and mash for your tea …
    with some onion gravy … OK, lad?
TUCKER: (*Voice over*) Yes, Mam …
    Cut to:

INT. TUCKER'S FLAT. BATHROOM. NIGHT

It is full of steam. TUCKER *stands in the bathroom and brings his hands to his face and luxuriously wipes his face and neck and chest.*
Cut to:

INT. LIVING-ROOM. NIGHT

Medium shot of TUCKER *on settee. TV is on.* TUCKER *is watching it.*

He looks across at his MOTHER. *Pan to* MOTHER. *She sits on the other side of the settee, her mouth open.*
Cut to close-up of TUCKER. *He is still looking at* MOTHER.
Cut to close-up of MOTHER, *her hands lying in her apron.*
Cut to close-up of TUCKER.
TUCKER: (*Very softly*) Oh, Mam …
　(*Cut to* MOTHER. *Her head droops. Her mouth is open. She stirs in her sleep.*)
MOTHER: (*Half-awake, half-asleep*) Oh, I'm dead licked …
　(*Dissolve to shot of living-room from behind the settee. TV is off.* TUCKER *is looking straight ahead,* MOTHER *is asleep. Silence. Dissolve to shot of* MOTHER *winding clock.*)
MOTHER: See you in the morning lad …
　(*Pan with her to the door.*)
　I'll lock up …
　(*Cut to side view of* TUCKER *in close-up from behind the settee.*)
TUCKER: OK Mam. D'you want some cocoa later on?
　(*Cut to* MOTHER *at door.*)
MOTHER: Yer … goodnight son …
　(*She exits.*
　Cut to side view of TUCKER *in mid-close-up.*)
TUCKER: Good night Mam. God bless.
　(*Cut to front view of* TUCKER *in close-up. He listens to the door being bolted then the sound of his* MOTHER *climbing the stairs. Dissolve to:*)

INT. LIVING-ROOM. NIGHT

Shot of TUCKER *pulling the hearthrug back several inches from the grate.*
Cut to shot of TUCKER *fluffing then rearranging the cushions on the settee.*
Cut to shot of TUCKER *switching off the lights in the living-room.*
Cut to shot of TUCKER *pouring hot milk into his* MOTHER'S *cup. Dissolve to:*

INT. MOTHER'S BEDROOM. NIGHT

Shot of TUCKER *coming into her bedroom carrying a cup of cocoa. The room is lit only by the landing light,* TUCKER *sits on the bed.*
TUCKER: (*Softly*) Mam …
　(*Gently shakes his* MOTHER.) Mam …
　(MOTHER *wakes up.*)

Here's your cocoa, Mam.
(*He gives her the cup of cocoa. Taking the cup she sits up in bed.*)
MOTHER: (*Sipping her cocoa*) Thanks lad … You're a good boy …
(*She continues sipping her cocoa,* TUCKER *continues sitting on the bed. They just look at one another.*
Dissolve to close-up of MOTHER *lying in bed asleep. Her mouth is open.*)

INT. TUCKER'S BEDROOM. NIGHT

Side view of TUCKER *in close-up. He is in bed, asleep. His face is turned away from the camera. He sighs and stirs in his sleep.*
VOICE OVER: (*Long, low and sibilant*) P–A–R–I–O–L–E–Y!
(TUCKER *turns. His face is now in profile.*)
VOICE OVER: But know thou that for all these things God will bring thee into judgement. For God shall bring every work into judgement, with every secret thing, whether it be good or whether it be evil.
(*Cut to:*)

EXT. FLAT'S LANDING. DAY

It is overcast. Grey. Slightly unreal. Four men carry a coffin down the landing. They are seen head on.
TUCKER'*s head immediately above and behind the coffin. He looks terror-stricken. The cortège moves towards the camera.*
VOICE OVER: And further, by these, my son be admonished … put away evil from thy flesh …
(*Cut to:*)

EXT. FLAT'S ENTRANCE. DAY

A very high shot of the coffin from the top of the flats looking directly down. The coffin comes into shot. It appears to float into frame as the four men carry it.
VOICE OVER: For the souls of the righteous are in the hands of God …
(*Cut to:*)

EXT. FLAT'S ENTRANCE. DAY

Head on shot of coffin carried by four men, with TUCKER'*s face and head immediately above and behind coffin,* TUCKER *looks terror stricken.*
VOICE OVER: And there shall be no torment to touch them …
(*Cut to:*)

INT. CHURCH. DAY

Low-angle shot of the feet of the four men carrying the coffin very low. Track with them down centre aisle. They place the coffin on trestles.

VOICE OVER: And the fruits that thy soul lusted after are departed from thee ... The time is at hand ... Thy judgement is come.

(*Cut to low-angled shot from inside the coffin. The faces of the four men look down at the camera. They are all impassive.*)

VOICE OVER: The judgement and the mercy of God.

(*A single stroke on the kettledrum is heard.*

Cut to high shot of coffin in centre aisle, TUCKER *is in it. His eyes are open. Begin a very slow zoom in on to his terror-stricken face. He tries desperately to speak but cannot. His mouth twitches as he tries to open it.*)

TUCKER: (*Trying desperately to speak*) ... A ... a ... shs ... st ... sti ... sti ... sti ... gu ... cru ... ddd ... drup ... cru ... c ... ccc ... cour ... age ... Cruda ... cru ... cruuuuuu ... A ... ha ... haha ... ha ... ha ... daas ... das ... de, de, de, de, ... De-eeeee ... De-eeeee ... nnnnnnnn ... nnnnnnooooooo!! ... nnnnoooo ... ppppppppooooorr, or ... Poor ... poor-ra-ta ... ahmmmmnoodahafirstistimmoommnna ... na ... ma ... ma ...

(TUCKER *in extreme close-up.*)

Mm!... Mm!...

(*Cut to:*)

INT. TUCKER'S BEDROOM. NIGHT

TUCKER *is seen head on in close-up sitting up violently.*

TUCKER: MM ... MM ... MA! ... HHHAAAHAAA!!

(*He is sobbing uncontrollably. Hold.*

Cut to shot of MOTHER *in bedroom doorway. She is a black silhouette in an 'Our Lady' stance.*)

MOTHER: Are you all right, lad?

(*Cut to* TUCKER *head on in close-up.*)

TUCKER: (*His sobs subsiding but a look of terror still on his face*) Yes ... Mam ...

(*He calms down a little as he realizes where he is. He lies back down.*

Cut to shot of MOTHER *closing bedroom door.*

Cut to side view of TUCKER *in close-up. He lies down, his head touching the pillow. He lies in profile looking at the ceiling. Pause. Then he turns his face towards the camera.*)
(*Tears in his eyes*) Yes …
(*He begins to sob – stifled and despairing. He continues to cry softly. Begin a very very slow fade to black. He continues crying.*
His face disappears altogether. Blackness. His crying is faintly heard.
It finally subsides altogether.
Blackness.
Absolute and complete silence. Then:)
TUCKER'S VOICE: (*Howling like an animal in peril*) M-A-M!!!
(*Silence. Pause. Fade to black.*)

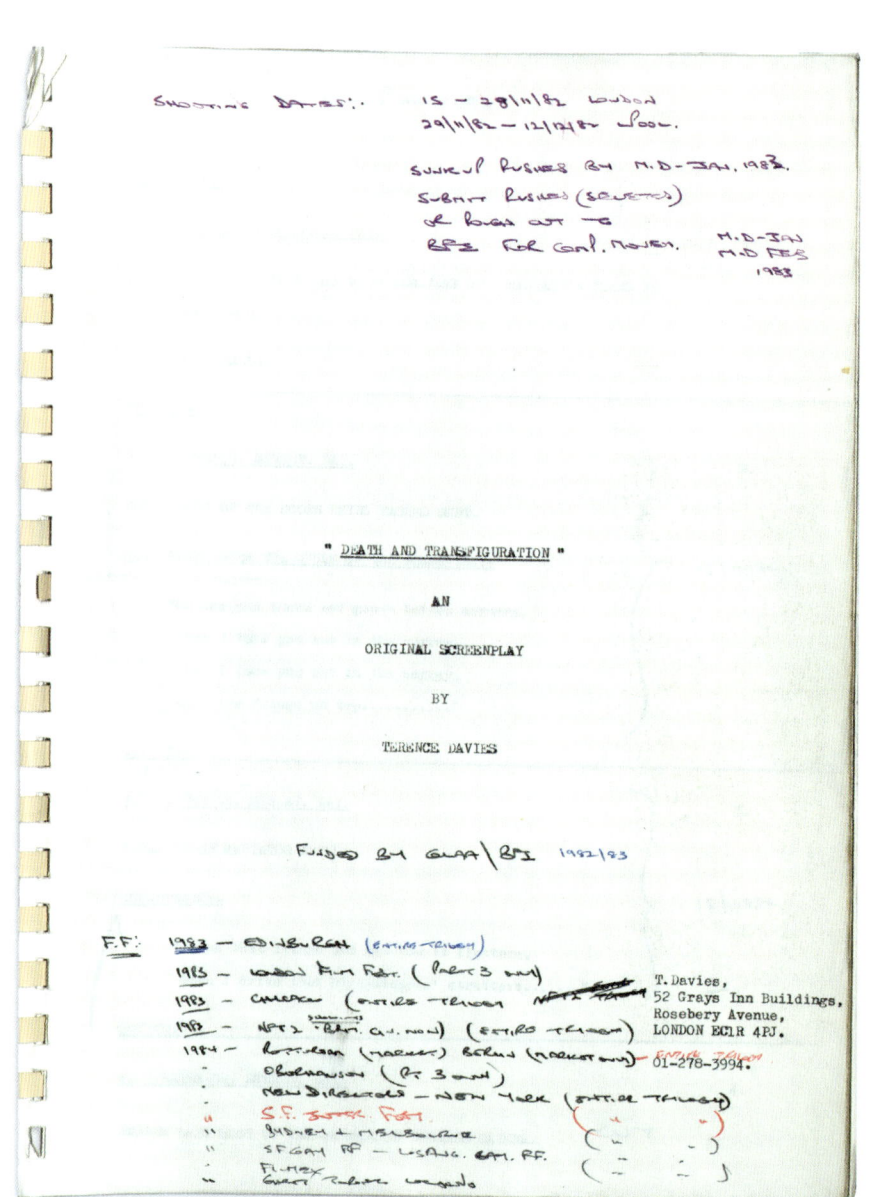

Death and Transfiguration, 1976: Shooting script, title page. (© The Terence Davies Estate, held by the Terence Davies Archive at Edge Hill University)

TRILOGY: PART III
DEATH AND TRANSFIGURATION (1983)

Death and Transfiguration (1983): leather man.

Cast and crew of *Death and Transfiguration* include:

TUCKER (as an old man)	Wilfrid Brambell	
TUCKER (middle-aged)	Terry O'Sullivan	
TUCKER (at eleven)	Iain Munro	
MOTHER	Jeanne Doree	
NURSE	Chrissy Roberts	
NURSE	Virginia Donovan	
NUN	Carol Christmas	
WARD SISTER	Angela Rooks	
DOCTOR	Brian Gilbert	
NURSE	Katharine Schofield	
NEIGHBOURS	Ron Metcalfe	Lisa Parker
	James Wilde	Ron Jones
	James Culshaw	Marie Smith
	Jim Penman	Gerry Shaw
	Mandy Walsh	
BOY AT WINDOW	Paul Oakley	

Children from The McKee School, Poulton Le Fylde, Lancashire

Written and Directed by	Terence Davies
Executive Producer	Maureen McCue
Production	Claire Barwell
Make-up Advisor	Fae Hammond
Art Director	Miki van Zwanenberg
Cameraman	William Diver
Continuity	Helena Barrett/Carine Adler
Sound Recordists	Mohammed Hassini/Charles Patey/Mark Frith
Editor	William Diver

A Greater London Arts production with the BFI (1983).

Fade up on:

EXT. LIVERPOOL. DAY

A shot looking out to sea with clusters of corporation flats in the foreground. It is very early.
Cut to:

EXT. STREET. DAY

Close shot of car doors being banged shut.
Soundtrack over the whole of the following of Doris Day singing: 'It All Depends On You'.
Cut to:

EXT. STREET. DAY

Close-up of radiator grill.
Cut to:

EXT. STREET. DAY

Medium long shot of people looking towards camera.
Cut to:

EXT. STREET. DAY

Low angled side view shot of wheels of limousine. They glide slowly away, left to right, followed by one other car.
Cut to:

EXT. STREET. DAY

Close shot of headlamps flashing as the first car turns left to right.
Cut to:

INT. PASSENGER CAR. DAY

Passenger's point of view of leading car – which is a hearse. It carries a coffin and wreaths.
Cut to:

INT. PASSENGER CAR. DAY

Side view of passenger. It is TUCKER, *aged about fifty-five years. He is in silhouette. The streets glide past.*

Cut to:

INT. PASSENGER CAR. DAY

Close-up of TUCKER's *hands.*
Cut to:

EXT. STREET. DAY

Medium long shot of hearse, head on, coming towards camera.
Cut to:

INT. HEARSE. DAY

Close-up side view of driver and SECOND MAN.
Cut to:

EXT. STREET. DAY

Medium close-up of coffin and wreaths seen through the glass of the hearse. The hearse glides past from left to right.
Cut to:
Shot of birds flying from the trees. Darkness is gathering.
Cut to:
A shot of the sun large and low in the sky.
Cut to:

EXT. CEMETERY GATES. DAY

Mid-shot of cars gliding in through the gates of Yewtree cemetery.
Cut to:

EXT. CEMETERY. DAY

High long shot of cars driving up the long gravel drive of the cemetery, seen from the gates.
Cut to:
Close shot of the cars coming to a halt.
Men get out of hearse.
Cut to:
Men carrying coffin shoulder high followed by a single mourner. It is TUCKER.
Song ends.

TRILOGY III: DEATH AND TRANSFIGURATION

Cut to:

INT. CREMATORIUM. DAY

End of coffin close-up gliding into the oven on rollers. The curtains and doors at the far end close. Pause. Then suddenly the oven flames burst upon the coffin. Title:

Death and Transfiguration

Cut to:

INT. GERIATRIC WARD. VERY EARLY MORNING

TUCKER is seen in medium long shot from the foot of his bed. He is much older now – in his late sixties.
Two nurses at either side of his bed have just finished washing him and rubbing his pressure areas. They finish.
FIRST NURSE: There you go, Pop ... spick and span.
SECOND NURSE: Spruce.
   (*As they draw towards the end of his bed brushing the bedclothes down, back in on* TUCKER. *He seems very ancient as he lies motionless in bed.*)
FIRST NURSE: (*Voice over*) What's pink, wrinkled and hangs out your underpants?
SECOND NURSE: (*Voice over*) I don't know.
   (*Track stops.* OLD TUCKER *in big close-up.*)
FIRST NURSE: (*Voice over*) Your mother!
   (*Both nurses giggle,* TUCKER *just looks at them, then his eyes flicker forward and he stares straight ahead. His mouth begins to move as he tries to form a word.*
   Cut to:)

INT. CAR. DAY

Side view of TUCKER *in close-up (aged fifty-five), returning from funeral. He tries to say 'mother' but cannot.*
PRIEST: (*Voice over*) I am the resurrection and the life.
   (*Cut to:*)

EXT. CORPORATION FLATS. DAY

The funeral cars drive into shot. Tucker gets out.

PRIEST: (*Voice over*) See, O Lord, and consider
How is the gold become dim,
How is the most fine gold changed.
(*Cut to:*)

INT. FLAT. DAY

TUCKER *in medium-long shot sitting at the kitchen table. A cup of tea beside him. Silence. Then slowly he begins to sip his tea. Pause.*
Cut to:

INT. TUCKER'S BEDROOM. DAY

TUCKER *sits on his bed with a scrap-book on his lap. He turns the pages. Cut to* TUCKER*'s point of view of scrap-book. It is filled with photographs of wrestlers and naked, muscular young men which he has cut out of magazines and pasted in. He stops at one page and passes his hand over a certain photograph. Then he leans down and kisses it.*
Cut to:

INT. MOTHER'S BEDROOM. DAY

Medium shot of MOTHER*'s wardrobe. The door is open. Her clothes hang neatly from the rail. Her shoes are on a neat row below them.*
Cut to:

INT. MOTHER'S WARDROBE. DAY

Close-up of garments hanging from the rail, TUCKER*'s hands enter shot and touch her clothes.*
Cut to:

INT. MOTHER'S BEDROOM. DAY

Side view of TUCKER *in close-up at wardrobe. He just stands there looking at her clothes. His eyes fill with tears as he buries his face in one of her coats.*
TUCKER: Mam … Mum … Mummy …
(*Cut to:*)

INT. GERIATRIC WARD. EARLY MORNING

Head on close-up of OLD TUCKER. FIRST NURSE *finishes feeding him his breakfast.* SECOND NURSE *plumps up his pillow.* TUCKER *eases back. One of the*

NURSES *walks towards a window at the end of the ward. Pan with her left to right until hospital window is framed. Outside it is pouring with rain.*
FIRST NURSE: (*Voice over*) Christ, what a day!

(*Pause.*)

SECOND NURSE: (*Voice over*) Roll on Christmas.

(*Cut to:*)

EXT. STREET. DAY

Shot of grey morning sky. It is pouring with rain. Pan down right to left from sky, past house fronts to TUCKER *from a three-quarter side view as a boy of seven or eight. He is hurrying to school. Track with him. He begins to hurry a little faster.*
Soundtrack:
CHILDREN: (*Voice over. Praying*) 'Jesus, Mary and Joseph,
   I give you my heart and my soul …'
   (*He breaks into a trot.*
   Soundtrack:)
   'Jesus, Mary and Joseph, I give you my body and blood …'
   (*He begins to run. Track stops. Pan with him as he runs past camera.*
   Cut to:)

INT. JUNIOR SCHOOL DAY

TUCKER *in close-up. Track back with him as he runs down corridor towards his classroom.*
Soundtrack:
CHILDREN: (*Voice over. Praying*) 'Jesus, Mary and Joseph, Assist me in
   my last agony …'
   (*Cut to* TUCKER's *point of view of classroom door at the end of the corridor. Track in on it.*
   Soundtrack:)
   'May I say when I am dying
   Jesus – mercy, Mary – help.'
   (*Track stops,* TUCKER *walks into shot and listens at the classroom door.*
   Soundtrack:)
   'In the name of the Father, and of the Son, and of the Holy Ghost, Amen.'

(*Sounds of the children sitting down. Then, quite suddenly, a cough is heard and* TUCKER *looks quickly back over his shoulder. From* TUCKER's *point of view in medium long shot cut to the* HEADMISTRESS *standing at the other end of the corridor. She is a nun and is in silhouette, her hands clasped in front of her.*)

HEADMISTRESS: (*Very softly*) There's no need to run inside the school, Robert.

(*Cut to side view of* TUCKER *in close-up from classroom door.*)

TUCKER: No, Sister.

(*Pause. He waits for a moment, then gingerly knocks on the classroom door. He enters.*

Cut to:)

INT. JUNIOR SCHOOL CLASSROOM. DAY

TUCKER *comes in and walks towards camera. To his left a coal fire blazes.*

TUCKER: I'm sorry I'm late, Miss Walsh.

MISS WALSH: (*Voice over. Kindly*) Stand by the fire until you're dry then go and see Sister.

TUCKER: Yes Miss.

(*He wipes his face with his hand, then gets out his handkerchief and begins to wipe his hair with it.*

Cut to:)

INT. MAIN CORRIDOR JUNIOR SCHOOL. DAY

Long shot. The main corridor is empty. Pause. Then footsteps are heard. TUCKER *enters frame right from around the corner. He is dressed as an angel. He walks towards camera. His steps slow to a stop. He stands there for a moment. Pause. Then he bursts into a fit of giggles. They eventually subside. Silence. He walks to the door of the* HEADMISTRESS's *study and knocks softly.*

HEADMISTRESS: (*Voice over. Softly*) Come in.

(*He goes in and closes the door.*

Cut to:)

INT. HEADMISTRESS'S STUDY. DAY

Side view of TUCKER *in close-up.*

TUCKER: Good morning Sister.

(*Cut to:*)

TRILOGY III: DEATH AND TRANSFIGURATION

INT. GERIATRIC WARD. DAY

Medium close-up of ward sister. She is switching off the lights.
WARD SISTER: Good morning boys!
>   (*Cut to first man in geriatric ward. He is seen from a three-quarter side view in medium long shot, sitting in a chair across from his bed. He stares straight ahead.*
>   *Soundtrack:*)

HEADMISTRESS: (*Voice over*) Who made you?
CHILDREN: (*Voice over*) God made me.
>   (*His hand goes up to the side of his head and scratches it. He then lays his hand down on the bed in front of him.*
>   *Cut to second man in geriatric ward. He is seen from a three-quarter side view in medium long shot. He is being helped on to a commode at the side of his bed by two nurses.*
>   *Soundtrack:*)

HEADMISTRESS: (*Voice over*) Why did God make you?
>   (*Cut to third man in geriatric ward. He is seen from a three-quarter side view in medium long shot. He eats porridge very slowly from a plate. When he has finished he lets the spoon fall into the plate.*
>   *Soundtrack:*)

CHILDREN: (*Voice over*) God made me to know Him, love Him and serve Him in this world and to be happy with Him for ever in the next.
>   (*Cut to side view of* TUCKER *in big close up in bed (à la Man Ray's photograph of the ageing Sibelius).* TUCKER *stares straight ahead.*
>   *Soundtrack:*)

HEADMISTRESS: (*Voice over*) What is God?
CHILDREN: (*Voice over*) God is love.
>   (*Cut to:*)

INT. CHURCH CONFESSIONAL. DAY

TUCKER *as a boy enters and closes confessional door. In the darkness,* TUCKER'*s form can just be made out as he stands there. Pause. He then begins feeling around the walls for the grille. Eventually he thinks he has found it and kneels down directly in front of the camera.*
TUCKER: Pray Father, give me your blessing, this is my first confession and I accuse myself of …
>   (*Over* TUCKER'*s right shoulder we see a curtain drawn back.*)

PRIEST: (*From behind the grille*) I'm over here.
(*Cut to:*)

INT. GERIATRIC HOSPITAL CORRIDOR. DAY

Long shot of OLD TUCKER *being wheeled up corridor in a wheelchair, towards camera, by a* NURSE. *As they get to a series of windows on their left which overlook an inner courtyard, the nurse stops and puts the brakes on the wheelchair.*

NURSE: (*To* TUCKER – *rather too loudly*) I'm just going for your X-rays, Mr Tucker ... So I'll leave you here for just a minute ... OK?
(*He doesn't respond. She walks away. Hold.*
Cut to close-up of OLD TUCKER *from the front. He looks old and sick. The right side of his mouth is slightly twisted. Hold.*
Soundtrack:)

DOCTOR: (*Voice over. Echoing slightly as if he were explaining to a group of medical students*) Cerebral thrombosis – stroke – stroke syndrome: a condition with sudden onset caused by acute vascular lesions of the brain ...
(TUCKER *turns and looks out of the window and down on to the inner courtyard. Pan slowly with him.*)
(*Soundtrack:*)
... such as haemorrhage, embolism, or rupturing aneurism ...
(*Pan stops when window is framed. Outside it is raining heavily.*
Soundtrack:)
... which may be marked by hemiplegia or hemiparesis, vertigo, numbness, aphasia and dysarthria ...
(*Hold camera on window. Pause.*
Soundtrack:)
It is often followed by permanent neurological damage and or death.
(*Hold camera. Pause. Then pan back to:*)

INT. HOSPITAL CORRIDOR. DAY

Pan stops when TUCKER *at fifty-five is framed in close up. He is looking out of the window at the rain.*
Soundtrack:
MOTHER: (*Voice over*) You mustn't grieve, lad ...

(*Doors are heard banging open.* TUCKER *looks around, full face to camera.*
Cut to – from behind TUCKER *– a medium long shot of ward doors opening. Visitors move towards them.* TUCKER *follows them, carrying an umbrella.*
Soundtrack:)

MOTHER: (*Voice over*) When I die … say you won't grieve …
(*Cut to:*)

INT. HOSPITAL WARD. DAY

Close-up of MOTHER *in bed. She lies in bed, semi-conscious, tubes up her nose and down her mouth. She has no teeth. She half-wakes, turns her head towards* TUCKER *– slowly – then smiles very weakly at him. Cut to* TUCKER *in close-up at the bedside. He tries to smile but is too close to tears.*

TUCKER: (*With great difficulty*) How are you Mam? … How do you feel?
(*Cut to* MOTHER *in close up. Her smile fades. Her eyes close again. Two-shot side view of* TUCKER, *left of bed.* TUCKER *gently takes* MOTHER'S *hand, rubs it then gently cradles it in his hand.*)

TUCKER: (*Very softly, through tears*) Mam, oh Mam …
(*Cut to:*)

INT. GERIATRIC HOSPITAL CORRIDOR. DAY

Side view of OLD TUCKER *in close-up sitting in wheelchair. Except for hospital noises, silence as he looks out of the window. Pause. Then the hospital noises begin to fade and we hear laughter echoing.* TUCKER *slowly turns his head and looks up. The laughter continues.*
Cut to:

INT. LIVING-ROOM. NIGHT

High two-shot of MOTHER *in her eighties and* TUCKER *at fifty-five seen over* MOTHER'S *shoulder. They are both laughing.* MOTHER *sits on the couch,* TUCKER *sits on a stool in front of her, cradling her foot in his lap.*

TUCKER: (*Through giggles*) Oh Mam, don't laugh … otherwise we'll never get it done …
(*Cut to medium long shot of* MOTHER *and* TUCKER *in side view from* TUCKER'S *position.*)

MOTHER: (*Through giggles*) Oh! ... you're a bloody case! ...
   (*The laughter subsides. He begins to bandage her lower ankle.*)
TUCKER: How has it been today, Mam?
   (*Cut to close-up of* MOTHER.)
MOTHER: It was aching a bit this morning ... not much though ...
   (*Cut to close-up of* TUCKER.)
TUCKER: You shouldn't stand on it, you know ... you're supposed to rest with a leg ulcer ...
   (*Cut to close-up of* MOTHER.)
MOTHER: I do rest it ... honest, lad ...
   (*Cut to close-up of* TUCKER.)
TUCKER: (*Finishes bandaging*) Oh, you'd say that ...
   (*Medium long shot of* MOTHER *and* TUCKER *in side view from* TUCKER's *position.*)
MOTHER: Read our stars ... Go on lad.
   (TUCKER *picks up the paper and finds the right page.*)
TUCKER: (*Reading*) Capricorn ... (*Reads stars.*)
MOTHER: And what's yours?
TUCKER: (*Reading*) Scorpio ... (*Reads stars.*)
   (*It is something improbable.*)
   Oh chance'd be a fine thing.
MOTHER: Well, you never know your luck in a big city.
   (*They both smile.*)
TUCKER: Fancy a cuppa?
MOTHER: Aye ... I wouldn't say no.
   (*He gets up to go out of the room. He gets to behind the sofa, immediately behind his* MOTHER.
   Cut to high two-shot over TUCKER's *shoulder looking down on to* MOTHER. *She looks up at him as he bends over her. He takes her face in his hands.*)
TUCKER: (*Looking down at her*) Oh – what would I do without you?
   (*Cut to:*)

INT. AGAINST BLACK DRAPES

Close-up of a head being pulled into shot. (NB: this is not TUCKER.) *The head is entirely encased in a leather head mask which has open zips over the eye and mouth holes. A dog collar is around this first man's neck. A dog lead is attached to the collar by a large d-ring.*

TRILOGY III: DEATH AND TRANSFIGURATION

Soundtrack:
SECOND MAN: (*Voice over*) Use your teeth ...
(*Cut to:*)

INT. BOOKSHOP. DAY

Close-up of TUCKER *at fifty-five seen through the window from inside the bookshop. As he looks into the shop his head is framed like a halo surrounding it by S+M and soft gay porn magazines which are hanging up.*
A customer, third man, enters frame. He is wearing tight leather jeans.
His buttocks entirely fill the frame.
Soundtrack:
SECOND MAN: (*Voice over*) Pull the zip down ...
   (*Cut to:*)

INT. AGAINST BLACK DRAPES

Medium long shot.
SECOND MAN *stands with his legs wide apart. He is stripped to the waist and very muscular. He is wearing tight leather jeans, boots, wrist straps, sunglasses and a motorcycle cap.*
In front of him kneels first man (head and shoulders only).
He is wearing the head mask and collar and is stripped to the waist also.
He faces SECOND MAN.
SECOND MAN *pulls first man to him.*
SECOND MAN: Use your fucking teeth!
   (*Cut to:*)

INT. BOOKSHOP. DAY

Close-up of third man's buttocks from inside shop.
Soundtrack:
SECOND MAN: (*Voice over, half in pain, half in ecstasy*)
   Nnnaaarrrhhh!
   (*Third man's buttocks clear frame.*
TUCKER *revealed in close-up still looking through window.*
He stands there a moment looking very tense.
Then lowers his eyes.
Cut to:)

INT. CHURCH. DAY

Side view of TUCKER *in close-up as a boy kneeling at the altar rails with his mouth wide open.*
Soundtrack:
CHILDREN: (*Voice over, singing*) 'Jesus thou art coming,
　　Holy as thou art …
　　(TUCKER, *with his mouth still open, is waiting to receive*
　　Holy Communion. He holds the paton under his chin.
　　Soundtrack:)
　　'By the God who made me,
　　To my sinful heart …'
　　(*The* PRIEST's *hands come into shot. They hold a chalice. The* PRIEST
　　takes a host from the chalice and puts it into TUCKER's *mouth.*
　　Soundtrack:)
　　'Jesus I believe it,
　　On thy only word …
　　(TUCKER, *having received the Eucharist, bows his head.*
　　Cut to.)

INT. GERIATRIC WARD. NOON

Mid-shot of ward sister sitting at her desk at the far end of the ward.
Soundtrack:
CHILDREN: (*Voice over, singing*) 'So shall I never, never part from thee.'
　　(*Singing fades. Two nurses come in, past desk, carrying a large natural*
　　Christmas tree into the ward.)
FIRST NURSE: Hello, Staff.
STAFF NURSE: Hello, girls … wouldn't this weather put years on you?
SECOND NURSE: They say it'll snow for Christmas.
FIRST NURSE: Oh, she's cheerful isn't she?
　　(*All smile. The two nurses exit frame.*
　　Cut to close-up of a cup of tea on bedside locker. A pair of hands slowly
　　enter frame and shakily pick up the cup. Pan right to left with cup until
　　three-quarter side view of OLD TUCKER *is framed in close-up.*
　　He is sweating profusely and looks weak. He sips his tea.
　　Cut to long shot of two nurses putting Christmas tree at the other end of
　　the ward. Through the window it is raining.
　　Cut to front view of OLD TUCKER *in close-up being lifted into an upright*

position by two nurses. As he is being lifted, he looks very weak. Clearly everything is becoming an extreme effort.)
FIRST NURSE: Now then … there we go …
(*Cut to:*)

INT. CHILDREN'S HOSPITAL. DAY

Medium close-up in side view of TUCKER, *as a boy, being lifted into an upright position by a* DOCTOR.
DOCTOR: Now then Robert … take a really deep breath in …
(TUCKER *does so.*)
… Hold it …
(TUCKER *does so.*)
And now … let it slowly out …
(TUCKER *does so.*
Cut to MOTHER *aged thirty-five with* TUCKER *as a boy walking down corridor away from camera.* TUCKER *looks up at her.*
Soundtrack:)
DOCTOR: (*Voice over*) Good boy, Robert …
(*Cut to:*)

INT. GERIATRIC WARD. AFTERNOON

Three-quarter side view medium long shot of OLD TUCKER *being helped to the side of his bed by two nurses. With every movement* TUCKER *keeps saying, very weakly, over and over again:*
TUCKER: Oh … Oh …
(*When they have got him to the side of his bed, they hold a bottle for him to urinate into.*
Soundtrack:)
TUCKER: (*Voice over, as a boy*) Why do I have to have breathing exercises, Mam?
MOTHER: (*Voice over*) It'll help your cough, lad.
(*Cut to:*)

INT. SHOPPING PRECINCT. DAY

MOTHER *aged eighty,* TUCKER *aged fifty-five, in medium long shot three-quarter side view walking down one of the aisles towards camera. They walk slowly.* TUCKER *carries the shopping.*

The shops are decorated and advertising for Christmas.
MOTHER: We've been invited to Elaine's twenty-first.
TUCKER: On Saturday?
MOTHER: Yer ... Christmas Eve.
TUCKER: Oh, smashin'.
> (*Soundtrack: voices singing 'Abie, Abie, Abie My Boy'.*
> *Cut to:*)

EXT. STREET. NIGHT

Medium-long shot of TUCKER *as a boy standing on the corner of the street outside a pub. Snow is on the ground.*
Soundtrack: they sing 'Abie, Abie, Abie My Boy'.
TUCKER *rises on tiptoe trying to see into the pub through the frosted glass.*
Soundtrack of the song continues.
Sound mix to next song.
Cut to long shot of group of adults coming down the street from pub, towards camera. They are in silhouette, and singing as they walk.
Soundtrack of people in the pub singing 'How You Gonna Keep Them Down on the Farm'.
Cut to TUCKER *as a boy in medium close-up sitting on the doorstep.*
The adults rapidly walk past him into the house, singing.
Cut to high shot of adults coming into the parlour as seen through the window from the street.
Through the window the parlour can be seen to have been decorated for Christmas. At the window a small natural Christmas tree. Everyone is dancing and singing.
Cut to close-up of a pair of woman's hands and arms, outstretched.
It is MOTHER *but we don't see her face.*
Soundtrack: RENEE'*s voice over, trying to sing above the general hubbub of the parlour 'There's a Someone to Watch Over Me'.*
MAN: (*Voice over, shouting*) Order! Go on Renee. Order please!
> (TUCKER *as a boy walks into shot and the outstretched arms and hands wrap around him.*
> *Soundtrack:* RENEE *singing.*
> TUCKER *hugs his* MOTHER *to him and smiles up at her.*)

MOTHER: (*Voice over*) Happy Christmas lad.

TRILOGY III: DEATH AND TRANSFIGURATION

TUCKER: Happy Christmas Mam.
> (*And slowly, in a small circle, they begin to dance to* RENEE's *singing.*
> *Cut to high shot of* MOTHER *and* TUCKER *slowly turning as they dance.*
> *It begins to snow.*
> Soundtrack: RENEE *finishes her song.*
> *The people in the parlour applaud,* MOTHER *and* TUCKER *keep dancing – silently in the falling snow.*
> *Soundtrack: people singing 'If You Knew Suzie'.*
> *Cut to:*)

INT. FLATS. NIGHT

Sound mix.
Soundtrack: continues song. Begin to fade singing. Singing gone.
MOTHER *aged eighty,* TUCKER *aged fifty-five get out of lift and walk along landing away from camera.*
TUCKER: (*Voice over*) It was a good night, wasn't it Mam?
MOTHER: (*Voice over*) Yer ... smashin'.
> (*Cut to:*)

INT. HOSPITAL. DAY

Close-up of two X-ray photographs illuminated. They are of TUCKER's *skull. One from the side, one from the front. Hold.*
Soundtrack:
PRIEST: (*Voice over*) 'And the Angel of the Lord said unto them ...'
> (*Cut to:*)

INT. GERIATRIC WARD. LATE AFTERNOON

Track slowly up TUCKER's *bed from foot of bed.*
Soundtrack:
PRIEST: (*Voice over*) '... Fear not, for I bring you tidings of great joy which shall be to all the world ...'
> (*Track stops. Side view of* TUCKER *in close-up. He is sweating very badly, breathing heavily and weakening.*
> *Soundtrack:*)
'... For this day in Bethlehem is born unto you a Saviour, which is Christ the Lord.'
> (*Cut to:*)

INT. JUNIOR SCHOOL. DAY

Close-up of three silver halos nodding and quivering across frame left to right. Pan with them.
Soundtrack:
CHILDREN'S CHOIR: (*Singing*) 'Oh come let us adore Him!
   Oh come let us adore Him!'
   (*Cut to:*)

INT. JUNIOR SCHOOL CLASSROOM. DAY

*Front shot. Tableau. The climax of the school nativity play. The three angels (*YOUNG TUCKER *is the middle one), their wings and halos quivering, their hands joined, enter shot, very embarrassed. They arrange themselves behind the Holy Family by standing on chairs. Soundtrack:*
CHILDREN'S CHOIR: (*Singing*) 'Oh come let us adore Him!
   Christ the Lord!'
   (*Cut to mid-shot of three boys. They have false beards on and each carries a gift. They are the three wise men. They walk towards camera.*)
THREE WISE MEN: (*Singing*) 'We three Kings of Orient are, Bearing gifts
   we travel so far …'
   (*Cut to front shot. Tableau. Holy Family and angels, three wise men enter left.*)
THREE WISE MEN: (*Singing*) 'Field and fountain,
   Moor and mountain,
   Following yonder star …'
   (*And an angel with a silver star on a stick moves across frame to left of Holy Family. The three wise men kneel to baby Jesus.*)
ALL: (*Singing*) 'Oh star of wonder, star of night,
   Star of royal beauty bright …'
   (*The* THREE WISE MEN *present their gifts.*)
ALL: (*Singing*) 'Westward leading,
   Still proceeding,
   Guide us with thy perfect light.'
   (*Cut to:*)

INT. JUNIOR SCHOOL CLASSROOM WINDOW. DAY

Pan along window right to left.
Soundtrack:

CHILDREN'S CHOIR: (*Singing*) 'Away in a manger no crib for a bed,
The little Lord Jesus lays down
His sweet head ...'
(*Continue panning. The window has been decorated with cotton snow and Christmas scenes.
Dissolve to pan right to left to the school crib, the Holy Family mounted on straw.
Soundtrack:*)
'The stars in the bright sky
looked down where he lay,
The little Lord Jesus
asleep on the hay ...
(*Dissolve to:*)

INT. GERIATRIC WARD. EVENING

*Close-up of star on top of ward Christmas tree.
Soundtrack:*
CHILDREN'S CHOIR: (*Singing*) 'The cattle are lowing, the baby awakes ...'
(*Pan slowly down tree right to left. Two nurses dressing tree.* FIRST NURSE, *standing on a set of steps, is on the right of the tree, dressing it.*
SECOND NURSE, *to the left of tree, is handing small Christmas ornaments to* FIRST NURSE.
Soundtrack:)
CHILDREN'S CHOIR: (*Singing*) 'The little Lord Jesus no crying he makes ...'
(*The two nurses talk softly. Pan down tree right to left until* SECOND NURSE *is framed in medium close-up, bottom left.*)
SECOND NURSE: (*Continuing to hand ornaments to* FIRST NURSE) I love Christmas Eve ... don't you, Staff?
(*Pan away from her right to left.
Soundtrack:*)
CHILDREN'S CHOIR: (*Singing*) 'Be near me Lord Jesus Look down from the sky ...'
(*Dissolve to pan right to left until* OLD TUCKER *is framed in close-up, head on, in bed. He looks very weak.
Soundtrack:*)
CHILDREN'S CHOIR: (*Singing*) 'And stay by my side until morning is nigh.'
(*Hold close-up.*

Cut to long shot of ward from sister's desk end. The two NURSES *walk towards camera as they go off duty.*)

TWO NURSES: Good night ... All the best lads ...

(*They exit. Then one by one the night nurse switches off the ward lights. Darkness. Pause.*

Soundtrack:)

PRIEST: (*Voice over*) And the glory of the Lord shone, round about them, and they were sore afraid.

(*Hold.*

Cut to:)

INT. GERIATRIC WARD. NIGHT

Long shot of ward from Christmas tree end looking up towards sister's desk. Pause. Then the night NURSE *gets up from the desk. She wears a cape and carries a torch, which she switches on.*

Soundtrack:)

CHOIR: (*Singing*) 'Silent night, Holy night,

All is calm, all is bright ...'

(*She begins walking along the beds, shining the torch on the faces of the patients to see if they are asleep.*

Cut to track along first row of beds right to left – NURSE'S *point of view. Torch shining on sleeping faces.*

Soundtrack:)

'Round yon Virgin, Mother and Child

Holy infant so tender and mild ...'

(*Dissolve to track along second row of beds right to left –* NURSE'S *point of view. Torch shining on the patients.*

Soundtrack:)

'Sleep in heavenly peace,

Sleep in heavenly peace.'

(*Fade singing. Track stops when* TUCKER *is framed from the foot of his bed. Torchlight on his face. His eyes flicker open, then close. He is obviously very ill.*

Cut to:)

INT. CHURCH

Low angled shot of huge crucifix.

TRILOGY III: DEATH AND TRANSFIGURATION

Soundtrack:
OLD TUCKER: (*Voice over*) Oh sacred heart of Jesus I give you my body and blood …
(*Cut to:*)

INT. GERIATRIC WARD. NIGHT

High-angled shot of OLD TUCKER *in bed.* NURSE *goes to him and examines him for a moment.*
Soundtrack:
OLD TUCKER: (*Voice over*) Oh sacred heart of Jesus I give you, my heart and my soul …
(*Cut to:*)

INT. CHURCH

Close-up of the sacristy light. A candle burns low in it.
Soundtrack:
OLD TUCKER: (*Voice over*) When the light goes out – God is dead.
(*Cut to:*)

INT. GERIATRIC WARD. NIGHT

Mid-shot side view of TUCKER's *silhouette in bed.* NURSE *leaning over him. She switches off the torch. Then she moves back towards the end of the bed and sits in a chair. They are both in silhouette.*
Soundtrack:
NURSE: (*Voice over*) They know when they're going – you go and sit by them but they know they're going.
(*The sound of rain can be heard very loudly. Hold.*
Cut to:)

INT. TUCKER'S CHILDHOOD HOME. LATE AFTERNOON

Close-up of window. Through the window it is pouring with rain. Pan down right to left away from the window across the room which is light only by firelight. Continue pan past a small natural Christmas tree hung with ornaments, past and along a sideboard filled with Christmas cards and fruit. And in the centre of the sideboard a photograph of MOTHER *when she was younger, about thirty-five. Continue pan until* TUCKER *as a boy is framed. He is asleep on the hearthrug.*

Toys are scattered about him. Everything glows in the firelight. And over all this, the continuous sound of the heavy rain.
Cut to:

INT. JUNIOR SCHOOL. DAY

The HEADMISTRESS's *study. Medium long shot of* HEADMISTRESS *from* TUCKER's *point of view as a boy.* TUCKER *however is not visible. The study is big, gloomy and over-furnished. The* HEADMISTRESS – *a nun* – *is seated at her desk, her back to the window. Through the window it is pouring with rain. As the room is lit only from the window the* HEADMISTRESS *appears in silhouette, making her appear like a shadow, a hooded figure whose features cannot be seen. Silence.*
HEADMISTRESS: Do you love God Robert?
TUCKER: (*As a boy, voice over*) Yes Sister.
    (*Cut to:*)

INT. GERIATRIC WARD. NIGHT

Long shot of OLD TUCKER *in bed – side view – from far end of the ward. His bed is lit by a white light coming in through a window directly opposite his bed. The light begins to flood in, making Tucker's bed appear to be the only object in the ward. Slowly track on* TUCKER *in his bed.*
Soundtrack: MOTHER *singing unaccompanied 'You're Still the Only Boy in the World'.*
TUCKER *begins to suffer great difficulty in breathing – long breaths getting progressively shallow – Cheyne–Stokes breathing. This gets louder as we get closer. Continue track.*
Soundtrack: MOTHER *singing unaccompanied.*
Continue track. We are now close enough to see TUCKER's *hands and arms rise slowly from the counterpane. Continue Cheyne–Stokes breathing.*
Soundtrack:
MOTHER: (*Voice over singing unaccompanied*) 'My love for you will
    ever be true …
    (*Dissolve to:*)

INT. WINDOW

Medium long shot of a young man standing naked at the window, his back to camera. The light floods in through the window. Track slowly in on him.

Soundtrack: continue Cheyne–Stokes breathing, MOTHER *singing. The young man half turns towards camera and smiles.*
Dissolve to:

INT. GERIATRIC WARD. NIGHT

Close-shot side view of TUCKER *in bed, his hands reaching towards the light. Continue Cheyne–Stokes breathing. Crab around to front of bed, then track back away from* TUCKER, *his hands reaching towards the light which is getting brighter all the time. Continue Cheyne–Stokes breathing.*
Soundtrack: MOTHER *singing unaccompanied 'You're Still the Only Boy in the World'.*
Dissolve to close shot of the window opposite TUCKER'*s bed. The light pours in, getting brighter still. Track in on it. Continue Cheyne–Stokes breathing.*
Soundtrack:)

MOTHER: (*Voice over, singing unaccompanied*) 'The one and only boy for me ...'
  (*The light gets brighter. The Cheyne–Stokes breathing more difficult and rapid, then suddenly it cuts out.*
  Light. Continue track. Silence. A momentary pause.
  Then fade to black.)

Distant Voices, Still Lives (1988): continuity shots. (© The Terence Davies Estate)

DISTANT VOICES, STILL LIVES (1988)

Distant Voices, Still Lives (1988): Eileen (Angela Walsh) and Father (Pete Postlethwaite).

Cast and crew of *Distant Voices, Still Lives* include:

MOTHER	Freda Dowie
FATHER	Pete Postlethwaite
EILEEN	Angela Walsh
TONY	Dean Williams
MAISIE	Lorraine Ashbourne
EILEEN (as a child)	Sally Davies
TONY (as a child)	Nathan Walsh
MAISIE (as a child)	Susan Flanagan
MICKY	Debi Jones
RED	Chris Darwin
JINGLES	Marie Jelliman
LES	Andrew Schofield
GRANNY	Anny Dyson
AUNTY NELL	Jean Boht
DOREEN	Pauline Quirke
MR SPAULL	Matthew Long
MARGIE	Frances Dell
UNCLE TED	Roy Ford
Written and Directed by	Terence Davies
Producer	Jennifer Howarth
Executive Producer	Colin MacCabe
Photography and Editing	William Diver
Photography	Patrick Duval
Costume Designer	Monica Howe
Art Directors	Miki van Zwanenberg
	Jocelyn James

A British Film Institute Production, in association with Channel 4 and ZDF, 1988.

Distant Voices

NB: *Distant Voices* is about memory and the mosaic of memory. Father is the central pivot around which Mother, Eileen, Maisie and Tony revolve and all have equal dramatic weight. Memory does not move in a linear or a chronological way – its pattern is of a circular nature, placing events (not in their 'natural' or 'real' order) but recalled for their emotional importance. Memory *is* its own validity.

Thus any 'story' involving memory is not a narrative in the conventional sense but of necessity more diffuse, more elliptical. Therefore conventional narrative expectation will not be satisfied in any conventional way, and I would ask you to bear this in mind when you are reading this piece.

I was trying to create 'a pattern of timeless moments'.

Distant Voices, Still Lives (1988): Terence Davies directing Freda Dowie.
(BFI National Archive)

Blackness.
Fade up main title 'Distant Voices'. *Sound of rain and thunder.*
Fade out main title.
Fade up to:

EXT. MORNING. MID-1950s

A terraced house. Rain. Thunder.
VOICE OVER: (*1950s BBC Radio announcer*) 'Faroes, Cromarty, Forth, Tyne …'

(MOTHER *opens the front door, picks up the milk, looks up and down the street, then closes the front door. Cut to:*)

INT. MORNING. MID-1950s

Hallway and stairs as seen from the front door.
MOTHER *walks down the hallway* (*away from camera*) *and stops at the foot of the stairs.*
MOTHER: (*Calling softly*) It's seven o'clock you three!
(*Walks away to kitchen.*)
VOICE OVER: (*1950s BBC Radio announcer*) 'Dogger, German Bight, Rockall, Mallin, Hebrides, Fastnet …'
(MOTHER *walks back up the hall to the foot of the stairs.*)
MOTHER: Eileen! Tony! Maisie!
You'd better get your skates on!
(*She exits down hall.*
Hold on empty hall and stairs.
Soundtrack of MOTHER'*s voice over, singing* 'I Get the Blues When It's Raining'
BBC Radio 'Lift up your Hearts'.
Footsteps on the empty stairs.)
TONY: (*Voice over*) Morning Mam.
MOTHER: (*Voice over*) Are those two sisters of yours up yet, Tony?
TONY: (*Voice over*) Yer – they're just coming down.
MAISIE: (*Voice over*) Hi yer Mam.
MOTHER: (*Voice over*) Morning Maisie.
EILEEN: (*Voice over*) Morning Mam.
MOTHER: (*Voice over*) Morning Eileen.
Nervous love?

EILEEN: (*Voice over*) A bit.
MOTHER: (*Voice over*) Have a cuppa and a ciggie.
> (*Track around 180 degrees and crane up from this camera position until the front door (which is closed) is framed. Hallway and door as seen from the stairs. Voice over of* MOTHER *singing 'I Get the Blues When It's Raining' continues.*
> *From the same camera position the front door opens in a dissolve. Sunshine. Through the front door a hearse is seen drawing up (right to left), early 1950s.*
> *Soundtrack of Jessye Norman singing, voice over 'There's a Man Goin' Round Takin' Names'.*
> *Dissolve to:*)

PARLOUR. EARLY 1950s. MORNING. FUNERAL

Tableau. Family group, MOTHER *flanked by* TONY *on one side and* EILEEN *and* MAISIE *on the other. All in black. Above them on the wall a photograph of* FATHER. TONY *and* MAISIE *grim.* MOTHER *and* EILEEN *tearful.*
Soundtrack, Jessye Norman singing 'There's a Man Goin' Round Takin' Names'.
They all stand. Track in on them. They all walk towards camera and exit. Keep tracking until photograph of FATHER *is framed in close-up. He is smiling and holding on to a horse.*
Hold. Dissolve to:

INT. MORNING. EARLY 1950s. FUNERAL

Camera position as at opening – from front door looking down hallway to stairs.
The family group entering shot.
They stand for a moment.
Dissolve to family funeral group seen through the bannisters.
They walk down the hall towards the front door.
Pan with them.
Soundtrack, voice over of Jessye Norman singing 'There's a Man Goin' Round Takin' Names' continues.
Front door closes.
Hold. Cut to:

INT. PARLOUR. AFTERNOON. WEDDING GROUP. MID-1950s

Tableaux, EILEEN (*the bride*) *flanked by* TONY (*on her right*), MOTHER *and* MAISIE *standing at the back of them.*
They all wear buttonholes. All smiling nervously.
Soundtrack, voice over of Jessye Norman singing, continues.
Track in on EILEEN. *Track stops when* EILEEN *and* TONY *are in two-shot, close-up.*

EILEEN: (*To* TONY, *who smiles uneasily*) I wish me Dad was here.
  (*Pause.*
  Pan to MAISIE.
  MAISIE *in close-up, looking grim.*)
MAISIE: (*Voice over*) I don't. He was a bastard and I bleedin' hated him!
  (*Cut to:*)

INT. HOSPITAL WARD. DAY. EARLY 1950s

Long shot of ward. Beds running down the long ward, MOTHER, EILEEN, MAISIE *and* TONY (*in army uniform*) *walking down towards* FATHER's *bed.*
MOTHER: (*Voice over*) They had to stretch his gullet.
  (*The group stop at* FATHER's *bed and look down at him. Favour* MAISIE *in this shot.*
  Cut to shot of FATHER *in bed from group's point of view. He is very frail and ill.*)
MAISIE: (*Voice over*) Can I have the money to go to the dance, Dad?
FATHER: (*Voice over*) You get that cellar done – never mind bleedin' dances.
MAISIE: (*Voice over*) But Dad, there's rats down there – I'm terrified of rats.
FATHER: (*Voice over, furious*) No cellar – no dance!
  (*Cut to:*)

INT. CELLAR. AFTERNOON. EARLY 1950s

Medium long shot. Stone-flagged cellar, MAISIE *kneeling scrubbing the flags.*
FATHER *walks across behind her kneeling figure.*
MAISIE *stops scrubbing.*
MAISIE: Can I go to the dance, Dad?
  (*He just throws the money on to the floor. She leans across and picks it up.*

Cut to close-up of MAISIE.)

MAISIE: (*With as much sarcasm as she can muster*) Thanks.

(*Cut to shot of* FATHER *from* MAISIE's *point of view.*

He picks up a yard brush and turns on her in a fury.)

FATHER: You're like your Aunty May and she was no bleedin' good! just

(*He begins to rain blow after blow down on* MAISIE *with the yard brush. She is screaming.*

Soundtrack: carry her screaming over the next shot, as we cut back to:)

INT. PARLOUR. DAY. MID-1950s. WEDDING GROUP

Two-shot of EILEEN *and* TONY.

EILEEN: I wish me Dad was here.

(*Pan to* TONY. TONY *in close-up. He looks at her. Hold.*

Cut to:)

INT. PARLOUR. NIGHT. EARLY 1950s

Close shot of windows.

Suddenly they are smashed from the outside – hands repeatedly coming in and out of the panes. TONY *is smashing the windows with his bare hands.* TONY *is now seen through the smashed windows. He is in army uniform, and is shouting in a paroxysm of rage and years of hurt.*

TONY: Come out and fight me you bastard! Come out and fight me you bastard!

(*He is now crying with fury and anger, his voice hoarse.*)

Come out and fight me! YOU BASTARD! Come out and *Fight!*

(*Over and over again.*

Cut to medium close-up of TONY *in uniform.*)

(*Pleading*) Will you have a drink with me, Dad?

(*Cut to medium close-up of* FATHER *at fireside.*)

FATHER: (*Unmoved*) No.

(*Cut to medium close-up of* MOTHER.)

MOTHER: (*Begging*) Have a drink with him, Tommy … Please.

(*Cut to two-shot – mid-long – of* TONY (*left of frame standing*) *and* FATHER (*right of frame sitting at fireside*).

TONY's *hands covered in blood. He is holding bottles of pale ale and Double Diamond.*)

FATHER: (*Angry*) I said No.

TONY: (*Taking two old pennies from his pocket and throwing them into the fire*)
Tuppence – that's all I've got.
(*Throws coins into fire.*)
But I wouldn't give *you* daylight.
(*Cut to medium shot (*side view*) of* FATHER *at fireside.*
He picks up the poker and prods the pennies deeper into the fire.
Cut to:)

EXT. STREET. NIGHT. EARLY 1950s

TONY *being bundled into a van by several military policemen.*
He starts to resist, then fight.
They begin to really beat him up as they manhandle him into the van.
Cut to:

INT. CORRIDOR OF GUARDHOUSE. NIGHT. EARLY 1950s

High shot looking down corridor. Cells on either side of corridor.
Grills in doors.
A face comes to a door grill on right hand side of corridor.
MAN: (*At cell-door grill*) Play 'Limelight', Scouse.
  (*Cut to:*)

INT. TONY'S CELL. NIGHT. EARLY 1950s

TONY *sitting on a bed (*with no mattress*). He bangs his harmonica on his thigh then begins softly to play 'Limelight'.*
Cut to:

INT. GUARDHOUSE CORRIDOR. NIGHT. EARLY 1950s

High shot.
The sound of the harmonica.
2ND MAN: (*Voice over*) Go on, Scouse … Give us a tune.
  (*Soundtrack: The sound of the harmonica being played into next shot.*
  Cut to:)

INT. TRAIN. DAY. EARLY 1950s

Train travelling right to left.
TONY *in two-shot with another soldier.*

Soundtrack: Cross-fade 'Limelight' with TONY *going through the list of heavyweight boxing champions from earliest times to the present day.*
SOLDIER: It was Schmelling, Scouse …
TONY: You're wrong – Schmelling never won the title … the heavyweight champions were Jack Sharkey, Primo Camera, Braddock, Baer – no, I tell a lie … Baer *then* Braddock then Joe Louis who held it from 1937 to 1948 and then –
2ND SOLDIER: Come on Scouse …
   (*Begins to sing 'It Takes a Worried Man to Sing a Worried Song'. They all join in.*
   Cut to:)

INT. PARLOUR. NIGHT. EARLY 1950s

MOTHER *and* TONY *in two-shot close-up, side view.*
MOTHER: Thanks for coming home, son.
TONY: I got compassionate leave, Mam.
   (*Cut to:*)

INT. HOSPITAL WARD. DAY. EARLY 1950s

Close-up of FATHER, *very ill.*
FATHER: I was wrong, lad.
   (*Cut to close-up of* TONY *standing in army uniform by foot of the bed.*)
TONY: OK, Dad. OK.
   (*Dissolve:*)

EXT. STREET. DAY. EARLY 1950s. FUNERAL

Mid-shot of front doorstep and hall.
Funeral group comes to the doorstep and stands there, MOTHER *and* TONY, *and behind them* EILEEN *and* MAISIE.
A small group of neighbours on either side of the door watch them. Pause.
A passenger car pulls up in front of them. Left to right, they enter it.
Cut to:

INT. HALLWAY. DAY. EARLY 1950s. FUNERAL

Funeral group walking down steps and into the passenger car. It moves off, right to left.
Cut to:

INT. PARLOUR. AFTERNOON. MID-1950s. WEDDING

Tableaux shot of wedding group, all nerves.
TONY: Are you ready, Ei?
EILEEN: Here goes.
   (*Cut to:*)

INT. CHURCH. DAY. MID-1950s

Close-up of two pairs of hands, EILEEN *and her husband-to-be.*
He puts the ring on her finger.
Priest's voice over intoning the Wedding Service.
Cut to:

INT. KITCHEN. EARLY SUMMER EVENING. MID-1950s

Close-up of EILEEN, *side view.*
EILEEN: (*Unbelieving*) Look what he's bought me.
   (*Cut to close-up of* JINGLES, *side view.*)
JINGLES: (*Awestruck*) It's Chanel No. 5!
EILEEN: (*Voice over*) I know.
   (*Cut to close-up of* MONICA, *three-quarter side view.*)
MONICA: (*Absolutely overcome as she puts her elbows on the table and cradles her face in her hands*) Oh … isn't that dead romantic!
   (*Cut to wide shot of all three girls just sitting looking at the bottle of Chanel which is on the kitchen table.*
   Cut to:)

INT. HALLWAY. DAY. MID-1950s. EILEEN'S WEDDING

Mid-long shot of street through open front door. Passenger car pulls up left to right. EILEEN *and* DAVE *get out of the car and come into the house. Neighbours throw confetti.*
EILEEN *and* DAVE *smiling as they come indoors, followed by* MOTHER, MAISIE *and* TONY *and other relatives and guests.*
Cut to:

INT. PARLOUR. DAY. MID-1950s. EILEEN'S WEDDING

Mid-wide shot of table in front of window.
EILEEN *and* DAVE *in centre. Their wedding cake in front of them. They are flanked by* MOTHER *and* MAISIE *on their right and* TONY *on their left.*

EILEEN *and* DAVE *stand and pose to cut the cake. All hold still.*
Silence.
Photographer takes a flash photo. All relax.
Applause. Laughter. Dissolve to:

INT. PUB. NIGHT. MID-1950s. EILEEN'S WEDDING

Pan around from left to right the smiling, singing faces.
They are finishing a song. Singing 'If You Knew Suzie'.
Pan stops on MAISIE, *who begins to sing solo 'My Yiddisher Momma'.*
Cut to two-shot of EILEEN *and* TONY.
EILEEN: (*Crying, howling like an animal*) I WANT MY DAD!
    (TONY *holding her. Both weeping.*)
    I want my dad …
    (*She cries and wails. He weeps.*
    Soundtrack, voice over of MAISIE *singing 'My Yiddisher Momma'.*
    Cross fade to:)
CHOIR: (*Voice over, singing*) 'In the bleak mid-winter
    Frosty winds made moan,
    Earth stood hard as iron
    Water like a stone …'
    (*Track, right to left, away from* EILEEN *and* TONY *into the darkness*
    of the street.
    It starts to snow.)
EILEEN: (*Voice over*) I know me Dad was bad – I know that – but
    I always try and think of the good times – like Christmas.
CHOIR: (*Voice over, singing*) 'Snow had fallen, snow on snow
    Snow on snow,
    In the bleak mid-winter
    Long ago …'
    (*Dissolve to:*)

INT. BEDROOM. NIGHT. EARLY 1940s

Continue tracking, right to left, to side view of a home-made altar/crib in blackness.
Candles and night lights being lit by five pairs of hands.
Continue tracking as EILEEN, TONY, MAISIE *as children and* MOTHER *and*
FATHER (*kneeling behind them*) *come into view. They are lighting the candles.*
All are radiant.

Soundtrack:

CHOIR: (*Voice over, singing*) 'Our God, Heaven cannot hold him Nor
  Earth sustain; Heaven and Earth shall flee away,
  When he comes to reign; ...'
  (*Dissolve to:*)

EXT. STREET. NIGHT. EARLY 1940s

Continue tracking, right to left, over the exteriors of the houses. Through the windows parlours that have been dressed for Christmas can be seen.
Soundtrack:

EILEEN:
MAISIE: (*Voices over – as children*) If I should die before I wake,
TONY:

  Pray the Lord my soul to take.
  God bless Mother,
  God bless Father,
  And keep them safe.

CHOIR: (*Voice over, singing*) 'In the bleak mid-winter
  A stable place sufficed
  The Lord God Almighty
  Jesus Christ ...'
  (*Track stops at third window.*
  Through it FATHER *can be seen decorating a small Christmas tree which is on the sideboard, his back to camera.*
  Soundtrack:)

CHOIR: (*Voice over, singing*) 'Enough for him, whom cherubim
  Worship night and day,
  A breast full of milk,
  And a manger full of hay;
  Enough for him, whom angels
  Fall down before,
  The ox and the ass and camel
  Which adore ...'
  (*Dissolve to* FATHER (*still with back to camera*) *as he finishes dressing the Christmas tree.*)

MOTHER: (*Voice over*) Say goodnight to your Dad.
  (FATHER *turns and smiles.*

Cut to shot of MOTHER *with* EILEEN, TONY *and* MAISIE *as children, ready for bed.*)
EILEEN: ⎫
TONY: ⎬ (As *children*) Goodnight, Dad.
MAISIE: ⎭
FATHER: (*Voice over*) Goodnight kids.
(MOTHER *and children exit.*
Soundtrack:)
CHOIR: (*Voice over, singing*) 'Angels and Archangels
May have gathered there
Cherubim and seraphim
Thronged the air …'
(*Cut to* FATHER *at sideboard turning back to the Christmas tree.*
Soundtrack:)
MOTHER: (*Voice over*) Come on – up the dancers!
(*Children giggling as they go upstairs.*
Cut to:)

INT. CHILDREN'S BEDROOM, NIGHT, EARLY 1940s

Pan with FATHER, *in close-up, creeping into bedroom.*
Cut to the three children sleeping in the bed, pan to them.
CHOIR: (*Voice over, singing*) 'But only his mother
In her maiden bliss
Worshipped the Beloved
With a kiss …'
(FATHER *places three Christmas stockings on the end of the bed.*
Cut to FATHER *in close-up.* FATHER *looking down at the sleeping children with love. His eyes fill with tears.*)
FATHER: (*Very softly*) God bless.
CHOIR: (*Voice over, singing*) 'What can I give him
Poor as I am?
If I were a shepherd
I would bring a lamb … '
(*Cut to:*)

INT. KITCHEN. NIGHT. EARLY 1940s

Shot of table.

FATHER *at the head of the table.* MAISIE *as a child to his right –* TONY *and* EILEEN, *as children, to his left.*
Soundtrack carol climaxes:
CHOIR: (*Voice over, singing*) 'If I were a Wise Man
    I would do my part;
    Yet what can I give him –
    Give my heart.'
    (FATHER *rises in a fury.*
    The table is laden with Christmas food.
    Suddenly he grabs the tablecloth and drags everything off the table.)
FATHER: (*In a fury*) NELLIE! CLEAN IT UP!
    (*Cut to:*)

INT. BEDROOM. NIGHT. EARLY 1940s

Pitch blackness.
Soundtrack:
EILEEN: (*As a child, very ill*) What's scarlet fever, Mam?
MOTHER: (*Quietly*) It's scarlettina, love. Scarlettina …
    (EILEEN, *lying in bed in foreground, gradually comes into focus.*)
    (*From the bedroom door*) How are you Ei?
EILEEN: (*Weakly*) I'm OK Mam.
    (MOTHER *comes to bed and sits down.*
    She begins to stroke EILEEN's *hair.*
    Clearly she is upset.
    Silence.)
    Where's our Tony, Mam?
    (MOTHER *doesn't answer.*
    Cut to:)

EXT. STREET. NIGHT. EARLY 1940s

Back view of TONY *as a child.*
Front door opens.
FATHER *standing there.*
TONY: (*As a child*) Why can't I come in, Dad?
FATHER: There's no place for you here – frigg off!
    (*Slams door in* TONY's *face.*
    Cut to side view close-up of TONY *as a child.*

He just stands there trying to prevent himself from crying.
He looks up at the bedroom window.
Cut to MOTHER *at the bedroom window from* TONY's *point of view.*
She just stands there in tears, shaking her head.
Cut to back view of TONY *as a child.*
Pause.
He backs away from the front door and moves left. Pan with him.
As he walks slowly down the street he puts his hands into his pockets then breaks into a trot.)
TONY: (*As a child, voice over*) Can I stay here, Gran?
GRANNY: (*Voice over*) You can have the sofa.
　(*Cut to:*)

　　INT. PARLOUR. NIGHT. MID-1950s. EILEEN'S WEDDING

Close-up of Aunty Nell singing 'Roll Along Kentucky Moon'.
AUNTY NELL: More band!
　(*Pan away from her, left to right.*)
GRANNY: (*Voice over*) Whoopie!
　(*Pan to* GRANNY *when she is in close-up.*
　Pan to GRANNY. *When she is in close-up pan stops.*
　GRANNY *sings 'A Little Bit of Cucumber'.*)
AUNTY NELL: (*Voice over*) More bleedin' band.
　(*Pan away to* MONICA *in close-up, left to right.*)
MONICA: Your Gran's in fine feckle.
　(*Continue pan to* EILEEN, *in close-up.*)
EILEEN: Yer – she's just come back from the Isle of Man.
　(*Continue pan to* MAISIE, *in close-up.*)
MAISIE: She should've stayed there – the auld cow – she's just like me Dad and I bleedin' hate her.
　(*Cut to:*)

　　INT. NIGHT. 1940s

Medium close-up of EILEEN, MAISIE *and* TONY *as children, their backs to camera but their faces seen in reflection in a mirror.*
Complete darkness surrounds them.
They are illuminated by a single nightlight in front of the mirror.

GRANNY: (*Voice over*) If you look into a mirror after midnight – you'll see the devil.
(*Her face looms up out of the blackness and appears disembodied above them in the mirror. They are terrified.*
GRANNY *half laughs, half grins.*
Cut to:)

INT. STABLE. DAY. LATE 1940s

Close-up of FATHER. *He is seen across the back of a horse which he is curry-combing.*
Cut to EILEEN, MAISIE *and* TONY *as children, painstakingly climbing a ladder which leads to a hayloft. They make no noise. Crane up with them. They reach the straw-filled loft and crawl commando-style across it.*
FATHER: (*Voice over, half whistling, half singing*) 'Irish Eyes …'
(*The three children reach the edge of the loft.*
Track in with them and over them.
FATHER *seen in high shot, curry-combing the horse as he half whistles, half sings.*
*Cut to stable floor (*FATHER'S *point of view) of hayloft.*
Slowly – very slowly – their three faces appear over the edge of the loft. They just look and listen as FATHER *continues half whistling, half singing* 'Irish Eyes'.
Cut to:)

EXT. STREET. DAY. LATE 1940s

Low-angle shot from street of MOTHER *cleaning bedroom windows. She sits on the outside window ledge with her legs inside the room.*
Cut to high shot of MAISIE *from* MOTHER'S *point of view, walking towards camera and looking up at the bedroom window.*
MAISIE: (*As a child, voice over*) Don't fall, Mam – Please don't fall.
(*Dissolve to:*)

INT. LANDING. DAY. LATE 1940s

Mid-shot, low-angle, of EILEEN *and* TONY *as children, their faces appearing and looking round banister towards camera.*

INT. BEDROOM. DAY. LATE 1940s

Long shot of bedroom window, the rest of the room dark but one or two objects catching the light: a corner of a bed, a little chest of drawers …
Sun blazing through the window, curtains billowing softly.
Right of the window, on the floor, a bucket.
Only MOTHER's *legs and feet can be seen as she sits on the outside of the window-ledge washing the windows. As she does so she is almost obliterated by the sun. Very slowly track in on her.*
Soundtrack:
MAISIE: (*As an adult, voice over*) Why did you marry him, Mam?
MOTHER: (*Voice over*) He was nice, he was a good dancer.
   (*Voice over of Ella Fitzgerald singing 'Taking a Chance on Love'.*
   Dissolve/cut to:)

INT. PARLOUR AND HALL. DAY. EARLY 1950s

A continuous tracking two-shot of MOTHER *and* FATHER *in parlour then ending in the hall.*
He is beating her relentlessly and she is screaming.
MOTHER: Tommy! Tommy! Oh stop Tommy! Stop!
   (*Soundtrack of Ella Fitzgerald voice over singing 'Taking a Chance on Love'.*
   FATHER *walks away back down the hall to parlour, leaving* MOTHER's *crumpled body on the floor.*
   Hold.
   Only her moans can be heard.
   Soundtrack of Ella Fitzgerald voice over singing 'Taking a Chance on Love'.
   Cut to:)

INT. PARLOUR. DAY. EARLY 1950s

Close-up of MOTHER's *face, side view. It is almost unrecognizable – like a boxer's after a particularly vicious fight. She is trying not to cry but clearly every movement is agony. She is polishing the sideboard. Blood trickles down from her nose and mouth and drips on to the sideboard. Pan down to top of sideboard. Blood drips on to the surface and* MOTHER *continues slowly to rub the polish and the blood into the surface of the wood.*
Cut to:

INT. COAL-HOLE IN CELLAR. DAY. EARLY 1950s

MAISIE *as an adult in coal-hole, shovelling coal into a bucket. She is lit only from above, from the pin-points of light coming in through the overhead iron coal-hole lid.*
She stops shovelling coal and looks up into the light.
MAISIE: (*In a quiet voice filled with impotent rage and furious hatred*)
    If anything happens to my Mam I'll bleedin' kill you!
TONY: (*Voice over*) Go on Ma – give us 'Barefoot Days'.
    (*Dissolve to:*)

INT. PARLOUR. NIGHT. MID-1950s. EILEEN'S WEDDING

Close-up of MOTHER*'s hands. As she begins to sing her hands beat time on her lap.* MOTHER *sings 'Barefoot Days'.*
Pan slowly up to her smiling face. She continues to sing.
She is now in close-up.
Guests begin to join in.
Pan slowly, from left to right, around the happy singing faces until EILEEN, TONY *and* MAISIE *are framed. They are singing too. Dissolve:*

INT. CELLAR. DAY. 1940

Continue panning shot, left to right.
FATHER, MOTHER, EILEEN, MAISIE, TONY, *as children, chopping wood and putting it into bundles.*
Soundtrack of voice over singing 'Barefoot Days' continues.
Pan ends.
Cut to tableau shot of entire family.
Soundtrack of voice over singing 'Barefoot Days' continues.
Silence.
They all continue chopping and bundling wood and putting it into piles.
Cut to:

EXT. ALLEY, DAY. 1940

EILEEN, MAISIE *and* TONY *as children, pushing a handcart laden with wood.*
Soundtrack: air-raid siren starts. They run faster with the cart. Air-raid siren wails louder. They stop running and get under the cart.
Cut to close-up of the three children under the cart.
Soundtrack: distant planes, sirens, bombs.

Cut to:

INT. AIR-RAID SHELTER. DAY. 1940

Soundtrack: sirens and distant bombs.
Close shot: MOTHER *and* FATHER *in the midst of the crowd being pushed into the air-raid shelter by the crowd's momentum.*
MOTHER: (*Frantic*) Where are the kids, Tommy? Where are the kids?
   (*Cut to:*)

EXT. STREET. DAY. 1940

High shot. A parade of shops.
EILEEN, MAISIE, TONY *as children running past them, right to left, followed by an ARP warden.*
Soundtrack: bombs, aircraft swooping down suddenly.
Cut to planes' point of view, swooping down and shattering the shop windows with tracer bullets.
Cut to:

EXT. SHOP DOORWAY. DAY. 1940

The children and ARP warden crashing to the ground inside shop doorway, glass showering them.
Soundtrack: bombs. Planes drone away.
Cut to:

AIR-RAID SHELTER. DAY. 1940

Close-up of FATHER.
Soundtrack: bombs getting progressively louder and closer.
FATHER: (*Furious*) Where the bleedin' hell have you been?
   (*Cut to three-shot of children,* EILEEN *in front,* TONY *and* MAISIE *behind,* FATHER *slaps* EILEEN *right across the face. She is more stunned than hurt.*
   Soundtrack: bombs very loud. People begin to panic.)
FIRST VOICE OVER: They're getting closer.
SECOND VOICE OVER: They're gonna bomb us!
   (*Cut to four shot,* FATHER *facing camera. The children backs to camera,* EILEEN *is lifted up by* FATHER.
   Cut to FATHER *holding* EILEEN *up. Mid-close up.*)
FATHER: Sing, Eileen! Sing!

(EILEEN *singing tentatively 'Roll Out the Barrel'.* FATHER *joins in.*
Cut to wide shot or pan around, right to left.
One by one people join in – singing quietly and afraid.
Soundtrack: bombs very loud.
All sing 'Roll Out the Barrel'.)

INT. KITCHEN. EARLY SUMMER EVENING. EARLY 1950s

Mid three-shot of EILEEN, MONICA *and* JINGLES *looking directly into camera, as if it were a mirror. They are getting made up.*
JINGLES: Wo – oh – it's Saturday!
　Yes! It's Sat – ur – day!
　(*Soundtrack: on the radio, Guy Mitchell and Cindy Carson sing 'Cos I Love Ya that's a Why'.*
　EILEEN, MONICA *and* JINGLES *finish getting made up, putting lipstick on as they finish, pursing their lips.*)
MONICA: (*Wetting her forefingers and running them over her eyebrows very quickly*) Oh kiss me you fool!
　(*They all smile.*
　A knock on the front door is heard.
　Cut to:)
EILEEN: (*Gathering herself together somewhat nervously*) That's him.
JINGLES: Bet he's come in a taxi.
MONICA: Well you know these seamen – money's no object. (EILEEN *exits.*
　Cut to:)

EXT. STREET. FRONT DOOR. EARLY SUMMER EVENING. EARLY 1950s

Close-up of EILEEN *opening front door. She is horrified by what she sees.*
EILEEN: (*More to herself than anything*) It's me Dad.
　(*Cut to:*)

INT. HALLWAY. EARLY SUMMER EVENING. EARLY 1950s

Shot of FATHER *from* EILEEN'S *point of view.*
He is swaying on the doorstep. He is very, very ill – like a Belsen victim.
FATHER: I've signed meself out of hospital.
　I've walked home.
　(*He literally falls into the hall.*
　Cut to:)

INT. PARLOUR. NIGHT. EARLY 1950s

Close-up of GRANNY.

GRANNY: (*In tears*) He's gone – my Tommy's gone …

(*Cut to shot of* MOTHER, EILEEN, MAISIE *and* TONY.

MOTHER *sits down in a chair.*

EILEEN *and* MAISIE *come and stand behind her.*

TONY *in a chair by the fireside, elbows on knees, lowers his head.*

They all look exhausted – more relieved than upset.

Cut to low-angled shot, side view, of FATHER's *head on bed.*

Pennies on his eyes.

Hold.)

MONICA: (*Voice over*) Arh – he was all right, your dad.

EILEEN: (*Voice over*) You were the only one who could get around him.

(*Cut to close-up of a pair of boots on the sideboard.*)

MONICA: (*Voice over*) What'll you give me for them, Mr. D.?

(*Cut to close-up of* FATHER.)

FATHER: (*Roaring with laughter*) Micky, they're your dad's working boots!

(*Cut to close-up of* MONICA.)

MONICA: But we've just *got* to have five bob.

(*Cut to close-up of* FATHER.)

FATHER: (*Incredulous*) What for?

(*Cut to close-up of* EILEEN.)

EILEEN: Oh Dad we've just *got* to go to the dance.

(*Cut to close-up of* FATHER.)

FATHER: (*Disbelieving*) I don't know – you two are bleedin' dance mad.

(*Cut to close-up of* MONICA.)

MONICA: (*Pleading*) Arh – go on Mr D. Just five bob – don't be snidey.

(*Cut to close-up of* FATHER.)

FATHER: All right – I'll *lend* you the money – but take the boots back home – OK?

(FATHER *throws her the money.*

Cut to mid-two-shot of EILEEN *and* MONICA. MONICA *catches the money.*)

MONICA: Arh – you're a pal, Mr D.

EILEEN: Thanks Dad!

(*Pan with them as they hurry out.*)

FATHER: (*Voice over*) And be back here by eleven!
   (*Cut to close-up of* FATHER.)
FATHER: (*Still incredulous*) Bleedin' dance mad!
   (*Cut to close-up of* MONICA *at the parlour door.*)
MONICA: How are we fixed for a few ciggies, Mr D.?
   (*Cut to close-up of* FATHER.)
FATHER: (*Mock anger*) OUT!
   (*Cut to:*)

          EXT. STREET. NIGHT. EARLY 1950s

Shot of EILEEN *and* MONICA *sitting on doorstep with their best dresses on.*
FATHER: (*Voice over from inside the house*) Eileen – it's nearly eleven o'clock.
EILEEN: OK, Dad.
MONICA: (*Coaxing*) Just one last ciggie, Mr D.
EILEEN: I'll only be a minute Dad.
   (*To* MONICA) You'll get me hung you will.
   (EILEEN *gives* MONICA *a cigarette and has one herself. They light up. Pause.*)
FATHER: (*Voice over*) Eileen – I won't tell you twice.
MONICA: (*Shouting back and coaxing*) Just a few more minutes and she'll be in – honest -
FATHER: (*Voice over*) Make sure it is only a few minutes and all.
   (*Silence as they savour their cigarettes.*)
MONICA: I'm sure I'm getting a brain tumour.
EILEEN: Oh Micky, behave! You're healthier than I am.
MONICA: No – honest kid – my head's been banging for days and –
FATHER: (*Voice over, roaring*) Eileen! What beedin' time do you call this!
   (EILEEN *and* MONICA *frightened out of their wits.*)
EILEEN: (*Choking on her cigarette*) Oh God blimey! (*Shouting in*) I'm coming Dad! I'm coming!
MONICA: Isn't it terrible the way we've got to be in by eleven o'clock?
EILEEN: I know. It's worse than Alcatraz, isn't it?
EILEEN/MONICA: See ya kid!
   (*Cut to:*)

EXT. STREET. NIGHT. MID-1950s. EILEEN'S WEDDING

Close-up of EILEEN *and* MONICA'*s feet.*
Track (left to right) as their feet dance in time to EILEEN/MONICA'*s voice over, singing* 'R-A-G-M-M-O-P-P- RAGMOP!'
Cut to MONICA *and* EILEEN *in two-shot close-up.*
Track with them, right to left, as they dance back.
EILEEN/MONICA: (Singing) 'R-A-G-M-M-O-P-P- RAGMOP!'
   (*They laugh and collapse on to the doorstep.*
   Pan with them. Wedding celebration going on inside the house. They fan themselves with their hands.)
MONICA: God isn't it hot? I'm sweating past myself.
   (*Pause.*)
EILEEN: Here's Red Donnelly.
MONICA: Oh, that's all I need.
EILEEN: Arh, he's harmless.
   (*Cut to* EILEEN *and* MONICA'*s point of view of Red Donnelly.*
   Pan with him as he walks to doorstep.
   He stops in front of them.)
RED: (*Winking at* MONICA) Hiya Mick!
   (*Cut to two-shot of* EILEEN *and* MONICA *on doorstep.*)
MONICA: (*Pointing her two forefingers at him*) Die!
   (RED *walks between them into the house.*)
RED: (*As he recedes into the house*) Oh what you're throwing away!
   (EILEEN *laughs.*)
MONICA: (*To* EILEEN) God help him – poor gobshite!
   (*Pause.*)
EILEEN: (*Laughing*) Remember Formby? And that tent?
MONICA: (*Embarrassed*) Oh God blimey!
   (*Cut to:*)

EXT. BEACH. DAY. EARLY 1950s

Mid three-shot. A tent being erected.
EILEEN, *left of frame, holds centre pole.*
MONICA, *right of frame, is kneeling on the ground knocking pegs in with a mallet.*
JINGLES *is inside the tent itself.*
MONICA: I never.

JINGLES: (*Popping her head outside the tent flap*) You did.
MONICA: I never.
　(*Cut to close-up of* JINGLES.)
JINGLES: (*Adamant*) You did!
　(MONICA *rising into shot.*)
MONICA: (*Adamant*) I never!
JINGLES: You did fart!
　(*Puts her head back inside the tent.*
　A momentary pause.
　MONICA *hits* JINGLES *on the head with the mallet.*
　Slowly JINGLES' *form collapses accompanied by a low groan.*)
MONICA: (*Quietly*) I never.
　(*Cut to:*)

　　EXT. STREET. NIGHT. MID-1950S. EILEEN'S WEDDING
EILEEN: I thought you'd killed her, Micky.
MONICA: I know – so did I. When I think about it I was a real cow with that mallet, wasn't I?
　(*Pause.*)
　Do you ever see Jingles?
EILEEN: No – not since she married Les Shone.
　(*Pause.*
　Cut to mid-shot of JINGLES.)
JINGLES: (*Throwing her arms wide and singing to the tune of Gershwin's "Swonderful"*) ''Swonderful!''
　(*Cut to two-shot of* EILEEN *and* MONICA *on doorstep.*)
EILEEN/MONICA: (*Singing*) ''Smarvellous.'
　(*They get up and go to* JINGLES. *Pan with them to mid three-shot.*
　All hug one another.)
EILEEN: Jingles! You came!
EILEEN:　⎤
MONICA:　⎬ (*Singing to the tune of 'Too Young'*) 'They tried to sell us Egg Foo Yung!'
JINGLES:　⎦
　(*All laugh.*)
EILEEN: How are you doing, kid?
JINGLES: Smashing.
MONICA: Still married?

JINGLES: Oh God yeah! Two kids and a radiogram to support, know what I mean?
(*Laughter. They walk towards the house. Pan with them. Dissolve to mid-long shot of the house. They go inside.*)
JINGLES: (*Voice over*) You haven't altered though, Ei – still not a pick on you.
EILEEN: (*Voice over*) Yeah – still eight stone soaking wet.
(*Wedding guests come out on to the doorstep as the three disappear into the house.*)
JINGLES: (*Voice over*) How do you do it?
EILEEN: (*Voice over*) Witchcraft.
(*Laughter.*)
JINGLES: (*Voice over*) You're looking well, Mick.
MONICA: (*Voice over*) Oh, but look at the size of me Jingles. I'm in a worse state than Russia.
JINGLES: (*Voice over*) Do you know who I saw in The Swan last week?
EILEEN: (*Voice over*) No. Who?
JINGLES: (*Voice over*) Jackie Mc-Gorrie.
EILEEN: (*Voice over*) Did you? Arh, remember the way we used to think that he was the dead spit of Burt Lancaster?
JINGLES: (*Voice over*) Yeah.
EILEEN: (*Voice over*) Arh, poor Jackie.
(*Their voices fade.*
Cut to:)

INT. TRAIN COMPARTMENT. DAY. EARLY 1950s

Train travelling left to right.
Two-shot of EILEEN *and* JINGLES *by the window.*
EILEEN, *left of frame, sitting opposite* JINGLES, *right of frame.*
Voice over of MONICA *singing 'Brr-Brr-Brr-Brr Busy Line'.*
  They both turn and look at her and smile.
  Cut to shot of MONICA *from* EILEEN *and* JINGLES' *point of view.*
  She is half in the compartment, half in the corridor.
  Cut to close-up of EILEEN. *She smiles but she is near to tears.*
  She turns and looks out of the window.
  Cut to:

INT. PARLOUR. DAY. EARLY 1950S

Close-up of EILEEN, *side view.*
EILEEN: (*Conciliatory*) Won't you say ta'ra, Dad?
   (*Silence.*)
   (*Hurt and angry*) I'm only going for the season.
   (*Cut to mid-long two-shot.*
     EILEEN *in front of the sideboard, left of frame,* FATHER *by the fire, right of frame; he just leans forward and looks into the fire.*)
   (*Looking at him*) Do you know what? If I ever get a gun I'll blow your bleedin' brains out!

EXT. STREET. DAY. EARLY 1950s

Close-up of EILEEN *at taxi window.*
EILEEN: (*Putting a brave face on*) Ta'ra Mam!
   (*The cab moves off, left to right. Pan with it.*
     EILEEN *waves.*
   Cut to:)

INT. CAB. DAY. EARLY 1950s

Shot of MOTHER *from* EILEEN's *point of view from moving cab.*
MOTHER *on doorstep.*
MOTHER: (*Waves tearfully*) Bye, love – don't forget to write now, will you?
   (MOTHER, *still waving, recedes.*
   Cut to:)

INT. HOLIDAY-HOTEL DINING ROOM. MORNING. EARLY 1950s

Mid long shot.
EILEEN, MONICA *and* JINGLES *in their black and white waitress uniforms, at the head of their respective stations of tables. They are very nervous. Silence.*
Cut to their point of view of the tables which are now filled with musicians taking breakfast and all beating time with hands and cutlery and singing 'R-A-G-M-O-P-P-P. RAGMOP!'
EILEEN, MONICA, JINGLES *serving and clearing away.*
Musicians' voices fade.
MOTHER: (*Voice over*) Please come home Ei, your Dad's *really* ill.
   (*Cut to:*)

INT. HALLWAY. DAY. EARLY 1950s

Shot of street from front door. A taxi pulls up, right to left.
EILEEN *gets out.*
MOTHER: (*Voice over*) He thought it was ulcers right up till the end.
   (EILEEN *looks up at the house and then enters.*
   Cut to:)

INT. EILEEN/DAVE'S FLAT. NIGHT. LATE 1950s

Firelight.
Close shot, back view of EILEEN *as she looks into the fire.*
Silence. She turns her head to face the frame right.
DAVE: (*Voice over*) You're married now – I'm your husband – your duty's to me, frig everyone else. Monica, Jingles, that's all ancient history now.
   (*She turns to look back into the fire.*
   Cut to:)

INT. PARLOUR. NIGHT. EARLY 1950s. EILEEN'S WEDDING

Close-up of MONICA, *side view, at an upright piano.*
MONICA *sings 'Buttons and Bows'.*
GUEST: (*Voice over*) Go on Mick!
   (*She really begins to vamp it. She puts the piano lid down and gets up and sits on it.*
   EILEEN *and* JINGLES *stand at the back of the piano.*
   Cut to three-shot of EILEEN, JINGLES *and* MONICA *singing.*
   Cut to:)

EXT. STREET. NIGHT. MID-1950s. EILEEN'S WEDDING

Close shot of doorstep.
EILEEN *on left of frame;* MAISIE, *right of frame and* TONY *sitting at a right angle behind them. He is very drunk.*
Soundtrack of EILEEN, MONICA *and* JINGLES' *voices over singing the finale of 'Buttons and Bows'.*
Applause and laughter, after a long pause.
MAISIE: Well, Ei – you're well and truly married now.
EILEEN: Yeah – but I don't feel *any* different, Maisie … I don't *feel* any different.
   (*Pause.*)

TONY: (*Drunk and sleepy, to no one in particular*) Don't be worrying we'll be all right …
(*Dissolve to slightly wider shot of doorstep. People coming out.*
EILEEN, MAISIE, TONY *no longer on it. Wedding celebrations continue.*
Soundtrack:)
MOTHER: (*Voice over*) They soon grow up … Maisie's engaged to Georgie Roughley and I don't think it'll be long before our Tony marries Rosie Forsyth …
(*Dissolve to slightly wider shot of house: front doorstep and parlour window. Front door closed. Window dark. Wedding celebrations over. All quiet.*
Pause.
Soundtrack:)
MOTHER: (*Voice over*) I'll leave the place till morning …
(*Silence.*
Then crane slowly up diagonally over the front of the house until the bedroom window is framed in darkness.
Track/zoom in on it.
Over the shot, soundtrack: the ending of Vaughan Williams' Pastoral Symphony No. 3. The soprano singing a wordless song. Song ends when bedroom window is framed.
Dissolve to:)

INT. BEDROOM. DAY

Track back very slowly from close-up of window.
A bright sunshine. Curtains billowing. Silence.
MOTHER: (*Voice over*) I love the light nights …
MAISIE: (*As an adult, voice over*) But they're starting to draw in now, aren't they, Mam?
MOTHER: (*Voice over*) Yeah.
(*Pause.*
Distant rolling thunder.
Pause.)
FATHER: (*Voice over*) Nellie … Nellie! … Nell! …
(*His voice fades.*
Thunder rolling vaguely in the background.
Dissolve.)

INT. KITCHEN. EARLY SUMMER EVENING

Panning shot to mirror on sideboard, make-up strewn in front of it. When mirror is framed hold.
Soundtrack:
EILEEN: (*As adult, voice over*) Sorry about the mess, Mam …
MOTHER: (*Voice over*) Go on – you're all right – I'll see to it …
EILEEN: ⎫   Thanks Mam …
MONICA: ⎬ (*Voice over*) See yer Mrs D….
JINGLES: ⎭   Ta'ra …
    (*The sound of them going out.*)
MOTHER: (*Voice over, calling after them*) Enjoy yourselves!
    (*Pan away from mirror.*
    Dissolve to panning shot of ironing board. Pan stops when ironing board is framed.
    MOTHER *is sprinkling water from a cup on to handkerchiefs, then – after ironing them with a flat iron – she folds them and puts them into a pile on the end of the ironing board.*
    Dissolve to close-up of MOTHER *at ironing board.*
    She picks up a flat iron, holds it close to her cheek, to test it for heat, spits on it, then continues ironing.
    Soundtrack:)
TONY: (*Voice over, as adult*) Goodnight, Mahsie.
MOTHER: (*Voice over*) Goodnight, son.
    (*Dissolve:*)

INT. PARLOUR. NIGHT

Parlour in firelight.
Mid-wide shot of MOTHER *sitting in a chair, reading newspaper.* EILEEN, MAISIE, TONY, *as children, sitting around her on the floor. They are ready for bed and drinking their cocoa.*
Silence.
MAISIE: (*As a child, quietly*) Look, Mam – my cocoa's got half a crown on it …
    (MOTHER *looks up and smiles. Children continue drinking.*
    MOTHER *stares into the fire and sighs.*
    Silence.
    Dissolve to panning shot across parlour.

Newspaper on chair, toys strewn across the mat in front of the hearth.
Firelight.
Soundtrack:)
MOTHER: (*Voice over*) Come on – up the dancers!
(*Children giggling as they go upstairs.*)
How much do you love me?
CHILDREN: A pound of sugar!
(*Laughter.*
Their voices fade.
Pause.)
MOTHER: (*Voice over, singing with a rocking motion*) Hush-a- bowee ...
Hush-a-bow ...
(*Her voice fades.*
Dissolve to MOTHER *in parlour in firelight.*
Track in on her.
She is sleeping in the chair, her head on her chest, her mouth open. The newspaper slips to the floor.
Soundtrack:)
(*Voice over*) The Sandman is coming ...
(*Dissolve to shot of* MOTHER *sitting in armchair in bright sunshine.*
She is bathed in and surrounded by light. Slowly she looks up and smiles.
Dissolve to firelight.
Pan to fire.
Track in on fire.
Soundtrack:)
(*Voice over*) How much do you love me?
(*Continue tracking in on fire.*
Fade to black.
Closing credits.)

Still Lives

NB: *Still Lives* continues the story of *Distant Voices* and takes place in Liverpool in the closing years of the 1950s.

It begins with a birth and ends with a marriage – these two great rituals forming the parameters within which the family's subtle but gradual disintegration takes place.

As in painting, the drama lies not so much in the bowl of fruit or the vase of flowers but the ways in which these objects are perceived – in effect, stasis as drama.

All the family history is packed into *Distant Voices*, while in *Still Lives* life has reached an even keel and ticks silently away.

Terence Davies on the set of *Distant Voices, Still Lives* (1988). (BFI National Archive)

LIVERPOOL 1955–59

Blackness.
Fade up on main title, Still Lives.
Fade out main title.
Fade up on:

EXT. NIGHT

Close-up of water. River Mersey, dark and rippling. Rain.
Track and pan.
Soundtrack: a choir singing unaccompanied Britten's
'A Hymn to the Virgin':

'Of one that is so fair and bright,
Velut maris stella,
Brighter than the day is light,
Parens et puella:
I cry to thee, thou see to me,
Lady, pray thy son for me,
Tam pia.
That I may come to thee Maria …'
(*Dissolve to:*)

INT. HOSPITAL LABOUR WARD. NIGHT

Close-up of hands grasping the bed-rail, side view.
Screaming is heard.
Hold.
Soundtrack: 'A Hymn to the Virgin' continued:

'All this world was forlorn
Eva peccatrice,
Till our lord was y-born,
De te genetrice …'
Track down the bed to close-up of MAISIE (*side view*).
She is in dry labour.

MAISIE: (*Screaming*) Oh God! God!
Soundtrack: 'A Hymn to the Virgin' continued:
'With ave it went away
Darkest night, and comes the day,

Salutis,
The well springeth out of thee,
Virtutis …'
(*Dissolve to:*)

INT. HOSPITAL. NIGHT

A newly born baby girl naked and screaming being handed from one pair of gloved hands to another, against blackness.
Dissolve to:

INT. CHURCH. SUNDAY. LATE MORNING

The baby in its christening robes being handed to PRIEST*'s hands.*
Dissolve to baby in PRIEST'S *arms.*
PRIEST: (*Voice over*) I baptize thee Elaine …
   (*Pours water on baby's head. Baby cries.*)
   In the name of the Father, and of the Son, and of the Holy Ghost …
   (*Dissolve to close shot of* MAISIE *and her husband* GEORGE *at the font.*
   The PRIEST *finishes baptising the baby and hands her to* MAISIE.
   MAISIE *cradles her.*)
Slowly track back.
Soundtrack: 'A Hymn to the Virgin' continued:
'Lady, flower of everything,
Rosa sine spina,
Thou bare jesu, heaven's king Gratia divina …'
Track stops when MAISIE, GEORGE, PRIEST *and entire family are seen in tableau at the font.*
Soundtrack: 'A Hymn to the Virgin' continued:
'Of all thou barest the prize
Lady, queen of Paradise,
Electa,
Maid mild, mother es effecta.'
Baby wailing. People smiling.
Dissolve to:

EXT. STREET. SUNDAY. MIDDAY

MOTHER*'s house seen in mid-long shot. Bright sunshine,* MAISIE*'s pram outside the front door. Front door open. Parlour window open. Curtains billowing.*

Soundtrack: 'Family Favourites' theme-tune is heard ('With a Song in My Heart').

BBC ANNOUNCER: This is Family Favourites introduced by Jean Metcalfe and Bill—

(*Fade* ANNOUNCER'*s voice.*

Soundmix to Dicky Valentine singing 'The Finger of Suspicion'. MAISIE *comes out of the house, takes the child from the pram, then goes back inside. Soundtrack of Dicky Valentine singing continues.*

Dissolve to:)

INT. MUM'S HOUSE. EARLY AFTERNOON. SUNDAY

Parlour. Close-up of GEORGE *asleep in the armchair, side view. Soundtrack:*

BILLY COTTON: (*Voice over*) Wakey! Way-kee!

(*Signature tune of 'The Billy Cotton Band Show'.*)

BBC ANNOUNCER: It's the Billy Cotton Band Show starring …

(*Soundmix: fade to music being played by Billy Cotton Band then cross-fade to voice over from show:*)

Hey you! You down there with the glasses! Don't I know you?

(*Laughter.*

Dissolve to close-up of TONY, *side view, listening to 'Beyond Our Ken' on radio. Soundtrack: soundmix to a 'Rodney and Charles' sketch or 'That was an excerpt from' at the show's opening.*

Laughter.

TONY *laughing.*

Applause. Laughter.

Soundtrack:)

BBC ANNOUNCER: You might have been listening to or have just missed 'Beyond Our Ken' – a sort of radio show in which you heard Kenneth Horne, Kenneth Williams, Hugh Paddick, Betty Marsden and Bill Pertwee. The script, believe it or not, was written …

(*Fade sound.*

Dissolve to:)

EXT. MOTHER'S HOUSE. SUNDAY AFTERNOON

MOTHER *is seen in medium close-up at the parlour window, from the street. Bright sunshine.*

The window is half open and she is sitting inside the parlour with her left arm lying along the outside of the windowsill. Her arm is the only part of her clearly seen – the rest of her face and body is behind the heavy net curtain. She looks out into the street.

MOTHER: (*Voice over*) Will you make us a lemon dash, Tony?
   (*Dissolve to:*)

INT. PARLOUR. SUNDAY AFTERNOON

Mid-shot of MAISIE *cradling the baby, side view.*
MAISIE *is singing 'The Birthday of the Little Princess' softly to the child. The child is asleep. She puts her in the cot.*
Soundtrack:
Soundmix to EILEEN'*s voice over singing 'Brown Skin Girl'.*
Cut to:

INT. PUB PARLOUR. CHRISTENING CELEBRATIONS. NIGHT

EILEEN *and* DAVE *in medium close-up.*
EILEEN *sings 'Brown Skin Girl'.*
The guests begin to join in except DAVE *who drinks silently.*
Pan around right to left on singing guests. Pan ends when MAISIE *and* MOTHER *are in medium close-up. All finish the song in chorus. Laughter. Applause. Smiles.*
Jib or crane up and track forward to the narrow passage leading from the parlour to the bar. It is crowded.
GEORGE *in medium close-up, ordering drinks.*
Soundtrack:
GUEST: (*Voice over, singing*) 'Oh my! What a rotten song,
   What a rotten song,
   What a rotten song,
   Oh my! What a rotten song,
   What a rotten singer too!'
   (*Laughter. Applause.*)
GEORGE: Can I have – a rum and pep, a rum and blackcurrant,
   a black and tan, half a shandy, a pint of bitter, a pint of mild,
   a mild and bitter mixed …
   (TONY – *preceded by his girlfriend* ROSE – *enters and they both walk towards the camera.*)

(*To* ROSE) Hiyer Rose – come to wet the baby's head?
ROSE: Oh, I wouldn't miss it for the world.
TONY: (*To* GEORGE) Well – how does it feel to be a dad?
GEORGE: Oh – made up!

(TONY *and* ROSE *walk into the parlour.*)
(*Calling after them*) What are you having?
(*Cut to medium close-up, two-shot.* MAISIE *and* MOTHER.)

MOTHER: ⎫ Hello Rose
MAISIE: ⎬ Hello son
(*Together*) ⎭ OK Tone?

(*Cut to medium close-up. Two-shot.* TONY *and* ROSE.)
TONY: Hi yer Maise.
How's Maisie eh?
ROSE: How are you, Mrs D?
Hello Maisie.
MAISIE: (*Voice over*) Smashing!
MOTHER: (*Voice over*) Still working at the English Electric, Rose?
ROSE: Oh God yer! I'm there for life I think.
DAVE: (*Voice over*) All right Tone?
EILEEN: (*Voice over*) Hi yer – Rose!
(ROSE *looks in their direction.*)
ROSE: Hello Ei, Dave.
(*Cut to medium close-up. Two-shot.* EILEEN *and* DAVE.)
DAVE: Hello girl.
EILEEN: How are you, Tone?
(*Cut to medium close-up. Two-shot.* TONY *and* ROSE, TONY *gives thumbs up sign.*)
(*Cut to medium close-up of a pint glass on the table, which is covered with drinks.*)
TONY: (*Voice over*) Let's have a kitty, eh? A pound a man?
(*Pound notes being put into the pint glass and thrown on to the table.*)
(*Cut to medium close-up. Two-shot.* MAISIE *and* MOTHER,
MOTHER *right of frame, full-faced,* MAISIE *in profile left of frame.*
MOTHER *begins to sing* 'When That Old Gang of Mine' *and everyone begins to join in.*
Pan slowly round guests left to right, as they sing along.

Fade singing and all sync sound, but guests continue to sing as we continue to pan.
Soundtrack:)
MR HYAMS: (*Voice over, calling*) **Rent!**
TONY: (*Voice over, calling*) **Spent!**
(*Fade to white.*
Soundtrack as we hold on white.)
MOTHER: (*Voice over*) **Oh don't, Tony – he'll think you're serious.**
(*Calling*) **Come in Mr Hyams – the money's on the sideboard.**
(*Fade from white to:*)

EXT. STREET. OUTSIDE MOTHER'S HOUSE.
EARLY FRIDAY EVENING. SUMMER

It is light. MR SPAULL, *the insurance man, riding a bike around the corner and stopping at* MOTHER's *front door. When riding the bike he is free-wheeling – standing on one pedal on one side of the bike. Pan with him to the front door, right to left.*
He props his bike up against the low wall in front of the house and goes to the front door.
Cut to:

INT. HALL. MOTHER'S HOUSE. EARLY FRIDAY EVENING. SUMMER

Looking down the hall towards the street.
MR SPAULL *comes to the door.*
MR SPAULL: (*Calling down the hall*) **Royal Liver!**
MOTHER: (*From the parlour, voice over*) **Come in, Mr Spaull.**
(*He comes down the hall and goes into the parlour.*)
(*Cut to:*)

INT. PARLOUR. MUM'S HOUSE. EARLY FRIDAY EVENING. SUMMER

Close-up of MOTHER.
MOTHER: **Can I surrender the policies on the two girls, Mr Spaull?**
(*Cut to mid-shot (head-on) of* MR SPAULL. *He is sitting on a chair near the door, next to the sideboard, which is on his left.*)
MR SPAULL: (*As he marks the books*) **Certainly, Mrs Davies.** (*Looking at the policies*) **You've had these some time now, haven't you?**
(*Cut to close-up of* MOTHER.)

MOTHER: Yer – I've had them since they were babies. I started paying them when it was only a penny a week – but as they're both married now there's no point in keeping them on. They've got their own insurance now.

MR SPAULL: (*Voice over*) All right, Mrs Davies, I'll take them into the office for you.

MOTHER: Thanks, Mr Spaull. See you next week.

(*Cut to medium close-up of* MR SPAULL *from* MOTHER*'s point of view.*)

MR SPAULL: (*Getting up and leaving*) Ta-ta.

(*Cut to medium close-up of sideboard. On it, rent book, insurance books, club book with money on it.*)

MOTHER: (*Voice over*) Tony!

TONY: (*Voice over*) Yer?

(*Fade to white.*)

MOTHER: (*Voice over*) I'm just running to Confession. Will you pay the clubman for me if he comes?

TONY: (*Voice over*) OK Mam.

(*Fade from white to:*)

INT. PUB PARLOUR. CHRISTENING CELEBRATIONS. NIGHT

Panning slowly around guests right to left. They are singing but no sync sound is heard.

Soundtrack:

MOTHER: (*Voice over*) I borrow £25 from the Leigh and Lend every Christinas then pay it back over the next twelve months – it's like a tontine really …

(*Fade up singing. Continue panning, as they sing. Pan stops on* MAISIE *and* MARGIE *in medium close-up two-shot.*

Singing finishes. Applause. Laughter.)

MARGIE: And how much did she weigh?

MAISIE: Just over seven pounds.

MARGIE: She was a big baby wasn't she?

MAISIE: Yeah.

MARGIE: Did you have her at Mill Road?

MAISIE: Yer – on the 6th.

MARGIE: What have you called her?

MAISIE: Elaine.

MARGIE: Arh – God love her! (*To* MOTHER) And how d'you like being a gran, Mrs D?
(*Cut to close-up of* MOTHER.)
MOTHER: Oh I wouldn't be without her – well she's my first – she's lovely.
(*Cut to medium close-up two-shot,* MARGIE *and* MAISIE.)
MARGIE: Well Maise – I'd better be making tracks.
MAISIE: Thanks for coming, Margie. I'll see ya.
MARGIE: (*Getting up*) See you Maisie.
Ta'ra Mrs D. (*Exits.*)
(*Pan to medium close-up two-shot,* MUM *and* MAISIE.)
MOTHER: (*To Margie*) Ta'ra love. (*To* MAISIE) You've known Margie for some years, haven't you, Maise?
MAISIE: Yer – we've all been mates since school …
(*Fade to white.*)
MAISIE: (*Voice over*) Margie, myself and Vera Large …
MOTHER: (*Voice over*) Vera's a nice girl, isn't she?
MAISIE: (*Voice over*) Arh smashing.
MOTHER: (*Voice over*) Is *she* still working?
(*Fade from white.*)
MAISIE: Yeah – she's still at Paton Calverts.

INT. HALL. MOTHER'S HOUSE. EARLY SATURDAY EVENING. SUMMER

It is light.
Medium close-up DOREEN MATHER'*s face at the front door. She is mentally retarded and constantly pushes her tongue in and out of her mouth between pursed lips. She knocks on the front door. No answer. She just stands there.*
Pause.
Silence.
DOREEN *sings from 'Dreamboat' softly to herself.*
DOREEN: (*Calling down hall*) Maisie!
(*Cut to mid-shot of empty hall from* DOREEN'*s point of view.*
Silence.
Cut to mid-long shot of DOREEN *from bottom of stairs.*
Pause.
She just stands there, looking down the hall.

Then slowly she begins to turn a circle on the doorstep, singing softly to herself as she does so.
She stops singing. Silence. She just stands there.)
MAISIE: (*Voice over*) Have you come to mind the baby Doreen?
DOREEN: Yeah.
MAISIE: (*Voice over*) Come in then, love.
  (*Slowly, clumsily,* DOREEN *walks down the hall towards the camera. Fade to white.*)
MAISIE: (*Voice over*) ... and Louis ... she went to live on that new estate they've just built in Kirkby ...
  (*Fade from white.*)

INT. PUB PARLOUR. CHRISTENING CELEBRATIONS. NIGHT
Medium close-up, two-shot, MAISIE *and* MOTHER.
MAISIE: (*To* MOTHER) ... you remember little Louis – she lived in Keble Street ... she always used to sing 'Deep Purple'.
MOTHER: Oh I know! Yer!
MONICA: (*Voice over*) Maisie Davies – you dirty mare!
MAISIE: (*Laughing*) Hi yer – Micky!
MONICA: (*Voice over*) Hi yer Mrs D!
MOTHER: (*Laughing*) You're looking well, Mick.
  (*Cut to medium close-up, two-shot,* MONICA *and her husband,* RED.)
MONICA: I know – the face that launched a thousand ships.
RED: The other way.
MONICA: That's wicked that – being married to you no wonder my poor face is destroyed. If I'd played my cards right I'd be in America now. (*To* MAISIE *and* MOTHER) Remember that yank I went out with, Mrs D? He thought I had lovely eyes ...
MONICA/RED: ... hated the rest of me but thought I had lovely eyes!
  (*Laughter*)
  And I end up by falling for a dwarf. There's no justice you know, is there?
  (*Cut to two-shot. Medium close-up.* MAISIE *and* MOTHER. *They laugh. Cut to two-shot. Medium close-up.* MONICA *and* RED. *He puts his arms around her waist from behind and cuddles her.*)
RED: (*Singing*) 'Chocolate eyes! Those great big chocolate eyes!'
MONICA: Get your hands off my body.

RED: (*Still cuddling her*) Arh – you've only got one tonsil but I love you all the same!
MONICA: Don't make mock of Mick! (*Aside*) Bastard!
(*Cut to medium close-up of* MAISIE.)
MAISIE: Now – you know you love the bones of him really.
(*Cut to two-shot. Medium close-up.* MONICA *and* RED.)
MONICA: Yer – I married him 'cos he's dead sensitive. Dead from the neck up – sensitive from the waist down.
(RED *cuddles her from behind even more.*)
RED: O O O H H H!
MONICA: (*To* MAISIE *and* MOTHER, *indicating* RED) The walking hormone.
(*To* RED – *laughing*) Oh you fool!
(*Walks off. Camera left.*
RED *sits down next to* MAISIE.
Pan down with him.)
RED: (*Clapping his hands together and looking at* TONY) Pound a man, is it?
(*Cut to medium close-up, two-shot,* EILEEN *and* DAVE.)
DAVE: (*Getting up and exiting frame*) 'E' are – Mick – sit here.
MONICA: (*Entering frame and sitting down beside* EILEEN) Thanks Dave.
DAVE: (*Voice over*) (*Calling to* RED) Go the match yesterday Red?
EILEEN: Oh eh Dave – you're not talking about football again, are you?
(*Cut to close-up.* DAVE *from* EILEEN's *point of view. Back view.*)
DAVE: (*Looking back over his shoulder as he walks to* RED)
Oh behave, will you!
(DAVE *walks towards* RED.
Cut to two-shot. Medium close-up. EILEEN *and* MONICA.)
EILEEN: Football mad.
MONICA: Aren't they all? Look at the thing I'm married to. He gets more worked up over a set of fixtures than me in my nude – d'you know what? If I was a centre forward I'd be laughing.
(*Cut to medium close-up of* RED, *already standing.*)
RED: (*Calling to* MONICA) What are you having, blossom?
(DAVE *enters shot.*
Cut to two-shot. Medium close-up of EILEEN *and* MONICA.)
MONICA: A rum and pep, love.
EILEEN: (*To* RED) And then *you*!
MONICA: He should be so lucky!

EILEEN: (*To* DAVE) Eh Dave will you get us some ciggies?
DAVE: (*Voice over*) Craven A?
EILEEN: Or Park Drive.
    (*Cut to two-shot. Medium close-up.* RED *and* DAVE.)
DAVE: (*To* EILEEN) OK. (*To* RED) What's your poison, Red?
    (*They walk to the bar in the passage.*
    Track or pan with them.)
RED: A brown over bitter thanks, Dave.
    (*Cut to medium close-up, two-shot,* TONY *and* ROSE, TONY *starts singing*
    'I Want a Girl'. Everyone begins to join in. Fade sound although TONY
    and ROSE *and all continue to sing. Hold.*
    Fade to white.)

MOTHER: (*Voice over*) You're home early lad. Come on in.
TONY: (*Voice over*) Oh but you've only just done the lobby mam.
MOTHER: (*Voice over*) No – go on – you're all right.
    (TONY'S *footsteps are heard along the hall.*
    Fade from white.)

  INT. HALL. MOTHER'S HOUSE. EARLY FRIDAY EVENING. SUMMER

It is light.

Low-angled medium close-up of MOTHER *looking out towards the street. She is kneeling and scrubbing the last part of the hall floor by the front door.*

MOTHER: (*Looking up*) Your tea's in the oven, son.
TONY: (*Voice over*) OK Mam.
    (*She continues scrubbing.*
    Hold.
    Cut to close-up of TONY *at the end of the hall by the kitchen door.*
    He is wearing only pants and a singlet and has just finished washing.
    He is drying his face with a towel. He stands for a moment just looking
    at MOTHER.)
TONY: Are you going to come and have yours, Mam?
MOTHER: (*Voice over*) I'll be in in a minute, lad.
    (TONY *continues looking at her. His eyes fill with tears.*)
TONY: OK Mam.
    (*Hold on* TONY.
    Fade to white.)

MOTHER: (*Voice over*) Your shirt is ironed, son – it's on the rack with the hankies.
TONY: (*Voice over*) Thanks, Mahsie.
   (*Fade from white.*)

INT. PUB PARLOUR. CHRISTENING CELEBRATIONS. NIGHT

Medium close-up, two-shot, TONY and ROSE. Everyone is singing though no sound can be heard. Gradually fade up sound of TONY and all singing 'I Want A Girl'.
Cut to medium close-up, two-shot, MAISIE and GEORGE. MAISIE starts singing 'Mississippi Honeymoon', which first GEORGE, then the others, join in.
Pan around left to right. All singing.
Pan ends on medium close-up of MONICA and EILEEN.

EXT. PUB CHRISTENING CELEBRATIONS, NIGHT

Two-shots of JINGLES and LES, head on.
JINGLES: (*Coaxing*) Come on, Les, just one drink.
   (*Soundtrack of all singing 'Mississippi Honeymoon' inside the pub.*)
LES: (*Bellicose*) All right, just one drink, just to wet the baby's head, but I'm not staying here all fucking night!
JINGLES: OK, Les, OK.
   (*They enter the pub – LES first, JINGLES after.*
   Cut to:)

INT. PUB CHRISTENING CELEBRATIONS. NIGHT

Mid-long shot, LES and JINGLES walk into the passage which leads from the parlour to the bar. LES stands at the bar with TONY, GEORGE, DAVE and RED. JINGLES continues towards camera and exits into the parlour.
Soundtrack:
EILEEN: (*Voice over*) What's the matter with Pontius?
JINGLES: (*Voice over*) Oh, yer know, the usual.
MONICA: (*Voice over*) Look at the face on that – stop a bleeding clock!
   (LES *is laughing and joking with the other men.*)
TONY: (*To* LES) Are you having a bevy or what?
   (*Hold on group in passage.*)
ALL: (*Singing*) 'We're all together again
   So here we are.

We're all together again
So here we are …'
(*Cut to mid-long shot.*
JINGLES, *back to camera, sitting on a stool facing* EILEEN *and* MONICA.)

ALL: (*Singing*) 'And the lord knows when
We'll be together again
So we're all together again
So here we are.'
(EILEEN *and* MONICA *start to sing 'Back in the Old Routine'.*
Everyone joins in but it is the three girls' special song.
Track in on the three girls very slowly as they sing.
Track continues in and around on JINGLES. *Track stops when she is in mid-shot, side view.*
Throughout the song she has been getting more and more upset. When the last verse is reached she breaks down completely. EILEEN *and* MONICA *kneel into shot by* JINGLES' *stool.*)

EILEEN: Oh, Jingles, don't get so upset.
MONICA: Arh – come on.
JINGLES: (*Bringing herself under control*) No – I'm all right – honest. It's just Les – you know what he's like when he turns.
EILEEN: The bastard! For two pins I'd go over there and tell him!
JINGLES: No – don't say anything, Ei.
MONICA: They're all the same – when they're not using the big stick, they're farting – aren't men horrible?
(*Cut to:*)

INT. PUB. PASSAGE LEADING TO THE PARLOUR. CHRISTENING CELEBRATIONS. NIGHT

Mid-shot. LES *in the passage on his own.*
LES: (*Looking at* JINGLES *and motioning her to come*) Eh! Come on!
(*Cut to:*)

INT. PUB PARLOUR. CHRISTENING CELEBRATIONS . NIGHT

Medium close-up of JINGLES, *side view.*
JINGLES *quickly looks around at* LES *and quickly finishes her drink.*
EILEEN: (*Voice over*) Oh you're not going are you Jingles?
JINGLES: I think Les wants to.

(*She looks anxiously around.*)
MONICA: (*Voice over*) But you've only been here five minutes.
(*Cut to:*)

INT. PUB. PASSAGE LEADING TO THE PARLOUR. CHRISTENING CELEBRATIONS. NIGHT

Close-up of LES *in passage.*
LES: (*Even more belligerent*) Come on!
(*Cut to:*)

INT. PUB PARLOUR. CHRISTENING CELEBRATIONS. NIGHT

Close-up of EILEEN and MONICA.
EILEEN: I feel like going over there and bursting him!
(*Cut to medium close-up of* JINGLES *from* MONICA *and* EILEEN's *point of view.* LES *is in the background walking out.*)
JINGLES: (*Getting up*) I'd better go Ei. See ya, Micky.
(JINGLES *walks away, very upset.*
Cut to two-shot, medium close-up. MAISIE *and* MOTHER. *They watch her go.*)
MOTHER: I wonder what's wrong.
MAISIE: I think Jingles is having a bad time with Les.
MOTHER: It's not right, you know.
(*Cut to mid-wide shot of* JINGLES.
She walks out behind a seated TONY.
Possibly pan with her.)
TONY: (*Sympathetic*) Never mind, girl.
JINGLES (*Breaking down again*) See yer, Tone.
(JINGLES *exits.*
Cut to mid three-shot of EILEEN, *centre frame,* DAVE, *left of frame,* MONICA, *right of frame.*)
EILEEN: Poor Jingles.
DAVE: You sit there! It's none of your business. Don't get involved.
(*Cut to close-up of* EILEEN.)
EILEEN: YOu callous bleeder! That's my friend that. You men – you're all the bleeding same – you only think of yourselves.
(*Cut to close-up of* DAVE.)
DAVE: Don't you tell me what I think. No one knows what's going on inside my mind.

(*Cut to close-up of* EILEEN.)
EILEEN: Including you.
  (*Cut to close-up of* DAVE.)
DAVE: You can't argue with you – women are different from men.
  (*Cut to two-shot, medium close-up of* EILEEN *and* MONICA.)
EILEEN: Oh, so you've noticed? (*To* MONICA) Isn't he quick?
  (*Cut to two-shot. Medium close-up of* DAVE *and* TONY.)
TONY: (*To* EILEEN) Heck! Heck! What's going on?
EILEEN: (*Voice over, angry*) Nothing!
TONY: All right, don't bite my head off.
DAVE: You know the way she flies off the handle for the least thing.
  (*Cut to close-up of* EILEEN *and* MONICA.)
EILEEN: (*Now very angry*) I don't! I've got good cause to! You closet!
  (*Cut to two-shot. Medium close-up of* MOTHER *and* MAISIE *from* EILEEN'S *point of view.*)
MOTHER: (*To* EILEEN) Now – come on! We don't want any upset.
EILEEN: (*Voice over*) OK Mam.
DAVE: (*Voice over*) OK Nell.
MOTHER: We're here to enjoy ourselves. Come on Micky – give us a song.
  (*Cut to two-shot. Medium close-up of* MONICA *and* EILEEN *from* MOTHER's *point of view.* MONICA *tries to diffuse the situation by singing* 'Bye Bye Blackbird'.
  Cut to close-up of RED.)
RED: (*Good-naturedly*) Oh God blimey – you're not singing again are you, Mick?
  (*Cut to close-up of* MONICA.)
MONICA: (*Equally good-natured*) Listen, bloated tonsils – just because you're dead miserable doesn't mean to say that the rest of us have got to go round looking like 'keep death off the road'. (*All sing* 'Bye Bye Blackbird'.
  Cut to close-up of RED.)
RED: Judy Garland in bad health.
  (*Cut to two-shot. Medium close-up of* EILEEN *and* MONICA.)
MONICA: Oh my arse!
  (*She joins in the singing and encourages* EILEEN *to do so.* EILEEN *responds reluctantly.*
  Then EILEEN *starts singing 'I Want To Be Around'.*)

MONICA: Go on Ei! I love this song.
   (*Pan to* EILEEN *in close-up, singing solo. Applause when she finishes song.*)
MONICA: (*Voice over*) Oh it's a smashing song, that.
   (*Cut to the passage leading to the parlour.* TONY *in mid-shot at the bar, side view, waiting to order drinks.*
   Soundtrack: *Guests in parlour singing 'I Loved the Ladies'.*)
TONY: (*To* BARMAID) Two halves of shandy. A mackies. A Double Diamond. A pale ale and lime. A Black and Tan. Mild over bitter. A rum and Pep. A rum and blackcurrant. And a Guinness.
   (*He stands at the bar getting the money ready. He acknowledges friends and neighbours as they pass him by while he waits for the drinks.*)
   Hello Moggie.
   Hiyer Ritchie (etc.).
   (*Soundtrack: Guests in parlour, singing.*
   The BARMAID *hands the drinks on a tray over the heads of the people at the bar.* TONY *takes them and pays her.*)
   Thanks Nora, and have one for yourself.
NORA: Thanks Tony.
   (*Soundtrack: Guests in parlour singing 'I Love the Ladies'.*
   TONY *turns and walks towards the parlour.*
   Cut to medium close-up of TONY *and* ROSE. *They all continue to sing.*
   Cut to medium close-up, three-shot of GEORGE, MAISIE *and* MOTHER.
   Cut to medium close-up, two-shot of DAVE *and* RED. *The song continues.*
   Cut to two-shot, medium close-up of MONICA *and* EILEEN. *Laughter. Applause.*)
RED: (*Voice over*) Come on Mick.
MONICA: OK. In a minute. I'll just finish my drink.
IVY: (*Voice over*) Come on! Let's have your glasses please!
   (EILEEN *and* MONICA *drink up.*)
   Cut to medium close-up of RED.
RED: Oh hey Mick – come on!
   (*Cut to two-shot, medium close-up of* EILEEN *and* MONICA *still trying to finish their drinks.*)
MONICA: Ignore him.
   (*Cut to wide shot, looking towards the door leading to the street.* TONY, GEORGE *and* DAVE *walk out, followed by* RED. *As he goes to the parlour door he turns to* MONICA.)

RED: Come on Keemosabbie!
(*Cut to two-shot. Medium close-up of* EILEEN *and* MONICA.)
MONICA: All right Tonto! Oh men – don't they mither? (*She puts down her still unfinished drink.*) I'd better go, otherwise he'll get a cobb on.
EILEEN: You're not frightened of him are you?
MONICA: Am I shite! He looks at me the wrong way I give him a dog's life.
(*They get up and leave.*
Cut to wide shot, looking towards the door which leads towards the street.
MONICA *and* EILEEN *enter the frame and walk towards the door.*)
EILEEN: Is he still handy around the house?
MONICA: You're joking aren't you? That thing won't do a tap. He changed a nappy once – nearly had a nervous breakdown.
(*As they exit, they are followed by a few people. Those remaining in the parlour begin to sing 'The Road to Anywhere'.*
Cut to:)

EXT. PUB. CHRISTENING CELEBRATIONS. NIGHT

Wide shot, head on, of TONY, GEORGE, DAVE *and* RED *in a heated but friendly discussion about football – the 1958/59 season. Soundtrack vaguely in the background of people in parlour singing inside the pub. Some people come out followed by* EILEEN *and* MONICA, *who stand talking.*
IVY: (*Voice over, from inside the pub*) Come on now! Can I have your glasses – PLEASE!
(*Cut to two-shot. Medium close-up, head on.* EILEEN, *left of frame profile,* MONICA, *centre frame full face.*
Soundtrack of people singing inside the pub.)
MONICA: (*To* RED) Red … Red! (*To* EILEEN) See what I mean? Doesn't take a blind bit of notice. It's like talking to a corpse. (*To* RED) Hey, soft shite! You said you wanted to go before.
(*Cut to mid-shot of group of* TONY, GEORGE, DAVE *and* RED, *side view,* MONICA'*s point of view.*)
RED: God blimey! It's worse than the SS this! I can have a talk can't I?
(*Continues talking to the others.*
Cut to two-shot, medium close-up, head on of EILEEN *and* MONICA.)
MONICA: Oh God help us – it's alive!
EILEEN: Men!

MONICA: (*American accent*) The little dears! (*To* EILEEN) So don't be a stranger – otherwise I'll not see you till next Preston Guild.
We're only in Jubilee Drive – you're only ten minutes away.
EILEEN: (*Half-hearted*) We'll see … I'll try and come round.
MONICA: Or I could come over to yours. You're only in Vane Street aren't you?
EILEEN: Oh you'd better not, Micky, he's funny about having visitors.
MONICA: (*A bit hurt at being put off*) OK. Then you try and come to me.
EILEEN: (*Still half-hearted*) We'll see, kid.
(*An awkward silence between them.*)
MONICA: Well, I'd better get Father Feck home.
(*She walks to* RED. *Pan with her.*)
(*To* RED) Come on Trigger – back to the reservation.
(*She takes him by the arm and they walk up the street. Goodnights all round,* MONICA *waves to* EILEEN *but without turning to her. Continue panning with* MONICA.
Cut to mid-shot of EILEEN, *full face. She watches* MONICA *and* RED *go. Her eyes fill with tears.*
Through the pub door behind EILEEN, MOTHER, MAISIE, ROSE *and other guests come streaming out into the street, singing 'I Will If You Will So Will I'.*)
MAISIE: (*Linking* EILEEN's *arm*) Come on Ei!
(EILEEN *turns and walks down the street with* MAISIE *and the others.* TONY, GEORGE *and* DAVE *follow. All sing 'I Will If You Will'.*)
GUEST: Hitchiecoo!
(*They all go down the street. Their voices drift away.*
Cut to:)

EXT. ALLEY LEADING TO GRAN'S HOUSE.
CHRISTENING CELEBRATIONS. NIGHT

DAVE *and* EILEEN *in medium close-up, back view, walking towards the house,* DAVE *drunk.*
Soundtrack of MAISIE's *voice singing 'Barney Google'.*
Track with EILEEN *and* DAVE.
DAVE: (*Very loud, very drunk*) I've had a ball!
EILEEN: (*An intense whisper*) Do you have to shout? You'll wake the dead.
GRAN: (*Voice over, angry, from inside the house*) Is that you Eileen?

EILEEN: Oh God blimey you have!
>(EILEEN *and* DAVE *stop walking.*
>*Track stops.*)
>(*Placatory*) Yer – it's only me and Dave Gran … we'll be in in a minute.

DAVE: I wanna wee.

EILEEN: Oh then do it over there – and be quick.
>(DAVE *goes to the wall, exiting camera left.*
>*Pause.*
>*Cut to mid-shot of* DAVE *at the wall, pissing and singing.*)
>(*Cut to medium close-up of* EILEEN, *front view.*)

EILEEN: Oh suffering Jesus! That's all we need – you singing. As if life isn't purgatory enough without that.
>(*The sound of torrential pissing.*)

DAVE: (*Voice over, singing*) '… a lazy river in the noonday sun …'

GRAN: (*Voice over*) Eileen! It's late!

EILEEN: Isn't this lively? (*To* GRAN, *placatory*) OK, Gran – we won't be much longer … (*To* DAVE) Come on dead hake! Hurry up!
And be quiet.
>(DAVE *comes into shot, singing, but very tired.*
>*Cut to medium close-up, two-shot of* EILEEN *and* DAVE, *back view.*
>*They go towards the house. Track with them.*)

GRAN: (*Voice over*) Eileen! Make sure that door's locked!
>(DAVE *wobbly on his feet.*)

EILEEN: Wouldn't this put years on you? (*To* GRAN) OK, Gran. (*They get to the door,* EILEEN *opens it, pushes* DAVE *inside.*) I'm sure I was put on this earth just to be tormented.
>(*Bangs door shut.*
>*Fade to white.*
>*Soundtrack: The sound of* DAVE *knocking something over and their feet on the stairs.*)
>(*An intense whisper as Dave falls upstairs, voice over*) Be careful!
>(DAVE *continues singing.*)
Oh, she's gonna have a right gob on her tomorrow.
>(*Fade from white to:*)

INT. EILEEN AND DAVE'S FLAT IN GRAN'S HOUSE. NIGHT

EILEEN *and* DAVE *in wide shot at the table, eating.*
A fire is lit.
Hold.
Soundtrack: on the radio, Take It from Here.
Cut to close-up of EILEEN *at the table. She is eating.*
Soundtrack from Take It from Here *continued.*
JUNE WHITFIELD: (*Voice over*) Ooh Ron! Beloved!
  (*Laughter.*
  EILEEN *stops eating and looks at* DAVE.
  Cut to close-up of DAVE *at table, eating loudly.*)
DICK BENTLEY: (*Voice over*) Yes Eth?
  (*Laughter.*
  Cut to close-up of EILEEN.
  Soundtrack: Fade Take It from Here *so that it is vaguely in the background.*)
EILEEN: Have you got to make that noise when you eat?
  (*Cut to close-up of* DAVE.)
DAVE: (*Making a noise while he eats*) What noise?
  (*Cut to close-up of* EILEEN.)
EILEEN: God blimey! What a future I've got to look forward to – twenty-five years with Mouth Almighty.
  (*Cut to medium close-up of door of flat. It opens.* UNCLE TED *is standing in the doorway carrying a candle at waist height so that his face is lit from directly beneath, making him look like a corpse. He switches off the light inside their flat.*)
UNCLE TED: (*In a sing-song voice*) I've switched the light off – I don't know whether I'm doing right or wrong-a!
  (*Slowly he closes the door.*
  Cut to two-shot. EILEEN *and* DAVE *sitting at the table in the firelight. They have both stopped eating.*)
DAVE: (*Really scared*) Who the bleeding hell was that?
EILEEN: (*A little scared too*) Uncle Ted – my Dad's brother.
DAVE: God blimey – what a family I've married into – crowd of nutters. He frightened the bleeding life out of me!
  (*Soundtrack: the* Take It from Here *signature-tune heard.*
  Cut to:)

INT. HALL AND STAIRS. GRAN'S HOUSE. NIGHT

Wide shot from the bottom of the stairs. Darkness except for a candle held by UNCLE TED. *He comes downstairs.*
Soundtrack: BBC serial announcer: 'This is The Man in Black'. Footsteps echoing in time with UNCLE TED *descending the stairs.* UNCLE TED *gets to the bottom of the stairs and is met by* GRAN *who is going into the kitchen.*

GRAN: (*Stern*) Teddy! Stop acting soft!

   (*She blows the candle out with a single, very definite blow. Blackness. Cut to:*)

EXT. ALLEY LEADING TO GRAN'S HOUSE. DAY

Late afternoon, the following Saturday. Hot summer's day.
Mid-wide shot, MOTHER *sits on a chair just inside the open door, left of frame. To the right of frame is* MAISIE's *pram by the railings which lead to cellar steps and the cellar. Above this area is the parlour window which is half open.* MOTHER *gently rocks the pram and fans herself with a newspaper. Pause and hold. Then* GRAN, *with a face like thunder, comes out followed by* EILEEN. GRAN *walks past* MOTHER *but neither of them speak.*

GRAN: (*Walking towards camera*) If you want me I'll either be at May Tobin's or in The Grapes.

EILEEN: In Phythian Street?

GRAN: (*Walking off camera*) Yer.

EILEEN: (*Calling after her*) Hey Gran – have you got a shilling for two tanners?

   (*Cut to mid-shot,* GRAN *from* EILEEN's *point of view.*)

GRAN: (*Not turning around*) There's enough money in the meter.

   (*She walks away down the alley and into the back entrance of an adjoining tenement building. As* GRAN *walks down the alley she passes* MAISIE, *but they don't speak,* MAISIE *carries shopping. Cut to mid-wide shot,* MOTHER *and* EILEEN *on doorstep.*)

EILEEN: She never leaves enough gas and the bleeding thing always goes.

MOTHER: (*Looking in her purse*) Way-o. 'E are love- I've got one.

   (*Gives a shilling to* EILEEN.)

EILEEN: Thanks Mam.

   (MAISIE *enters shot and joins them on the step.*)

MAISIE: Isn't she an auld cow? How can you live with her Ei?

EILEEN: Beggars can't be choosers Maisie – you know how hard it is to get a place of your own.

MOTHER: (*To* MAISIE) Did you get anything for a sarnie love?
MAISIE: Yer – I got a quarter of corned beef and a Hovis ... oh and four Devon Delights.
EILEEN: (*Taking the shopping from* MAISIE) I've just made a pot of tea.
   (EILEEN *goes inside the house.*)
MAISIE: (*Looking into the pram at the baby*) Has she been good Mam?
MOTHER: As good as gold.
   (MOTHER *fans herself with the paper,* MAISIE *looks into the pram and rocks it.*
   Track away from them and into the parlour window, left to right. When window is in close-up, hold.
   Soundtrack: BBC Radio football results, 1958/59 season.
   Cut to:)

INT. PARLOUR. GRAN'S HOUSE. DAY

Medium close-up. DAVE, *side view, listening to the results and marking his coupon.*
Soundtrack: The football results finish, the racing results start.
EILEEN: (*Voice over*) Any luck?
DAVE: (*Turning to her*) No. Couldn't pick my nose.
   (*Cut to:*)

INT. PARLOUR. MUM'S HOUSE. SAME SATURDAY. DAY

Close-up, side view of TONY, *listening to the racing results.*
Footsteps heard.
Soundtrack:
MOTHER: (*Voice over*) We're back!
TONY: Any pea wack Mam?
MOTHER: (*Voice over*) Yer – I've made a pan.
MAISIE: (*Voice over*) Did you back the winner?
TONY: With the donkeys I do? It had three legs. It's probably still running.
   (*Cut to:*)

EXT. GAUMONT CINEMA. NIGHT

Mid-wide shot.
Heavy rain. Queue waiting to get into cinema for the second house.

The bottom of the frame is filled with black umbrellas.
Soundtrack from 'Guys and Dolls'.
Begin to crane up from the umbrellas in the cinema queue over the exterior of the cinema.
On the wall two posters are seen. On the left marked 'All This Week' is the poster for 'Love is a Many-Splendoured Thing'.
On the right marked 'Coming Soon' the poster for 'Guys and Dolls'.
Soundtrack: theme tune 'Love is a Many-Splendoured Thing'.
Dissolve to:

INT. GAUMONT CINEMA. NIGHT

Continue craning up over rows of people watching the film on the screen until MAISIE *and* EILEEN *are framed in medium close-up two-shot, head on.*
Soundtrack: 'Love is a Many-Splendoured Thing' throbs out.
The two girls weeping profusely.

INT. WAREHOUSE. DAY

Low-angle shot looking straight up at a glass roof.
In slow motion two bodies come crashing through it. They are GEORGE *and* TONY.
Soundtrack:
EILEEN: (*Voice over*) Wasn't that marvellous?
  (*Cut to:*)

INT. HOSPITAL CORRIDOR. NIGHT

Wide shot. MAISIE *running frantically down the corridor towards the camera.*
MAISIE: (*Voice over*) When he dies and she ran up that hill – I thought I was going to cry my eyes out.
  (*Cut to:*)

INT. HOSPITAL WARD. NIGHT

Two-shot. Medium close-up. Side view of bed. MAISIE, *full faced, is lit.*
GEORGE, *in profile, is not, so that he is in silhouette.*
MAISIE *holds* GEORGE's *right hand in hers. He is heavily bandaged and sedated and drifts in and out of sleep.*
MAISIE *is very upset.*
MAISIE: (*Cradling his hand in hers and very close to tears*) How are you love?
  (*Silence.*)

GEORGE: (*With great difficulty*) We fell off the bleeding scaffolding May ...
(*She just looks at him.*)
MAISIE: (*Trying not to cry*) Anything for notice ...
(GEORGE *drifts back into unconsciousness,* MAISIE, *unable to control herself any longer, breaks down and sobs.*)
(*Through sobs*) Oh George! George!
(*Hold.*
Soundtrack: Tommy Riley plays 'Galway Bay' on the harmonica.
Crane up and around into the hospital window. Outside, it is pouring with rain.
Hold on window.
Then without a dissolve crane back down and around to the first camera position, side view, medium close-up of hospital bed, only this time it is Tony's bed.
At his bedside MOTHER, EILEEN, ROSE *and* DAVE, *all very upset,* TONY *is heavily bandaged and sedated. He is in silhouette. They are lit.*)
MOTHER: (*Very upset*) Oh Tony! Oh son!
(*Soundtrack: Tommy Riley on the harmonica continues.*)

INT. KITCHEN. MOTHER'S HOUSE. MORNING OF TONY'S WEDDING DAY

Medium close-up, two-shot, MOTHER *and* MAISIE. MOTHER *facing camera,* MAISIE *with her back to it.*
MAISIE *is fixing a carnation to* MOTHER'*s coat. She is having difficulty in pinning it on.*
MOTHER: They're dead fiddly these, aren't they?
(*Cut to medium close-up, two-shot,* MOTHER *and* MAISIE.)
MAISIE: Yer ... did you get the carnations from Annie Gaffney?
(*Cut to medium close-up, two-shot,* MOTHER *and* MAISIE.)
MOTHER: Yer.
MAISIE: (*Finishing*) The' are.
(*Cut to:*)

INT. PARLOUR. MOTHER'S HOUSE. THE MORNING OF TONY'S WEDDING DAY

Medium close-up. GEORGE *at the window, back to camera.*
Pause.

Silence. Then GEORGE *turns around to camera.*
GEORGE: (*To* TONY) Well – aul' arse – are you ready?
(*Cut to mid-shot,* TONY *sitting in Dad's chair next to the fireplace from* GEORGE's *point of view.* TONY *stands up. He wears a calliper.*)
TONY: (*Clapping his hands together nervously*) Fighting fit!
(*Cut to mid-shot. Parlour door from* TONY's *point of view.* MOTHER *and* MAISIE *enter from the right,* EILEEN *and* DAVE *from the left. They all have their coats on and are wearing buttonholes.*)
MAISIE: (*To* TONY) Well – let's be having you!
MOTHER: (*To* ALL) Are we all ready?
(EILEEN *walks off camera right, to* TONY.
Cut to mid-shot from GEORGE'S *point of view of* TONY.
EILEEN *walks into shot.*)
EILEEN: (*To* TONY) Well – sun-bun – mustn't keep the bride waiting.
(TONY – *very nervous, very uncomfortable – fiddles with his collar then puts his hands in his pockets.*)
TONY: Oh God blimey – I'd never live it down.
(*Cut to mid-shot of parlour door from* TONY's *point of view.*
They all exit – TONY *last.*
Hold on door.
Soundtrack: EILEEN *singing 'From the Candy Store on the Corner'.*

INT. CHURCH. MORNING OF TONY'S WEDDING DAY

Medium close-up. TONY *and* GEORGE *at the altar rails, backs to the camera. Hold.*
Soundtrack: EILEEN *singing. Then* GEORGE *and* TONY *turn around and look up the aisle, directly at camera.*
Cut to medium close-up. Two-shot, ROSE *and* MR FORSYTH, *her* FATHER, *walking down the aisle towards the camera from* TONY's *and* GEORGE's *point of view,* ROSE *is wearing a white wedding dress and veil. The veil is very heavy so that she is almost invisible behind it.*
Cut to low-angle, two-shot of TONY *and* ROSE *seen from behind. Crane up to medium close-up three-shot of* TONY *and* ROSE, *backs to camera, and* PRIEST, *facing camera, conducting the marriage service.*
Hold as they exchange vows.
Soundtrack: EILEEN *singing.*

Cut to mid-shot of pews, MOTHER, MAISIE, EILEEN *and* DAVE *in the front one – other relatives, including* GRAN, *behind, watching the wedding ceremony. A mixture of happiness tinged with sadness.*
Cut to two-shot, medium close-up of TONY *and* ROSE *at the altar rails from* PRIEST'*s point of view.*
Wedding service continues.
Applause from wedding guests.
Cut to:

EXT. CHURCH. MORNING OF TONY'S WEDDING DAY

Wide shot.
TONY *and* ROSE *come out of the church followed by both families and they arrange themselves on the church steps for a group photo.*
MOTHER *slightly behind* TONY.
Family tableau.
They all pose for the photographer. They all smile. Then MOTHER'*s face crumbles into tears.*
Soundtrack: MOTHER *singing 'Thanks to You'.*
Dissolve to:

INT. PARLOUR. ROSE'S PARENTS' HOUSE.
TONY'S WEDDING NIGHT

MOTHER *in close-up surrounded by wedding guests continues song.*

EXT. ROSE'S PARENTS' HOUSE.
TONY'S WEDDING NIGHT

Medium close-up. TONY *standing on the doorstep – hands in pockets – listening to his* MOTHER *singing. He begins to weep.*
Soundtrack: MOTHER *singing.*
TONY *now weeping uncontrollably.*
Soundtrack: MOTHER *singing last verse of song.*
Wedding guests applaud.
TONY'*s weeping subsides but he continues just to stand there.*
Soundtrack: MR FORSYTH *singing 'I got into a Boxing Ring with a Fella Named Big-nosed Jim':*
RITCHIE: (*Voice over*) Oh hey Dad – you're not gonna sing that auld bleeding thing are you?

(*Whoops and laughter.*)
CATHY: (*Voice over*) Come on, let's have some records.
(*Pause.*
Then 'Oh Mein Papa', played by Eddie Calvert, is heard.
Hold on TONY.
Soundtrack: Fade wedding sounds.
Fade in:)
TONY: (*Voice over*) Your dad enjoyed himself.
ROSE: (*Voice over*) I think everyone did.
TONY: (*Voice over*) Yer – it was a good do, wasn't it?
ROSE: (*Voice over*) Yer – but your Mam got a bit upset.
TONY: (*Voice over*) Arh-don't be worrying. She'll be all right.
(*Dissolve to:*)

EXT. STREET OUTSIDE ROSE'S PARENTS' HOUSE, TONY'S WEDDING, NIGHT

Mid-shot, side view looking up the street. People come streaming out of the house. TONY *and* ROSE *at their head, followed by* MOTHER, MAISIE, EILEEN, GEORGE *and* DAVE, *and* ROSE's *family.*
Pan with them to taxi, which draws up. TONY *and* ROSE *get into the taxi, everyone waving their goodbyes. The taxi moves off into the darkness.*
Track with it and fade to black.
Soundtrack: 'O Waly, Waly', sung by an unaccompanied soprano in the arrangement by Benjamin Britten:
'The water is wide I cannot get o'er
And neither have I wings to fly
Give me a boat that will carry two
Then both shall row my love and I …'
Dissolve to three-quarter angle shot of both families waving to the taxi. They all go back into the house.
Dissolve to mid-shot, side view, looking down the street, MOTHER, MAISIE, GEORGE, DAVE *and* EILEEN *coming out of the house with their coats on.*
They say their goodbyes to MR *and* MRS FORSYTH *and family.*
Soundtrack: 'O Waly, Waly' continued:
'Down in the meadow the other day
A-gathering flowers both fine and gay
A-gathering flowers both red and blue

I little thought what love can do ...'
MOTHER *and her family walk down the street into the darkness. Pan with them, then track with them and fade to black.*
Dissolve to:

EXT. ALLEY. LEADING TO GRAN'S HOUSE. TONY'S WEDDING. NIGHT

EILEEN *and* DAVE, *mid-shot, back view, walking towards the house.*
Soundtrack:
DAVE: (*Voice over*) Goodnight Nell.
MOTHER: (*Voice over*) Goodnight Dave.
EILEEN: (*Voice over*) See you tomorrow Mam.
MOTHER: (*Voice over*) OK Ei ...

('*O Waly, Waly*' continued:)
'I leaned my back up against some oak
Thinking that it was a trusty tree.
But first it bended and then it broke
And so did my false love to me ...'
(DAVE *and* EILEEN *continue to walk towards the house. Track with them into the darkness and fade to black.*
Dissolve to:)

EXT. STREET. LEADING TO MOTHER'S HOUSE. TONY'S WEDDING. NIGHT

Mid-long shot. Back view of MAISIE, MOTHER *and* GEORGE, MOTHER *walking slightly behind them.*
Track with them.
Soundtrack: '*O Waly, Waly*' *continued:*
'A ship there is and she sails the sea
She's loaded deep as deep can be
But not so deep as the love I'm in
I know not if I sink or swim ... '
MAISIE *and* GEORGE *stop and look back at* MOTHER.
MAISIE: (*To* MOTHER) Come on Mam.
GEORGE: (*To* MOTHER) Come on girl.
(MOTHER *walks between them. They all link arms and continue walking down the street.*

Continue tracking with them into the dark.
Track stops and they recede into the darkness.
Then fade to black.
Hold on black.
Soundtrack: 'O Waly, Waly' continued:
'O love is handsome and love is fine
And love's a jewel while it is new
But when it is old
It groweth cold
Then fades away like morning dew.'
(*Hold on darkness.*
Silence.
Fade up end credits.)

Terence Davies, with Freda Dowie, on the set of *Distant Voices, Still Lives* (1988). (BFI National Archive)

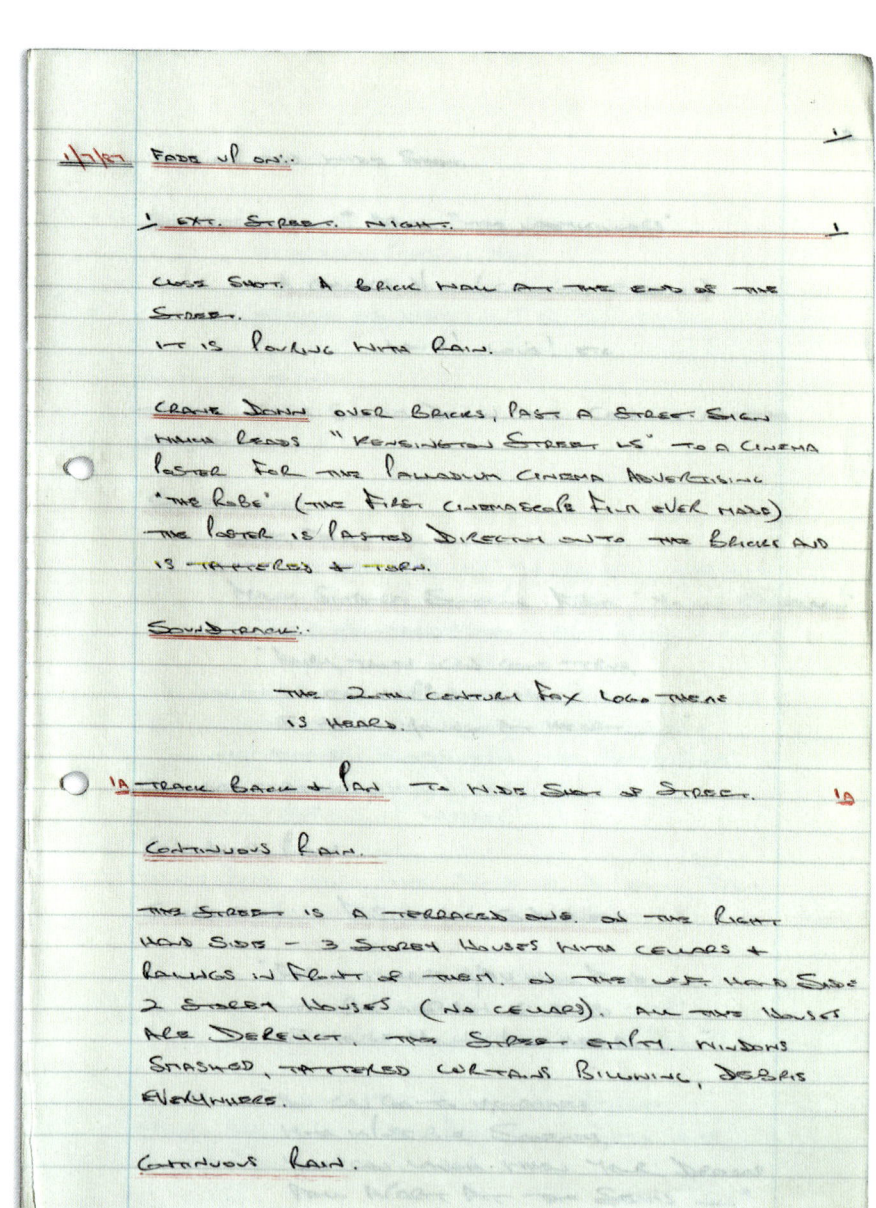

The Long Day Closes (1992): first draft, opening scene. (© The Terence Davies Estate, held by the Terence Davies Archive at Edge Hill University)

THE LONG DAY CLOSES
(1992)

The Long Day Closes (1992): shooting the scene where Mother (Marjorie Yates), Bud (Leigh McCormack) and Helen (Ayse Owens) watch *Carousel*.

Cast and crew of *The Long Day Closes* include:

MOTHER	Marjorie Yates
BUD	Leigh McCormack
KEVIN	Anthony Watson
JOHN	Nicholas Lamont
HELEN	Ayse Owens
FRANCES	Joy Blakeman
JEAN	Denise Thomas
AMY	Patricia Morrison
EDNA	Tina Malone
CURLY	Jimmy Wilde
MR NICHOLLS	Robin Polley
MR BUSHELL	Peter Ivatts
BILLY	Gavin Mawdsley
LABOURER/CHRIST	Kirk McLaughlin
BLACK MAN	Marcus Heath
NUN	Victoria Davies
NURSE	Brenda Skeggs
ALBIE	Karl Skeggs
1ST BULLY	Lee Blennerhassett
2ND BULLY	Peter Hollier
3RD BULLY	Jason Jevons
Written and Directed by	Terence Davies
Producer	Olivia Stewart
Director of Photography	Michael Coulter
Production Designer	Christopher Hobbs
Editor	William Diver
Costume Designer	Monica Howe
Art Director	Kate Naylor
Music Director	Robert Lockhart

A British Film Institute and Channel 4 (Film Four International) Production, 1992.

LIVERPOOL 1955–56

Fade up on black.
First titles then main title:
'The Long Day Closes'.
Fade out main titles.
Fade up on:

EXT. STREET. NIGHT

Close shot. A brick wall at the end of the street. It is pouring with rain. Crane down over bricks, past a street sign which reads 'Kensington Street L5' to a cinema poster for the Palladium cinema advertising 'The Robe (*the first Cinemascope film ever made*)'. *The poster is pasted directly on to the bricks and is tattered and torn.*
Soundtrack: The 20th Century-Fox logo theme is heard. Track back and pan to wide shot of street. Continuous rain.
The street is a terraced one. On the right-hand side – three storey houses with cellars and railings in front of them. On the left-hand side – two-storey houses. All the houses are derelict. The street empty. Windows smashed, tattered curtains billowing, debris everywhere. Continuous rain.
Hold on this wide shot.
Soundtrack from The Ladykillers.
Track very slowly down the centre of the street.
Soundtrack: Cross fade to Nat King Cole singing 'Stardust'.
Continue track.
Continuous rain.
Soundtrack: Cross fade to the sound of a gong from The Happiest Days of Your Life: *Margaret Rutherford voice over:* 'Tap, Gossage, I said "tap" – you're not introducing a film.'
As we get halfway down the street track around to the right and into one of the derelict houses. Continuous rain inside the house. Soundtrack from The Ladykillers: *Alec Guinness voice over:* 'Mrs Wilberforce? I understand that you have rooms to let?'
Cross fade to 'Meet Me in St Louis'.

Continue tracking into the hallway and crane up the stairs. Continuous rain inside the house. Crane and track stop halfway up the stairs.
   Dissolve to:

INT. HALL AND STAIRCASE. DAY

The same camera position halfway up the stairs. The house is no longer derelict but bathed in brilliant sunshine from an internal skylight, open bedroom windows and open front door.
Bud, a boy of eleven, sits on the stairs, half bored. He plays with his shoelaces, his chin on his knees.
BUD: (*Calling*) Mam! ... Mam! ...
   (*Silence.*)
Can I go to the pictures, Mam?
   (*Silence. Her footsteps are heard. He races downstairs.*
   Cut to:)

INT. HALLWAY. DAY

Foot of the stairs. Mid-wide shot.
BUD *comes rushing to the foot of the stairs.*
MOTHER *comes up the hall towards camera from the backyard and goes into the kitchen, which is opposite the stairs.*
BUD: Mam.
MOTHER: (*Going into kitchen*) Yer?
BUD: I've got a penny.
MOTHER: (*Voice over from the kitchen*) So?
BUD: If you gave me elevenpence I'd have a shilling.
MOTHER: (*Coming out of the kitchen and going down the hall and into the yard*)
   You're not soft, are you?
BUD: (*Leaning over the banister and calling after her*) Arh, go on Mam ...
   Mam!
   (*Silence.*)
   Our Titchie said she'd take me ...
   (*Silence.*)
   Mam ... Arh ... go on Mam ...
   (*Silence.*)
MOTHER: (*Voice over, from the yard*) Eh Bud – will you get me those nets
   from the lads' bedroom?

(*Pause.*)
BUD: (*His voice drenched in boredom*) OK Mam ...
(*Lethargically he goes upstairs, trailing his hand along the banister.*
Hold on empty stairs.
Cut to:)

EXT. BACK BEDROOM WINDOW. DAY

From the outside close-up of BUD *kneeling at the open window, nets in his hands. Bright sunshine.*
MOTHER: (*Voice over from the yard*) Oh, come on, lad! Where's those nets? I want to wash them.
(*He drops the nets on to her.*
Cut to:)

EXT. BACK YARD. DAY

High shot of MOTHER *in yard – from* BUD'*s point of view directly overhead.*
MOTHER *is hanging out washing as the nets descend on her, covering her head.*
Cut to close-up side view of MOTHER, *the nets descending over her head.*
MOTHER: (*Taking the nets from her head*) That's before he'll bring them down ...
(*Cut to high shot of* MOTHER *from* BUD'*s point of view.*
Looking up and pretending to be annoyed) You little bugger!
(*Cut to:*)

EXT. BACK BEDROOM WINDOW. DAY

Close-up of BUD *at back-bedroom window, head on from the outside.*
He giggles. Laughter and shouting is heard and he looks up. The smile fading from his face.
Cut to:

EXT. GARAGE WALL. DAY

BUD'*s point of view of Smitten's Garage. The garage lies beyond the back-yard wall.*
Three labourers are building a wall. All are stripped to the waist and very muscular, one in particular. They are lifting bags of cement over their heads.
A bag bursts, showering one of them with powdered cement. They all roar with laughter. One of the labourers – the particularly muscular one – looks up at BUD *and waves and smiles at him.*

Cut to:

INT. BACK BEDROOM. DAY

Mid-shot back of BUD. *He comes back inside the room and squats on the floor beside and below the window. He looks back at the open window and the labourers' laughter can still be heard. He then puts his face to his knees.*
He looks faintly, vaguely disturbed. Hold.
Dissolve to:

INT. CHURCH. LATE AFTERNOON

Close-up of one of the Stations of the Cross. Christ on his way to Calvary but depicted in High Victorian Catholic revival.
Cut to close-up high shot looking down of BUD *performing the Stations of the Cross. He blesses himself and starts silently to pray. Pause. He stops praying and looks up.*
Cut to special effects shot of BUD's *point of view, but it is not the Station of the Cross he saw. It is a big close-up of the right hand of Christ being nailed to the cross.*
Cut to close-up of BUD *as he drops his joined hands and stares straight up.*
Cut to special effects shot of close-up of Christ's hand. They finish hammering the nail in. Hold. The hand quivers then is still. Then as we track back and crane up the cross begins to turn so that eventually as the camera rises above it and comes to rest the whole of the cross and Christ crucified are revealed – only we are above and looking down on to them. Christ and the cross are suspended at a terrible height. Below the cross is infinite black space.
Hold.
This Christ is young and handsome and muscular. Pause. Then Christ looks up at the camera and BUD. *It is the labourer at the garage. Slowly he grins then barks a terrifying human bark at* BUD.
Cut to close-up of BUD. *He jumps out of his skin, then, realizing where he is, he bows his head and resumes his praying in the unbroken quiet of the silent, dark church.*
Soundtrack of MOTHER *singing from the yard 'If You Were the Only Girl in the World'.*
Dissolve to:

INT. HALL. DAY

Shot of BUD *coming down and sitting on stairs. Looking through the banisters,* MOTHER'*s singing continues.*
Cut to:

INT. HALL AND STAIRS. DAY

Shot of Mum through banisters. She comes up the hall from the yard and goes into the kitchen, continuing to sing softly.
Cut to:

INT. STAIRS. DAY

Close-up of BUD *sitting on the stairs looking at* MOTHER *in the kitchen as she sings.*
Cut to:

INT. KITCHEN. DAY

Close-up, side view, of MOTHER *from* BUD'*s point of view. She is making an egg custard. She stops singing.*
Silence. She stands there rolling pastry with a sterilized milk bottle. Pause. Then she looks towards the stairs and BUD *and smiles.*
MOTHER: Go on … get me purse.
BUD: (*Voice over*) Arh, thanks Mam!
   (*She goes back to rolling pastry and humming softly to herself. Hold. Then:*)

INT. KITCHEN/LEAN-TO. DAY

Track and pan right to left to half-open window opposite MOTHER.
KEVIN *is seen through the window, bent over the sink in the lean-to washing himself. He is stripped to the waist. He stands up into shot and begins to get dry.*
MOTHER: (*Voice over*) Your tea's ready, Kev.
KEVIN: OK, Mam.
   (*Continue track and pan right to left to kitchen door.* JOHN *and* HELEN *are coming down the hall.*
HELEN *goes halfway up the stairs and* JOHN *stops at the door.*)
HELEN: (*Leaning over the banister*) Hey John, will you get the flat irons out for me?

JOHN: (*Taking off his coat and rummaging in the space below the stairs*) OK, Titch.

HELEN: (*Running upstairs*) Hiyer, Mam!

JOHN: Where's our Bud, Mam?

MOTHER: (*Walking out of kitchen to lean-to*) The pictures – where else?
(*Soundtrack: the orchestral introduction to 'At Sundown' from* Love Me or Leave Me *sung by Doris Day.*
Cut to:)

EXT. CINEMA. EARLY EVENING

The Hippodrome picture house advertising Love Me or Leave Me. *It is pouring with rain. Wide shot of the side of the building which has a series of exit doors running down its entire length.* BUD *is standing inside one of them sheltering from the rain.*
Soundtrack: Doris Day sings 'At Sundown' from Love Me or Leave Me.
A man passes by BUD.

BUD: (*Offering him his money*) Take us in, Mister?
(*The man hurries by without responding.*
Soundtrack of Doris Day continued.
It starts to get dark.
BUD *still waits and tries to keep warm and dry. A couple pass.*)

BUD: Will you take us in, please?
(*They hurry by without answering.*
Soundtrack: Doris Day.
A second man walks by and off camera right.)

BUD: Will you take us in, Mister?

MAN: (*Voice over*) OK, come on then.

BUD: Arh, thanks Mister!
(BUD *runs off, camera right. Hold.*
Soundtrack: Doris Day singing. Continued.
Orchestral interlude in song. Hold on empty frame.
The rain stops. It is now completely dark.)

EXT. CINEMA. NIGHT

Track in on cinema.
Soundtrack: Doris Day sings end of song.

Continue track right to left as all the doors of the cinema open and the audience comes streaming out. The stalls seats can be seen immediately beyond the doors. BUD *is amongst the crowd. He walks into a close shot. He begins to run and as he passes another boy, he sings sarcastically to him.*
BUD: 'Tiddle – iddle – iddle
    Tiddle – iddle – iddle
    Tiddle – iddle – iddle Hodge!'
TIDDLE HODGE: (*Voice over*) I'll get you Mavis!
    (*Continue tracking with* BUD *right to left as he runs away. Dissolve to:*)

INT. HALLWAY. BONFIRE NIGHT

Side view of BUD *in medium close-up as he walks slowly down the hall. Track with him right to left.*
Soundtrack: Sound of BUD *running down the hall.*
MOTHER: (*Voice over*) What are you running for?
BUD: (*Voice over*) (*Breathless*) Tiddle Hodge was chasing me.
MOTHER: (*Voice over*) Why?
BUD: (*Voice over*) I was skitting him.
MOTHER: (*Voice over*) You be careful – one day he'll catch you and give you a right go-along.
    (*The house and hall are dark but are lit from the light from the bonfire outside in the street. The whole hall is aflame.*
    Dissolve to:)

INT. PARLOUR. BONFIRE NIGHT

Continue tracking with BUD *in medium close-up, right to left. Everything is flame-coloured.*
BUD: (*Moving to the window and looking out*) Tiddle – iddle – iddle – Hodge.
    (*The sound of the bonfire, fireworks and people. Track stops when he gets to the window. He looks out through the nets.*
    Cut to:)

EXT. STREET. BONFIRE NIGHT

BUD's *point of view. The bonfire is surrounded and thronged with people and children from the street.*
Directly opposite BUD's *point of view one man is standing by the bonfire, laughing and talking. He is short but very powerfully built. His shirt is*

collarless and open on the chest. His shirt sleeves have been rolled up as far as they will go.
Cut to close shot of window with BUD's *face in it behind the nets. He stares at the man for a long time.*
Cut to:

INT. PARLOUR. BONFIRE NIGHT

Side view close-up of BUD *staring at the man. Slowly* BUD *sinks down until only his chin touches the window sill on which his arms are crossed. Everything is flame-coloured.*
Soundtrack of Kathleen Ferrier singing 'Blow The Wind Southerly'.
Dissolve to:

EXT. STREET. DAY

Side or three-quarter back view of BUD *as he runs to school. He is late. Track with him right to left. He passes the bottoms of three streets. At each street bonfires are smouldering from the night before.*
Soundtrack of Kathleen Ferrier singing:

> 'They told me last night there were
>   ships in the offing
> And I hurried down to the deep
>   rolling sea
> But my eyes could not see it
>   wherever might be it
> The barque that is bearing
>   my lover to me …'

Cut to:

EXT. SCHOOL. DAY

High shot looking in through the window at BUD.
On the outside of the school track into 'Board Schools' and 'Junior Boys', chiselled into the sandstone façade.
Cut to:

INT. CLASSROOM. DAY

All the children are working quietly. Pause. The rest of the classroom goes dark and motionless. Only BUD *is lit. He looks up.*
Soundtrack, Kathleen Ferrier singing:

'Blow the wind southerly, southerly, southerly
Blow balmy breeze o'er the bonny blue sea ...'

He looks to his right out of the school window.

Dissolve to BUD's *point of view of window. But instead of seeing the Liverpool skyline he sees a huge sailing ship moving across the frame right to left. It sails in slow motion through huge, heavy seas, wind and rain.*

Soundtrack of Kathleen Ferrier singing:

'Blow the wind southerly, southerly, southerly
Blow balmy breeze and bring him to me ...'

Cut to close-up of BUD. *Wind and rain on his face and hair. He gasps as he tries to keep gazing at the ship.*

Cut to:

SAILING SHIP

Wind and rain in the rigging as the ship glides from right to left across frame. The storm still raging, still lashing the ship.

Soundtrack, Kathleen Ferrier singing:

'Is it not sweet to hear the breeze singing
As like he is come o'er the deep
    rolling sea ...'

The ship passes from view and fades.

Cut to:

INT. CLASSROOM. DAY

Front view close-up of BUD *at desk. The storm subsides. He keeps looking for the ship.*

Soundtrack, Kathleen Ferrier singing:

'But sweeter and dearer by far 'tis
When bringing the barque of my true love
    in safety to me.'

The lights go back on.

He turns away from the window. A look of infinite disappointment comes over his face. His head drops. He and the other children go back to work as the lesson continues.

A triangle of vertical white light from a cinema projection booth appears above their heads.

Soundtrack: 'Carousel Waltz'. Hold. Then track and pan left to right from BUD *at desk to front of classroom but instead of seeing the teacher at her desk, dissolve to:*

INT. CINEMA. NIGHT

Pan left to right to MOTHER, BUD *and* HELEN *in close three-shot in the balcony of a cinema – the sort that has been converted from a theatre,* BUD, *sitting between* MOTHER *and* HELEN, *leans on the parapet. They are watching* Carousel. *The projection light is above their heads.*
Hold for a moment.
Soundtrack: 'Carousel Waltz'. Then crane down from three-shot in balcony and then dissolve to:

EXT. FAIRGROUND. NIGHT

Crane down to two-shot of MOTHER *and* HELEN.
HELEN: There's our John and Kevin, Mam.
MOTHER AND HELEN: *(Calling)* Kev! John!
  (Continue crane down to BUD *in close-up.)*
BUD: *(Calling)* John! Kevin!
  (And track away left to right.
  Soundtrack: 'Carousel Waltz' begins to fade. Fade all natural sound.
  Dissolve to track left to right to two-shot of KEVIN *and* JOHN *in side view. They are holding rifles and are firing them and laughing – they haven't heard the calls.*
  Soundtrack: A man singing 'She Moved Through the Fair', a cappella.
    'My young love said to me "My mother won't mind
    And my father won't slight you
    For your lack of kind" –'
Dissolve to track left to right to BUD *in close-up eating candyfloss and following* MOTHER *and* HELEN. *Track with him as he walks left to right behind* MOTHER *and* HELEN. *He looks up at* MOTHER *and smiles.*
Soundtrack of MAN *singing:*
    'And she stepped away from me
    And this she did say
    It will not be long, love, 'til
    our wedding day'

Two-shot of MOTHER *and* HELEN (*who is slightly in front of* MOTHER), MOTHER *and* HELEN *are eating candyfloss.* MOTHER *looks back at* BUD *and smiles though no sound can be heard.*
Track with MOTHER *left to right as she moves beyond* HELEN *and* BUD, *into close-up. She looks radiant as she walks.*
Soundtrack of MAN *singing:*

>'She stepped away from me
>And she went thro' the fair
>And fondly I watched her
>Move here and move there
>And then she went homeward
>With one star awake
>As the swan in the evening
>Moves over the lake ...'

Dissolve to:)

INT. PARLOUR. NIGHT

Pan to two-shot of MOTHER *and* BUD *in an armchair, sitting in the firelight. Hold.*
Soundtrack of MAN *singing:*

>'Last night she came to me,
>She came softly in
>So softly she came that
>her feet made no din ...'

As we track in on them.
Soundtrack: MAN's *voice becomes* MOTHER'S *voice, singing:*

>'And she laid her hand on
>me and this she did say
>"It will not be long, love,
>till our wedding day".'

Track stops in mid-close two-shot. Long silence as they both sit there looking into the fire, BUD *snuggles up against* MOTHER *as she strokes his hair.*

MOTHER: (*More to herself*) My dad used to sing that.
BUD: Granddad O'Brien?
MOTHER: (*Her eyes filling with tears*) Yer.

(*She continues stroking his hair – but crying silently so that* BUD *won't hear her or be disturbed. Hold on both of them as they sit in the firelight. Silence. Cut to:*)

INT. HALLWAY AND STAIRS. NIGHT

Wide shot of MOTHER *going upstairs.*
MOTHER: (*Dead beat*) Lock up, will you Kev?
KEVIN: (*Voice over*) OK, Mam.
   (*She moves slowly up the dark stairs. Hold on stairs.*
   Soundtrack: Tom Drake and Judy Garland from Meet Me in St Louis.
   (MOTHER *gone. Hold on empty dark stairs.*
   Cut to:)

INT. PARLOUR. NIGHT

Close-up on BUD *in firelight.*
Cut to two-shot of KEVIN *and* FRANCES *from* BUD*'s point of view on the sofa which they have pulled in front of the fire.* FRANCES *is in the foreground.* KEVIN *behind her. They both look at* BUD. FRANCES *talks softly to him.* KEVIN *points at* BUD *then points to the ceiling indicating bed for* BUD. KEVIN *caresses* FRANCES.
Cut to close-up of BUD *by sideboard. He looks crestfallen and moves to the parlour door which is a curtain. Pan with him right to left.*
FRANCES: (*Voice over*) Goodnight Bud.
   (*He doesn't answer.*
   Cut to:)

INT. HALL. NIGHT

Close-up two-shot of JOHN *and* JEAN *by the open front door in the dark kissing and talking softly to each other.*
Soundtrack of Judy Garland singing.
The vestibule door slowly closes over on JOHN *and* JEAN *leaving their silhouettes reflected behind the decorated glass.*
Cut to:

INT. HALL AND STAIRS. NIGHT

Shot of BUD *climbing softly, slowly up the dark stairs.*
BUD *disappears.*
Cut to:

INT. MAIN BEDROOM. NIGHT

Shot of ceiling directly over main window. Outside it is raining heavily. The window is reflected on the ceiling, it ripples like V-shaped water.
Cut to close-up side view of BUD *in bed. Outside it is raining heavily – the rain being reflected on the wall by Bud's bed. He turns on his back and touches the rain's reflection on the wall.*
Soundtrack: Judy Garland's singing continues.
BUD: (*Calling softly*) Mam! Mam!
   (*Cut to two-shot of* MOTHER *and* HELEN *in bed asleep but favour* MOTHER.
   Soundtrack of Judy Garland singing.
   Absolute silence except for the rain.
   Cut to special effects top shot looking straight down on BUD *in bed. The bed looks coffin-like. He lies perfectly still in the silence.*
   Then a pair of hands – the hands of CHRIST/LABOURER *complete with stigmata – come through the back wall behind the head of the bed and grasp* BUD *around the head and face,* BUD *is paralysed with fear.*)
CHRIST/LABOURER: You're mine!
   (BUD *screams in terror.*
   Cut to BUD *sitting up into shot, screaming and screaming. Hands enter shot and hold his face. Track back to two-shot of* MOTHER *and* BUD *on bed in side view,* MOTHER *holding* BUD *to her.* BUD *is sobbing and sobbing, the rain reflected on the wall behind them.*)
BUD: (*Sobbing*) It was a man. It was a *man!*
MOTHER: (*Calming him*) You're all right. You're all right …
   (*Pan left to right to bedroom floor. Rain reflected on it. Hold on floor. Dissolve to:*)

INT. PARLOUR. LATE AFTERNOON

Floor of parlour. The parlour window is reflected on the floor. It is pouring with heavy rain. Hold on floor.
Soundtrack: Orchestral version of 'A Shropshire Lad'.
The rain stops. The sun comes out weakly, fades and comes out again so that the reflection of the window on the floor appears and disappears.
A blazing fire in the grate. Hold on floor.
Then track and pan left to right to window to back close-up of BUD *at the window standing inside the nets looking out at the street. Odd squalls of rain*

against the glass, BUD *sighs and kicks his foot and trails his fingers along the panes looking very bored. Hold on* BUD.
Dissolve to:

EXT. STREET. LATE AFTERNOON

Medium close-up of BUD *at the window looking out. It is snowing and he looks excitedly at the falling snow. In the background a blazing fire bathes the whole of the dark parlour with warmth.* BUD *strains to look up at the sky and the falling snow.*
Soundtrack: 'A Shropshire Lad' ends.
He disappears from behind the nets into the dark, warm parlour.
BUD: (*Voice over*) What am I going to get for Christmas, Mam?
MOTHER: (*Voice over*) Don't be so nosey.
   (*Dissolve to:*)

INT. PARLOUR. LATE AFTERNOON/EARLY EVENING

Close-up of sideboard in parlour lit only by the blazing fire. Early evening. Pan right to left along sideboard. It is covered with fruit and Christmas cards. Continue panning right to left to fire in close-up. It blazes.
Dissolve/cut to:

INT. CLASSROOM. DAY

The end of the school nativity play. The play has taken place at one end of a classroom on the lower floor. It has been staged in front of the fireplace.
The Holy Family are already seated. Behind them desks and chairs form a semi-circle. Mary, seated behind a cradle, holds a doll – the baby Jesus. Joseph stands on her right. The rest of the class troop in as shepherds, the magi, angels.
CHILDREN: (*Singing*) 'Oh come all ye faithful
   Joyful and triumphant
   Oh come ye, oh come ye,
   To Beth-eth-le-hem …'
   (*As they sing, they arrange themselves on top of the desks and chairs. The angels take the highest position behind the Holy Family on the desks. The shepherds stand by Joseph's left,* BUD, *one of the shepherds, carries a crook with a lantern suspended from it.*)
CHILDREN: (*Singing*) 'Come and behold him
   Born the king of angels

Oh come let us adore him
Oh come let us adore him
Oh come let us adore him
Christ the Lord.'
(*A pause as they settle into a tableau. Then they start to sing 'Silent Night'.*)

CHILDREN: (*Singing*) 'Silent night, Holy night
All is calm, all is bright
Round yon virgin, mother and child
Holy infant so tender and mild ...'
(BUD *looks at his* MOTHER *and smiles as he sings.*
Cut to shot of group of MOTHERs *watching their children in the play, all very proud,* BUD'S MOTHER *is in the middle of the group. She looks at him and smiles but is choked with tears.*)

CHILDREN: (*Singing*) 'Sleep in heavenly peace
Sleep in heavenly peace.'
(*Cut to:*)

INT. HALL AND STAIRS. NIGHT

Mid-shot front view of BUD *sitting halfway up the stairs. The stairs and hall are dark but he is lit from the brilliant light flooding from the kitchen. Voices are heard in the kitchen – laughing and talking. Hold on shot of* BUD. *He looks at them.*
Cut to:

INT. KITCHEN. NIGHT

BUD's *point of view of his* MOTHER, HELEN, JOHN *and* KEVIN *in the kitchen. They are talking about Christmas.*
Cut to:

INT. HALL AND STAIRS. NIGHT

Close-up front view of BUD *on the stairs. He smiles and looks towards the front door. The light from the kitchen fades as do the voices of his family and a light in front of him begins to flood his face. He smiles. His face becoming radiant. Soundtrack: Bing Crosby, Vera Ellen, Rosemary Clooney and Danny Kaye singing 'White Christmas'.*
Dissolve to:

INT. HALLWAY. NIGHT

BUD'S *point of view of the dark hallway and front door.*
Soundtrack of 'White Christmas' continues.
The dark is gradually giving way to a wonderfully soft glowing light as the whole of the front of the house opens up.
It is snowing outside and all Bud's family are dressed in red and white Santa Claus outfits and miming to 'White Christmas'. They gather themselves around a huge, decorated Christmas tree. They are singing just for BUD.
Soundtrack of 'White Christmas' continues.
Dissolve to:

EXT. STREET AND BUD'S HOUSE. NIGHT

Mid long shot. Real time. Snow.
The family are no longer singing but the house is filled with people and is a blaze of light in the midst of darkness. Someone has put a record of 'White Christmas' on the radiogram and everyone joins in.
Soundtrack: all sing 'White Christmas'.
Track away left to right down the street away from Bud's house. Continue tracking through the snow and into the darkness. All real sounds fade as we track over the dark house fronts. There is a sudden wind and a flurry of snow.
Soundtrack: Orson Welles in The Magnificent Ambersons.
Continue tracking left to right into the darkness. Then crane up out of darkness to a high shot of the main road. Fade up natural sound. The main road is crammed with people doing the Hokey-Kokey. Traffic has been stopped or slowed to a crawl. All are singing 'The Kokey-Kokey'.

A VOICE: It's twelve o'clock!

>   (*Everyone begins shouting, kissing, wishing each other 'All the best', 'Happy New Year'. People bang bats on the pavements, bang pots and pan lids with spoons, car horns hoot, fog horns bleat from the river.*)

ALL: (*Singing*) 'Should old acquaintance
be forgot
And never brought to mind
Should old acquaintance
be forgot
For the sake of Auld Lang Syne …'

>   (*Crane down to a small circle of people consisting of* MOTHER, BUD, HELEN, JOHN *and* JEAN.)

ALL: (*Singing*) 'For Auld Lang Syne my dear
For Auld Lang Syne
We'll take a cup of
Kindness yet
For the sake of Auld Lang Syne.'
MOTHER: (*Kissing* BUD) All the best, Bud!
BUD: All the best, Mam!
(*The rest do the same. Track and pan right to left away from them – past* KEVIN *and* FRANCES *kissing in a pub doorway to the darkness of the street. Fade all natural sound. Continue tracking right to left into the darkness then out of it. Out of the darkness emerges* MOTHER, BUD, HELEN, KEVIN *and* JOHN *walking down the street towards their house. Track slowly with them right to left.*)
BUD: (*To* MOTHER) What's 'Kinnershet', Mam?
MOTHER: What's what?
BUD: In that song … 'We'll take a cup of "Kinnershet"'.
MOTHER: Oh! It's 'kindness yet'.
NEIGHBOUR: All the best!
ALL: All the best, Frank! Happy New Year Mr Campbell!
(*Track stops when they all reach the house. Medium-long shot front view of house. They all go in. The house lights have been left on.*)
MOTHER: Will you lock the back door, Kev?
KEVIN: I locked it before we went out.
JOHN: (*Resigned air*) You don't half panic, Mam.
(*They all begin to drift upstairs except* MOTHER, *who closes the front door. The hall and parlour lights go off and we hear them troop upstairs. The house is dark except for the fairy lights on the Christmas tree in the parlour window, flashing on and off.*
KEVIN *and* JOHN'S *laughter and talk fades into silence as they drift into sleep. Silence.*)
MOTHER: (*Voice over*) Good night, Titch.
HELEN: (*Voice over*) Good night, Mam.
(*Silence.*)
MOTHER: (*Voice over*) God help anyone with no home tonight.
(*Silence. It starts to rain. Hold on the dark house. Pan down to street and snow. The rain turning the snow into a dirty slush.*)
MOTHER: (*Voice over*) Well, I wonder what 1956 'll bring.

(*Dissolve to:*)

INT. HEADMISTRESS'S STUDY. PRIMARY SCHOOL. AFTERNOON

Two-shot side view of BUD *seated and in front of him the* HEADMISTRESS *who is a nun. Her face cannot be seen. Only her hands move as she bathes the back of* BUD*'s neck as he bends over.*

HEADMISTRESS: Stay here until your nose stops bleeding.

BUD: (*Bending his head right back*) Thank you, Sister.

(*Dissolve to shot of the study looking towards the window. The study is dark – made even darker by the brilliant sunshine flooding in through the bay windows, sash bay windows from floor to ceiling – fully opened. In front of the window, in the bay, a large desk.*)

TEACHER: (*Voice over*) Put something cold on his neck – like keys -that'll do the trick.

(*Shot of* BUD *– his head still held back – walking towards the desk and open window. Track with him. Beyond the window but directly outside it is the back school yard. At the far end of the school yard is a strip of grass and a perimeter wall beyond that.*

In the centre of the wall a permanently locked wooden door. To the right of this door, a pear tree. The schoolchildren are not allowed to play on this grass area, BUD *stops at the desk by the study window. He brings his head back up to see if his nose is still bleeding. It isn't. Track continues,* BUD *looks out the window at the children playing in the school yard. In a kind of unofficial sports day – teams compete in sack race, three-legged race, egg and spoon race, supervised by teachers. Parents look on.*

Track past BUD.

Dissolve to track back from the open study window – only now there is no desk. In its place is a piano in front of which is seated a teacher – Miss Delaney. Her class is arranged in front of and below the study window – in the school yard. BUD *included.*

Miss Delaney strikes a note. Her class hum it. She strikes the note again. Again they hum. She begins to play. Continue track back.)

CHILDREN: (*Singing*) 'Faith of our Fathers sanctify my breast
Body of Christ be, now, my saving guest
Deep in thy wounds Lord hide and shelter me
So that I'll never, never part from thee.'

(*In front of the choir the rest of the schoolchildren are sitting facing the choir, with their teachers. On either side the parents, sitting on chairs, looking on. All very formal. Brilliant sunshine. Choir fades. Continue track back. Dissolve to:*)

EXT. BACK SCHOOL YARD. PRIMARY SCHOOL. AFTERNOON

Shot of the grass area and the pear tree and the door in the perimeter wall.
Breeze in the pear tree.
Track in on door for a moment then track stops.
Hold for a moment.
Then the door in the perimeter wall opens of its own accord – debris and the city beyond. Hold.
Cut to:

EXT. SECONDARY SCHOOL. MORNING

Close-up (back view) of BUD. *It is his first day at secondary school. A crisp cold morning. Boys everywhere. He walks towards the school gates. Track with him. A boy walks past him then stops.*
FIRST BOY: (*To* BUD) Are you Povey?
  (BUD *shakes his head.* FIRST BOY *stops at school gates against which two other* BOYS *are leaning.*)
FIRST BOY: (*Laughing to the two others*) I thought he was Povey.
SECOND BOY: (*To* BUD) Are you from Bernard Street?
BUD: No – Canon Kennedy's.
  (*The three boys bar his entrance into the school yard. Then just stand looking at him. Track stops.*)
THIRD BOY: (*To* BUD) Who's a fruit then, eh?
  (*Cut to close-up front view of* BUD. *He is terrified.*
  Cut to:)

INT. MR NICHOLLS' CLASSROOM. DAY

Close-up of BUD *standing in a line which moves slowly from left to right. Pan with him. He looks petrified.*
Soundtrack: The sound of the cane as all the boys are systematically beaten. It comes to BUD's *turn. He holds out his hand. The sound of the cane. He is caned. He is close to tears.*

Cut to shot of BUD *sitting down at one of the front desks. He is trying not to cry.* MR NICHOLLS *brings the cane down hard on* BUD's *desk frightening him still further.*
MR NICHOLLS: (*Voice over*) That's just to show you who's boss …
   (*Cut to close-up of* MR NICHOLLS.)
MR NICHOLLS: … I'm Mr Nicholls … you play ball with me, I'll play ball with you.
   (*Cut to:*)

INT. DINNER CENTRE. LUNCHTIME

Line of boys – BUD *among them – moving towards the still where food is being served. Pan/track with them right to left side view. All the boys carry steel trays as they each in turn get their lunch at that still. Chaos. Terrible noise.* BUD *looks both bewildered and terrified,* BUD *gets served.*
Cut to shot of BUD *-from the other side of the still counter – getting served. Beyond him rows and rows of large trestle tables filled with boys eating. Chaos. Noise.*
Cut to mid-shot side view of BUD. *Pan/track with him right to left past row upon row of trestle tables, crowded with boys all eating their food rapidly and without relish. Terrible noise,* BUD *looking more and more demoralized. Track stops when he sits down at the end of a table and starts to eat. Just as he does so:*
DINNER LADY: (*Voice over*) Seconds!
   (*A mad scramble for more unappetizing food.*
   BUD *sits there in the pandemonium just looking and picking at his food. Soundtrack: Noise of boys playing in playground, then the sound of a whistle.*
   Cut to:)

EXT. PLAYGROUND. AFTERNOON

Close-up of MR BUSHELL *with the whistle still in his mouth. He is the* HEADMASTER *– short, spruce, correct. A military man. Silence as he eyes the entire playground. Pause. Then he blows his whistle.*
Cut to wide shot of boys standing where they stopped when the whistle blew.
MR BUSHELL: Get into line!
   (*They all get into their respective class lines. Silence.*)
   (*Blowing on his whistle*) S4! … Right wheel! Quick march!
   … Left, right, left …

(*S4, BUD's class, go into the school. Line by line they go into the school from the playground in absolute silence.*
Cut to:)

INT. CHURCH HIGH ALTAR. LATE AFTERNOON

Wide shot from high altar looking up the body of the church. Benediction has not yet begun. The church interior is dark. The pews filling up rapidly and silently with boys from the whole school. They genuflect at the pews before entering them. The last few boys settle in pews. The whole church is full. Silence except for the odd cough. Hold. Then the whole congregation rises. Cut to mid-shot of BUD *in pew surrounded by the three boys he met on his first day at secondary school.*

SECOND BOY: (*Imitating* BUD) I'm from Canon Kennedy!

THIRD BOY: Who's a fruit then, eh?

FIRST BOY: (*Laughing*) Povey!

(BUD *is frightened.*
All begin to sing the Tantum Ergo.)

ALL: (*Singing*) 'Tantum ergo sacramentum
Veneremur cernui
Et antiquum documentum
Novo cedet ritui …
Genitori genitoque
Laus et jubilatio
Salust honor virtus quoque
Sit et benedictio …'
Soundtrack: Cross fade to:

HELEN: (*Voice over, a regular weekly ritual*) Well, did you get me stuff for me?
(*Cut to:*)

INT. CHURCH CORRIDOR. LATE AFTERNOON

Corridor running down the entire length of church. All the boys are filling the corridor pushing towards the doors at the far end. BUD *in close-up amid the seething mass of boys. Crane with him as he looks back over his shoulder anxiously.*
Soundtrack:

BUD: (*Voice over*) Yer – two pairs of nylons – 15 denier. American Tan, fully fashioned – Panstick, nail varnish …

HELEN: (*Voice over*) Majestic Red?

BUD: (*Voice over*) Yer ... Imperial Leather and the Picture Goer and Picture Show ...
(*Dissolve to:*)

INT. BUD'S HOUSE. EARLY EVENING

Track back with BUD *in close-up from the dark hall to the bright kitchen. The kitchen seems magical and bright to* BUD. *He is in the midst of a sea of pastel-coloured dresses – coming in from the dark hall to the bright kitchen. He is surrounded by* FRANCES, JEAN *and* AMY *but only the dresses are seen.*

HELEN: (*Voice over*) Evening in Paris?
BUD: They didn't have any.
AMY: (*Voice over*) 'e' are Titch – you can have a bit of mine.
    (*Pan to wide shot. Girls –* FRANCES, JEAN *and* AMY *walk into shot.* HELEN *is finishing her make-up. All are getting ready to go out.*)
HELEN: Thanks Amy.
AMY: Can I borrow a bit of your lippy, Helen?
HELEN: Yer.
    (*Pan to window which is half open.* JOHN *and* KEVIN *are in the dark lean-to getting washed and ready to go out. They are lit from the kitchen light flooding through into lean-to. They catch sight of* AMY.)
BOTH: (*Singing*) 'Once in love with Amy! ...'
    (*Cut to:*)

INT. LEAN-TO. EARLY EVENING

Two-shot from behind of JOHN *and* KEVIN *in lean-to. They are in silhouette in the foreground.* AMY *and the girls are in the bright kitchen beyond.*

AMY: (*Blushing to her roots*) Oh, I feel ashamed!
JOHN and KEVIN: (*Singing*) '– Always in love with Amy'
HELEN: Oh, leave her alone you two!
    (*The boys laugh.*)
FRANCES: Take no notice, Amy.
JEAN: They're just letting their soft out.
JOHN and KEVIN: (*Singing*)
    'Her lips are much too close to mine,
    Take care my foolish heart!'
HELEN: Couple of head-the-balls!
    (*Cut to:*)

INT. KITCHEN. EARLY EVENING

Close-up (side view) of JEAN.
JEAN: Eh, Bud, will you go and get us some ciggies?
   (*Cut to:*)

INT. KITCHEN. EARLY EVENING

Medium wide shot of kitchen looking towards the door and hall,
BUD *squatting on a chair left of door.*
BUD: (*Jumping off chair*) OK Jean! Throw us the money – go on! – I'll cop it.
   (*She throws the money and he catches it and runs out of the kitchen into the hall.*
   Cut to:)

INT. HALLWAY. EARLY EVENING

BUD *running out of kitchen. Runs into close-up, stops and screams, then slowly backs away. The girls come to the kitchen door. The lads run in from the lean-to.*
Cut to shot of a tall BLACK MAN *standing in the hall from their point of view.*
BLACK MAN: (*Speaking in a soft, gentle, polite, heavy Jamaican accent*)
   Is this 18 Kensington? I'm looking for Mona …
   (*Cut to shot of girls at kitchen door –* BUD *backs towards them.*
   The lads move up to the camera threateningly.)
HELEN: (*Scared*) No – it bloody well isn't. This is 18 Kensington Street.
   Kensington's the main road. There's no Mona here.
JOHN: (*Aggressively*) Go on! Frigg off!
   (*Cut to shot of* BLACK MAN *backing down the hall towards front door, all the time smiling.*)
BLACK MAN: (*Soft and polite*) Thank you … thank you …
   (*Cut to track and pan with girls and boys and* BUD *in tow down the dark hall to the front door.*
   Cut to:)

EXT. STREET. EARLY EVENING

Wide shot side view. They all come spinning out of the front door into the street – BUD *remains on the step. Track with them.*
BUD: (*Calling after them*) My Mam said don't be late.

ALL: (*Calling and waving back*) OK Bud! See yer!
> (*Cut to* BUD *on the doorstep from their point of view. But closer. He waves then sits down on step, crane down with him. He sits on the step watching them go away down the street and into the night laughing and joking. Hold.*
> *Cut to medium close-up of* BUD *in side view through cellar railings.* BUD *switches on the torch he's been carrying, first shining it into the cellar then into the night sky, as he sits on the step.*
> *Cut to:*)

EXT. SUMMER NIGHT SKY

Shot of torchlight beam raking the night sky.

BUD: (*Voice over*) If you shine a torch into the sky – the light goes on forever.

MOTHER: (*Voice over*) Who says?

BUD: (*Voice over*) Our teacher.
> (*Cut to:*)

EXT. STREET. DOORSTEP. NIGHT

Close-up of BUD *on doorstep head-on. The house and hall are dark behind him. The light from the kitchen has been switched off. He continues shining the torch into the sky then brings the torch down so that it shines directly into the camera. For a brief moment the screen goes white. Then the beam of light is taken away and we are at the far end of the hall looking down towards* BUD *at the front door. He takes the beam of light away from camera then switches the torch off. He stands at the door for a moment looking into the dark house. Dissolve to same angle as previous shot, although much later. The front and vestibule doors are closed and the only light in the hall is the light from the kitchen.*

MOTHER: (*Voice over*) Go on up lad – I'll bring the Cocoa.
> (BUD *comes out of kitchen and goes into the hall then up the dark stairs.*)

BUD: Arh – thanks Mam.
> (*A short pause then the light in the kitchen is switched off. He is followed by* MOTHER *carrying two cups of cocoa. She goes up the dark stairs. Hold on empty dark hall,* MOTHER *sings 'Me and My Shadow' in the dark. Hold. Then soundtrack:*)

BBC RADIO ANNOUNCER: 'This is the BBC Home Service. 'Lift up Your Hearts'.

(*Dissolve/cut to:*)

INT. HALLWAY. EARLY MORNING

Long shot looking down the hall towards the front door. MOTHER *comes down the stairs and goes to the front door. She opens it and collects the milk. Looks up and down the street. The weather is cold and wet with squalls of wind and rain blowing down and across the empty street. She closes the front door and comes down the hall. She stops at the foot of the stairs.*

MOTHER: (*Calling up the stairs*) Come on you four! Make a shape! It's well past seven! (*Shivering against the cold.*) Jesus tonight – it's cold. (*She goes into the kitchen and switches on the light. The light floods into the grey hall.*
Cut to:*)

INT. PARLOUR. EARLY MORNING

Close shot of fireplace. MOTHER *puts a match to the set fire then puts a shovel against the front of the grate, then a newspaper over this for draught. Hold.*
Cut to:

INT. LEAN-TO EARLY MORNING

Close shot of MOTHER *holding a kettle beneath the cold water tap. Water splashing into kettle. Hold.*
Cut to:

INT. PARLOUR. EARLY MORNING

Close-up side view of HELEN *putting her turban on. She stands on the hearth to see in the mirror. Hold. She finishes her turban.*
Cut to:

INT. KITCHEN. EARLY MORNING

Mid wide shot from kitchen door looking into room. JOHN *is seated at the table eating his breakfast left of the gas fire. He wears only trousers and a singlet. Right of the gas fire is a bowl of water on a chair –* KEVIN *in front of the chair getting washed. He is just in his underpants.*
Cut to mid-wide shot-reverse angle of above looking towards kitchen door, KEVIN *in foreground getting washed,* BUD *comes to door and looks at* KEVIN.
KEVIN: Eh, Bud – will you do my back?

(BUD *hesitates for a moment then comes forwards to* KEVIN. *He takes the flannel from* KEVIN *and begins to wash* KEVIN's *back. The expression on* BUD's *face is a sad and lonely one.*
Cut to:)

INT. HALLWAY. EARLY MORNING

Three-quarter shot of KEVIN, JOHN *and* HELEN *going through the front door into the street.*
KEVIN: (*As front door opens*) God blimey! It's bleeding freezing!
 (*They go out into the street.*
 Cut to:)

EXT. STREET. EARLY MORNING

Side shot of KEVIN, JOHN *and* HELEN *coming out of the house. The weather is getting nastier – rain and a strong wind. They go down the street.* HELEN *crosses to other side of street and runs to work,* KEVIN *and* JOHN *bend into the wind then turn right into a side street.*
Cut to:

INT. PARLOUR. EARLY MORNING

Medium wide shot of BUD *standing in front of the fire. In front of him a bowl on chair. He is taking his pyjama-top off.*
MOTHER: (*Voice over*) I could've slept till the Lord called me this morning …
 (BUD *looks at her and smiles sadly.*)
MOTHER: (*Voice over*) Go on – get washed and I'll bring you your tea and toast …
BUD: (*Looking at her for a while – sad and lonely*) OK Mam.
 (*Slowly he begins to get washed.*
 Cut to:)

INT. PARLOUR. EARLY MORNING

Two-shot side view of MOTHER *and* BUD *looking towards the parlour window. The curtains have been drawn back making everything seem grey.* MOTHER *buttons* BUD's *mac. Then holds his face in her hands.*
MOTHER: You'll soon *be* grown up, won't you *lad?*
 (BUD *doesn't answer. He just looks at her. Hold.*
 Cut to:)

EXT. STREET. EARLY MORNING

Wide shot of BUD *running up street to school. Squally wind and rain. Hold.*
Cut to:

EXT. SCHOOLYARD. MORNING

Pan with BUD *as he races through the empty school yard into the school. Wind and rain.*
Cut to:

INT. SCHOOL CORRIDOR. DAY

Medium long shot of BUD *coming in through door. He walks towards camera and stops at his class door. He listens for a moment then taps lightly on the door and goes in.*
Cut to:

INT. CLASSROOM. DAY

Close-up of BUD *at door. He looks both surprised and distressed.*
Cut to long shot from BUD'*s point of view of empty classroom except for* MR NICHOLLS *sitting at his desk correcting exercise books. He looks up.*
MR NICHOLLS: You're late! Report to Mr Bushell, the Headmaster, then go upstairs to nurse in Room 10.
BUD: (*Voice over*) Yes, sir. Thank you, sir.
    (*Cut to:*)

INT. HEADMASTER'S STUDY. DAY

Mid-shot of MR BUSHELL *head-on at his desk from* BUD'*s point of view.*
MR BUSHELL: Why have you come?
    Cut to:

INT. HEADMASTER'S STUDY. DAY

Mid-shot of BUD *head-on from* MR BUSHELL'*s point of view.*
BUD: Mr Nicholls told me to report late, Sir.
    (*Cut to mid-wide two-shot of* BUD *and* MR BUSHELL. MR BUSHELL *walks into shot holding a cane.*)
MR BUSHELL: Come on.
    (BUD *lifts his hand and is caned. This time he does not cry or even respond.*)

MR BUSHELL: In future, be punctual.
BUD: Yes, sir. Thank you, sir.
   (*Cut to:*)

INT. ROOM 10. DAY

Mid-close shot of BUD *in a line of boys which moves slowly from left to right. Pan with* BUD *as the line moves slowly.*
NURSE: (*Voice over*) Lice … Lice … Clean … Lice.
   (*It comes to* BUD's *turn. The nurse swirls a spatula in white disinfectant and inspects his head.*)
NURSE: Lice …
   (*He walks off camera.*)
   (*Cut:*)

INT. ROOM 10. DAY

Mid wide shot of two groups of boys, BUD *joins the group on the right – the boys with lice.*
NURSE: (*Voice over*) Clean … Clean … Lice …
   (*Cut to:*)

INT. ROOM 10. DAY

Close-up of BUD. *He looks at the windows – squalls of wind and rain. He is very close to tears. Pan left so that* BUD *is on edge of frame right. Soundtrack: Laughter is heard and the sound of running water. Special effects: In the space to the left of* BUD *appears the window of the kitchen which looks into the lean-to.* HELEN *is crouched over the sink and* BUD *is pouring water over her hair. Both are laughing.*
   Pan/dissolve to:

INT. MR NICHOLLS' CLASSROOM. DAY

Shot of MR NICHOLLS' *desk. He is marking the class register. As he calls boys' names out they answer 'Present Sir'.*
MR NICHOLLS: (*Calling the register*) Andrews, Aughton, Barnes, Bedson, Bell, Clotworthy, Crowley, Davies …
   (*Begin to fade his voice.*
   Cut to shot of class standing at their desks, hands joined, saying morning prayers, BUD *at the front.*)

BOYS: (*Praying*) 'Glory Be to the Father and To the Son and To the Holy Ghost.'
(*Cut to shot of window. Outside it is raining.*)
BOYS: (*Voice over*) (*Praying*) As it was in the beginning, is now, and ever shall be, world without end. Amen.
(*Dissolve to:*)

INT. CHURCH. LATE AFTERNOON. SUMMER SATURDAY

The icon of the face of Jesus on the cloth of St Veronica. Candles burn below it.
BUD: (*Voice over*) Jesus Mary and Joseph
I give you my heart
and my soul …
(*Dissolve to a shot of the crucifix in the church looking along the crossbar at Christ crucified, his head droops and is turned slightly away.*)
Jesus Mary and Joseph
I give you my body and blood.
(*Dissolve to shot of the high altar bathed in lighted candles and covered in flowers for Quarant'ore.*)
Jesus Mary and Joseph
assist me in my last agony …
(*Dissolve to two-shot of* MOTHER *and* BUD *in a pew in the dark body of the church. Both are kneeling and praying.*)
May I say when I am
dying – Jesus mercy,
Mary help.
(*Blessing himself*) In the name of the Father
and of the Son and of the
Holy Ghost. Amen.
(MOTHER *remains kneeling,* BUD *goes back into the pew. Silence.*
BUD *looks at the altar for a while then at* MOTHER. *Silence.*
Soundtrack: Isabel Buchanan singing a capella, 'Ae fond kiss'.
    'Ae fond kiss and then we sever
    ae farewell alas for ever.'
Dissolve to shot of the pietà – Mary holding the dead Christ.
Soundtrack:
    'Deep in heart-wrung tears
    I'll pledge thee'

Track or pan right to left.
Dissolve to:

EXT. STREET. LATE AFTERNOON. SUMMER SATURDAY

Pan right to left to a shot of MOTHER *and* BUD *crossing the main road and walking slowly down the street.*
Track and pan right to left.
Soundtrack:

    'Warring sighs and moans I'll wage thee'

Dissolve to:
Pan right to left to a group shot of BUD, MOTHER, HELEN, JOHN, KEVIN *and* JEAN *and* FRANCES *sitting in and around the front door.* MOTHER *sits on a chair just inside the front door,* BUD *stands behind the railings. Everyone else sits on the steps. They are having an impromptu picnic – lemonade and sandwiches.*
Soundtrack:

    'Had we never loved sae kindly
    Had we never loved sae blindly –
    Never met or never parted
    We had ne'er been broken-hearted'

Dissolve to:
Pan right to left to shot of BUD *behind railings. He gets a bottle of lemonade from the windowsill, walks along behind the railings and hands it to* MOTHER.
Pan/track right to left with him to her.
Soundtrack:

    'Fare thee weel thou first and fairest
    Fare thee weel thou best and dearest'

Dissolve to:

EXT. BUD'S HOUSE. LATE AFTERNOON. SUMMER SATURDAY

Pan right to left to two-shot of FRANCES *and* KEVIN *on doorstep.*
They are laughing and talking.
Pan right to left from them.
Soundtrack: 'Thine be ilka joy and treasure.'
Dissolve and pan right to left to shot of HELEN, JEAN *and* JOHN *on doorstep laughing.*

Soundtrack: 'Peace enjoyment love and pleasure.'
Pan right to left from them.
Dissolve to:

EXT. STREET. MAIN ROAD. LATE AFTERNOON. SUMMER SATURDAY
Pan right to left to shot of the three school bullies bored at the top of BUD's *street.*
Pan from them, right to left.
Dissolve to:

EXT. BUD'S HOUSE. EARLY EVE. SUMMER SATURDAY
Pan right to left to shot of JOHN *and* JEAN *talking quietly at the railings then drifting down the street.*
Soundtrack: 'Ae fond kiss and then we sever'.
Dissolve and pan right to left to shot of KEVIN *and* FRANCES *at railings.*
They talk softly and KEVIN *yawns.*
Soundtrack: 'Ae farewell alas for ever'.
Dissolve and pan right to left to BUD *alone at railings.*
Pan or track right to left to MOTHER *sitting inside the front door. Pan stops on* MOTHER.
We are looking straight down the dark hall.
She gets up and takes the chair inside and disappears into kitchen.
Soundtrack: 'Deep in heart-wrung tears I'll pledge thee'.
BUD *walks into shot and goes in.*
Soundtrack: 'Warring sighs and moans I'll wage thee'.
Silence.
Hold.
Dissolve to:

INT. BUD'S HOUSE. EARLY EVENING. SUMMER SATURDAY
Shot of MOTHER *from lean-to, hanging ironing on to rack. She finishes then pulls the rack up.*
Dissolve to:

INT. LEAN-TO. LATE AFTERNOON
Shot of BUD *in lean-to.*
He is listening to the rain hammering down on to the lean-to roof of doors.

He looks up then tries to touch the lean-to roof with his hand. Follow his hand. Thundering rain.
Dissolve to:

INT. BUD'S HOUSE. NIGHT

Pitch blackness.
MOTHER, HELEN, JOHN *and* KEVIN, *holding candles below their faces, move in blackness towards camera.*
Dissolve to pitch blackness.
MOTHER, HELEN, JOHN *and* KEVIN *with candles moving up the stairs.*
Dissolve to:

INT. BUD'S HOUSE. MAIN BEDROOM. NIGHT

Pitch blackness. The light from candles on BUD's *face.*
BUD: (*Slightly scared*) Oh, put the light on!
  (*As the light goes on a string of apples drops down in front of him.*)
  (*Recognizing the joke*) Oh, it's duck apple night!
  (*Laughter Cut to:*)

INT. LEAN-TO. LATE AFTERNOON

Close-up of BUD *behind lean-to window. Outside it is pouring with rain.*
Silence.
MOTHER: (*Voice over*) Come on Bud, we'll go the Hippy – Danny Kaye's on.
  (*Cut to:*)
BULLY: (*Voice over laughing*) I thought he was Povey.
  (*Cut to:*)

INT. KITCHEN. SUMMER EVENING

Left of BUD *so that* BUD *and* HELEN *fill frame.* HELEN *bends over sink as she shampoos her hair.*
Dissolve to:

INT. LEAN-TO. SUMMER EVENING

Mid three-quarter shot from back. HELEN *bent over sink, pans of water on window sill,* BUD *standing on a chair to* HELEN's *right.*
HELEN: OK, you can rinse it now, Bud.

(BUD *dips his finger into one of the pans. He pulls it out very quickly as the water is still too hot. He picks this pan up from the window sill and, giggling, pours it over* HELEN's *head.*)
HELEN: Oh, God blimey! It's scalding.
(BUD *laughs all the more and picks up another pan and quickly pours it over her head,* BUD *giggling uncontrollably.*)
HELEN: You little sadist!
(BUD *jumps down from chair and runs to kitchen.*
Cut to:)

INT. LEAN-TO. KITCHEN WINDOW. SUMMER EVENING

Close-up of BUD.
BUD: Can we go to second house, Titch?
(*Cut to:*)

INT. KITCHEN. SUMMER EVENING

Helen coming into close-up from BUD's *point of view drying her hair.*
HELEN: Oh give us a chance will you? I haven't looked at the *Echo* yet
 – what's on?
(*Cut to close-up of* BUD *at kitchen window.*)
BUD: Can we go and see 'Young at Heart'? It's on at the Forum.
HELEN: (*Voice over: pretending reluctance*) Oh – I suppose so.
BUD: Arh, thanks Titch!
HELEN: Go to Tyrers and get some sweets.
BUD: What sort?
HELEN: Oh – er – 'Misshapes' – the money's in me coat.
(*Pan left to right to wall then dissolve to:*)

INT. KITCHEN. LATE AFTERNOON

Pan left to right to side view mid-shot – BUD, MOTHER *and* HELEN. *They are de-lousing* BUD's *hair.*
Soundtrack over dissolve and pan.
HELEN: Are you ready?
BUD: Yer!
HELEN: Well get your coat on. We don't want to miss the beginning do we?
(*Cross-fade their voices.*)
BUD: (*As* HELEN *fine toothcombs his hair*) Arh! Ey, Mam!

HELEN: Keep still!
BUD: Arh, Titch!
   (*She starts to rub Lorexene into his hair.*)
BUD: Arh – it – stinks!
MOTHER: D'you prefer having nits?
BUD: No.
HELEN: Then you'll have to put up with the stink, won't you?
   (HELEN *continues combing nits out of his head.*)
MOTHER: The' are – all done.
   (*Cut to:*)

EXT. STREET. AFTERNOON

Close two-shot of the backs of the heads of two boys BUD *and his friend* ALBIE. *They are seen through the window of 'The Only Jones's' barber shop. Hold. The barber beckons them and they go into the main shop where the haircutting takes place. Crane down the window to where it is opaque then track left to right to the door of shop.*

ALBERT DRAKE *and* BUD *come out – short back and sides.* BUD *wets his fingers and touches* ALBIE *on the back of his neck.*

BUD: First wet Albie!
   (*They run off.*
   Cut to:)

INT. KITCHEN. LATE AFTERNOON

Shot of EDNA CLOTWORTHY, *the next-door neighbour. She is married to* CURLY *and they have two children.* EDNA *has a good sense of humour but gets terribly irritated with* CURLY *if he starts doing impressions of his favourite American film stars.*

She drinks tea.

HELEN: All right, Ed?
EDNA: Oh, I'm dead chokka! Cook, wash, clean – that's all I do – I never go anywhere. I'm like the bleeding Prisoner of Zenda.
   (*Looks at hands.*) Look at them hands – putrid!
   (*Her son* BILLY *aged eleven runs along hall and stands at kitchen door.*)
BILLY: My dad's coming, Mam.
EDNA: Tell him his tea's in the oven and I'll be in in a minute.
   (*He runs off.*

Cut to close-up of MOTHER *and* BUD. *They are having their tea, gentian violet on his right ear lobe.*)

MOTHER: Little Billy isn't half going like you, isn't he?

(*Cut to medium close-up of* EDNA.)

EDNA: I know – poor little swine – I mean you could chop wood with my face, couldn't you? God Blimey what nature has in store for us.

(CURLY *appears at kitchen door.*)

CURLY: Hello, girl!

EDNA: See what I mean?

(*Cut to three-shot of* MOTHER, BUD *and* HELEN. *Continue their tea.*)

HELEN: Still on the electric, Curly?

CURLY: No – I spewed it.

HELEN: Why?

(*Cut to two-shot of* CURLY *and* EDNA.)

EDNA: He didn't like the fella, did he?

MOTHER: (*Voice over*) How are you managing?

CURLY: (*Beating time to a song on the chair*) I'm doing foreigners.

EDNA: Thank Christ – otherwise we'd all be eating bleeding fuse wire.

(*Cut to close-up of* MOTHER.)

MOTHER: (*Indicating* CURLY) He's full of rhythm, isn't he?

(*Cut to two-shot of* EDNA *and* CURLY.)

EDNA: Yer – like St Vitus.

(CURLY *does an impression of famous Hollywood film star.*)

EDNA: (*Very irritable*) Oh don't start doing those bleeding stupid impressions!

(*Cut to Close-Up of* HELEN.)

HELEN: (*To* EDNA) Arh – he does them good though, doesn't he?

(*Cut to two-shot of* CURLY *and* EDNA.)

EDNA: Oh God blimey Helen, don't encourage him – if he thinks he's got an audience he'll do it all the more – I'm tormented enough now.

(CURLY *does a very good impression of Edward G. Robinson.*)

(*Really annoyed.*) Who's that supposed to be?

CURLY: Edward G. Robinson.

EDNA: Sounds more like bleeding Cardew Robinson.

(*Cut to three-shot of* BUD, MOTHER *and* HELEN. *They laugh.*

Cut to two-shot of EDNA *and* CURLY.)

EDNA: He does it just to annoy me you know. It doesn't half get on my nerves.

CURLY: Come on girl where's me scoff?

EDNA: It's in the oven – steak and onions.

CURLY: Oh, I had that last week.

EDNA: If you're not careful I'll hit you with it. Isn't it bleeding lively turning his nose up at steak and onions. Some poor bastards never get it. Oh tomorrow night it'll be dog food.

CURLY: Sounds – ruff.

(*Cut to three-shot of* BUD, MOTHER *and* HELEN. *They laugh. Cut to their point of view of* EDNA.)

EDNA: (*Smiling in spite of herself*) See what I've got to put up with? I should never have married. What the bleedin' hell did I ever see in you?

BILLY: (*Voice over*) Mam!

EDNA: (*Irritated*) What!

BILLY: (*Voice over*) I'm hungry!

EDNA: (*Really irritated*) Oh – eat someone!

(EDNA *and* CURLY *get up.*)

EDNA: I'll swing for those kids one of these days. (*To* CURLY.) Come on soft ollies – we'd better go.

CURLY: (*Stopping in the doorway. To* HELEN *and* MOTHER) Have you heard the latest? They're burying Catholics in Protestant cemeteries now – they're dead like.

EDNA: (*Smiling, long-suffering*) The next bus'll be along in a few minutes – be under it.

(*Cut to three-shot of* BUD, MOTHER *and* HELEN. *They laugh.*)

MOTHER: See *you*, Ed.

HELEN: T'ra, Curly!

(*Cut to:*)

INT. HALLWAY/KITCHEN. EARLY EVENING

Two-shot back view of CURLY *followed by* EDNA *going down hall.*

EDNA: ⎫
       ⎬ See yer! T'ra
CURLY: ⎭

EDNA: You need a shave.

CURLY: So do you.

(*Both laugh.*)

EDNA: Oh stop messing! Tant!

(*Cut to:*)

INT. KITCHEN. EARLY EVENING

Special effects: Three-shot side view of MOTHER, BUD *and* HELEN *finishing their tea.*
Pan right to left so that this group is on the edge of frame right. In the space left of them BUD *comes through the clinic doors.*
Pan or dissolve to:

INT. SCHOOL CLINIC. MORNING

Shot of BUD *coming through the double doors of the school clinic. He comes into close-up and stops. He has gentian violet where his right earlobe meets his cheek. He stands in the silence. Hold.*
Cut to: very wide shot of school clinic. It seems large and bare to BUD. *Eau de nil walls and brown lino. Right of frame the treatment cubicle inside which a* NURSE *moves. Left of frame a large highly polished refectory table. At the far end of it sits the* NURSE *who was inspecting the boys for lice,* BUD *walks into shot frame right and walks to the table and stops halfway down it, a few feet away from the* NURSE. *Silence as she writes, taking no notice of him. Hold.*
Cut to mid-shot of NURSE, BUD's *point of view; she is about fifty, bespectacled and intensely clean. White and all ice. Her voice is soft and cool. Pause.*
NURSE: (*Without ever looking at him*) Your card.
    (*Cut to mid-shot of* BUD *from* NURSE'S *point of view. He puts the card on the table and just looks at her. Hold. Silence.*
    Cut to BUD's *point of view of* NURSE.)
NURSE: (Looking at his card) Is it your ear again?
    (He doesn't answer.)
    I suppose you've been picking at it, haven't you?
    (*Cut to* NURSE's *point of view of* BUD. *He's too afraid to reply. He just stands there.*)
    (*Voice over*) What nasty little creatures you little boys are.
    (*Cut to:*)

EXT. SCHOOL PLAYGROUND. MORNING

Close shot of the three bullies dragging and punching BUD *into a secluded part of the school yard. Track quickly with them right to left. The whistle is heard. All activity stops.*
THIRD BOY: (*To* BUD) If you snitch we'll get you tonight!
    (*Cut to:*)

INT. MR NICHOLLS' CLASSROOM. MORNING

Medium wide shot of MR NICHOLLS *head-on at his desk. He is taking the geography lesson.*

MR NICHOLLS: (*Dictating from a textbook*) 'The Process of Erosion. Erosion is the cumulative effect of a great variety of processes …'
(*Cut to medium wide shot of classroom from* MR NICHOLLS *'point of view, head-on.* BUD *at the front desk of the second row. All the boys write quickly as* MR NICHOLLS *continues to dictate.*)

MR NICHOLLS: (*Voice over*) '… in general these can be divided into five groups …'
(*Cut to close-up of* MR NICHOLLS. *Pan with him right to left to blackboard at window.*)

MR NICHOLLS: (*Reads off blackboard*) '… 1. River Erosion.

2. Rain Erosion

3. Glacial Erosion.

4. Wind Erosion.

and

5. Marine Erosion.'

(*Cut to close-up of* BUD *at desk writing, head-on.*)

(*Voice over*) '… life also co-operates in the work of destruction,

1. Rivers and their valleys …'

(*Cut to:*)

INT. SWIMMING BATHS. MORNING

Close shot of the wooden doors of the cubicles running down the entire length of the pool. Suddenly the hand of the games master bangs open a door. BUD *half dressed, is startled and embarrassed.*

GAMES MASTER: Come on! Hurry up! We all know what you're trying to hide!
(*The rest of the doors open and boys come out.*
Cut to close shot of the water in the pool. Bodies splashing into and out of the water. BUD *comes wading gingerly into shot – scared of the water. Suddenly someone from beneath the water takes* BUD*'s legs from under him. He falls backwards into the water – terrified. Hold for a moment – all natural sound fades. Then crane down and over the placid surface of the pool. The water gently lapping.*)

Soundtrack (over and through dissolve): all in the pub singing 'Slow Boat to China'.
(*Dissolve to:*)

EXT. STREET PUB. NIGHT

Continue crane down.
Soundtrack of 'Slow Boat to China'.
Continue crane down to mid-wide shot of BUD, *back to camera, looking towards the pub.* BUD *stands centre frame in front of the pub door which is flanked by two large ornate windows. The pub is an ornate Victorian one – marble facings and elaborate carved, frosted glass windows, which read* 'Ind Coope Traditional Ales' 'Fine Wines and Spirits'. *People drift in and out.*
Soundtrack of the singing continues.
Applause, laughter.
BUD *walks towards the pub door. Track in on it with him and past him into back parlour.*
JOHN: (*Voice over doing a very bad impression of Jack Palance*)
  Who's this Curly? 'I am Attila-Attila the Hun'.
CURLY: (*Voice over*) Esther Williams.
  (*Laughter.*)
JOHN: (*Voice over*) You bastard!
KEVIN: (*Voice over*) Eh, Edna tell him to behave will you?
EDNA: (*Voice over*) I know – people have been strangled for less haven't they?
  (*By now* EDNA *and* CURLY *and all Bud's family can be seen at an end table near the door leading to the toilets. Continue tracking towards toilets.*)
CURLY: (*To* EDNA *who gets up*) Want a drink girl?
EDNA: In a minute – I'm just going for a twinkle.
CURLY: Say one for me.
EDNA: Oh, shut it!
  (*She goes into the ladies' toilet. Continue track into the darkness.*
  Hold on darkness.
  Dissolve to:)

INT. HALL. BUD'S HOUSE. NIGHT

Hold on darkness of the lean-to. Then track back into hall.
EDNA *comes through the door leading from the lean-to.*

EDNA: (*To* BUD – *putting her cold hands on either side of his face*) It's perishing out there!
(BUD *squeals and giggles. He runs and sits on the stairs.* EDNA *stops at the kitchen door.*)

CURLY: (*Singing and tipsy*) 'Civilization! Bongo! Bongo! Bongo!'

EDNA: (*Smiling in spite of herself*) Isn't that singing bleeding terrible? Like an ollie in a bottle.
(*Cut to:*)

INT. HALL. BUD'S HOUSE. NIGHT

Shot looking up the hall towards CURLY *who is standing with* JOHN *and* KEVIN *in front of the open vestibule – by the parlour.* CURLY *carries on singing.*

EDNA: (*Voice over*) Oh, choke him, somebody!
(*Cut to mid-wide shot of* CURLY's *point of view of* BUD – *amidst all the girls – on the stairs,* EDNA *is framed right at foot of stairs.*)

JEAN: (*To* CURLY) Now, Curly, behave yourself! Otherwise Edna'll give you forty lashes.

EDNA: (*To* CURLY) That'd be an incentive wouldn't it love?
(*Cut to shot looking up hall towards* CURLY. JOHN *and* KEVIN *go into parlour.*)

JOHN: (*To* CURLY) Have you got a bevvy Curly?

CURLY: You're all right, John, me Judy'll get me up one.
(*Cut to group shot with* EDNA *at the foot of the stairs.*)

EDNA: You've had enough. You can't have just one drink, you've got to get pallatic.
(*Cut to shot of* CURLY *by parlour door.*)

CURLY: (*Even tipsier – one too many*) Arh, go on girl – be nice nice to be nice – (*To himself*) People are people –
(*Cut to group shot with* EDNA *in close-up.*)

EDNA: Well they're not grapefruit are they? (*To girls*) God help him. He's in a world of his own.
(*Cut to mid-wide shot of* CURLY *at parlour door,* CURLY *does another impression,* EDNA *enters shot.*)
(*Irritated*) And don't start doing those stupid bleeding impressions – otherwise wooden overcoat – savvy?

CURLY: (As *Edward G. Robinson*) See here kid – !

EDNA: (*Pushing him into parlour, really annoyed*) Oh shut up! Bleeding screwball!

(*Cut to:*)

INT. PARLOUR. BUD'S HOUSE. NIGHT

Medium close-up two-shot of EDNA *and* CURLY. *She sits in a chair and he sits on the arm to her left.*
CURLY *sings 'When I Leave the World Behind'.*
   (*Laughter.*)
   (*Half-way through the first verse,* EDNA *begins to cry and* CURLY *slips his arm around her shoulder,* CURLY *sings second verse. All join in the chorus.*)
EDNA: (*Through tears*) That was my Mam's song, that.
CURLY: (*Hugging her*) Come on girl – you give us one.
   (EDNA *sings 'I Don't Know Why I Just Do'.*
   She gestures everyone to join in and they do so. Pan around room left to right past JOHN, KEVIN, JEAN, FRANCES, AMY *then finish on* MOTHER *in close-up by the fire.*
   All join in the song.
   Applause.)
MOTHER: Come on – our Bud now!
   (*Cut to wide shot – looking at the curtain which serves as a door for the parlour.*
   A guest draws the curtain back to camera left and BUD *and* HELEN *come in, singing 'A Couple of Swells'.*
   Big finish. Curtain drops. Applause.
   Cut to:)

EXT. STREET OUTSIDE BUD'S HOUSE. NIGHT

Medium close-up head-on from outside of BUD *and* HELEN *at the open parlour window – they lean out and look to their right towards the front door. Pan from them right to left.*
CURLY: (*Voice over*) Well you're always saying I never take you anywhere …
   (CURLY *and* EDNA *come out of the front door and into the street.*
   Pan with them.)
CURLY: … We'll go the Dance.
EDNA: The Grafton's for bits of kids – we're too old.
   (*Continue panning with them as they walk in front of the parlour window.*)
CURLY: You're as old as you feel.

EDNA: Look – you may think you're Peter Pan but I'm not bleeding Wendy. (*Determined.*) We're not going!

CURLY: (*Stopping in front of the parlour window*) Yes Edna. No Edna. Three bags full Edna. (*Suddenly realizing he has no jacket on.*) Eh, where's me jacket? It's cold.

(EDNA *trying to put his arms in the armholes.*)

Eh, what's happening?

EDNA: Get your arms in!

CURLY: My tiny hand is frozen.

EDNA: If it was any bigger it'd have frost-bite.

CURLY: (*Singing*) 'Oh you beautiful doll!
You great big beautiful doll …!'
(*Walks off frame left.*)

EDNA: Whatever you do, Helen, don't get married – you could end up with someone like this soft bastard –

(CURLY *continues to sing.*)

(*Walks after him*) Oh button it!

CURLY: (*Singing fades.*)

(*Cut to medium close-up head-on of* BUD *and* HELEN *at open window. They wave their good nights to* EDNA *and* CURLY *then* HELEN *disappears back into parlour,* BUD *stays at the window looking into the sky then down into the dark cellar.*

Pan down away from window and crane over the cellar steps and railings to the street. The railings are reflected on the pavement, splayed out. Hold. Dissolve to:)

EXT. STREET. DAY

Same camera position as above.
Sunday morning. Bright sunshine. Church bells.
Crane down to street level to two-shot of BUD *and his friend* ALBIE *standing on the cellar steps looking out through the railings. They seem fascinated by something.*
Cut to close-up of a man walking by on the opposite side of the street. He looks completely emaciated, his face and neck eaten away. He looks weary from pain. He seems to glide and drift painfully by.

ALBIE: (*Voice over*) That's Mr Yates.

(*Cut to two-shot head-on of* ALBIE *and* BUD. *They move away from the railings and sit down on the cellar steps.*)

ALBIE: (*Quietly*) He's got cancer.

(*Silence.*)

MOTHER: Come on Bud! Time for Mass.

BUD: OK, Mam! See you after, Albie.

ALBIE: OK.

(*They run up the steps.*
Cut to:)

INT. KITCHEN. DAY

Medium-wide shot of an upturned bike – resting on two chairs – fills the screen. KEVIN *– just wearing dungarees is centre frame.* BUD *is seen behind the wheel frame right. He is bored.* KEVIN *mends a puncture.*

BUD: Are you going to Cast Iron Shore, Kev?

KEVIN: No. Woolton Woods.

BUD: Can I come with you?

KEVIN: You haven't got a bike, Bud lad.

(*Silence.*)

BUD: Will you bring us some pears back, Kev?

KEVIN: Yer.

(*Silence.* KEVIN *takes a drink from a bottle of Double Diamond.*)

BUD: Can I have some of your drink, Kev?

KEVIN: You won't like it.

(BUD *drinks and makes a face.*)

BUD: Arh, it's horrible!

KEVIN: (*Laughing*) I told you you wouldn't like it.

(KEVIN *finishes and turns the pedals of the bike. The wheels spin and* BUD *is obliterated by them.*
Cut to:)

EXT. STREET. DAY

Sunday afternoon – bright sunshine.
Close-up of BUD *on doorstep, bored and lonely.*

BUD: Can't I come with you? Arh, go on! Let me!

(*Cut to wide shot from* BUD's *point of view of* FRANCES, JOHN, KEVIN, JEAN, HELEN *and some others, all on bikes. The group cycle up the street.*

Track with them. They disappear into the main road.)
BUD: (*Voice over, calling after them*) Don't forget the pears!
    (*Cut to close-up three-quarter side view of* BUD *on doorstep looking up the empty street. He walks down the step. Pan with him left to right as he trails his hand along the railings.*
Soundtrack:
BBC Radio's Rays A Laugh. *A last joke is heard. Laughter. Applause.*)
BBC RADIO ANNOUNCER: 'That was *Rays a Laugh* starring Ted Ray with Kitty Bluett, Kenneth Connor, Laidman Brown, Rosalind Knight, and Pat Coombes ...'
    (*Fade sound,* BUD *gets to the top of the cellar steps and stops. There is an iron bar which runs from just below the window sill to the railings. He looks at this bar for a moment then jumps.*
Dissolve to shot directly overhead of the cellar steps, BUD *swings on the bar. Hold.*
Soundtrack: the passing bell is heard.
Then still directly overhead crane and track away right to left from swinging BUD.
Dissolve to:)

INT. MR NICHOLLS' CLASSROOM. AFTERNOON

Continue craning and tracking right to left still directly overhead.
MR NICHOLLS: Get into line.
    (*The boys do so.*)
    Turn.
    (*The boys do so.*)
    Good night, boys.
BOYS: Good night, Sir.
MR NICHOLLS: Off you go.
    (*Soundtrack: Terry Thomas's voice over from 'Private's Progress'.*
The boys snake out. Continue craning and tracking directly overhead – right to left.
Dissolve to:)

INT. CINEMA. NIGHT

Continue craning and tracking right to left directly overhead. The projection light flickers over the heads of a full cinema audience. MOTHER *and* BUD *walk*

down the aisle and take seats at the end of the row. The aisle runs down centre of frame. Continue craning and tracking.
Soundtrack: Debbie Reynolds singing the title song 'Tammy' from the film Tammy and the Bachelor.
Dissolve to:

INT. CHURCH. DAY

Continue craning and tracking right to left directly overhead. The church is full. The congregation standing. The altar bell is rung three times. The congregation sinks to its knees.
CONGREGATION:
 Holy! Holy! Holy!
 Lord God of Hosts!
 Heaven and Earth are full of thy Glory!
 (*Continue craning and tracking.*
 Priest comes into shot. He elevates the host. The altar bell rings three times.
 Dissolve to:)

EXT. STREET. DAY

Continue craning and tracking right to left down street directly overhead. Crane and track comes to rest when the pavement and cellar outside BUD'S *house is reached.*
ALBIE *and another boy enter shot.*
Cut to close-up of BUD *head-on leaning out of front bedroom window watching* ALBIE *and another boy walk up street.*
Cut to:

INT. FRONT BEDROOM. DAY

Three-quarter back view of BUD *rushing from window to downstairs. Pan with him left to right.*
Cut to:

INT. HALLWAY. DAY

Shot of BUD *rushing downstairs and to front door. Pan with him right to left. He stops at the front door.*
Cut to:

EXT. STREET AND FRONT DOOR. DAY

Close-up of BUD *at door. He looks up the street after* ALBIE *and then looks crestfallen.*
Cut to:

EXT. STREET. DAY

Shot of ALBIE *and other boy disappearing down street from* BUD'S *point of view.*
Cut to:

INT. HALLWAY. DAY

Long shot of BUD *at the front door. He comes down the hall towards camera and into close-up – very dejected. He stops at kitchen door and looks towards his* MOTHER.
Cut to:

INT. KITCHEN. DAY

Close-up side view of MOTHER *at kitchen table rolling pastry. She is humming to herself. Silence.*
MOTHER: (*To* BUD) Aren't you going to the pictures?
  (*Cut to:*)

INT. HALLWAY. DAY

Close-up of BUD *–* MOTHER'S *point of view.*
BUD: I've got no one to go with.
  (*Cut to:*)

INT. KITCHEN. DAY

Close-up side view of MOTHER *–* BUD'*s point of view.*
MOTHER: What about Albie?
  (*Cut to:*)

INT. HALLWAY. DAY

Close-up of BUD *–* MOTHER'*s point of view.*
BUD: He's just gone past with John Hughes.
  (*Cut to:*)

INT. KITCHEN. DAY

Close-up (side view) of MOTHER – BUD's *point of view.*
MOTHER: Why don't you run after them and ask can you go with them?
   (*Cut to:*)

INT. HALLWAY. DAY

Close-up of BUD – MOTHER's *point of view. He shakes his head. Hold.*
Cut to:

INT. KITCHEN. DAY

Close-up of MOTHER – BUD's *point of view. She continues rolling pastry and humming softly to herself. Hold.*
Cut to:

INT. HALLWAY. DAY

Shot looking directly up the hall towards the front door, BUD *drifts towards the front door. He stops at it for a while then drifts into the street.*
Cut to:

EXT. STREET. LATE AFTERNOON

Low-angle shot of BUD *behind cellar railings. He looks up the street. Cut to* BUD'S *point of view. Low-angle shot of a coal cart being pulled by a horse. The horse and cart slop outside* BUD's *house. The coalman jumps down and secures the horse. He jumps back upon the cart to select a bag of coal for delivery.*
Cut to:

INT. CELLAR. LATE AFTERNOON

Wide shot of coal-hole (right of frame), cellar door (centre frame) and cellar window (left of frame): through it BUD *can be seen.*
BUD *moves away from the railings and moves down the cellar steps towards the cellar door – which is closed.*
Special effects: the coalman lifts up the iron lid which covers the coal-hole. Simultaneously the cellar door opens of its own accord. A shaft of conical light comes pouring through the coal-hole, BUD *just stands there – trance-like – looking into the quiet, dark cellar. Then the coalman delivers a rush of coal. Black dust billows out of the coal – hole, the sound of the unloading coal*

getting louder and louder and huge black clouds of coal dust gradually filling the cellar, BUD *continues just to stand there.*

Through the coal dust the shaft of light is just discernible then the coal-hole lid is slammed back on – like a door shutting – a tomb. BUD *continues to stand there – terrified – as black coal dust silently fills the silent, dark cellar. Soundtrack: Jean Simmons' voice over from* Great Expectations.

'He's just a boy. A common labouring boy ...'

(BUD *starts coming into the cellar towards the camera. He is crying uncontrollably. He moves past the camera.*

Dissolve to:)

EXT. CELLAR. LATE AFTERNOON

Wide shot of cellar from cellar door.
BUD, *his back to camera, looking into, being consumed by, the black coal dust. He disappears from view. Silence. The coal dust is still billowing out. Soundtrack: Martita Hunt's voice over from* Great Expectations.
BUD: (*Voice over, crying uncontrollably*) Mam! Mam! It's dark in here!

(*His crying fades.*

Soundtrack: laughter is heard from decades ago.

It fades. Silence.

The black clouds of coal dust begin to disperse and the cellar is empty and quiet and derelict. It is now night. Plaster and powder fall, then all is silence. Then pan around to cellar door and crane up – simultaneously – through the derelict house.

Soundtrack:)

BUD: (*Voice over*) What did you get for Christmas, Albie?
ALBIE: (*Voice over*) A cowie outfit and a Bren gun.
BUD: (*Voice over*) Our Kevin bought me a watch.

(*As crane rises to front door level, everywhere is derelict.*

BUD *and* ALBIE *are seated on the front step, their backs to camera, and are in silhouette. They are shining their torches up into the night sky. They are silent with just the torchlight.*

Crane past them to the sky along the line of the torchlight. The light from the torches raking the night sky – a sky full of sudden clouds and crystal clear dark blue/black.)

BUD: (*Voice over*) Some of those stars are dead – the light from them started out when Jesus was alive …
(*Pause.*)
ALBIE: (*Voice over*) How d'you know?
BUD: (*Voice over*) Our teacher said …
(*Crane comes to rest on a wide shot of the night sky.*)
Soundtrack: the crackle of radio waves heard from deep space.)
TEACHER: (*Voice over, still dictating*) '4. Wind Erosion. The waters of the seas readily respond by movement to the brushing of the wind over the surface; to the variations of temperature and salinity; to the gravitational attraction of the moon and sun and to the coriolis force. A. Tides and Currents …'
(*Fade his voice.*
Soundtrack: his voice fades back into the crackle of radio waves heard from deep space. The torches continue to rake the night sky. Hold on sky.
Soundtrack:)
MOTHER: (*Voice over*) Come on lad! Down the Red Lane!
BUD: (*Voice over*) OK, Mam.
HELEN, JOHN, KEVIN: (*Voice over*) Happy Christmas, Bud.
MOTHER: (*Voice over*) Happy Christmas, lad.
BUD: (*Voice over*) Happy Christmas, Mam.
(*The torchlight fades.*
Soundtrack: the radio waves crackling fades.
Hold on sky. Some white clouds scud across the night sky. All is silence.
Then soundtrack: a four-part choir singing a cappella, 'The Long Day Closes' by Arthur Sullivan.)

> 'No star is o'er the lake
> Its pale watch keeping
> The moon is half awake
> Through gray mist creeping
> The last red leaves fall round
> The porch of roses
> The clock has ceased to sound
> The long day closes …'

(*Hold on sky. The sky continues to change.*
Soundtrack:)

> 'Sit by the silent hearth

> In calm endeavour
> To count the sounds of mirth
> Now dumb forever
> Heed not how hope believes
> And fate disposes
> Shadow is around the eaves
> The long day closes … '

(*Hold on sky. The sky continues to change. Soundtrack:*)

CHOIR: 'The lighted windows dim
> Are fading slowly
> The fire that was so trim
> Now quivers lowly
> Go to the dreamless bed
> Where grief reposes
> Thy book of toil is read
> The long day closes …'

(*Hold on the sky. It continues to change. Soundtrack:*)

CHOIR: 'Go to the dreamless bed
> Where grief reposes
> Thy book of toil is read
> Thy book of toil is read
> Go to the dreamless bed
> The long day closes.'

(*The radio waves are heard from deep space. Fade to black.*)

OF TIME AND THE CITY (2008)

Of Time and the City (2008): 'The Long Walk' (© Bernard Fallon, 1969).

Crew of *Of Time and the City* includes:

Written and Directed by	Terence Davies
Narrator	Terence Davies
Producers	Solon Papadopoulos
	Roy Boulter
Archive Producer	Jim Anderson
Director of Photography	Tim Pollard
Editor	Liza Ryan-Carter
Music Director	Ian Neil

A Hurricane Films (2008) production with:
Digital Departures / Liverpool Culture Company / BBC Films / Northwest Vision and Media / Merseyside Film and Television Fund / Northwest Regional Development Agency / Regional Attraction Fund / UK Film Council.

IMAGE	SOUND
Philharmonic screen rising. (*Consolation No.3 In D Flat Major – Franz Liszt*) Track into screen, as lights change colour on curtain.	Into my heart an air that kills from yon far country blows: What are those blue remembered hills, What spires, what farms are those? That is the land of lost content, I see it shining plain, The happy highways where I went And cannot come again. (*From:* 'A Shropshire Lad, Poem 40 – *A. E Housman*)
Images appear on the screen – Overhead railway. Title – 'Of Time and the City'. Image on screen, looking down on the Overhead Railway. Fade into the image. Various shots of railway.	I met a traveller from an antique land who said: two vast and trampless legs of stone stand in the desert … And on the pedestal these words appear: My name is Ozymandias, King of Kings, look on my works he mighty and despair! Nothing besides remains. Round the decay of that colossal wreck, boundless and bare, the lone and level sands stretch, far… away. (*Excerpt:* 'Ozymandias' – *Shelley*)

IMAGE	SOUND
	If Liverpool did not exist, it would have to be invented (*Myrbach*)
Enter tunnel and into darkness. Darkness.	
Emerge from darkness, and the tunnel, into Liverpool. (*Music for the Royal Fireworks - George Frideric Handel*)	
St. George's Hall. Portico. Engravings. Front columns. SPQL on door. Inside the Great Hall.	
Track to Organ.	We love the place we hate, then hate the place we love. We leave the place we love, then spend a lifetime trying to regain it.
	Come closer now, and see your dreams, Come closer now and see mine.
Fade to Altar at Sacred Heart.	No meat on Friday, confession on Saturday, emerging cleansed and pleasing to God. Mass on Sundays and Holy days of obligation.
Fade to religious painting.	Despite my dogged piety, no great revelation came, no divine

IMAGE	SOUND
Fade to statue of Jesus and Mary, with candles in front. Fade to religious triptych. Fade to Altar.	balm to ease my soul, just years wasted in useless prayer. If I pray long enough I will be forgiven, if I am forgiven I will be made whole, all I'll need then is the girl. Suddenly I knew, suddenly I thought, it's all a lie, paradise betrayed, there was no God, only Satan sauntering behind me with a smirk saying 'I'll get you in the end'.
Fade to petals falling past camera in the Alma de Cuba. Various shots of church converted into a bar (Alma de Cuba).	'Tu Es Petrus' – you're a brick Pete. Here people married. Here people died and were buried. In deconsecrated Catholic churches, now made into restaurants as chic as anything abroad.
Shots of the bar.	Now the congregation can eat and drink in the sight of God. Who will no doubt disapprove of cocktails in Babylon. Is this happiness, is this perfection?
Fade to shots of people walking circa 1970s.	As you are now, we once were. (*James Joyce*)

IMAGE	SOUND
Fade to Bernard Fallon tugboat photo. B&W.	They that go down to the sea in ships and that do business in great waters, these see the works of the Lord and his wonders of the deep.
(*Protecting Veil – John Tavener*)	Anno Domini.
B&W. Cut to boat moving along the water. B&W. Various shots of packed ferry, docking, people getting off. B&W. People playing at lido and the beach in New Brighton.	Removed from the sight of happier classes, poverty may struggle along as it can – (*Friedrich Engels*)
B&W. Getting back on board the ferry. Fade to shot of a packed football crowd.	*Fade in Radio broadcast of football results.* Preston North End 2, Blackpool 3. Everton 2, West Ham United 0, Leicester City 0, Leeds United 2. Manchester United 3, Nottingham Forrest 1.
B&W. Footage of the 1955 FA Cup Final. B&W. End of match. Players shake hands. Shots of the crowd.	On slow Saturdays, when football like life was still played in black and white, and in shorts as long as underwear. When it was still not venal, when sports men and woman knew how to win and lose with grace, and never to punch the air in victory. Match over, pea soup made, my mother calling from the kitchen, my eldest brother listening to the

IMAGE	SOUND
	football results in front of the bakelite radio, marking his coupon hoping to win millions. Accrington Stanley, Sheffield Wednesday, Hamilton Academicals, Queen of the South.
B&W. Fade to Sefton Park. Various shots around the park.	
	And on even slower Sundays when it felt as if the whole world was listening to the light programme, Kenneth Horne, promptly at two o'clock, and long before the repeal of the Sexual Offences Act would regularly visit two of his very special friends…
	(*Radio archive – Round The Horne.*) (*Slang*)
B&W. Sefton Park lake.	*Kenneth Horne: … I was recommended to a fashionable firm of solicitors in Lincoln's Inn, the brass plate on the door read 'Bona Law' (Laughter).* *Kenneth Horne: Hello anybody there?* *Julian: Oh hello, I'm Julian and this is my friend Sandy. I've got me articles and he's taken silk… frequently. Well Mr Horne how nice of you to varder your dolly old eek again, oh what brings you trolling in here?* *Kenneth Horne: Can you help me? I've erred.*

IMAGE	SOUND
	Julian: Yes we've all 'eard, ducky.
Sandy: I mean its common knowledge, isn't it Julian?
Kenneth Horne: Will you take my case?
Julian: Well it depends on what it is, we've got a criminal practice that takes up most of our time (laughter).
Kenneth Horne: Yes, but apart from that.
Julian: Oh, ain't he bold! (laughter).
B&W. Fade to the Ritz cinema. (*Hooray for Hollywood* – Benny Goodman and his Orchestra)

Premiere. Lights.
Crowds. Stars arriving. | But the law proscribed and was anything but tolerant, as when, contemporaneously, two gay men were arrested and convicted, and were to be made an example of, and the judge said to them before he was passing sentence, 'not only have you committed an act of gross indecency but you did it under one of London's most beautiful bridges.'

Pathe News Reel.
V/O: Showplace of the North, the Ritz Theatre, Birkenhead, again, presents a replica Royal film performance. |
| Stars talking and joking on stage. | (*'Hooray for Hollywood'* – Benny Goodman and his orchestra). |

IMAGE	SOUND
	At seven I saw Gene Kelly in *Singin' in the Rain*, and discovered the movies, loved them, and swallowed them whole.
Last shot of the Ritz cinema with the spotlights spinning in the sky.	And my love was as muscular as my Catholicism, but without any of the drawbacks. Musicals, melodramas, Westerns, nothing was too rich or too poor, for my rapacious appetite and I gorged myself with a frequency that would shame a sinner.
B&W. Fade to wrestling ring, a fight is in action.	
	But soon darker pleasures, at fifteen, I saw Dirk Bogarde in *Victim*, and discovered something entirely different.
B&W. A masked wrestler looms in the ring.	And when I was not at the movies, on Friday nights I was at the Liverpool Stadium watching the wrestling. Not for its pantomimic villainy, but for something more illicit, and in short, I was afraid. As I struggled with my adolescent desires, as I waited at the top of the aisle as the wrestlers swaggered up from the ring, their trunks tight across the buttocks, I could feel their body heat as I furtively touched a back or a thigh, choking with schoolboy guilt and trembling with the fear of the wrath of God.

IMAGE	SOUND
B&W. Fade to a track across the religious stations in Sacred Heart church. (*Beata Viscera* – Andrew Pickett)	Oh save me from those dark desires which thrill and compel. The world, the flesh, and the devil.
B&W. Wide shot, track across Altar in Sacred Heart. B&W. Cut to a painting of Christ's face, lit by candles underneath. B&W. Face of a young boy in church. A nun. Cut to a cityscape full of smoking chimneys.	Caught between canon and the criminal law, I said goodbye to my girlhood. Here I wept, wept and prayed, until my knees bled, but no succour came, no peace granted. Here was my whole world; home, school, the movies, and God. You who damn, but give no comfort. Why do I plead? Why do you not respond Angel Eyes? Jesus mercy, Mary help, lull me to safety.
Cut to: trains in action. People on trains. Travelling. Disembarking. City life beginning to stir into action.	Between sleeping and waking, earth does not revolve, and slow turns a life of meagre timbre, of dullest breath.
B&W. People starting there days, walk past the Liver buildings. Various shots of the city continue.	Between birth and dying, some lovely moments grow, and sorrows (not known until tomorrow) cloud the happy hours spent dreaming in the sun.

IMAGE	SOUND
	Between joy and consolation, no easy path … some flights of fancy, some colour, (glorious old Hollywood), small comic England (black and white).
	Between loving and hating, the real journey starts, let go the latter, embrace the former, then fall to heaven on a gentle smile.
B&W: Cut to: two women walk along with their bags of washing perched on their heads.	Between waking and sleeping, the earth resumes its turn, the soft light fills the room, the nightly demons perish from the bed, and all humanity braves another day.
Shots inside the washhouse.	('Untitled' – TD)
Woman walks back along street, washing on top of her head.	Audio archive: WOMAN: *We used to help one another out, and go the washhouse. Do washin' for anyone, careful – nursing them if they're sick.*
B&W. Two ships on the Mersey. Worker on ship loading bananas.	*And then, of course, my Mother died, on Christmas Eve, and she left me at fourteen, a little baby twelve months old, and another one, erm,*
Wall daubed with the graffiti: 'God bless Fr Maxwell'.	*four. Me dad stayed with us eight weeks, and then he got a ship and went away and left us, so of course, he died after, y'know. Then I had*
('*Dirty Old Town*' – *The Spinners*)	*more trouble on me plate like, me*

IMAGE	SOUND
B&W. Cut to: Montage: various shots of the city. Trains going along the tracks. Liver buildings. Ships. Hustle and bustle of the city. Cars, buses, people.	*husband never ever got much work and I had to work all me life, but thank God, God's been very good to me, and his Holy Mother.*
Cars entering Mersey tunnel.	
A bonfire goes on. People with torches light the bonfire.	
Children gather round and watch the fire.	
The bonfire burns; fireworks are set off, people smile and laugh.	The year moves towards November, Bonfire Night, a penny for the Guy, someone singing, "Keep the Home Fires Burning".
	As Jimmy Preston and me, the only ones left now, roast potatoes on sticks. We sit, quiet at the last, Jimmy Preston who was a real boy, and whom I envied, Jimmy Preston who once put his hand on my shoulder and I didn't want him to remove it.
Fade to black.	
	Don't go in just yet, please, not just yet. But he does.
B&W. A wide cityscape, down a sloping, terraced street. Track along a terraced street. Empty streets and playgrounds as dawn breaks. Milk is delivered on the step. An elderly woman lights the fire.	"Twilight and evening bell, and after that the dark". (*Tennyson*)

IMAGE	SOUND
Scenes of life in the home. Mum cooking, dad shaving, children stirring in bed. Women scrub the front step, clean windows. Young girls sing and play.	('Watch and Pray' – Angela Gheorghiu)
Boys on the playground play a 'dip' between each other. Women scrub and work in the washhouse. Men work in the street. People on the streets. Children play in the playground.	
Young boy swings from a lamppost. Various shots of children playing.	GIRLS SINGING: *Good bye Betty while you're away, send me a letter to tell me that you're better. . Good-bye Betty, and while you're away, and don't forget you're old pal Anne. Good-bye Anne while you're away, send me a letter to tell me that you're better. Good-bye Anne, and while you're away, don't forget you're old pal Pat.*
B&W: Cut to: A woman walking and looking into shop windows. Old lady walks down the street.	CHILD SINGS: *He bought me a shawl of red, white, and blue. And when we got married he tore it in two. Oh gee I love him, I can't deny it, I'll be with him wherever he goes…* Audio archive:

IMAGE	SOUND
B&W. Cut to: Hands folded into a lap. An old woman sits and looks. Fade to young girls smiling. Shots of streets.	WOMAN: *I would have liked to have worked on but they threw me out, because I was old. It's a sin to grow old you know. We had an old lady here, and erm, she, everybody would run and get her a cup of tea, and they'd wait on her, and do all those little things, but she'd always say "nobody wants me". Well, I mean, if you take that attitude you can't expect anyone to want you, can you?*
B&W. Cut to: Christmas holly in close-up. A woman picks out a turkey from a shop-front. Children play with fruit.	Oh watch and pray, watch and pray. Do you remember, you who are no longer young, and you who still are, do you remember the months of November and December? Wet shoes and leaking galoshes, and for the first time, chilblains, with Christmas in the air. God was in his heaven, and oh, how I believed, oh, how fervent I was. And on Christmas Eve, pork roasting in the oven, the parlour cleaned, with fruit along the sideboard. A pound of apples, tangerines in tissue paper, a bowl of nuts, and our annual, exotic pomegranate.
People hustle round shop displays, eyeing the goods.	Do you remember? Do you? Will you ever forget?

IMAGE	SOUND
Shots of cinema fronts. Neon signs identifying each cinema by name.	*Archive Audio:* (*Laughter*) *Happy days.*
Cut to: A wintry park. Snow covered trees and roads.	My mother, generous with her small nest-egg of twenty-five pounds, borrowed from the 'Leigh and Lend'. Love and cellophane. My brothers with their made-to-measure suits, bought on HP, my sisters and a dab of scent, maybe only 'Evening in Paris', but making it seem as if the whole world was drenched in Chanel. Being taken to the pictures and in all those movies, it was always Christmas, and it was always perfect.
Snow covered buildings. Cut to: Gunships blazing as they fire. ('*He Ain't Heavy, he's my brother*' – The Hollies) Soldiers march in driving snow. Montage of war scenes. Colour. Soldiers on parade. Gates of Buckingham Palace. B&W. Various shots of street parties.	*Seven Brides for Seven Brothers, Young at Heart, All That Heaven Allows*, but all, all are gone, the old familiar faces. And yet, time renders, deceive the eye, deceive the heart. A valediction and an epitaph. Now voyager, go forth, to seek and find. But my eldest brother, lying in an army hospital in Leamington Spa, He will not go to war, he will be safe. Cometh the hour, cometh the man, cometh the Korean War.

IMAGE	SOUND
Colour. Scenes of the Coronation. The Queen in an extravagant horse-drawn carriage.	For Queen, country, and the civil list. And yet all over the country street parties were held to celebrate the start of The Betty Windsor Show.
	When the golden couple married in 1947, the following was lavished on the ceremony; jewellery from other Royals, a washing machine, a fridge, 76 handkerchiefs, 148 pairs of stockings, 38 handbags, 16 nightgowns, 500 cases of tinned pineapple, 10,000 telegrams, 2000 guests, 5 Kings, 7 Queens, 8 Princes, and 10 Princesses. And for the 10,000 pearls sewn onto her wedding dress, Her Majesty allegedly saved all her clothing coupons.
Colour. The Coronation ceremony proceeds down the aisle. Colour. Marching soldiers.	Even more money was wasted on her coronation, as yet another fossil monarchy justified its existence by 'tradition', and deluded itself with the notion of
More Coronation footage. B&W. Queen waves from a balcony.	'duty', privileged to the last, whilst in England's green and pleasant land the rest of the nation survived on rationing in some of the worst slums in Europe.
B&W. The 21 hose salute in Scotland.	And in bonny Scotland, they gave Her Majesty a 21 hose salute – or maybe they were just taking the piss.

IMAGE	SOUND
	After Korea, EOKA, and Mau-Mau, India had gone, soon Africa would go, then Suez as a last hurrah, leaving only a fading memory of when most of the globe was red, and Victoria was the first and only diminutive bourgeoisie imperatrix.
B&W. Shawlie and Husband (Bernard Fallon).	Betty and Phil with a thousand flunkies.
	The trouble with being poor is that it takes up all your time – Willem DeKooning.
	The trouble with being rich is that it takes up everybody else's.
	After farce, realism.
B&W. Cut to: Photo of women standing on front step. (*'Folks Who Live On the Hill'* – Peggy Lee) Montage of people. Derelict and broken down housing. Children vandalising. Houses being knocked down.	The heart that beats beneath the heart is tender, is not savage. It beats, in time though years apart from struggles silent marriage, of storm and stress, of quiet love, as when the lights begin to fall and he just smiles, or she just hums a tune that fitted like a glove, that tapped its rhyme, still and small into their room, when nightfall thrums a kind of peace, that soothes the heart and lets the years fall from nought and down,

IMAGE	SOUND
Long Walk' (Bernard Fallon photo).	as they shuffle off to bed, apart, then meet again beneath the Eiderdown.
New roads, tower blocks, suburbs.	(Cocoa – TD)
B&W. Stormy waters crash against the pier.	
B&W. Beatles sing on stage.	
(*Hippy Hippy Shake Shake* – *Swinging Blue* Jeans)	
B&W. Cut to: Crowds of fans screaming and waving.	By the waters of Babylon, there we sat down, yea we wept when we remembered Zion, and they that carried us away captive, required of us a song, saying, sing us one of the songs of Zion. But how shall we sing in a strange land?
Beatles struggling through hordes of fans.	Yeah, yeah, yeah, yeah.
B&W. Police struggle to contain crowd. People pass out. The Beatles wave from a balcony.	And in an era when pop music was still demure, before Presley,

IMAGE	SOUND
(*Elizabethan Serenade* – Ronald Binge)	before the Beatles; John, Paul, George, and Ringo, not so much a musical phenomenon, more like a firm of provincial solicitors.
B&W. People queue to enter the Cavern Club. Dancing inside. A band plays on stage. People dance.	When they are given the freedom of the City, Teddy Johnson and Pearl Carr, Dicky Valentine, Lita Rosa, Alma Cogan, sedate British pop was screamed away on a tide of Merseybeat – and the witty lyric, and the well crafted love song seeming as antiquated as antimacassars or curling tongs.
People dancing in the Cavern and similar clubs. Cut to:	After the rise of rock and roll, my interest in popular music waned and as it declined, my love of classical music increased, Sibelius, Shostakovich, and my beloved Bruckner.
Elegant hall with people ballroom dancing in synch.	Then in my overwrought adolescent state of mind, I discovered Mahler, and responded completely to his every overwrought note. And in classical music they had such
Dancers finish in perfect position.	wonderful foreign names; Amy Shuard, Otto Klemperer, Elizabeth Schwarzkopf, Annalisa Rottenberger. Furtwangler and
Cut to: Young girls in a circle clap and play singing games.	Munch, Knapperts Busch and Gauk, Robert Merrill and Jussi Bjorling "The Pearl Fishers".

IMAGE	SOUND
Cut to: A football crowd clapping and chanting. Cut to: People in umbrellas queue at Aintree racecourse. Horses line up.	But there was still ballroom dancing, as staid as a funeral parlour, hectares of tulle, brylcream, and the fish-tail. Accompanied by Victor Silvester and his famous orchestral whine, as thin as a two-step, as quick as a foxtrot.
The race commences. People watch through binoculars. Race continues.	V/O: A thousand-throng Aintree racecourse for the biggest event in the steeple-chasing world, the Grand National. Even umbrella weather won't stop the crowds coming to this almost legendary racing classic…
The race finishes, crowds surround the winner.	All of Britain listened to the Grand National on radios as small and brown as Hovis, made bets, off-course and absolutely illegal, but it was only once a year and a shilling win, so where was the harm? Sundew, ESB, Early Mist. Even mum opened her purse, for her annual little flutter and said, I really fancy Quare' Times – each way. *Radio commentary.*
Cut to: The Orange Lodge parade.	Bob Danvers-Walker, the voice of British Pathe, Michael

OF TIME AND THE CITY

IMAGE	SOUND
	O'Hehir, Peter O'Sullevan, the voices of racing, listening to their controlled excitement pouring through the wireless.
	Radio commentary – And Quare' Times who cost his owner only three hundred guineas, wins the National.
Cut to: B&W. Children out playing together on a long terraced street.	Mum, smiling at her small win, and those who've lost think, well there's always next year. God willing.
Girl skips along an empty road by herself. Two boys stand, looking glum. Children play in a puddle.	The twelfth of July and the Orange Day Parade through the city, winding their way towards Exchange Station and Southport, to toast King Billy in a perrouque, and say 'fuck the pope, and all those Fienian bastards' – whatever, whoever they were. And on the train coming home, slightly the worse for wear, howling at the papist moon.
Shots of fairs, fetes, jumble sales, and races.	But no religious divide in my street, just quiet acceptance that Catholics did everything in mysterious Latin, while protestants sang 'Jesus Wants me

IMAGE	SOUND
	for a Sunbeam', in plain, no-nonsense English.
Fête.	Although sometimes it felt as if one's entire world was one long Sunday afternoon. Nothing to do, nowhere to go.
	Then mum or one of my sisters would say, "lets have a day out next week", and the ensuring seven days were streaked and gilded.
B&W. Masses of people wait to board the ferry.	But you still had to wait. Those days, queuing was De Rigeur, queuing modestly for modest entertainment at the local fete, in posh parts of the city, like Stoneycroft, where they sounded their 'Hs' and knew what 'sculleries' were.
Colour. People disembark the ferry.	A jumble sale, a fancy dress parade, a foot race, with someone collapsing of heat-stroke because the temperature rose a couple of degrees above freezing.
Colour. Montage of beach scenes.	The scouts, darts, and a May Queen crowned, a nation deprived of luxury relishing these small delights. Decorated prams and bicycles, a smattering of applause, all the fun of the fair.

IMAGE	SOUND
	So, to New Brighton, only ferry ride away, but happiness on a budget.
Colour. Beauty competition goes on.	They board in black and white…
	Then disembark in colour, for things were changing.
	World War Two was over, peacetime and hardship eased.
Various New Brighton footage.	And all day on the beach, completely unsupervised, with no factor two hundred sun block, and safe as houses, little baby Joyce – Tarquin, and Gemma being as yet, unknown.
	Stiff at joy time with Aunty Lil'.
	Bathing beauty competitions, in their day harmless, now as quaint as the bustle, now as unacceptable as Chinese foot-binding.
The fairground lights spin against the night sky. (The House Band – *Paul Baile, Jacques Degraine*)	Pretty young women being kissed by the Lord Mayor, given a sash, a trophy, and some small modest fame, and oh, how we laughed.
	A stroll along the prom, deck chairs and the Floral Clock, sand in the egg sandwiches, tea at three, then a snooze.

IMAGE	SOUND
	New Brighton rock as sweet as sick, and gobstoppers that would last until your middle age.
Colour. The sun slowly sets over New Brighton pier.	A ride or two, then the miniature railway, then maybe to the dance, maybe a jive, maybe a gin and orange, and maybe love.
(*Concertino for Guitar and Orchestra in A Minor Opus 72 – Bacarisse*)	Kiss me quick and roll me over, announce an engagement, plan a wedding, taffeta skirts and blue serge, youth that cannot end and hopes as high as Blackpool Tower, when all the world was young and knew no bounds.
Colour. Cut to: Driving through terraced streets. People on the streets, kids playing, etc. Children playing in tower blocks.	
Colour. Montage: deprived and rundown areas. Shabby tower blocks. Graffiti. Derelict and vandalised housing.	Then, the journey home, tired, cocoa and toast – and happiness unlimited.
People in snow. Kids play on rope swing. Poor area, in the shade of the Catholic Cathedral.	The golden moments pass and leave no trace – Chekhov.
Colour. Priests walk up the steps of the Cathedral and enter.	We had hoped for paradise, we got the Annus Mundi.

OF TIME AND THE CITY

IMAGE	SOUND
Various shots of the Cathedral's inauguration. (*Symphony No.2 in C minor "Resurrection"* – Mahler)	Rise, oh rise, oh surely thou shalt rise.
Colour. Cut to: Various images of people. Liver Buildings. Tug boats coming into dock. Building work. Rundown areas.	But not before the opening of the Metropolitan Cathedral of Christ the King, inaugurated by Cardinal Heenan in his brand new frock. The Vatican's response to Schiaparelli. I had lived my spiritual and religious life under Popes Pious the Twelfth, John the Twenty-Third, and Clitoris the Umpteenth, which is enough to turn anyone pagan. As far as I knew Holy Mother church still wanted me, but I no longer wanted her, for I was now a very happy, very contented, born again atheist. Thank God, Oh Come All Ye Faithful have another plateful.
Colour. Grim tower block.	
(*Brahms' Wiegenlied – Jennifer John*) Colour. Various shots around the industrial area of the docks.	
B&W. Cut to: Still – warehouse workers caught in a shaft of light.	
Cut to: Colour. Modern recreation of Overhead Railway footage.	Municipal architecture dispiriting at the best of times but when combined with the British genius for creating the dismal makes for a cityscape that is anything but Elysian.

IMAGE	SOUND

	Out to sea the dawn wind wrinkles and slides, I am here or elsewhere.
	…
	    in my end is my beginning.
	    (*T. S. Eliot, excerpts from 'Four Quartets'*)
	
	We meet our destiny on the road we take to avoid it – Carl Jung.
	
	I said to my soul be still, and let the dark come upon you
	Which shall be the darkness of God.
	…
	I said to my soul be still, and wait without hope,
	For hope would be hope for the wrong thing;
	wait without love,
	For love would be love of the wrong thing: there is yet faith but the faith and the love and the hope are all in the waiting.
	…
	The rest is not our business.
	At the still point of the turning world.
	
	Suspended in time between pole and tropic.
	
	And all is always now.

OF TIME AND THE CITY

IMAGE	SOUND
	Home is where one starts from, as we grow older The world becomes stranger, the pattern more complicated Of dead and living. There is a time for the evening under starlight, A time for the evening under lamplight,
(*Dolly Suite*, Op. 56, No. I. "Berceuse" – Fauré)	(the evening with the photograph album), Love is most nearly itself When here and now cease to matter. (*T. S. Eliot, excerpts from 'Four Quartets'*)
Colour. Modern Liverpool. Wind farm in Mersey. People, children in prams in city centre. Williamson Square, etc. Men drinking in pub, laughing.	I said to my soul be still, and accept this my chanson d'amour, for all that has passed, but where oh where are you, the Liverpool I
(*Symphony No.2 in C minor "Resurrection"* – Mahler) Cut to: Colour. Sefton Park Palm House, modern day. Various shots of the Palm House. Plaque, 'Olive and Bob Dryhurst – If wishes could be granted and dreams really could come true…xx'	knew and loved, where have you gone without me? And now I am an alien in my own land. Oh Tempora, oh Mores. Oh the times, oh the fashions. Tread gently stranger as you softly turn the key, to unlock time and cause the years to fall towards their end. Speak low love, but speak wisely for frail time hangs by a thread above the world with only

IMAGE	SOUND
Peter Pan Statue. Cut to: Colour. Modern footage of the Catholic Cathedral. The Three Graces. Modern aerial footage of Liverpool city centre. Liver buildings, etc. Container ships, docks.	hope to keep us safe. Tap lightly at the door, then close it with a silent shock, but never ever yield to the night. We shall return with hope to the good earth, and you my dear children, you are the earth.
Modern footage continues. Night time on the busy streets of Liverpool bars and clubs.	But, I reason, earth is short – And anguish – absolute – And many hurt, But what of that? I reason, we could die – The best Vitality Cannot excel Decay, But, what of that? I reason that in heaven – Somehow it will be even – Some new equation given – But what of that? (*Emily Dickinson*) We shall not cease from exploration, And the end of all our exploring Will be to arrive where we started And to know the place for the first time,

IMAGE	SOUND
	Through the unknown, remembered gate, When the last of earth left to discover Is that which was the beginning; … A condition of complete simplicity (costing not less than everything) And all shall be well, and All manner of thing shall be well.. (*T. S. Eliot, excerpts from 'Four Quartets'*)
Cut to: Colour. Mother and child in street. Sun sets over Mersey.	If all the world and love were young, And truth in every shepherd's tongue these pretty pleasures might me move To live with thee and be thy love. But time drives flocks from field to fold, When rivers rage, and rocks grow cold And Philomel becometh dumb;
Modern shots of Sefton Park, with sunset.	The rest complains of cares to come.
(Symphony No.2 in C minor "Resurrection" – Mahler – resumes)	The flowers do fade, and wanton fields To wayward winter reckoning yields: A honey tongue, a heart of gall, Is fancy's spring, but sorrows' fall.

IMAGE	SOUND
B&W. Montage of old Liverpool. Old footage of St George's Hall. Colour. Various old footage of ships. Statues outside St. George's Hall. Colour. Cut to: Modern St. George's footage,	Thy gowns, thy shoes, thy beds of roses, Thy cap, thy kirtle, and thy posies Soon break, soon wither, soon forgotten – in folly ripe, in reason rotten.
Liver buildings, etc. City skyline with rainbow. Fade to: Skyline at night erupting with fireworks.	Thy belt of straw and ivy buds, Thy coral clasps and amber studs, All those in me, no means can move, To come to thee, and be thy love. But could youth last and love still breed, Had joys no date, nor age, no need, Then those delights my mind might move To live with thee and be thy love. (Sir Walter Ralegh – Reply to Marlowe – 'The nymph's reply to the shepherd') We are being gathered in – at gloaming. Is it sleep … or is it death.
(*Consolation No.3 In D Flat Major – Franz Liszt*) END CREDITS	Goodnight ladies, goodnight sweet ladies, goodnight, goodnight. (*T. S. Eliot* – excerpt from 'The Waste Land')

BIOGRAPHY – THE POETS

Benediction (2021): Jack Lowden as the young Siegfried Sassoon.

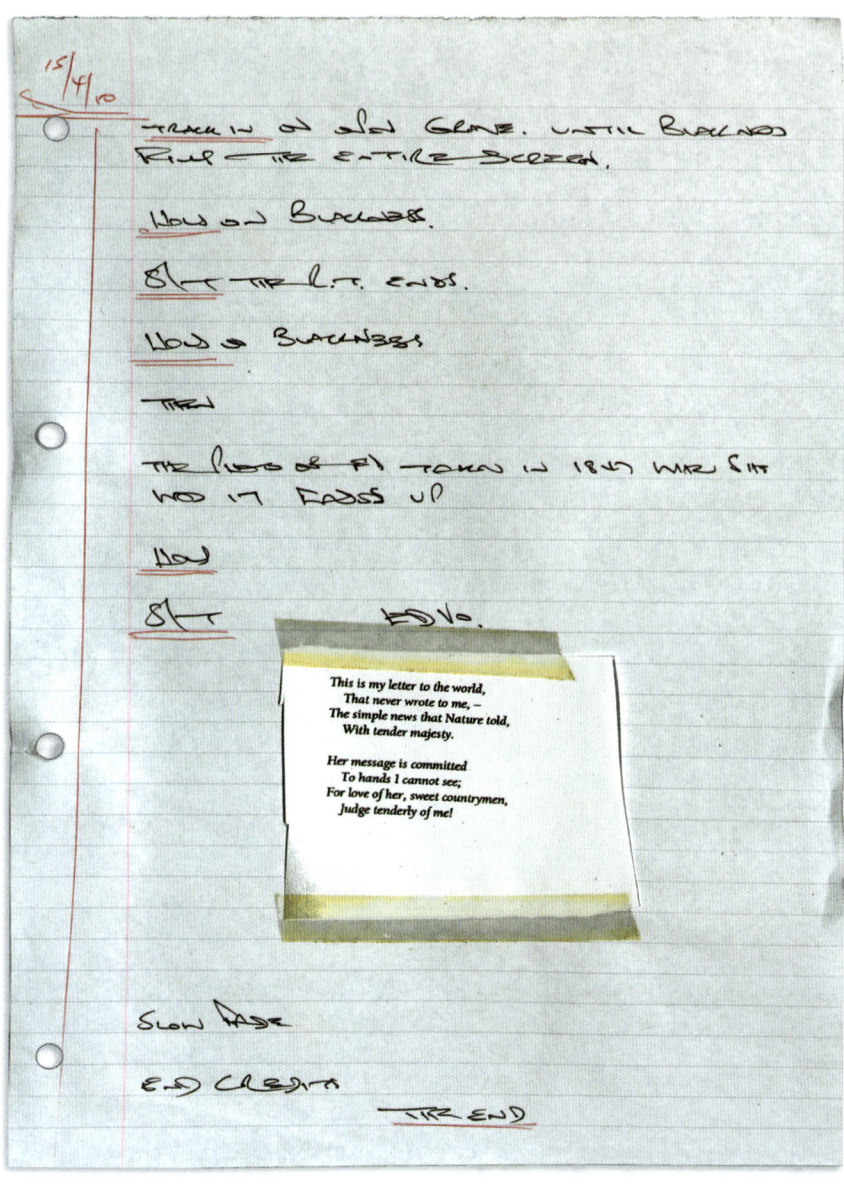

A Quiet Passion (2016): first draft, closing scene. (© The Terence Davies Estate, held by the Terence Davies Archive at Edge Hill University)

A QUIET PASSION (2016)
(EMILY DICKINSON)

A Quiet Passion (2016): Emma Bell as the young Emily Dickinson.

A Quiet Passion
SHOOTING SCRIPT – 23 APRIL 2015

Cast and crew of *A Quiet Passion* include:

EMILY DICKINSON	Cynthia Nixon
VINNIE DICKINSON	Jennifer Ehle
SUSAN GILBERT	Jodhi May
EDWARD DICKINSON	Keith Carradine
MOTHER	Joanna Bacon
AUSTIN DICKINSON	Duncan Duff
VRYLING BUFFAM	Catherine Bailey
AUNT ELIZABETH	Annette Badland
YOUNG EMILY	Emma Bell
REVEREND WADSWORTH	Eric Loren
MRS WADSWORTH	Simone Milsdochter
Written and Directed by	Terence Davies
Producers	Roy Boulter
	Solon Papadopoulos
Director of Photography	Florian Hoffmeister
Editor	Pia Di Ciaula
Production Designer	Merijn Sep
Costume Designer	Catherine Marchand
Music Director	Lesley Barber
Casting	John Hubbard and Ros Hubbard

A Hurricane Films (2016) production with:
Potemkino / Scope Pictures / Gibson & MacLeod / WeatherVane Productions / Screen Flanders / Double Dutch International / Indomitable Entertainment.

FADE UP ON

THE OPENING CREDITS WILL INCLUDE GRAPHIC RECREATION OF CURSIVE HANDWRITING AND CONTEMPORANEOUS IMAGERY, ENDING ON THE ONLY KNOWN IMAGE OF EMILY DICKINSON (AGE 17) – A DAGUERREOTYPE IN ITS ORIGINAL WORN VELVET CASE.

THIS THEN MORPHS AND DISSOLVES INTO EMILY DICKINSON AT 17 SITTING IN THE MIDST OF A ROOM FULL OF SCHOOLGIRLS

1   INT. MOUNT HOLYOKE LADIES SEMINARY. DAY   1

HOLD ON EMILY DICKINSON

S/TRAX OVER MORPH AND DISSOLVE

                     MISS LYON
               (VO)
             You have now come to the end of
             your second semester here. Some of
             you will remain here to complete
             your education, some of you will go
             out into the world…

                                                      CUT TO

2   INT. MOUNT HOLYOKE LADIES SEMINARY. DAY   2

MISS LYON ON A SMALL STAGE FLANKED BY HER FEMALE TEACHING STAFF. THEY ARE ALL STANDING

                     MISS LYON
             And, as is my custom at the end of
             each semester, I put to you a
             question of the utmost importance
             which concerns your spiritual
             wellbeing.
               (pause)
             Do you wish to come to God and be
             saved? All those who wish to be
             Christian and saved will rise.

A LARGE PORTION OF THE ASSEMBLED FEMALE STUDENTS DO SO.

                   MISS LYON (CONT'D)
             You will move to your right.

THEY DO SO

                   MISS LYON (CONT'D)
             Of those of you who remain - rise
             those of you who hope to be saved.

THE REST RISE EXCEPT FOR EMILY WHO, ALONE, REMAINS SEATED

MISS LYON (CONT'D)
You will move to your left.

THEY DO SO LEAVING EMILY SITTING ALONE

MISS LYON (CONT'D)
(to Emily)
Have you said your prayers?

YOUNGER EMILY
Yes - though it can't make much difference to the Creator.

MISS LYON
Do I understand you correctly? Do you think that your Creator is indifferent to your sins?
That, in his mercy, he sees you slumber?

YOUNGER EMILY
You misunderstand me. I have not got so far. I am not even awakened yet, and how can I repent? I am somewhat troubled, to be sure, but my feelings are all indefinite.

MISS LYON
Do you think your not having got so far is any valid excuse for not repenting, and giving your heart to God? The question is not, how far you have advanced, but how far you ought to have advanced - not how you feel, but how you ought to feel.

YOUNGER EMILY
I do not feel anything. I have no sense of my sins, and how can I have? I wish I could feel as others do, but it is impossible.

MISS LYON
My dear young friend, do stop and think what you are saying. You do not feel! You have no sense of sinfulness! Astonishing! A sinner against a Holy God and under condemnation, and liable every moment to drop into a burning hopeless eternity - and yet cannot feel, cannot be alarmed, cannot "Flee from the wrath to come". The true question is - are you in The Ark of Safety?

                    YOUNGER EMILY
          I fear I am not.

                    MISS LYON
          You are alone in your rebellion,
          Miss Dickinson. I fear that you are
          a "no-hoper".

                    YOUNGER EMILY
          Yes Miss Lyon.
               (smiling)
          But I love the danger!

HOLD ON HER

                                                  CUT TO

3   EXT. HOLYOKE LADIES SEMINARY, BOARDING ROOM WINDOW. DAY   3

     EMILY LOOKS OUT OF THE WINDOW. SHE SEES SOMETHING/SOMEONE,
     SMILES AND RUNS AWAY

                                                  CUT TO

4   INT. ENTRANCE HALL OF MOUNT HOLYOKE LADIES SEMINARY. DAY   4

     SHOT OF EMILY RUNNING IN AND THEN STOPPING

                    YOUNGER EMILY
               (breathless but happy)
          Father! Austin! Vinnie! My
          happiness would be complete if
          Mother were here with you.

     CUT TO THREE SHOT OF FATHER, BROTHER AUSTIN AND SISTER VINNIE

                    FATHER
          The journey would have been too
          fatiguing for her. We have come to
          take you home Emily.

                    YOUNGER AUSTIN
          We were concerned by your last
          letter.

                    YOUNGER VINNIE
          You spoke of being ill.

                    FATHER
          Yes. What is it that you are
          suffering from?

CUT TO EMILY

                    YOUNGER EMILY
               (smiling)
          An acute case of "evangelism".
               (pause)
          Am I really to go home?

CUT TO FATHER

                    FATHER
          Yes. We will go to Amherst via
          Boston and stay for a short
          while with Aunt Elizabeth.

                                                    CUT TO

5   INT. STAGE, CONCERT HALL. NIGHT   5

     JENNY LIND IS SINGING, ACCOMPANIED BY A PIANIST. SHE FINISHES
     HER SONG 'AH NON CREDEA MIRARTI' IN THE BEL CANTO TRADITION
     BY VINCENZO BELLINI)

     APPLAUSE

     SHE BOWS, THEN WALKS OFF STAGE

     AN INTERVAL

     CRANE UP FROM THE STAGE TO THE BOX THAT THE DICKINSON ARE IN

                                                    CUT TO

6   INT. BOX, CONCERT HALL. NIGHT.   6

     IN THE BOX FATHER, AUNT ELIZABETH, AUSTIN, EMILY AND VINNIE

                    YOUNGER AUSTIN
          I fear you don't approve Father?

                    FATHER
               (who has not applauded)
          I do not like to see a woman on
          stage.

                    YOUNGER EMILY
          But she has a gift!

                    FATHER
          A gift is no excuse for a female to
          exhibit herself in that way.

                    YOUNGER EMILY
                (tart)
            What would you have her do -
            perform an act of congress - aloud?

                    FATHER
                (equally tart)
            That would depend upon what key it
            was in.

                    YOUNGER AUSTIN
                (trying to lighten the
                 atmosphere)
            Well the rest of her programme is
            in respectable German.

                    YOUNGER EMILY
            And the Germans are wonderful in
            music.

                    AUNT
            That's true. English - thank Heaven
            - is not a language that can be
            sung.

                    YOUNGER AUSTIN
            But Aunt Elizabeth, you love your
            hymn tunes.

                    AUNT
            Hymns are different. They have
            absolutely nothing to do with
            music.

                                                        CUT TO

7   INT. STAGE, CONCERT HALL. NIGHT   7

        JENNY LIND COMES ONTO THE STAGE TO GREAT APPLAUSE. SHE
        PERFORMS SCHUBERT'S 'NIGHT AND DREAMS' (IN GERMAN)

                                                        CUT TO

8   INT. BOX, CONCERT HALL. NIGHT   8

        CRANE UP TO THE DICKINSON FAMILY

                    YOUNGER EMILY
                (indicating JENNY LIND)
            Ah, the devil in music!

                    FATHER
            Don't be trite Emily.

CRANE BACK DOWN TO JENNY LIND

DISSOLVE TO:

9   INT. SOUTH PARLOUR. THE HOMESTEAD. NIGHT   9

CONTINUE TO CRANE DOWN TO EMILY FROM BEHIND AS SHE WATCHES THE DARK RAIN OUTSIDE.

S/TRAX

          EMILY
        (v/o)
"For each ecstatic instant
We must an anguish pay
In keen and quivering ratio
 To the ecstasy.
For each beloved hour
Sharp pittances of years,
Bitter contested farthings And
coffers heaped with tears."

         YOUNGER EMILY
     (in a quiet ecstasy,
      throwing her arms wide
then hugging herself)
Oh life!
Oh home!
How wonderful you are!

CUT TO FATHER

COMING OUT OF THE LIBRARY AND TOWARDS THE PARLOUR

          FATHER
Emily - why are you up so late?

         YOUNGER EMILY
May I speak with you father?

          FATHER
Of course.

         YOUNGER EMILY
As you may know I like to write… letters mostly… but some poetry…

          FATHER
Yes…?

                    YOUNGER EMILY
          May I have your permission to write
          during the night - for quiet's sake
          - I shall not disturb the rest of
          the household, I promise.

                    FATHER
          Yes. You may. It was very
          considerate of you to ask.

                    YOUNGER EMILY
          But it is your house father.

                    FATHER
          But it is our home Emily.

HE MAKES TO GO

                    YOUNGER EMILY
          I have one more favour to ask of
          you father.

                    FATHER
          What is it?

                    YOUNGER EMILY
          You are, I believe, on cordial
          terms with Dr. Holland. Editor of
          "The Springfield Republican"…

                    FATHER
               (smiling)
          And "The Springfield Republican"
          publishes poetry…

EMILY SMILES TOO

                    FATHER (CONT'D)
          I will write to him - and if he
          agrees - you may send him some of
          your work.

CUT TO EMILY SMILING

THE RAIN STILL LASHES DOWN

FATHER GOES BACK INTO THE LIBRARY AND CLOSES THE DOOR

CUT TO HIGH SHOT

EMILY IS STANDING IN THE DARK WATCHING THE RAIN

                                        DISSOLVE TO

| 10 | INT. HALLWAY AND SOUTH PARLOUR, HOMESTEAD. DAY | 10 |

AUNT ELIZABETH COMING THROUGH THE FRONT DOOR ACCOMPANIED BY FATHER, AUSTIN AND VINNIE

AS AUNT ELIZABETH COMES IN SHE TAKES OFF HER BONNET AND CAPE AND GIVES THEM TO ONE OF THE DOMESTICS

GENERAL GREETINGS AS THEY ALL GO INTO THE PARLOUR THROUGH THE DOOR NEAREST THE FRONT DOOR, WHERE MOTHER IS SITTING

> AUNT
> (as they do so)
> Where's Emily?

> FATHER
> She'll be down presently.

CUT TO

| 11 | INT. EMILY'S ROOM. THE HOMESTEAD. DAY | 11 |

VINNIE COMES IN SUDDENLY AND EMILY STOPS WRITING AND SPINS AROUND ALMOST AS THOUGH SHE'S GUILTY

> YOUNGER VINNIE
> What are you doing Emily?

EMILY DOESN'T ANSWER

SHE TURNS TOWARDS THE WINDOW AND AS SHE GETS UP THE PAPER ON WHICH SHE WAS WRITING FALLS TO THE FLOOR

VINNIE COMES TO HER AND PICKS UP THE PAPER

VINNIE LOOKS AT THE PAPER, PUZZLED

CUT TO THE PIECE OF PAPER

IT IS COVERED WITH "EMILY DICKINSON" WRITTEN OVER AND OVER AGAIN

CUT TO VINNIE

> YOUNGER VINNIE (CONT'D)
> What does it mean?

> YOUNGER EMILY
> (half laughing)
> I'm trying to discover who I am.

> AUNT'S VO
> Emily! Vinnie! Come here at once!

A QUIET PASSION

                    YOUNGER VINNIE
          Quickly! Quickly! It's Aunt
          Elizabeth!

                    YOUNGER EMILY
          The only other male on father's
          side of the family.

                                            CUT TO

12   INT. HALLWAY AND SOUTH PARLOUR, THE HOMESTEAD. DAY   12

VINNIE AND EMILY COMING DOWN STAIRS ALONG THE HALL AND INTO
THE SOUTH PARLOUR

                    YOUNGER VINNIE
          Remember Aunt Elizabeth has
          celebrated the Dickinson dynasty in
          55 stanzas.

                    YOUNGER EMILY
          And every one of them dull.

                    YOUNGER VINNIE
          I'll fix some refreshment.

EMILY GOES INTO THE PARLOUR ALONE

                    YOUNGER EMILY
              (breathless)
          Aunt Elizabeth!

                    AUNT
          Ah, at last. Emily. I was nearly
          kept waiting.
              (pause)
          And what is your opinion of my poem
          Emily?

                    YOUNGER EMILY
          I'm sure your verse is equal to
          your talent, Aunt.

                    AUNT
          If I were clever enough I should
          probably take offence at that
          dubious compliment.

                    YOUNGER EMILY
              (charming)
          But Aunt, all the best compliments
          are dubious...that's part of their
          charm.

> AUNT
> (to AUSTIN)
> Did you enjoy my verses, Austin?

> YOUNGER AUSTIN
> (just as wicked)
> Very much Aunt. They put 'Paradise Lost' to shame.

AUNT ELIZABETH KNOWS SHE IS BEING GENTLY MOCKED AND IS CHARMED BY IT

> AUNT
> (to FATHER)
> Your children are far too sophisticated, Edward — I'm sure part of me disapproves.

> FATHER
> (equally playful)
> Disapproval is a heavy thing. It always helps to confirm one's own waywardness. Besides if I had to choose between having sophisticated children and ones that were merely docile… I think I should choose the former… docility is too much like slavery…

> AUNT
> That sounds like abolitionist talk…

> FATHER
> No it is not. But no Christian can ever make a case for slavery.

> AUNT
> Please let us not discuss this subject. It is both improper and tiresome.

> YOUNGER EMILY
> Not to those who are enslaved.

> AUNT
> I see we have a Robespierre in our midst.

> YOUNGER EMILY
> Not Robespierre. Charlotte Corday perhaps.

> AUNT
> Edward, they're as bad as you are.

PAUSE.

> AUNT (CONT'D)
> (to EMILY)
> I believe you've had your first poem published.

> YOUNGER EMILY
> (awkward)
> Yes… in "The Springfield Republican"…

EMILY PICKS UP A MAGAZINE FROM THE TABLE AND GIVES THE MAGAZINE TO AUNT

> YOUNGER EMILY (CONT'D)
> It was printed anonymously.

> AUNT
> That seems a little eccentric…
> (she reads the poem then quickly puts it down)
> But in the circumstances probably a good thing.

> YOUNGER EMILY
> (very hurt)
> We can't all be Milton.

> AUNT
> Don't pout Emily. It's unbecoming.

> YOUNGER EMILY
> (quietly)
> Poems are my solace for the eternity which surrounds us all.

> AUNT
> Who said that?

> YOUNGER EMILY
> I did.

> AUNT
> Well don't. It sounds unchristian. And where's Vinnie?

VINNIE COMES IN WITH A TRAY OF WINE. SHE SITS IT DOWN ON A TABLE

> YOUNGER VINNIE
> Here Aunt.

> AUNT
> And what of you?

> YOUNGER VINNIE
> Oh I'm like a pilgrim trying to improve.

                    AUNT
          A pilgrim should only ever be
          conscious of other peoples' self-
          improvement - consciousness of his
          own is mere vanity.

                    YOUNGER VINNIE
          But Aunt, vanity is such a harmless
          vice - it's as shallow as the
          people who indulge in it.

                    AUNT
          No vice is harmless Vinnie. Look no
          further than Babylon for that.
               (pause)
          What of you, Austin?

                    YOUNGER AUSTIN
          Oh I'm on no pilgrimage at all.

                    AUNT
          And what of vice?

                    YOUNGER AUSTIN
          Surely vice is only virtue in
          disguise.

                    AUNT
               (to Mother)
          And what is your opinion of your
          children's moral laxity Emily?

                    MOTHER
          Oh I prefer to listen and remain
          silent. That way a prejudice
          doesn't seem like an opinion.

                    AUNT
          That reply was so sphinx-like I'm
          none the wiser.

                    YOUNGER EMILY
          Oh cherish your ignorance Aunt
          Elizabeth - you never know when you
          will need it!

                    AUNT
          Edward, your children astound me!
          They ought to be sent to their
          rooms and pummelled. Hourly.

FATHER GIVING HER A GLASS OF WINE

                    FATHER
          Calm down Aunt Elizabeth. Have a
          glass of currant wine and turn vice
          into a medicinal pleasure.

                        AUNT
            Medicinal?

                        FATHER
            For your circulation.

                        AUNT.
                  (sipping the wine and as
                  it warms her she begins
                  to thaw. Smiling)
            There is nothing wrong with my
            circulation.

                                            DISSOLVE TO

13   INT. THE PARLOUR. THE HOMESTEAD. NIGHT   13

        IN THE LAMPLIGHT

        IN THE FIRELIGHT

        C/U EMILY. SHE SITS QUIETLY READING AND THEN LOOKS UP AT HER
        FAMILY

        PAN (L TO R) AWAY FROM HER TO;

        1 MOTHER STARING AT THE FIRE, WARMING HER FEET

        2 FATHER READING

        3 VINNIE SEWING

        4 AUSTIN STUDYING

        5 AUNT ELIZABETH LOOKING INTO THE FIRE

        PAN ENDS ON C/U OF EMILY (PAN HAS DESCRIBED A COMPLETE
        CIRCLE)

        S/TRAX OVER THIS PAN

                        EMILY
                  (v/o)
            "The heart asks pleasure first,
             And then, excuse from pain;
             And then, those little anodynes
                That deaden suffering;

             And then, to go to sleep;
             And then, if it should be
             The will of it's inquisitor,
                The liberty to die."

CUT TO VINNIE

>   YOUNGER VINNIE
>   Would you play something Emily?

CUT TO EMILY

>   YOUNGER EMILY
>   Of course.

CUT TO MOTHER

>   MOTHER
>   (in deep thought)
>   One of the old hymn tunes…

SHOT OF EMILY GOING TO THE PIANO. SHE BEGINS TO PLAY SOFTLY

CUT TO MOTHER

>   MOTHER (CONT'D)
>   When I was very young… a young man
>   who came to our church used to sing
>   that… he had a lovely voice… so
>   pure!… he was only 19 when he died…
>   (she starts to cry)
>   There!
>   (calming down)
>   There.

                                                          CUT TO

14   EXT. OUTSIDE THE HOMESTEAD. DAY   14

AUNT LEAVING

MR. AND MRS. DICKINSON, VINNIE, AUSTIN AND EMILY ESCORTING AUNT ELIZABETH TO HER CARRIAGE. THEY ARE SAYING THEIR GOODBYES AS THEY ALL WALK FROM THE PORCH TO THE STEPS WHICH LEAD TO THE STREET. BUT JUST AS AUNT ELIZABETH GOES TO GET INTO HER CARRIAGE EMILY GOES TO HER AND KISSES HER

>   YOUNGER EMILY
>   God keep you well.

>   AUNT
>   When He is ready He will call me.

>   YOUNGER EMILY
>   (fervently)
>   I hope you live for a hundred
>   years.

                         AUNT
               What a repellent idea!

                         YOUNGER EMILY
                    (suddenly near to tears)
               Oh Aunt, don't say that!

                         AUNT
                    (tenderly)
               I'm not afraid of death Emily. Nor
               should you be. If we keep our souls
               in readiness for God there can be
               no fear. He will smooth our way.

SILENCE FOR A MOMENT AS THEY ALL JUST STAND THERE

                         AUNT (CONT'D)
                    (skittish)
               I shall pray for you all and
               remember keep atheism at bay and
               watch the clock that ticks for us
               all.

SHE GETS INTO HER CARRIAGE

                         YOUNGER AUSTIN
               Tick…

                         YOUNGER VINNIE
               Tock…

                         YOUNGER EMILY
               Tick…

AUNT RAPPING THE FLOOR OF HER CARRIAGE WITH HER STICK AND AS
THE CARRIAGE MOVES OFF

                         AUNT
               Oh! You are all impossible!

HOLD ON   HER AS SHE DRIVES AWAY

S/TRAX

                         EMILY
                    (v/o)
                 "I went to thank her,
                    But she slept;
                 Her bed a funneled stone,
               With nosegays at the head and foot,
                  That travellers had thrown…"

WE WATCH AUNT DRIVE AWAY

S/TRAX

                    EMILY (CONT'D)
        V/o
               "Who went to thank her;
                   But she slept.
               'Twas short to cross the sea
               To look upon her like, alive,
               But turning back 'twas slow."

                                                    DISSOLVE TO

15   INT. PHOTOGRAPHIC STUDIO. DAY   15

        SHOT OF FATHER SITTING FOR HIS PHOTOGRAPH. HE'S VERY STIFF,
        VERY UNCOMFORTABLE

        CUT TO

        PHOTOGRAPHER

        HE IS READY TO TAKE FATHER'S PHOTOGRAPH

                          PHOTOGRAPHER
                    Do you think you might smile Mr.
                    Dickinson?

        CUT TO

        FATHER IN LONG SHOT

                          FATHER
                    (unsmiling)
                 I am smiling!

        TRACK IN ON HIM

        AS WE GET CLOSER HE MORPHS INTO HIS OLDER SELF

                                                    DISSOLVE TO

16   INT. PHOTOGRAPHIC STUDIO. DAY   16

        LONG SHOT OF YOUNGER AUSTIN

        TRACK IN ON HIM AND HE MORPHS INTO HIS OLDER SELF

                                                    DISSOLVE TO

| 17 | INT. PHOTOGRAPHIC STUDIO. DAY | 17 |

LONG SHOT OF YOUNGER VINNIE

TRACK IN ON HER AND SHE MORPHS INTO HER OLDER SELF

                                                                                                   DISSOLVE TO

| 18 | INT. PHOTOGRAPHIC STUDIO. DAY | 18 |

LONG SHOT OF YOUNGER EMILY

HOLD

S/TRAX

                            DR. HOLLAND
                              (v/o)
            "Dear Miss Dickinson, thank you for
            your other poems which I have read
            with interest but I must confess
            that the genuine classics of every
            language are the work of men, not
            of women…"

TRACK IN ON YOUNGER EMILY AND SHE ALSO MORPHS INTO HER OLDER SELF

S/TRAX

                            DR. HOLLAND (CONT'D)
                              (v/o)
            "Women, I fear, cannot create the
            permanent treasures of literature…"

                                                                                DISSOLVE TO

| 19 | INT. EMILY'S BEDROOM, THE HOMESTEAD. DAY | 19 |

EMILY SITTING AT HER DESK IN ROUGHLY THE SAME POSITION AS HER PHOTOGRAPH

S/TRAX

                    DR. HOLLAND
                        (v/o)
                    "I have decided to publish "Sic
                    transit Gloria mundi" as it is the
                    least wayward and shows some wit –
                    although at 17 stanzas, the wit
                    outstays its welcome… as to the
                    rest of the poetry it is in the
                    common metre…childish like nursery
                    rhymes…"

HOLD ON EMILY

                    EMILY
                        (smiling ruefully)
                    "Old King Cole was a merry old soul
                    And a merry old soul was he…"

SHE FINISHES READING DR.HOLLAND'S LETTER, PUTS IT IN HER DESK
AND LOCKS THE DRAWER

                    VINNIE'S VO
                    Emily! Emily! We have a guest!

EMILY JUMPS UP AND RUSHES DOWNSTAIRS

                                                    CUT TO

20   INT. HALL, THE HOMESTEAD. DAY   20

EMILY COMES RUSHING DOWN BREATHLESS BUT HAPPY AND STOPS

                    VINNIE
                        (introducing the young
                        lady to EMILY with a
                        flourish)
                    This is Miss Vryling Buffam!

                    MISS VB
                        (pert, vivacious, pretty
                        and irreverent)
                    It sounds like an anagram doesn't
                    it?

THEY SHAKE HANDS

                    MISS VB (CONT'D)
                    You see before you a life blighted
                    by Baptism.

                    VINNIE
                    I hope you brought to the attention
                    of your parents their lack of
                    thought in that respect.

MISS VB
I have. It makes them very cross.

EMILY
(laughing)
I'm sure they will forgive you!

MISS VB
Ah! But will I forgive them?
Weren't you at a ladies seminary at…
Fort Sumter or somewhere?

EMILY
(laughs)
Mount Holyoke.

MISS VB
Yes! I thought it had a military ring to it.

EMILY
But that was many years ago now.

MISS VB
And were your studies as disciplined?

EMILY
Arithmetic, algebra, geometry and, for the sake of decorum, ecclesiastical history.

MISS VB
I believe all women should have the same educational advantages as men – but – ecclesiastical history? It sounds as dreary as paradise.

VINNIE
We brought her home.

MISS VB
Did you dislike Mount HOLYOKE so much?

VINNIE
She was bullied there.

EMILY
There's bullying and there's coercion.

MISS VB
Which did you suffer?

EMILY
(smiling wryly)
A unique combination of both.

                    VINNIE
          It was appalling.

                    EMILY
          Yes - but it puts iron in the soul.

                    MISS VB
          But what's the point of that? When,
          in the end, we are all
          extinguished.

                    EMILY
          Do you fear death?

                    MISS VB
          No. But I fear Heaven. I'm afraid
          it will seem like an anti-climax.
          Perfection usually does.

                    EMILY
          And what of Hell?

                    MISS VB
          I'm sure that it will be even
          duller that Heaven. That will be
          the agony.

THEY GO DOWN THE HALL TOWARDS THE FRONT DOOR

                                                    CUT TO

21   EXT. OUTSIDE THE HOMESTEAD. DAY   21

      THREE PARASOLS (ALREADY OPEN) CLEAR THE FRAME TO REVEAL
      EMILY, VINNIE AND MISS VB

      THEY WALK TOWARDS THE STREET

      TRACK BACK WITH THEM

                    EMILY
          Will you come to church with us
          Miss Buffam?

                    MISS VB
          Of course not. Going to church is
          like going to Boston - you only
          enjoy it after you've gotten home.

                    EMILY
          But we are to pray for the repose
          of our late Pastor's soul.

                    MISS VB
          Doesn't that rather depend on where
          it's gone?

THEY ALL LAUGH

                    EMILY
          We shall become fast friends!

                    MISS VB
          Of course we shall! I'm
          irresistible. Everyone says so.
          When the new Pastor does arrive you
          must point him out to me.

                    EMILY
          So that you too can be saved?

                    MISS VB
          No - so that I'll know whom to
          avoid.
               (walking away)
          Don't enjoy your praying too much -
          it might become habit forming.

SHE WALKS OFF

VINNIE AND EMILY CONTINUE WALKING TOWARDS THE CHURCH.

                                                  CUT TO

22   INT. THE SOUTH PARLOUR. HOMESTEAD. DAY   22

      THE DICKINSON FAMILY GATHER TOGETHER

                    PASTOR
          Do you come to God sir?

                    FATHER
          We do sir.

                    PASTOR
          Do you come humbly sir?

                    FATHER
               (stiffly)
          I come as myself Pastor.

                    PASTOR
          You want to come to Christ as a
          lawyer? But you must come to him as
          a poor sinner.

SILENCE

>   Get down on your knees and let me
>   pray for you… and then pray for
>   yourself…

FATHER HESITATES FOR A MOMENT, SHOCKED AT THE IDEA

A TENSE SILENCE

THEN HE KNEELS AND ALL THE FAMILY DO THE SAME – EXCEPT FOR EMILY WHO REMAINS SEATED.

>   PASTOR (CONT'D)
>   (standing)
>   And you Miss Dickinson?
>   (quietly angry)
>   What of you?
>
>   EMILY
>   (quietly furious)
>   What of me sir?
>
>   PASTOR
>   Will you not kneel and give
>   yourself to God?
>
>   EMILY
>   No sir, I will not kneel. Though I
>   think that God has already given
>   himself to me.
>
>   PASTOR
>   (furious)
>   That is profane.
>
>   EMILY
>   It was not meant so sir.
>
>   PASTOR
>   Do you guard your soul Emily?
>
>   EMILY
>   As best as I am able sir.
>
>   PASTOR
>   And Hell? What of Hell?
>
>   EMILY
>   Avoid it if I can. Endure it if I
>   must.
>
>   PASTOR
>   That was irreligious young lady.
>
>   EMILY
>   Then I beg God's pardon for my
>   impiety.

A VERY TENSE SILENCE

> PASTOR
> (kneeling)
> Let us pray for all sinners.

CUT TO

23 INT. THE LIBRARY. HOMESTEAD. NIGHT   23

> FATHER
> (very angry)
> How dare you behave in that manner! It is both unchristian and unseemly.

> EMILY
> (equally angry)
> I will not be forced to piety!

> FATHER
> You will do as you are instructed!

SILENCE

> EMILY
> (trying mollify him)
> I know your Christian shore is safer father and I know I must seem recalcitrant – but my soul is my own.

> FATHER
> Your soul is God's!
> (pause)
> You neglect it at your peril.

> EMILY
> (giving way)
> Yes father.

> FATHER
> And, in future, you will conduct yourself in a manner that is befitting to the station in life to which it has pleased God to call you.

> EMILY
> Yes father.

> FATHER
> Goodnight Emily.

                            EMILY
                    Goodnight father.

                                                    DISSOLVE TO

24   INT. DINING ROOM. THE HOMESTEAD. DAY   24

        EMILY FINISHES LAYING THE TABLE

        IT LOOKS PERFECT

        THEN THE FAMILY COME IN AND SIT DOWN. EMILY ON FATHER'S RIGHT
        AT THE HEAD OF THE TABLE

        THEY ARE JUST ABOUT TO SAY GRACE WHEN FATHER LOOKS AT HIS
        PLATE AND STOPS

                            FATHER
                       (picking up the plate)
                    This plate is dirty.

        EMILY TAKES IT FROM HIM AND SMASHES IT AGAINST THE SIDE OF
        THE TABLE

                            EMILY
                    It is dirty no longer.

                                                        CUT TO

25   EXT. GARDEN BETWEEN THE EVERGREENS AND THE HOMESTEAD. DAY 25

        EMILY AND MISS BUFFAM WALKING IN THE BRILLIANT SUNSHINE
        TOGETHER

                            MISS VB
                    I wouldn't have gone that far. If I
                    had father would have packed me off
                    to a good military school and
                    mother would have tearfully
                    embroidered something.

        THEY CONTINUE TO WALK TOGETHER

                                                        CUT TO

                            AUSTIN
                    Ah! The eternal Miss Buffam!

                            MISS VB
                    Alas no sir! Father Time knocks at
                    my door also.

AUSTIN
And what precautions do you take?

MISS VB
I contrive never to be at home when he calls.

AUSTIN
All women should aspire to that state of readiness.

MISS VB
No. Women should only aspire to be younger than their waistlines…then the unpleasant topic of "age" becomes almost irrelevant.

AUSTIN
And what should men aspire to?

MISS VB
Tobogganing.

AUSTIN
And in warmer weather?

MISS VB
Philately – it has all the dangers of sport without any of the rigour.

AUSTIN
Your banter Miss Buffam is, as always, delightful.

MISS VB
Take it Mr. Dickinson as the mere outpourings of a poor tormented soul.

AUSTIN
(touching his hat)
Ladies.

BOTH EMILY AND MISS VB DO A QUICK CURTSY

AUSTIN (CONT'D)
(smiling and walking away)
Now you go too far.

MISS VB
We were trying to be ironic.

AUSTIN WALKS AWAY

DISSOLVE TO:

25a   EXT. GARDEN AT THE SIDE OF THE HOMESTEAD - DAY   25a

   EMILY AND MISS VB CONTINUE THEIR WALK

   SILENCE IN THE SUMMER HEAT

   THEY SIT DOWN ON A BENCH IN THE SHADE OF A LARGE TREE

   SILENCE

                        EMILY
              Will you marry?

                        MISS VB
              I suppose in time I shall. Isn't
              that what we all do in the end.

                        EMILY
              I don't know. I cannot imagine
              myself beyond my family – amongst
              strangers.

   SILENCE IN THE SUMMER HEAT

                        MISS VB
              You are a strange creature, with
              more depth I suspect, than any of
              us.

                        EMILY
              How can you say that? I haven't
              demonstrated that at all.

                        MISS VB
                   (smiling)
              Oh my dear you don't
              "demonstrate"… you "reveal".

                        EMILY
                   (sadly)
              When you do eventually go away will
              you write?

                        MISS VB
              No. I don't possess the propensity
              for long correspondence. I suspect
              I have a trivial mind.

                        EMILY
              But a good heart.

                        MISS VB
              Don't let sentiment cloud your
              judgment Emily. Should my future
              husband put me out of humour he
              will think he has married one of
              the minor Borgias.
                        (MORE)

> MISS VB (CONT'D)
> (pause)
> Will you marry?

> EMILY
> I only want my family. It is not perfect. It is not paradise but it is far better than anything I could know… or want.
> (sadly)
> When you do marry, I shall miss you.

> MISS VB
> Of course you'll miss me! I refuse to be forgotten!

CUT TO

26 INT. EMILY'S BEDROOM. HOMESTEAD. DAY   26

EMILY AT HER DESK, WRITING

A SOFT TAP ON THE DOOR, THEN FATHER COMES IN DRESSED FOR OUTDOORS

EMILY CONTINUES TO WRITE THROUGHOUT THIS SCENE

> FATHER
> Will you come to church Emily?

> EMILY
> No father.

> FATHER
> Why will you not come?

> EMILY
> God knows what is in my heart – he doesn't require me to be in a pew to remind him.

> FATHER
> I hope that remark isn't as frivolous as it sounds. Your soul is no trivial matter.

> EMILY
> I agree father. Which is why I'm so meticulous in guarding its independence.

SILENCE

FATHER LEAVES CLEARLY DISMAYED BUT NOT ANGRY

EMILY GOES ON WRITING, THEN STARTS TO SEW GROUPS OF POEMS INTO SMALL BOOKS.

S/TRAX

> EMILY'S VO
> "I reckon - when I count out all -
> First - poets - then the sun -
> Then summer- then the heaven of God
> And then - the list is done -
>
> But, looking back - the first so seems -
> To comprehend the whole -
> The others look a needless show -
> So I write - poets - all -
>
>
> Their summer - lasts a solid year -
> They can afford a sun
> The East - would deem extravagant -
> And if the further heaven -
>
> Be beautiful as they prepare
> For those who worship them -
> It is too difficult a Grace -
> To justify the dream."

CUT TO

27 INT. HALLWAY, HOMESTEAD. DAY   27

TRACK BACK WITH EMILY, VINNIE AND MISS VB FROM THE PORCH INTO THE HALL

> MISS VB
> This is my third commencement ball and not a hint of romance. Do you suppose that men are frightened of a woman who teaches and is used to her independence?

> EMILY
> Men are supposed to be fearless aren't they?

> MISS VB
> In war, yes. In religion, always. In love - never.
>   (she pauses as she
>   embraces Emily)
> Emily my own! This is a luxury that is almost Parisian!

                    EMILY
          Let's not be anything today except
          superficial.

                    MISS VB
          Yes! And superficiality should
          always be spontaneous – if its
          studied it's too close to
          hypocrisy.

                    EMILY
          We may be superficial but we're not
          stupid!

                    MISS VB
          Heaven forbid!

THEY LAUGH AS THEY GO INTO THE PARLOUR

28   INT. BOTH PARLOURS, THE HOMESTEAD – DAY   28

THE TWO PARLOURS HAVE BEEN OPENED OUT SO THAT DANCING CAN
TAKE PLACE FOR THE COMMENCEMENT BALL

EMILY, VINNIE AND MISS VB SIT DOWN

                    MISS VB
          Look at that divine creature.

CUT TO A YOUNG MAN IN A SOLDIER'S UNIFORM

HE IS TALKING TO A GROUP OF CIVILIAN YOUNG MEN

CUT BACK TO THE TRIO

                    MISS VB (CONT'D)
          What a noble head he has.

                    VINNIE
          Like a Roman emperor.

                    MISS VB
          Nero!

                    EMILY
          Let's hope he's just as wicked.

                    MISS VB
          As long as he has a fortune we can
          take his wickedness as merely a
          lapse in virtue.

CUT TO SOLDIER COMING TOWARDS THEM

CUT TO TRIO

                    EMILY
          I think you must prepare yourself
          for a polka.

THEY FAN THEMSELVES FURIOUSLY IN UNISON

                         SOLDIER
                    (to Miss VB)
               May I be permitted to have the next
               dance on your card Miss Buffam?

                         MISS VB
               I don't have a dance card sir. I
               prefer to "improvise".

                         SOLDIER
                    (offering his hand)
               Isn't that rather dangerous?

                         MISS VB
                    (taking his hand and
                    getting up)
               That is precisely why I do it.

SOLDIER BOWS TO VINNIE AND EMILY

                         SOLDIER
               Ladies.

THEY NOD THEIR HEADS AND CONTINUE FANNING THEMSELVES

MISS VB AND SOLDIER COMMENCE TO DANCE

CUT TO SOLDIER AND MISS VB DANCING. HE IS NOT VERY GOOD AT IT

CUT TO VINNIE AND EMILY SEATED

MISS VB ESCORTED BY THE SOLDIER BACK TO HER SEAT - SHE SITS
DOWN HEAVILY

                         EMILY
               How was the divinity?

                         MISS VB
               He dances like a polar bear. And a
               prig.

                         EMILY
               Did you say something to shock him?

                         MISS VB
               Only that I had just finished
               reading "Wuthering Heights" and he
               was scandalised.

                         VINNIE
               Had he read it?

> **MISS VB**
> No. So I told him that to condemn a novel he had not read was like going to Sodom or Gomorrah and being disappointed that neither were Philadelphia.
>
> **EMILY**
> I hope he had the presence of mind to laugh.
>
> **MISS VB**
> He didn't. He went very silent and the air became charged with unspoken profanity. It was delicious! Now I must go - Miss Buffam has a "tryst".
>
> **EMILY**
> That sounds sinful.

EMILY GETS UP WITH MISS VB AND ESCORTS HER OUT TO THE HALLWAY

TRACK BACK WITH THEM

29 EXT. OUTSIDE THE HOMESTEAD - DAY   29

EMILY ESCORTS MISS VB TO HER CARRIAGE

> **MISS VB**
> I was told once (by a clergyman) that I should repent my sins, otherwise I would be pursued by the devil. "Oh, a sort of spiritual Wells Fargo", I said. He promptly went silent - like patience on a monument - appalled but dumb.
>
> **EMILY**
> (half seriously)
> For the lost soul there will be no tomorrow.
>
> **MISS VB**
> For the lost soul, today is quite enough.
>
> **EMILY**
> Oh I shall miss you if you ever go - your honesty is sublime!
>
> **MISS VB**
> In the long term honesty is not the best policy.
>
> **EMILY**
> Is dishonesty?

                    MISS VB
          I prefer to call it "diplomacy",
          that way one can turn a tactical
          defeat into a victory.

                    EMILY
          Who proposed that?

                    MISS VB
          Oh I don't know! Probably George
          Washington as he was crossing The
          Delaware – the wrong way. Now my
          own! I must fly. A "Mr Wilder" is
          waiting.

                    EMILY
          With bated breath?

                    MISS VB
          I hope not – that always sounds too
          much like asthma.

SHE GETS INTO HER CARRIAGE

                    EMILY
          Drive carefully and don't do
          anything against God.

                    MISS VB
          I'll stop yodelling then.

                    EMILY
             (smiling)
          Very wise.

                    MISS VB
             (starting the horse)
          Quick Pendennis, a gentleman's
          health is at stake!

                                                    CUT TO

30   INT. LANDING / MOTHER'S ROOM HOMESTEAD. DAY   30

     DURING THE COMMENCEMENT BALL

     EMILY OUTSIDE HER MOTHER'S ROOM

     SHE GETS TO THE DOOR – WHICH IS AJAR AND SHE WALKS SOFTLY IN

     SHOT OF HER MOTHER LYING IN BED HER HAND BEATING TIME WITH
     THE MUSIC, TAPPING ON THE COUNTERPANE

                    MOTHER
              (seeing Emily)
        Oh come in Emily.

SHOT OF EMILY

                    EMILY
        Shall I close the door?

                    MOTHER
              (smiling)
        No, leave it open… it's lovely
        to hear the music…

SHE CLOSES HER EYES AND HER HAND WAVES IN TIME TO THE MUSIC

                    MOTHER (CONT'D (CONT'D)
              (almost to herself)
        It makes me recollect when your
        father and me went to our first
        commencement ball…all those years
        ago…

                                        DISSOLVE TO

31   INT. KITCHEN. HOMESTEAD. DAY   31

        MEDIUM C/U EMILY SITTING DOWN

                    VINNIE'S VO
        Make sure your bread is ready for
        the agricultural fair tomorrow
        Emily.

                    EMILY
              (calling back but
               distracted by pain)
        Yes, I haven't forgotten.

EMILY LOOKS DOWN AT HER HANDS

                    EMILY'S VO
        They feel swollen.

SHE RUBS HER HANDS TOGETHER

        They are swollen…like my feet…

SHE GETS UP. SHE THEN FALLS BACK INTO THE CHAIR HOLDING HER
SIDE

THE PAIN IS ACUTE BUT PASSING

SHE HAS BROKEN OUT INTO A SWEAT

SHE SITS THERE FOR A MOMENT

CUT TO THOMAS AND MARGARET AND MAGGIE, THE THREE DOMESTICS EMPLOYED BY THE DICKINSONS COME IN

> THOMAS
> (in unison)
> Miss Emily…

> MARGARET
> (in unison)
> Miss Emily…

> MAGGIE
> (in unison)
> Miss Emily…

> EMILY
> (trying to hide her pain
> as she winces as it
> returns)
> Would you please take my bread from
> the oven?

MAGGIE DOES SO BUT IN DOING SO DROPS THE BREAD ON THE FLOOR

THOMAS, MAGGIE AND MARGARET PICK UP THE BREAD AND DROP IT AGAIN

> EMILY (CONT'D)
> (very sharply)
> It doesn't take all three of you to
> pick it up!

CUT TO

32   INT. THE LIBRARY. HOMESTEAD. DAY   32

> FATHER
> I believe you spoke sharply to
> Thomas, Margaret and Maggie
> yesterday?

> EMILY
> Yes father.

> FATHER
> You must never forget that they
> must be treated with respect. They
> are not servants, but employees.

EMILY GOES TO HIM AND KISSES HIM

> FATHER (CONT'D)
> What was that for?

                    EMILY
          For pointing out so eloquently the
          distinction between the two.

                                                        CUT TO

33   INT. THE KITCHEN. HOMESTEAD. DAY   33

       THREE SHOT OF THOMAS, MARGARET AND MAGGIE ALL STANDING.
       LOOKING VERY UNEASY

       CUT TO EMILY

                    EMILY
          I was very impolite yesterday. I
          would like to apologise to all
          three of you.

                    THOMAS
               (clearly relieved)
          No offence taken.

       CUT TO EMILY

                    EMILY
          Then may I take it that I am
          forgiven? For I am truly sorry.

       CUT TO THREE SHOT

       ALL VERY RELIEVED. NODS AND SMILES

                    MAGGIE
          But we have good news miss…

                    THOMAS
          Your bread won five dollars!

                    EMILY
          You must keep the money - it'll
          ease my conscience.

                    MARGARET
          It took second prize!

       CUT TO EMILY

                    EMILY
               (clearly disappointed)
          Ah…second prize…

                                                    DISSOLVE TO

34   INT. PARLOUR. HOMESTEAD. DAY

VINNIE COMES RUNNING INTO THE PARLOUR

SHE STOPS IN MEDIUM C/U. SHE IS HOLDING AN OPEN PARCEL BUT KEEPING THE CONTENTS AGAINST HER CHEST

CUT TO EMILY

> EMILY
> What is it?

CUT TO VINNIE

> VINNIE
> (breathless)
> From Austin!

SHE LOOKS DOWN AT THE TWO PHOTOGRAPHS - WHICH IS WHAT THEY ARE - SHE THEN TURNS THEM TOWARDS EMILY

> VINNIE (CONT'D)
> Likenesses of Austin and his bride-to-be Susan Gilbert.

SHE TURNS THEM AROUND FOR EMILY TO SEE

CUT TO EMILY

> VINNIE'S VO
> Austin - as handsome as ever!

> EMILY
> But she looks terrified.
>   (a forced enthusiasm)
> But we must make her welcome and reassure her that we are not all forbidding!

CUT TO BOTH PHOTOGRAPHS

                              DISSOLVE TO

35   INT. SOUTH PARLOUR. HOMESTEAD. DAY   35

AUSTIN AND SUSAN STANDING IN THE PARLOUR HAVING ARRIVED HOME. LATE AFTERNOON

> AUSTIN
> (to Susan)
> This is my sister Lavinia.

SUSAN SMILES

CUT TO TWO SHOT OF EMILY AND VINNIE

                VINNIE
    But everyone calls me "Vinnie".

              AUSTIN'S VO
    And this is my other sister Emily.

              EMILY
    And everyone calls me "Napoleon".

CUT TO AUSTIN AND SUSAN. SUSAN LAUGHS AND THE TENSION IS BROKEN

CUT TO EMILY

              EMILY (CONT'D)
    You come back a lawyer and married!
    Harvard clearly agreed with you.

CUT TO AUSTIN

              AUSTIN
    Even more agreeable is that we now
    shall be neighbours - Susan and I
    are moving into The Evergreens,
    next door.

CUT TO VINNIE

              VINNIE
    Another thunderbolt!

CUT TO EMILY

              EMILY
    But a welcome one!

CUT TO FATHER AT THE PARLOUR DOOR

              FATHER
    Austin and I are to practise law.
    Together.

CUT TO EMILY

              EMILY
    Oh shingle has never sounded so
    lovely! Is there no end to these
    wonders?

CUT TO FATHER AT THE PARLOUR DOOR. AFTER A MOMENT MOTHER JOINS HIM QUIETLY

              MOTHER
       (shyly to Austin and
        Susan)
              (MORE)

                    MOTHER (CONT'D)
            I welcome you both - my son and his
            lovely bride.

CUT TO EMILY

                    EMILY
            ... his very lovely bride.

CUT TO MOTHER. EMILY RUNS TO HER AND EMBRACES HER

                    EMILY (CONT'D)
            And this is the greatest wonder of
            all... Mother coming down from Mount
            Olympus!

                    MOTHER
              (embarrassed but kindly)
            Emily, as usual, dramatizes... I live
            a very quiet life. No one would
            know I was here.

                    EMILY
            But if you weren't, oh what a chasm
            you would leave!

                                              DISSOLVE TO

36   INT. SOUTH PARLOUR. HOMESTEAD. EARLY EVENING   36

SUSAN SITTING HOLDING HER NEWBORN BABY. AUSTIN STANDING NEXT
TO HER. EMILY, VINNIE AND MOTHER COMPLETE THE GROUP

                    EMILY
              (to Austin)
            And what does it feel like to be a
            father?

                    AUSTIN
              (beaming)
            Fatherly.

                    EMILY
            Let me hold him.

AUSTIN TAKES THE BABY FROM SUSAN AND GIVES HIM TO EMILY

                    SUSAN
            We're calling him Edward.

                    AUSTIN
            Ned for short.

EMILY HOLDS THE CHILD VERY TENDERLY

THEN SPEAKS SOFTLY TO HIM

                    EMILY
        "I'm nobody! Who are you?
        Are you nobody too?
        Then there's a pair of us – don't
        tell!
        They'd banish us, you know.
        How dreary to be somebody!
        How public, like a frog
        To tell your name the livelong day
        To an admiring bog!"

HOLD ON HER AND BABY

CUT TO FATHER COMING INTO THE PARLOUR FROM THE LIBRARY –
CLEARLY UPSET

                    AUSTIN
        Father what is it?

                    FATHER
        Fort Sumter has been fired upon.

CUT TO GROUP SHOT VINNIE, EMILY, MOTHER, SUSAN AND AUSTIN

                    AUSTIN
        What does this mean?

CUT TO FATHER

                    FATHER
        It is thought that the South will
        secede from the Union.

CUT TO GROUP SHOT AGHAST

CUT TO AUSTIN

                    AUSTIN
        Then it means Civil War.

CUT TO SUSAN

                    SUSAN
        Does this mean that you will be
        drafted Austin?

CUT TO AUSTIN

                    AUSTIN
                  (quietly)
        Yes… almost certainly …

CUT TO FATHER

                    FATHER
        You will remain here…

                    AUSTIN
          But Father my friends will fight. I
          cannot stay at home.

                    FATHER
          You will not go sir.

SILENCE

                    FATHER (CONT'D)
          I will pay the $500 bond so that a
          substitute may fight in your place.

                    AUSTIN
          But what about my honour sir?

                    FATHER
          Your honour sir will be safe in my
          hands.

                    AUSTIN
          And my conscience, Father, what of
          that?

                    FATHER
          It will be best if your conscience
          found solace in doing your filial
          duty.

                    AUSTIN
          For those who will die in this
          Civil War "filial duty" will seem
          like cowardice.

                    FATHER
          No young man of breeding would make
          such a remark.

                    AUSTIN
          No gentleman would provoke it.

AN ANGRY TENSE SILENCE

                    FATHER
               (trying to bend)
          Austin, you are my only son. I
          cannot see your life put at risk.

                    AUSTIN
               (pleading)
          Please Father… don't make me stay…

                    FATHER
               (furious)
          You are not to go! I forbid it! In
          this matter I will be obeyed!

A LONG SILENCE

                    AUSTIN
                  (crushed)
            I will remain here.

FATHER TURNS TOWARDS AUSTIN WHO QUICKLY LEAVES. FOLLOWED BY THE REST OF THE FAMILY

S/TRAX

                    EMILY'S VO
            "To fight aloud is very brave,
              But gallanter, I know,
            Who charge within the bosom,
              The cavalry of woe.

            Who win, and nations do not see,
              Who fall, and none observe,
            Whose dying eyes no country
              Regards with patriot love.
            We trust, in plumed procession,
              For such the angels go,
            Rank after rank, with even feet
              And uniforms of snow."

                                        DISSOLVE TO

A SERIES OF PHOTOGRAPHS FROM THE CIVIL WAR

THEN DISSOLVE TO A PHOTOGRAPH OF THE CONFEDERATE DEAD. TITLE "THE BATTLE OF ANTIETAM". SEPTEMBER 1862. COMBINED DEAD 23,134

DISSOLVE BUT KEEP TRACKING IN ON A PHOTOGRAPH OF THE CONFEDERATE DEAD. TITLE "THE BATTLE OF CHANCELLORVILLE". MAY 1863. COMBINED DEAD 30,099

DISSOLVE BUT KEEP TRACKING IN ON A PHOTOGRAPH OF THE UNION DEAD. TITLE "THE BATTLE OF GETTYSBURG". JULY 1863. COMBINED DEAD 51,112

DISSOLVE BUT KEEP TRACKING IN ON A PHOTOGRAPH OF A YOUNG BOY DRESSED IN A CONFEDERATE UNIFORM

DISSOLVE BUT KEEP TRACKING IN ON A DEAD CONFEDERATE SOLDIER. HE IS ONLY A BOY

S/TRAX   CANNON AND RIFLE FIRE OVER ALL THIS

DISSOLVE TO SMOKE. THE CONFEDERATE FLAG COMES INTO FRAME LEFT. IT WAVES IN A STRONG WIND. SMOKE AND CANNON FIRE

THEN THE UNION FLAG COMES INTO FRAME LEFT, ALMOST OBSCURING THE CONFEDERATE FLAG

> EMILY'S VO (CONT'D)
> "There is a word
> Which bears a sword
> Can pierce an armed man.
> It hurls it's barbed syllables –
> And once is mute again.
> But where it fell
> The saved will tell
> On patriotic day
> Some epauletted brother
> Gave his breath away.
>
> Wherever runs the breathless sun,
> Wherever roams the day,
> There is it's noiseless onset,
> There it's victory!
>
> Behold the keenest marksmen!
> The most accomplished shot!
> Time's sublimest target
> Is a soul "forgot"!"

DISSOLVE TO

37 INT. SOUTH PARLOUR. NIGHT   37

AUSTIN, VINNIE AND EMILY SITTING QUIETLY IN THE FIRELIGHT

SILENCE

> EMILY
> Is Susan well?

> AUSTIN
> As well as an expectant mother can be – but always sanguine.

> VINNIE
> Perhaps this time it will be a little girl?

> AUSTIN
> Yes… that would be lovely…

SILENCE

> AUSTIN (CONT'D)
> Civil War is a terrible thing. Surely anything is better.

> EMILY
> I wonder what the butcher's bill will be today?

                    VINNIE
              (reading from the
              newspaper)
          They say that over 600,000 men have
          perished.

                    EMILY
          And for what? To end slavery which
          should never have flourished in
          this country in the first place.

                    AUSTIN
          Miss Buffam has had too great an
          influence over you Emily.

                    EMILY
          If more people were like her we may
          not have had a war.

                    AUSTIN
          How dare you trivialise it in that
          way! The conflict was not about
          gender!

                    EMILY
          Any argument about gender is war
          because that too is slavery!

                    AUSTIN
          That's a contemptible thing to say!

                    EMILY
          Live for a week as a woman, Austin,
          and you will find it neither
          congenial nor trivial.

A TENSE SILENCE

                    VINNIE
              (trying to calm things)
          So you leave tomorrow... How long
          will you be gone?

                    AUSTIN
          Several weeks, two months maybe.
          Both cases are difficult and both
          are being tried by Judge Lord... and
          you know how fierce he can be...

SILENCE

                    VINNIE
          Must you go for such a length of
          time?

                    AUSTIN
          Yes. A man must make his way in the
          world - he can't be merely
          decorous.

                    EMILY
          And a woman? What should she do? Or
          is she destined only for
          decorousness?

                    AUSTIN
          Let's not argue. Not on my last
          night at home.

SILENCE FALLS FILLED WITH SUPPRESSED TEARS

                    AUSTIN (CONT'D)
          I'll write. It'll ease my
          unhappiness.

                    EMILY
          But increase mine.

                                                  CUT TO

38   EXT. HOMESTEAD. DAY   38

          AUSTIN LEAVING

          THE FAMILY, EXCEPT EMILY, SAY THEIR GOOD-BYES, INCLUDING
          SUSAN WHO IS HEAVILY PREGNANT

                    AUSTIN
                (looking around)
          Where's Emily?

          THEY ALL START CALLING HER, AND AFTER A MOMENT SHE COMES OUT
          OF THE HOUSE AND GOES TO AUSTIN

                    AUSTIN (CONT'D)
          Won't you say goodbye Emily?

                    EMILY
                (shaking her head)
          But I will say, "Goodbye until we
          meet again."

          THEY EMBRACE AND AUSTIN LEAVES

          S/TRAX

                    EMILY'S VO
          "It's all I have to bring today,
             This, and my heart beside,
                    (MORE)

> EMILY'S VO (CONT'D)
> This, and my heart, and all the fields,
> And all the meadows wide.
>
> Be sure you count, should I forget -
> Someone the sum could tell -
> This, and my heart, and all the bees
> Which in the clover dwell."

DISSOLVE TO

39 INT. STAIRWAY/HALL, THE HOMESTEAD. NIGHT 39

WE SEE A LAMP MOVING THROUGH THE DARK HOUSE BUT NOT WHO'S CARRYING IT

40 INT. SOUTH PARLOUR THE HOMESTEAD. NIGHT 40

WE SEE THE LAMP AND EMILY CARRYING IT QUIETLY INTO THE PARLOUR

EMILY SETS THE LAMP DOWN AND SITS DOWN

THEN THERE IS A LIGHT TAP ON THE FRENCH WINDOW - IT IS SUSAN WHO COMES IN QUIETLY

> SUSAN
> (quietly)
> What are you doing at this hour?

> EMILY
> (quietly)
> This is my time for writing. Between 3am and morning. My father allows it. No husband would.

> SUSAN
> I came over... I thought something was amiss.

> EMILY
> No.

SILENCE

> This is the best time... when it feels as if the whole world is asleep and still.

SILENCE

> Did you wake Austin?

> SUSAN
> No. He sleeps very soundly.

SILENCE

> EMILY
> Why did you take so long to consent to marry Austin?

> SUSAN
> In truth, the thought of men – in that particular respect – turned me to stone. Although Austin is very tender and yielding to my… reservations.

> EMILY
> Is that particular part of married life so terrible?

> SUSAN
> I do my duty.

Pause

> (brightly)
> But I not only gained a husband but two sisters also.

> EMILY
> (eagerly)
> And we will be sisters!

> SUSAN
> And we will share and read everything!

> EMILY
> The Brontes, George Elliot, and – heaven save us Mrs. Gaskell too!

THEY BOTH LAUGH QUIETLY

SILENCE

> SUSAN
> And you have your poetry.

> EMILY
> But you have a life. I have a routine. It's God's one concession to a "no-hoper".

SILENCE

> SUSAN
> Does nothing bring you solace?

> EMILY
> For those of us who live minor lives and are deprived of a... particular... kind of love... we know best how to starve.

LONG SILENCE

> EMILY (CONT'D)
> We deceive ourselves and then others – it's the worst kind of lie.

> SUSAN
> But in matters of the soul you are rigorous.

> EMILY
> Rigour is no substitute for happiness.

DISSOLVE TO

41 INT. KITCHEN. HOMESTEAD. DAY 41

EMILY IS AT THE TABLE PREPARING BREAD. SUDDENLY SHE FEELS AN ACUTE PAIN IN HER KIDNEYS. SHE ALMOST CRIES OUT BUT DOESN'T

S/TRAX

> EMILY'S VO
> "While I was fearing it, it came,
> But came with less of fear,
> Because that fearing it so long
> Had almost made it dear.
> There is a fitting a dismay,
> A fitting a despair.
>
> 'Tis harder knowing it is due,
> Than knowing it is here.
> The trying on the utmost,
> The morning it is new,
> Is terribler than wearing it
> A whole existence through."

DURING THIS THE PAIN COMES AND GOES AND SHE REMAINS SEATED, EXHAUSTED BY THE PAIN

DISSOLVE TO

42 INT. EMILY'S ROOM. HOMESTEAD. DAY   42

EMILY IS SEATED AT HER WRITING DESK

ABOVE HER THE WINDOW

LIGHT COMES STREAMING IN

THEN REVEREND WADSWORTH APPEARS WITHIN THE LIGHT

          REV. WADSWORTH
      (v/o)
      (ecstatically)
Oh what a call is this? The spirit and the bride call and he that heareth calls. The voices of all God's bright and blessed things take up the utterance. The dear ones in your earthly homes – mother and sister and brother and child – whose names are written in the lamb's book of life cry, "Come, Come!" And the church below, Christ's witness unto the world, in all her ordinances and utterances, "Come, Come!" And the church above with the rustling of white robes, and the sweeping of golden harps, cries, "Come, Come!" And the angels of Heaven, lo! Rank above rank, immortal principalities, as they circle the eternal throne, they have caught up the sound, and cry…

REV. WADSWORTH'S VOICE CROSS FADES TO EMILY'S VOICE

          EMILY'S VO
"I have no life but this,
To lead it here;
Nor any death but lest
Dispelled from there;
Nor tie to earths to come,
Nor action new,
Except through this extent,
The realm of you."

SHE KEEPS ON WRITING FURIOUSLY

          VINNIE
      (coming in)
Rev. Wadsworth's sermons take the breath way.

          EMILY
That kind of religious ecstasy is wonderful but back in the quiet of one's room it seems as remote as Spitzbergen.

SILENCE

> EMILY (CONT'D)
> (jocular)
> But he is as handsome as he is ecstatic! And he's so clean! Like a cherub after bathing.

> VINNIE
> And happily married.

EMILY JUST SMILES

> EMILY
> Ah, to be betrothed - without the swoon. But a person may hope.

> VINNIE
> If you are too quick to hope you will always be disappointed.

> EMILY
> And if I am too quick to despair - what then?

> VINNIE
> Then you will be too slow to hope.

> EMILY
> I set too much store by friendships… when we lose friends to death that is the most profound loss… when we lose them to marriage the grief is subtler but felt just as keenly.

> VINNIE
> We cannot keep the world or life at bay Emily. Neither can we ignore it.

> EMILY
> We can do better than that - we can be vigilant against it.

> VINNIE
> And when that vigil is over - what then?

> EMILY
> Eternity. And in that place no loss is felt.

> VINNIE
> But what of the kingdom to come?

EMILY
That may be a gain - but only after the fact.

VINNIE
But one day you may marry.

EMILY
I think not. You and Austin are the handsome ones - I am a kangaroo amongst beauties.

VINNIE
No! You have a lovely face and a fine soul!

EMILY
Then let us hope that the man who courts me will have an interest in zoology and all things spiritual!

THEY BOTH LAUGH

EMILY (CONT'D)
Let's invite Rev. Wadsworth to tea.

VINNIE
And Mrs. Wadsworth.

EMILY
Oh very well.

VINNIE
But you must promise me that you'll behave… I know how provocative you can be.

EMILY
I will muster as much dignity as I can.

VINNIE
That's what I'm afraid of.

CUT TO

43 INT. SOUTH PARLOUR. HOMESTEAD.DAY   43

THE TABLE IS SET WITH TEA AND COFFEE. EMILY, VINNIE, REV. WADSWORTH AND HIS WIFE. HE IS ABOUT 40 AND AFFABLE. SHE IS A WOMAN COMPLETELY DEVOID OF EITHER CHARACTER OR HUMOUR

ONE OF THE DOMESTICS COMES IN WITH A TRAY OF WATER, LEMONADE AND GLASSES, SETS IT DOWN AND EXITS

AN AWKWARD PAUSE

>   EMILY
>   Will you take coffee Mrs.
>   Wadsworth?

MRS. WADSWORTH SHAKES HER HEAD BUT DOES NOT SPEAK

>   EMILY (CONT'D)
>   Tea then?
>
>   REV. WADSWORTH
>   No thank you. Mrs. Wadsworth is an
>   abstainer.
>
>   EMILY
>   I thought abstention was only for
>   alcohol.
>
>   MRS. WADSWORTH
>   For me it extends to tea also.

SILENCE

>   EMILY
>   They say the Chinese drink tea for
>   remedial purposes.
>
>   MRS. WADSWORTH
>   I am glad to say that I am not
>   Chinese.

ANOTHER AWKWARD SILENCE

>   VINNIE
>   Some lemonade then?
>
>   EMILY
>   Surely God would not disapprove of
>   lemonade?
>
>   MRS. WADSWORTH
>   Levity and the will of God are, I
>   think, incompatible, almost
>   improper. Just plain water would be
>   pleasant.
>
>   EMILY
>   Rev. Wadsworth?
>
>   REV. WADSWORTH
>   Just a cup of hot water for me
>   thank you.

THE SILENCE BROKEN ONLY BY VINNIE POURING THE COLD AND HOT WATER FOR REV. WADSWORTH AND HIS WIFE

>   REV. WADSWORTH (CONT'D)
>   I understand from Vinnie that you
>   are a poet?
>
>   EMILY
>   (suddenly shy)
>   I write verses, yes.
>
>   REV. WADSWORTH
>   And what of your contemporaries?
>   Mr. Longfellow for instance.
>
>   EMILY
>   His genius lies in stating the
>   obvious.
>
>   MRS. WADSWORTH
>   Oh that is too harsh. There are
>   many fine things in "Hiawatha".
>
>   EMILY
>   (imitating "Hiawatha"
>   rhyme scheme)
>   "I am sorry I was cruel
>   But, madam, I must say in truth
>   Hiawatha is but gruel
>   Just read one stanza for the
>   proof".

REV. WADSWORTH SMILES APPRECIATING THE JOKE, BUT THIS HAS NOT GONE DOWN TOO WELL WITH MRS. WADSWORTH

>   EMILY (CONT'D)
>   No - give me something pressed from
>   truth and that is poetry.
>
>   REV. WADSWORTH
>   I suppose you feel The Brontes do
>   that?
>
>   EMILY
>   Yes. And a few others.
>
>   MRS. WADSWORTH
>   What do you find in all that
>   Yorkshire gloom?
>
>   EMILY
>   The beauty of truth. The poetry of
>   the known.
>
>   MRS. WADSWORTH
>   But why can't they dwell on
>   something wholesome?
>
>   EMILY
>   If they wished to be wholesome I
>   would imagine they would crochet.

THIS HAS NOT GONE DOWN TOO WELL WITH MRS. WADSWORTH EITHER

ANOTHER AWKWARD SILENCE

> EMILY(CONT'D)
> (to Rev. and Mrs. Wadsworth)
> Would you like to take a turn in the garden?
>
> MRS. WADSWORTH
> No thank you. I find this heat oppressive. But Charles loves to be out of doors. I myself prefer the shade.
>
> EMILY
> In that case I shall take the liberty of escorting your husband around our modest garden…

VINNIE GOES TO PROTEST BUT EMILY AND THE REV. WADSWORTH HAVE ALREADY RISEN

> EMILY (CONT'D)
> … and my sister can have you all to herself!

THEY LEAVE

VINNIE INWARDLY GROANING

SILENCE

> VINNIE
> More water?

CUT TO

44 EXT. SIDE GARDEN, HOMESTEAD. DAY 44

GLORIOUS WEATHER

EMILY AND REV. WADSWORTH COMING FROM THE HOUSE

SUDDENLY EMILY SEEMS EXTREMELY EMBARRASSED AND ILL AT EASE.

> REV. WADSWORTH
> Thank you for your invitation Miss Dickinson.
>
> EMILY
> I was very moved by your sermon sir, and very much wanted to tell you.

SILENCE

SHE TAKES FROM HER POCKET ONE OF THE SMALL SEWN BOOKS OF POETRY

          EMILY (CONT'D)
  This is all I have to give in return.

HE SITS DOWN IN THE SHADE. SHE STANDS BEHIND THIS TREE - WAITING.

HE BEGINS TO READ HER POEMS

THE PAUSE SEEMS IMMENSE

TRACK IN ON EMILY

          EMILY (CONT'D)
  Please - say something. Does my poetry have any worth?

          REV. WADSWORTH'S VO
     (he stops reading and for a moment is unable to speak)
  They are remarkable! Uncompromising yes! But this is wonderful poetry!

EMILY SAYS NOTHING BUT IS CLEARLY DELIGHTED, THRILLED EVEN - ALMOST TO TEARS

          REV. WADSWORTH
  How many have been published?

          EMILY
  Seven…eleven…I cannot recall…

          REV. WADSWORTH
     (shocked)
  And no more?

          EMILY
  And no more.

          REV. WADSWORTH
  How can you be so stoic?

          EMILY
  It is easy to be stoic when no one wants what you have to offer.
     (half laughs)
  There's always posterity, I suppose… but posterity is as comfortless as God.

                    REV. WADSWORTH
            That sounds like despair.

                    EMILY
            No. It's bitterness. Besides a
            posthumous reputation is only for
            those who - when living - weren't
            worth remembering. But ah, to be
            wracked by success!
                (full of longing)
            But I would like some approval
            before I die.

HOLD ON EMILY

                                            DISSOLVE TO

45   INT. EMILY'S ROOM. HOMESTEAD. DAY   45

        SHE SITS AT HER DESK WRITING FURIOUSLY

        BRILLIANT SUNSHINE POURING THROUGH THE WINDOW

        S/TRAX

                    EMILY'S VO
                (in a hushed but thrilled
                 voice)
            "If you were coming in the Fall,
                I'd brush the summer by
            With half a smile, and half a
                        spurn,
                As housewives do a fly.

            If I could see you in a year,
                I'd wind the months in balls,
            And put them each in separate
                        drawers,
                Until their time befalls.

            If only centuries delayed,
                I'd count them on my hand,
            Subtracting 'till my fingers
                        dropped
                Into Van Diemen's land…"

        SHE STANDS UP IN THE SUNLIGHT AND SPEAKS THE REST OF THE POEM
        ALOUD
            "…If certain, when this life was
                        out,
                That yours and mine should be,
            I'd toss it yonder like a rind,
                And taste eternity.

            But now, all ignorant of the length
                    (MORE)

> EMILY'S VO (CONT'D)
> Of time's uncertain wing,
> It goads me, like the goblin bee,
> That will not state it's sting."

THE DOOR IS KNOCKED UPON AND VINNIE ENTERS

EMILY TURNS AROUND

> VINNIE
> (cautiously)
> Rev. Wadsworth has sailed for San Francisco.

EMILY NEAR TO TEARS BUT TRYING TO HIDE THEM AT THE SHOCK OF THE NEWS

> EMILY
> They all go. They all leave. They all desert you.

VINNIE TRIES TO CONSOLE HER BUT EMILY BREAKS AWAY

> EMILY (CONT'D)
> Don't touch me! I will not be pitied! It makes me feel repulsive!

PAUSE

> VINNIE
> You set too much store by physical beauty Emily.

> EMILY
> The only people who can be sanguine about not being handsome are those who are already beautiful. The rest of us have only our envy to keep us warm.

> VINNIE
> But you have an exquisite nature.

> EMILY
> What's the use of that in this world?

> VINNIE
> I sometimes think that you are too harsh with yourself Emily.

> EMILY
> I have many defects. There is much to rectify.

> VINNIE
> Emily, it is just as punitive to admit to too many faults as it is to deny too few virtues.
> (MORE)

VINNIE (CONT'D)
(cautious)
The Rev. Wadsworth is a married man Emily.

EMILY DOESN'T ANSWER

VINNIE (CONT'D)
This kind of attachment is improper.

EMILY
(angry)
We can't all possess your smug rectitude.

VINNIE
(equally angry)
Don't sneer at anyone's morals Emily when your own could do with some little correction.

EMILY
By that I assume you mean Rev. Wadsworth?

VINNIE
Yes! He's married! And you should not attach yourself to someone who is not free to return that… attachment. You hardly know the man except through his sermons.

A TENSE SILENCE

VINNIE (CONT'D)
Besides he and Mrs. Wadsworth are very happy. She has led a blameless life.

EMILY
(rather spiteful)
She hasn't led a "life" at all! She's too inert for that! If docility were love we'd all live happily ever after!

VINNIE
(warmly)
She's a good wife! And to be truthful I have never understood the attraction of her husband for you… he's hardly a Mr. Rochester and you are certainly not Jane Eyre!

A TENSE SILENCE

VINNIE STARTS TO THAW

                    VINNIE (CONT'D)
          That was unkind of me.

                    EMILY
          I'm sorry too. You are not smug.

                    VINNIE
          But I do sermonise.

                    EMILY
          And I do over dramatize. But it was
          news that was, is hard to bear.

EMILY CATCHES HERSELF IN THE MIRROR AND COLLAPSES INTO A
CHAIR

                    EMILY (CONT'D (CONT'D)
              (utter despair)
          Oh you wretched creature - will you
          never achieve anything!

PAN AWAY FROM EMILY (L TO R) BLAZING WITH SUNLIGHT

                    EMILY'S VO
          "We outgrow love like other things
           And put it in the drawer,
           'Till it an antique fashion shows
           Like costumes grandsires wore."

                                        DISSOLVE TO

46   EXT. GARDEN, THE HOMESTEAD. DAY   46

       TWO SHOT OF EMILY AND MISS VB WALKING THROUGH THE GROUNDS

       TRACK WITH THEM

                    MISS VB
          I must have someone with a sense of
          humour, someone who can laugh at
          the world. Taking life seriously is
          the shortest route to disaster.

                    EMILY
          And have you found such a one?

                    MISS VB
          Someone has found me. A Mr. Wilder -
          a professor of mathematics. And if
          he can find comedy in a vulgar
          fraction - I'm his!

> EMILY
> But do you love him?

> MISS VB
> Love? I cannot say. It's a very beguiling idea… they even say it exists.

> EMILY
> But how will you know?

SILENCE

> What if you make an error?

> MISS VB
> If he is a bad choice I'll have him killed quietly and tell everyone that he died of some sort of algebraic shock.

THEY BOTH SMILE. EMILY RUEFULLY

> EMILY
> I hope you'll be happy.

> MISS VB
> That can't be guaranteed. I'll settle for consideration.

> EMILY
> That sounds like surrender.

> MISS VB
> No. It's practicality. And who knows? Perhaps love will come in it's wake. Then I can relax into smugness.

> EMILY
> You could never be smug.

> MISS VB
> Life catches you out Emily. In the end we all become the thing we most dread.

> EMILY
> Then I shall reject the world and not fulfil that prophecy.

> MISS VB
> Then you will make the greatest of mistakes for you will deny yourself what your spirit needs most.

> EMILY
> And what is that?

MISS VB
Truth. And experience. Otherwise your vow will be an act of cowardice.

EMILY
(hurt)
That was hurtful.

MISS VB
(kindly)
But honest. Don't resist your vices Emily - it is your virtues you should be wary of.

A PAUSE AND THEN THEY BOTH LAUGH

EMILY
Austin once told Aunt Elizabeth that our virtues are just vices in disguise.

MISS VB
Now there is a man with a sense of humour!

EMILY
And does Mr. Wilder possess one?

MISS VB
Of a kind. He proposed to me by letter - so if the marriage is unhappy I shall blame the US mail.
(more seriously)
Always conform Emily. Keep disobedience secret. Be outwardly docile but in here…
(she touches her heart)
You can be as revolutionary as you like.

EMILY
Isn't that hypocrisy?

MISS VB
Of course it is! But in America we cherish it… we think it makes us incorruptible… you must not, you must never confuse the outer with the inner piety. Only Episcopalians do that.

EMILY
But I am rebellious and far from the grace of God.

> MISS VB
> Emily you are closer to Him than anyone I know.
> (pause)
> Always look below the surface Emily. But don't be afraid of what you find there.

> EMILY
> Chaos?

> MISS VB
> Yes.

> EMILY
> Then I shall confront everything.

> MISS VB
> Don't be too radical Emily. Radicals don't thrive in this country.

> EMILY
> But you're a radical.

> MISS VB
> But I'll eventually conform. For the sake of peace… or a quiet life.
> (pause)
> But I know that you will not and I envy you your courage.
> (pause)
> You seem a little distant… or is it just my overactive imagination.

EMILY DOESN'T REPLY. THEY CONTINUE WALKING TOGETHER SLOWLY BUT DO NOT LINK ARMS

> EMILY
> (subdued)
> I suppose you will carry some lovely flowers and have Mr. Mendelssohn's wedding march.

> MISS VB
> Flowers – yes. Mendelssohn – no. Never play happy music at a wedding Emily, it's too misleading.

> EMILY
> But you will be completely gone from us.

> MISS VB
> You make it sound like dying.

> EMILY
> Isn't it?

                    MISS VB
          No. And even if it were you must
          force yourself to think otherwise.
          America is the only country in the
          world that looks upon death as some
          kind of personal failure.

PAN AWAY FROM THEM (L TO R)

                                                  DISSOLVE TO

47   EXT. HOMESTEAD. DAY   47

       MISS VB ARRIVING IN A CARRIAGE. PAN WITH HER (R TO L)

       VINNIE FOLLOWED BY EMILY COMES TO THE GATE. EMILY RELUCTANTLY

                    MISS VB
               (to the horse)
          STOP!!

                    VINNIE
          Aren't you supposed to say "Whoa"?

                    MISS VB
          Not with clever Pendennis - he went
          to Princeton.

                    VINNIE
          How fares Mr. Wilder?

                    MISS VB
          I've met him several times know but
          he never speaks. Just sits there
          smiling and going pink… which
          always makes him look like a roll
          of highly polished linoleum… until
          yesterday - when he pounced.

                    VINNIE
          Pounced?

                    MISS VB
          Pounced. I use the word advisedly.
          Then he told me that I reminded him
          of Pocahontas.

                    VINNIE
          Did he know her?

                    MISS VB
          No - but his mother probably did.
          But he is a gentle creature and
          seems to be amused by my…
          unladylike ways.

                    EMILY
               (rueful)
          So you have found your Capt. Smith?

                    MISS VB
          It would seem so. Ah me! I had
          always wanted a high romance - but
          instead all I get is some wampum
          and a very small wigwam.

                    VINNIE
          On your wedding day we'll do a rain
          dance and send you a tomahawk.

                    MISS VB
          Send two tomahawks. The first one
          might miss my mother-in-law.
               (to the horse)
          Quickly Pendennnis - before second
          thoughts set in!

     SHE DRIVES OFF

48   EXT. LOOKING AWAY FROM THE HOMESTEAD (DIFFERENT LOCATION)   48

                    VINNIE
               (to Emily)
          You're very quiet Emily.

                    EMILY
          This is the way it always happens.
          A flirtation and then they
          marry…already she is going, already
          she is lost to us…

                    VINNIE
          Surely you don't begrudge her, her
          happiness?

                    EMILY
          No. But I am selfish. Change
          frightens me.
               (tries to smile)
          I set too much store by worldly
          things.

                                                  DISSOLVE TO

49   EXT. STREET AND CHURCH. DAY   49

S/TRAX OVER THE DISSOLVE

      EMILY'S VO
  Bees in the lavender then the lazy
  owl.

MISS VB AND MR. WILDER EMERGE FROM THE CHURCH MARRIED

A SMALL CROWD VINNIE AND EMILY AMONG THEM

AS MISS VB GOES TO HER WAITING CARRIAGE SHE STOPS BY VINNIE AND EMILY AND EMBRACES VINNIE

      VINNIE
  We wish you all the happiness in
  the world.

MISS VB AND VINNIE KISS

MISS VB TURNS TO EMILY WHO IS FIGHTING TEARS

      MISS VB
   (embracing Emily)
  No tears Emily.
   (near to tears herself)
  No tears.

SHE GOES TO THE CARRIAGE AND HER HUSBAND DRIVES HER AWAY

S/TRAX

      EMILY'S VO
  "The dying need but little, dear –
   A glass of water's all,
   A flowers unobtrusive face
    To punctuate the wall,

  A fan, perhaps, a friend's regret,
   And certainly that one
   No colour in the rainbow
  Perceives when you are gone.

  Look back on time with kindly eyes,
   He doubtless did his best;
  How softly sinks his trembling sun
   In human nature's west!"

AS THEY DRIVE AWAY IT SLOWLY GOES DARK

               DISSOLVE TO

50   INT. SOUTH PARLOUR/ HALLWAY. HOMESTEAD. LATE AFTERNOON   50

AUSTIN AND SUSAN BEING ESCORTED TO THE FRONT DOOR BY EMILY AND VINNIE

> AUSTIN
> We went to Gettysburg to hear the speeches. Mr. Edward Everett spoke for nearly two hours!

> SUSAN
> Very splendid! Very rousing!

> EMILY
> And The President's speech?

> AUSTIN
> Mr. Lincoln was shocking in his brevity. He spoke for about three minutes. Not memorable.

> VINNIE
> Were there many there to hear the orations?

> SUSAN
> Thousands. Some said fifteen thousand.

> AUSTIN
> Most of them looking for breakfast or trying to find souvenirs of the battle. Macabre. We travelled back with Mr. and Mrs. Todd… Mr Todd is to teach astronomy at Mount Holyoke.

> SUSAN
> Mabel Todd is a very accomplished young lady… she paints in oils on canvass and in watercolour… she plays the piano seriously well and sings in a lovely trained soprano and is splendidly upholstered.

> EMILY
> She sounds like an armchair…

ALL GIGGLE

> VINNIE
> … or a phenomenon.

> AUSTIN
> (absentmindedly)
> Yes… I suppose she does…

AUSTIN AND SUSAN LEAVE AND THE FRONT DOOR IS CLOSED

OUTSIDE THE HOUSE THE SUN IS LOW

EMILY AND VINNIE MOVE TO THE STAIRS AND GO UP THEM SLOWLY

SILENCE

                                                                            DISSOLVE TO

51   EXT. HOMESTEAD. LATE AFTERNOON   51

THE SUN IS LOW

THE SHADOWS ARE LENGTHENING

HOLD

S/TRAX   THE "THREE RAVENS" (A MEDIEVAL TEXT) SETTING BY JOHN HERLE SUNG BY A SOPRANO

"Since first I saw your face I resolved
To honour and renown you.
If now I am distained, I wish
My heart had never known you.
What! I that loved, and you that liked,
Shall we begin to wrangle?
No, no, no, my heart is fast,
And cannot disentangle.

If I admire or praise you too much,
That fault you may forgive me;
Or if my hands had strayed to touch,
Then justly might you leave me.
I asked you leave, you bade me love,
Is't now a time to chide me?
No, no, no, I love you still,
What fortune e'er betide me.

If I have wronged you, tell me wherein,
And I will soon amend it;
In recompense of such a sin,
Here is my heart, I'll send it.
If that will not your mercy move,
Then, for my life I care not;
Then, oh then, torment me still,
And take my life and spare not."

SONG FINISHES

                                                        DISSOLVE TO

52   INT. SOUTH PARLOUR. HOMESTEAD. LATE AFTERNOON   52

MOTHER ON A DAY BED

CUT TO EMILY

                     EMILY
          May I get you something Mother?

CUT TO MOTHER

                    MOTHER
         (shaking her head)
         No Emily.

SILENCE

CUT TO EMILY

                     EMILY
         You have always seemed so sad
         Mother.

EMILY JOINS HER MOTHER

                    MOTHER
         (still far away)
         My life has passed as if in a dream
         - as if I'd never been part of it.
         After Vinnie was born a kind of
         melancholia settled over me which I
         mistook for contentment…

                    EMILY
          Were we such a terrible price to pay?

                    MOTHER
          No! I would not be without all three
          of you…to have my children about me –
          there could be no better medicine…

SILENCE
                    MOTHER (CONT'D)
          But sometimes, at a certain hour,
          when the sun is low and the shadows
          lengthen…
                    (she begins to weep)
          … I'm filled with such a sense of
          longing that I feel such a weight on
          my heart!… oh how it aches…

EMILY VERY MOVED HOLDS HER MOTHERS HAND AND FATHER COMES IN

HE GOES TO THE DAY BED AND EMBRACES MOTHER

                    MOTHER (CONT'D)
                    (weeping)
          Oh my dear! Oh my dear!

                    FATHER
                    (murmuring softly)
          There my lamb! There!

                    EMILY'S VO
          "Of so divine a loss
          We enter but the gain
          Indemnity for loneliness
          That such a bliss has
                    been."
                    FATHER'S VO
          Mr. Lincoln is assassinated.

                                        DISSOLVE TO

53   INT. SOUTH PARLOUR. HOMESTEAD. NIGHT   53

FATHER'S OPEN COFFIN

EMILY, VINNIE, AUSTIN, SUSAN AND MRS. DICKINSON SITTING THERE
STUNNED BY GRIEF

HOLD ON COFFIN

THEN

A QUIET PASSION

HOLD ON THEM

MOTHER AND VINNIE WEEPING BUT AUSTIN AND EMILY PARALYSED WITH SHOCK

EMILY RUNS FROM THE ROOM

SHE GOES TO HER ROOM. SHUTS THEN BOLTS THE DOOR

                                                    DISSOLVE TO

54   INT/EXT. HOMESTEAD. DAY   54

FATHER'S FUNERAL PROCESSION SEEN FROM EMILY'S WINDOW

CRANE UP TO C/U OF EMILY WATCHING THE PROCESSION FROM HER WINDOW. HER FACE SWOLLEN WITH WEEPING, THE NET CURTAIN DROPS, COVERING EMILY'S FACE

HOLD ON HER

THE PROCESSION MOVES OFF

                  VINNIE'S VO
        Shall I call Emily?

                  MOTHER'S VO
        No. She grieves privately. That is
        enough.

HOLD ON PROCESSION

S/TRAX

                  VINNIE'S VO
        If we reach into the silence then
        we cannot be afraid for where there
        is nothing - there is God.

                  EMILY'S VO
        It sounds beautiful but
        comfortless.

                  VINNIE'S VO
        But the comfort is God.

                                                  DISSOLVE TO

55   INT. LANDING, HOMESTEAD. DAY   55

VINNIE CLIMBS THE STAIRS TO EMILY'S ROOM

SHE STOPS AT THE BEDROOM DOOR

OUTSIDE THE DOOR A TRAY OF UNTOUCHED FOOD

     VINNIE
   (knocking softly on the
    door)
  Emily… Emily…you must eat… you must come down… it's been three days now…

SILENCE

THEN WE HEAR THE DOOR BEING UNLOCKED

EMILY OPENS THE DOOR AND IS DRESSED IN A WHITE PIQUE DRESS WHICH SHE WILL WEAR UNTIL THE END OF THE FILM

     VINNIE (CONT'D)
  Emily you're wearing white!

     EMILY
  Yes.

     VINNIE
  But we're still in mourning!

     EMILY
  So am I.

          DISSOLVE TO

56 INT. TOP OF THE STAIRS. HOMESTEAD. DAY 56

PAN (R TO L) TO EMILY'S ROOM THE DOOR OF WHICH IS CLOSED

     VINNIE'S VO
   (calling up)
  Emily – it's Mr. Bowles. He has come to Amherst specially to see you.

     SAMUEL BOWLES VO
  Come down damn you! I refuse to speak to anyone who's a flight of stairs above me!

EMILY COMING MEEKLY OUT OF HER BEDROOM. SHE STANDS AT THE TOP OF THE STAIRS. SHE IS CLEARLY IN PAIN, HER FACE PUFFY

     EMILY
  Forgive me if I am frightened. I never see anyone and hardly know what to say.

CUT TO SAMUEL BOWLES

>SAMUEL BOWLES
>You could say "thank you" for my publishing some of your verse!

CUT TO EMILY

>EMILY
>For that Sir, you get more than my thanks. You get my gratitude. But you have altered some of my punctuation.

CUT TO SAMUEL BOWLES

>SAMUEL BOWLES
>Good Lord! What's a hyphen here or a semi-colon there?

CUT TO EMILY

>EMILY
>To many – nothing. But to me the alteration of my punctuation marks is very hard to endure.

CUT TO SAMUEL BOWLES

>SAMUEL BOWLES
>(still rather irritable)
>Then I apologise. I was merely trying to make your meaning clearer to my readers.

CUT TO EMILY

>EMILY
>Clarity is one thing sir. Obviousness quite another. The only person qualified to interfere with a poet's work is the poet herself. From anyone else it feels like an attack.

CUT TO SAMUEL BOWLES

>SAMUEL BOWLES
>(still tetchy)
>Miss Dickinson, this is no way to speak or behave. If you treated a suitor like this he would not return.

CUT TO EMILY

>EMILY
>Are you sure there will be one?

CUT TO SAMUEL BOWLES

> SAMUEL BOWLES
> Of course! Even for someone as hard to please as yourself.

CUT TO EMILY

> EMILY
> Well if he does come, he will have to be as spectacular as Disraeli and as sincere as Gladstone.

CUT TO SAMUEL BOWLES

> SAMUEL BOWLES
> And as upright as George Washington?

CUT TO EMILY

> EMILY
> George who?

DISSOLVE TO

57   INT. LANDING, HOMESTEAD. DAY   57

VINNIE AT EMILY'S DOOR

> VINNIE
> Emily, Mr. Emmons is here to see us.

> EMILY
> (sitting in the door which is slightly ajar)
> Our "beautiful friend"?

> VINNIE
> Will you come down?

> EMILY
> No.

> VINNIE
> This is discourteous. Why will you not come down to meet him?

> EMILY
> Because he is so beautiful and I am not beautiful enough.

                    VINNIE
          He has read some of your published
          poems…and admires them.

                    EMILY
          Admiration always masks envy.

                    VINNIE
          And what does envy mask?

                    EMILY
          Oh, that masks admiration.

SILENCE

                    EMILY (CONT'D)
              (uncompromising)
          He may come to the foot of the
          stairs.

                    VINNIE
              (embarrassed)
          But he has come to see…

                    EMILY
          … you!…

                    VINNIE
          Both of us!

                    EMILY
          Well - he has seen you at any rate.

VINNIE GOES DOWNSTAIRS

SILENCE

58   INT. HALLWAY, HOMESTEAD - DAY   58

     THEN HENRY VAUGHN EMMONS COMES TO THE FOOT OF THE STAIRS

                    MR. EMMONS
          Miss Dickinson?

                    EMILY
          Yes.

                    MR. EMMONS
          I cannot see you.

                    EMILY
          That, Sir, is no matter.

SILENCE

                        MR. EMMONS
                    (trying to make light of
                    it)
                It is the first time I've conducted
                a visit in this fashion.

SILENCE

                It seems unfair that you can see me
                but I can only hear you.

                        EMILY
                That can be no hardship, sir, since
                I am best heard and not seen.

SILENCE

                        MR. EMMONS
                Will you take a ride with Vinnie
                and me?

                        EMILY
                No. I do not cross my father's
                ground to any house or town.

                        MR. EMMONS
                That seems such a shame, especially
                in such lovely weather.

                        EMILY
                The weather will remain lovely
                whether I drive through it or not.

                        MR. EMMONS
                Then I'll wish you good day, Miss
                Dickinson.

                        EMILY
                Good day, Mr. Emmons.

HE LEAVES

SHE REMAINS SITTING JUST INSIDE THE HALF OPENED DOOR

THE SOUNDS OF VINNIE AND MR. EMMONS LEAVING

THEN SILENCE

HOLD ON EMILY

                                                DISSOLVE TO

59   INT. LANDING/HALLWAY - DAY   59

        EMILY STILL SITTING AT HER HALF OPEN DOOR

        IT SLOWLY GOES FROM DAY TO NIGHT

DARKNESS, EXCEPT FOR HER LAMP BURNING LOW

SILENCE

SHE SITS AS IF ANTICIPATING SOMEONE OR SOMETHING

SILENCE

S/TRAX   FOOTSTEPS ARE HEARD COMING UP THE STAIRS BUT WE DON'T SEE ANYONE

HOLD ON EMILY EXPECTANT AND FLUSHED

                        EMILY'S VO
          He will mount the stairs at midnight…

CUT TO A MANS FIGURE SEEN IN BLACKNESS MOVING SOFTLY UP THE STAIRS

CUT TO EMILY

HER NERVES SEEM STRUNG OUT AS SHE WAITS

                      EMILY'S VO (CONT'D)
          He will be my mirror, my volcano…

CUT TO THE FIGURE OF THE MAN AS HE REACHES THE LANDING AND WALKS TOWARDS HER DOOR

CUT TO EMILY AT HER DOOR. IT OPENS WIDE AS IF BY ITSELF

SHE SMILES A RADIANT SMILE

TRACK IN ON HER

                      EMILY'S VO (CONT'D)
          The looming man in the night…

TRACK STOPS ON HER

SHE OPENS HER EYES

THERE IS ONLY THE DARK – NO FIGURE OF A MAN AT ALL. SHE TURNS OFF HER LAMP AND SITTING IN THE DARK SHE SLOWLY CLOSES THE DOOR

                      EMILY'S VO (CONT'D)
          No ordinary bridegroom he… but I will wait all my days… I will wait… and he will come before the afterlife… 47, 48… 49… oh please let him come, let him not forget me…

                                                  DISSOLVE TO

60   INT. EMILY'S BEDROOM – EVENING   60

EMILY STILL SITTING THERE BY HER HALF OPEN DOOR WAITING FOR VINNIE AND MR. EMMONS TO COME BACK. DAY

THEN WE HEAR VINNIE AND MR. EMMONS RETURN AND COME TO THE FOOT OF THE STAIRS

          VINNIE
Oh Emily, you should have come – it was radiant!

          MR. EMMONS
Yes! And I'm sure you would have made it even more radiant, Miss Emily.

          EMILY
Ridicule is not the way to any woman's heart sir. Least of all mine.

          MR. EMMONS
It was meant sincerely. Or should I judge beauty by the common standard.

          EMILY
Any standard may be "common", familiarity as they say breeds contempt.

          VINNIE
Perhaps contempt breeds familiarity?

          MR. EMMONS
At any rate – beauty is in the eye of the beholder.

          EMILY
That is only true sir, after a truism has become a cliché.

          MR. EMMONS
        (rather hurt)
Miss Dickinson, you are just a little too sharp.

          EMILY
        (taking offence)
And you sir, are just a little too quick to play the martyr.

          MR. EMMONS
        (making to leave)
Then I'll take my leave before any blood is spilt.

EMILY
(bristling)
There are some wounds which don't bleed but which aggrieve nonetheless.

MR. EMMONS
I just assumed that you wanted to be rid of me. I meant no injury.

EMILY
Nor did I sir. I only wished to be honest.

SILENCE

MR. EMMONS
May I call again?

EMILY
If it gives you no pleasure, what is the point?

MR. EMMONS
I had hoped that my company wouldn't be a burden.

EMILY
A burden can always be laid down sir. You are not required to be another Sisyphus.

MR. EMMONS BOWS THEN LEAVES, VINNIE SEEING HIM TO THE DOOR

CUT TO

61   INT. SOUTH PARLOUR. HOMESTEAD. EVENING   61

VINNIE
Oh Emily, why do you behave like this? He is a kind man and he was hurt.

EMILY
I don't know. But as soon as they get too close I feel as if I'm suffocating… I long for… something but I'm afraid of it… a man may love then cool - but it's not that way with me…

VINNIE
But you cannot be equal to a man.

                    EMILY
          If I cannot have equality then I
          want nothing of love! I will not be
          so confined that I cannot breath!

                    VINNIE
          A rebellious spirit only invites
          retribution.

                    EMILY
          Then I will be silent in my
          rebellion, so that no one will know
          what my true feelings are.

                    VINNIE
          God will know.

                    EMILY
          But I will not be married to God.

                    VINNIE
          But you are God's possession and
          answerable to him.

                    EMILY
          He will know of my struggle and be
          merciful. And if he does not exist
          then I will be eternally free.

                                        DISSOLVE TO

62   INT. EMILY'S BEDROOM. HOMESTEAD. DAY   62

          EMILY SITS IN HER ROOM. SHE IS CLEARLY ILL

          THE CHERRYWOOD CUPBOARD IS OPEN AND FILLED WITH PAPERS - HER
          POEMS

          SLOWLY, METHODICALLY, SHE SEWS SOME OF THE POEMS INTO A SMALL
          BOOK

          THEN STARTS AGAIN

                                        DISSOLVE TO

63   INT. EMILY'S BEDROOM - DAY   63

          HER SMALL WRITING TABLE IS NOW COVERED WITH THESE LITTLE SEWN
          TOGETHER BOOKS

          SHE PICKS THEM UP AND PUTS THEM IN THE CUPBOARD WITH LOTS OF
          LOOSE PAPERS ON WHICH HER POEMS ARE WRITTEN

          THEN SHE CLOSES THE CUPBOARD

SHE FEELS FAINT AND STEADIES HERSELF THEN COLLAPSES TO THE FLOOR

> EMILY'S VO
> "We never know we go, – when we are going
> We jest and shut the door;
> Fate following behind us bolts it,
> And we accost no more."

SHE THEN STARTS SHAKING UNCONTROLLABLY. WITH GREAT DIFFICULTY SHE GETS TO HER FEET AND MANAGES TO GET ON THE BED – SHE IS STILL SHAKING VIOLENTLY

DISSOLVE TO EMILY UNDER THE COVERLET, SHAKING VIOLENTLY

DISSOLVE TO EMILY AND THE SHAKING GRADUALLY SUBSIDES

DISSOLVE TO EMILY LYING IN BED, HER FACE SWOLLEN AND SHE IS CLEARLY IN PAIN

A DOCTOR EXAMINES HER FACE AND HANDS

> EMILY'S VO
> (over all the foregoing)
> "He fumbles at your spirit
> As players at the keys
> Before the drop full music on;
> He stuns you by degrees,
>
> Prepares your brittle substance
> For the ethereal blow,
> By fainter hammers, further heard,
> Then nearer, then so slow
>
> Your breath has time to straighten,
> Your brain to bubble cool, –
> Deals one imperial thunderbolt
> That scalps your naked soul."

DOCTOR
Have you noticed any blood in your urine?

EMILY
Yes Doctor.

DOCTOR
Back pain?

EMILY
Yes Doctor.

DOCTOR
Severe?

EMILY
Very severe.

                    VINNIE
            She has had fever and vomiting.

                    DOCTOR
            And your breathing?

                    EMILY
            Very restricted.

SILENCE

VINNIE AND EMILY WAIT FOR THE DIAGNOSIS

                    DOCTOR
            You have all the common symptoms of
            Bright's Disease - it is a disease
            of the kidneys.

                    VINNIE
            Is there a cure?

                    DOCTOR
            Not to my knowledge.

SILENCE

                    EMILY
            What is your prognosis Doctor?

                    DOCTOR
            Diuretics and laxatives may ease
            some of the symptoms.

                    EMILY
            But there is definitely no cure?

                    DOCTOR
            No.

                    EMILY
            Thank you Doctor.

VINNIE CLEARLY UPSET LEADS THE DOCTOR OUT.

EMILY JUST LIES THERE LOOKING AT THE SUN STREAMING IN THROUGH THE WINDOWS

ALL IS STILL, ALL IS CALM

                    EMILY'S VO
            "This world is not conclusion;
              A sequel stands beyond,
                Invisible as music,
              But positive, as sound
            It beckons and it baffles;
              Philosophies don't know,
            And through a riddle, at the last,
                Sagacity must go.
                    (MORE)

A QUIET PASSION

> EMILY'S VO (CONT'D)
> To guess it puzzles scholars;
> To gain it men have shown,
> Contempt of generations,
> And crucifixion known."

THEN SLOWLY THE LIGHT FADES AND IT TURNS TO NIGHT

                                        DISSOLVE TO

64   INT. EMILY'S BEDROOM. HOMESTEAD. NIGHT   64

EMILY AT HER DESK WRITING BY LAMPLIGHT

SILENCE

THEN A PIANO IS HEARD BEING PLAYED FOLLOWED BY A WOMAN SINGING. IT IS A SONG BY SCHUBERT, CALLED "NIGHT AND DREAMS." IT WOULD BE SUNG IN GERMAN BUT I GIVE THE ENGLISH TRANSLATION BELOW

S/TRAX - NIGHT AND DREAMS

> MABEL LOOMIS TODD
> (o/s)
> (in German)
> "Holy night, sink you down;
> Dreams, too, float down,
> Like your moonlight through space,
> Through the silent hearts of men,
>
> They listen with delight,
> Crying out when day awakes;
> Come back Holy night!
> Fair dreams return!"

EMILY STOPS WRITING AND LISTENS

SHE GOES TO THE DOOR OF HER ROOM, OPENS IT AND LISTENS

64A   LANDING - NIGHT   64A

THE VOICE IS STRONG AND CONFIDENT AS IS THE PIANO ACCOMPANIMENT

64B   STAIRS / HALLWAY - NIGHT   64B

EMILY GOES SOFTLY DOWNSTAIRS. SHE IS CLEARLY IN PAIN

S/TRAX   THE SINGING AND THE PIANO GETTING LOUDER AS EMILY GETS NEARER TO IT

EMILY GETS TO THE DOUBLE DOORS OF THE PARLOUR WHICH ARE SLIGHTLY OPEN

EMILY STANDS IN THE DARK AND LISTENS THEN LOOKS THROUGH THE SLIGHTLY AJAR DOORS

                                                                                  CUT TO

65   INT. NORTH PARLOUR. HOMESTEAD. NIGHT   65

AT THE PIANO MABEL LOOMIS TODD SINGING AND PLAYING. AUSTIN STANDS JUST TO HER RIGHT AND SLIGHTLY BEHIND HER. OBVIOUSLY HE IS ENJOYING THE SINGING AND MABEL

AUSTIN LEANS FORWARD AND TURNS A MUSIC PAGE AND AS HE DOES SO HIS HAND BRUSHES MABEL'S SHOULDER

PAN AWAY (R TO L) FROM AUSTIN AND MABEL AT THE PIANO. TO MR. TODD

                  VINNIE'S VO
         Your wife plays beautifully Mr.
         Todd.

MR. TODD JUST SITS THERE. HE HAS NOTICED THE MOMENT OF INTIMACY BETWEEN MABEL AND AUSTIN

                  MR. TODD
         My wife does everything
         beautifully… and with here
         whole being.

HE HALF SMILES THEN DROPS HIS EYES

CONTINUE PANNING (R TO L) TO A TWO SHOT OF VINNIE AND SUSAN

                  SUSAN
         (quietly to Vinnie)
         They say every man who meets her
         falls in love with her.

                  VINNIE
         (sharp)
         No - she says that.

CONTINUE PANNING (R TO L) UNTIL WE FRAME EMILY THROUGH THE SLIGHTLY OPEN DOORS

EMILY STANDS THERE FOR A MOMENT. THERE IS A PROFOUND SADNESS ON HER FACE. SHE SILENTLY CLOSES THE DOORS THEN MOVES AWAY, BACK UPSTAIRS

                                                       DISSOLVE TO

66   INT. STAIRS AND HALLWAY. HOMESTEAD. NIGHT   66

AS USUAL EMILY GOES DOWNSTAIRS WITH HER LAMP IN ORDER TO WRITE

SHE MOVES AS SLOWLY AS HER CONDITION ALLOWS. IT HAS MADE HER SWOLLEN

AS SHE GETS DOWNSTAIRS SHE SEES THE PARLOUR SLIDING DOORS ARE SLIGHTLY AJAR AND THE HUSHED EXCITED VOICES OF A MAN AND WOMAN

SHE TURNS OFF THE LAMP AND MOVES TOWARDS THE PARLOUR DOORS

THE VOICES ARE ANIMATED AND LOW

SHE GOES TO THE SLIDING DOORS AND LOOKS IN

                                                            CUT TO

67   INT. NORTH PARLOUR. HOMESTEAD. NIGHT   67

EMILY'S POV

MABEL LOOMIS TODD AND AUSTIN TOGETHER KISSING PASSIONATELY - SHE IS LYING DOWN HE ON TOP OF HER - THEY ARE BOTH VERY PASSIONATE AND AROUSED. THEY ARE ENGAGED IN FROTTERISM

CUT TO EMILY SEEN FROM INSIDE THE PARLOUR

SHOCKED

SHE OPENS THE SLIDING DOORS A LITTLE WIDER

> EMILY
> Is this a private rehearsal or is it open to the general public?

CUT TO MABEL AND AUSTIN EMBARRASSED BUT BRAZEN

CUT TO EMILY AT THE DOORS

> EMILY (CONT'D)
> Mrs. Todd the exit is to your right!

EMILY SLAMS THE DOOR SHUT

                                                            CUT TO

68 INT. EMILY'S BEDROOM DOOR / LANDING / STAIRS. DAY 68

VINNIE KNOCKS ON EMILY'S DOOR

                VINNIE
    Emily…

EMILY OPENS THE DOOR A LITTLE

                VINNIE (CONT'D)
    Emily…Mrs Todd is about to depart…

                EMILY
    This life or just the house?

                VINNIE
    Stop it Emily! She'll hear you.

CUT TO THE BOTTOM OF THE STAIRS. MABEL TODD AND AUSTIN

                MABEL
    Goodbye Emily.

                EMILY
    (from inside her bedroom
     door)
    Goodbye Mrs. Todd. Please give my
    regards to Mr. Todd… a man of
    rare patience and fortitude.

                MABEL
    (annoyed)
    I'll remember you to him.

SHE LEAVES

AUSTIN STAYS FOR A MOMENT

                AUSTIN
    (furious)
    Perhaps next time Emily when you
    wish to say goodbye to a guest you
    might consider using semaphore.

CUT TO EMILY AND VINNIE

                EMILY
    There aren't enough flags for what
    I wish to say.

CUT TO AUSTIN WHO IS FUMING

                EMILY'S VO
    Use the backstairs Austin, it's
    quicker.

AUSTIN LEAVES

CUT BACK TO VINNIE AND EMILY

      VINNIE
Oh Emily why do you behave like this? Now there'll be hostilities for days!

SHE LEAVES

HOLD ON EMILY FOR A MOMENT THEN SHE CLOSES THE BEDROOM DOOR

                CUT TO

69 INT. SOUTH PARLOUR. HOMESTEAD. DAY   69

VINNIE AND EMILY BOTH READING

AUSTIN COMES IN AND SITS DOWN

A TENSE SILENCE

      EMILY
How is Susan?

      AUSTIN
Well, thank you. She's taking tea with Mabel.

      EMILY
Ah, Mrs. Todd! And her dull narcissism.

VINNIE VISIBLY STIFFENS AS SHE KNOWS THERE WILL BE ANOTHER QUARREL

      AUSTIN
   (keeping his temper)
You mistake confidence for narcissism and womanly reticence for dullness.

      EMILY
Whatever else can be said of Mrs. Todd, no one could ever accuse her of reticence. Or does one only require reticence in a wife?

      AUSTIN
My wife is perfectly happy.

      EMILY
Yes, of course. I'm sure she sees infidelity when accompanied by Schubert as a delightful pastime. A kind of musical adultery.

                    AUSTIN
              (heated)
     Real artists cannot be confined by
     narrow convention!

                    EMILY
              (heated)
     Real artists don't deceive
     themselves or their public!

                    AUSTIN
     When you acquire any "public" to
     speak of I'm sure your reputation
     will no doubt be very secure!

                    EMILY
     In all of this Susan is the
     innocent party.

                    AUSTIN
     If you take the trouble to look
     you'll see that there is more to
     that innocence that meets the eye.

                    EMILY
     That's a despicable thing to say!

                    VINNIE
     Oh stop bickering!

SILENCE

                    EMILY
              (smouldering)
     My sympathies lie entirely with
     Susan - if she had a liaison with a
     married man how would you respond?

                    AUSTIN
     I would not forgive her.

                    EMILY
     Yet you "admire" Mrs. Todd.

                    AUSTIN
     An admirable woman is one thing - a
     wife quite another.

                    EMILY
     I don't think that I have ever been
     closer to despising you.

                    AUSTIN
     Don't lecture me on how to live!

                    EMILY
     Don't you dare try to justify your
     position.
                    (MORE)

                    EMILY (CONT'D)
          It's both immoral and vicious.
          Susan is a good and intelligent
          wife - or do you prefer more
          obvious charms?

                    AUSTIN
          By that I assume you mean Mabel
          Loomis Todd?

                    EMILY
          Mrs. Todd - yes!

AUSTIN GOES TO SPEAK

                    EMILY (CONT'D)
          And don't tell me that your
          intentions towards her are
          fraternal - especially in that semi-
          recumbent position.

AUSTIN SEETHING BUT STILL DOESN'T SPEAK

                    EMILY (CONT'D)
          I wonder if she is that
          "percussive" with her husband?

                    AUSTIN
          Sometimes Emily you are as ugly as
          your poetry!

HE STORMS OUT

SILENCE

                    VINNIE
          There's nothing to be done. Mabel
          has made up her mind to continue
          the status quo.

                    EMILY
              (furious)
          She's incapable of making up her
          mind because she's too stupid to
          have one.

                    VINNIE
          That's a horrible thing to say!

PAUSE

                    EMILY
          Yes. It is. You see what a vile
          person I've become.

                    VINNIE
          That's too harsh. You lash out
          because you're hurt or angry.
                    (MORE)

> VINNIE (CONT'D)
> Your anger is, I think, a defence against the world.

> EMILY
> (very moved)
> How can you go on loving me when I don't deserve it?

> VINNIE
> Because you are so easy to love.

> EMILY
> (weeping)
> Oh Vinnie, Vinnie!

> VINNIE
> (embracing Emily)
> And you are not the only one who has had horrible thoughts… yes, me also… I once hoped that Mabel would go up in a balloon then explode!

> EMILY
> (laughing through tears)
> Oh Vinnie! If that is the extent of your wickedness your sainthood is assured - explosions notwithstanding.

> VINNIE
> I know we differ in our allegiance and mine is with Austin.

> EMILY
> And mine with Susan.

> VINNIE
> Try not to provoke him.

EMILY DOES NOT RESPOND

CUT TO

70 INT. SOUTH PARLOUR. HOMESTEAD. EARLY EVENING 70

A TENSE MEETING OVER TEA. EMILY, VINNIE, AUSTIN AND SUSAN

> EMILY
> (unable to keep silent)
> And how is Mrs. Todd? Or are you too discreet to say?

AUSTIN READING BUT BRAZEN AND BIDING HIS TIME TO STRIKE

                    AUSTIN
          Mabel is in fine voice - especially
          at the piano.

                    EMILY
          What a pity she isn't married to
          one - then her bliss would be
          complete.

SILENCE

                    AUSTIN
          Have you read this article in "The
          Springfield Republican", Emily?

                    EMILY
              (disturbed)
          No. Why.

                    AUSTIN
              (nonchalant)
          It is by Mr. Bowles, who publishes
          some of your work and whom you
          admire, I think, and who is also
          married.

                    EMILY
              (alarmed)
          What does it say?

                    AUSTIN
              (reading aloud)
          "Why should we write. There is
          another kind of writing only too
          common, appealing to the sympathies
          of the reader without recommending
          itself to its subject. It may be
          called the literature of misery.
          The writers are chiefly women,
          gifted women maybe, full of thought
          and feeling and fancy, but poor,
          lonely and unhappy. Also that
          suffering is so seldom healthful.
          It may be a valuable discipline in
          the end, but for the time being it
          too often clouds, withers,
          distorts. It is so difficult to see
          objects distinctly through a mist
          of tears. The sketch or poem is
          usually the writer's…"

EMILY STUNNED AND VERY CLOSE TO TEARS AS SHE RUNS OUT

                    VINNIE
          That was cruel Austin.

                    AUSTIN
          Life is cruel.

                        SUSAN
              And cruelty knows no morality.

                                                    CUT TO

71   INT. EMILY'S BEDROOM. HOMESTEAD. EVENING   71

        VINNIE COMES IN. EMILY IS STANDING BY THE WINDOW WITH HER
        BACK TO VINNIE. EMILY DOESN'T TURN AROUND

        SILENCE

                        VINNIE
              Are you alright? Austin was cruel.

        SILENCE

                        EMILY
                  (still not turning around)
              He was I suppose "defending" his
              position… or should we call it
              "poetic licentiousness"?

        SILENCE

                        EMILY (CONT'D)
              I must confess I cannot understand
              his infatuation with her when she
              already has a husband who should
              satisfy her in all aspects of
              married life.

        PAUSE

                        VINNIE
                  (tentatively)
              They say with Mr. Todd that it is a
              venereal case.

                        EMILY
                  (turning around shocked)
              How do you know this?

                        VINNIE
              There are rumours…perhaps now you
              will be able to view Mabel in a
              more favourable light.

                        EMILY
              I doubt that. Mrs. Todd may have
              her private troubles but it is
              still no excuse for Austin's
              infidelity. Susan has been betrayed
              in the vilest way by a brother whom
              I once adored.

PAUSE

> VINNIE
> People aren't saints Emily. You judge too harshly because you judge too highly.

> EMILY
> Lowering a standard is the first excuse for every villainy.

> VINNIE
> And keeping only to one high principle is the last refuge of the intolerant.

> EMILY
> And what of integrity? Austin was once fierce in his defence of it and now it seems merely an encumbrance to be easily discarded.

> VINNIE
> Integrity, if taken too far, can be equally ruthless Emily.

> EMILY
> And do I fall into that category?

> VINNIE
> Sometimes - yes.

SILENCE

> VINNIE (CONT'D)
> (softly)
> We are only human, Emily, don't pillory us for that.

> EMILY
> You're right of course. I wish I had your gentle spirit. If I castigate Austin it is because my own failings are equally as great.

A LONG SILENCE

> EMILY (CONT'D)
> We become the very thing we dread and I have become embittered.

> VINNIE
> Despite your vehemence yours is a soul anyone would be proud of.

EMILY SINKS INTO A CHAIR AND BURSTS INTO TEARS

                        EMILY
             Oh Vinnie! Vinnie! Why has the
             world become so ugly!

VINNIE GOES TO HER AND COMFORTS HER. EMILY SOBS
UNCONTROLLABLY

                                              DISSOLVE TO

72   INT. MOTHER'S BEDROOM. HOMESTEAD. DAY   72

        HOLD ON MOTHER IN BED

        S/TRAX OVER THE DISSOLVE

                        EMILY'S VO
                "Our journey had advanced;
                 Our feet were almost come
               To that odd fork in Being's road,
                     Eternity by term.

                  Our pace took sudden awe,
                  Our feet reluctant led,
               Before where cities, but between,
                  The forest of the dead.

                  Retreat was out of hope, −
                    Behind, a sealed route,
                Eternity's white flag before,
                   And God at every gate."

        MOTHER GROANING LOW AND STEADY

                        VINNIE'S VO
                Emily − Mother has had a stroke.

        SILENCE EXCEPT FOR MOTHER'S GROANING

                        EMILY'S VO
                I can hear her sigh before she
                        makes one…

                                              DISSOLVE TO

73   INT. MOTHER'S BEDROOM. HOMESTEAD. DAY   73

        MOTHER IN BED WITH A SEVERE STROKE. EMILY SITS DOWN BESIDE
        HER BUT MOTHER SHOWS NO SIGN OF RECOGNITION

        EMILY SITS IN THE SILENCE HOLDING MOTHER'S HAND

(THIS SEQUENCE OF DISSOLVES INDICATES THE PASSING OF YEARS - RATHER THAN ONE SINGLE DAY)

DISSOLVE TO

74 INT. MOTHER'S BEDROOM - LATER, AFTERNOON 74

MOTHER IN BED. EMILY AND VINNIE WASHING HER

DISSOLVE TO

75 INT. MOTHER'S BEDROOM - LATER, EVENING 75

EMILY AND VINNIE COMBING MOTHER'S HAIR

DISSOLVE TO

76 INT. MOTHER'S BEDROOM - LATER, NIGHT 76

VINNIE AND EMILY FEEDING MOTHER

DISSOLVE TO

77 INT. MOTHER'S BEDROOM - LATER, NIGHT 77

EMILY AND VINNIE AT MOTHER'S BEDSIDE. MOTHER COMES AROUND SLIGHTLY AND TRIES TO SPEAK BUT CAN'T. SHE TRIES AGAIN. IT IS TERRIBLE TO WATCH THIS EFFORT

VINNIE AND EMILY COME CLOSE TO MOTHER.

      MOTHER
    (with great difficulty)
  Why?

SILENCE

THEN AUSTIN AND SUSAN COME IN JUST AS MOTHER'S BREATHING GENTLY STOPS AND SHE JUST LIES THERE

      AUSTIN
  We've come to say goodnight mother.

DISSOLVE TO

| 78 | INT. MOTHER'S BEDROOM. HOMESTEAD. DAY | 78 |

MOTHER'S BED REMADE BUT EMPTY

HOLD ON IT

          VINNIE'S VO
    Father believed…

          AUSTIN'S VO
    … and Mother loved…

          EMILY'S VO
    She achieved in sweetness what she
    lost in strength.

                                                     DISSOLVE TO

| 79 | INT. EMILY'S BEDROOM. HOMESTEAD. LATE AFTERNOON/EARLY EVENING |

EMILY IS WRACKED WITH SEVERE SHAKING

IT DOES NOT STOP

SHE IS BY THE WINDOW

THE SHAKING IS SO SEVERE THAT SHE IS UNABLE TO MOVE

THE SHAKING GETS WORSE AND SHE MANAGES, VERY SLOWLY, TO GET TO HER BED AND PULL THE COVERLET OVER HERSELF

THE VIOLENT SHAKING CONTINUES

                                                   DISSOLVE TO

| 80 | INT. EMILY'S BEDROOM. HOMESTEAD. NIGHT | 80 |

EMILY IN BED. HER BREATHING PROTRACTED AND RASPING. ALMOST TO ASPHYXIA. SHE THRASHES ABOUT. SHE IS STRUGGLING SIMPLY TO BREATHE

          AUSTIN
     (to doctor)
    Is there nothing you can do,
    Doctor?

          DOCTOR
    Hold her down - I'll administer
    some more chloroform.

AUSTIN HOLDS THE STRUGGLING EMILY DOWN. SHE FIGHTS FOR HER BREATH AND FIGHTS BOTH DOCTOR AND AUSTIN

CUT TO SUSAN AND VINNIE UTTERLY WRETCHED AS THE SOUND OF EMILY'S BREATHING DOES, IF ANYTHING, GET WORSE

                                                                         DISSOLVE TO

81   INT. EMILY'S BEDROOM – NIGHT   81

EMILY IS CALMER NOW BUT THE DIFFICULT RASPING BREATHING CONTINUES

AUSTIN AND VINNIE GIVE EMILY WHAT COMFORT THEY CAN – VINNIE WITH COLD COMPRESSES, AUSTIN STROKING EMILY'S HAND

EMILY'S BREATHING LOW, DIFFICULT AND RASPING

                                                                         DISSOLVE TO

82   INT. EMILY'S BEDROOM NIGHT   82

EMILY IN BED. VINNIE AND AUSTIN EITHER SIDE OF HER

HER BREATHING RASPING, DIFFICULT AND SLOW

TRACK IN ON HER

SUDDENLY HER BREATHING STOPS

SILENCE

VINNIE AND AUSTIN ARE EXHAUSTED AND JOINED BY SUSAN EQUALLY EXHAUSTED

SILENCE

VINNIE BENDS FORWARD AND KISSES EMILY, AUSTIN STROKES HER HAND, SUSAN BEHIND AUSTIN COMFORTING HIM

THEY ALL WEEP

THEY STRAIGHTEN HER BODY THEN REMAIN SITTING THERE, WEARY FROM EXHAUSTION AND GRIEF

HOLD

                                                                         DISSOLVE TO

| 83 | INT. EMILY'S BEDROOM - DAY | 83 |

EMILY IN BED WASHED AND DRESSED IN HER WHITE PIQUE DRESS

HOLD

                                                    DISSOLVE TO

| 84 | INT. SOUTH PARLOUR. HOMESTEAD. DAY | 84 |

                    EMILY'S VO
"My life closed twice before it's close;
It yet remains to see
If immortality unveil
A third event to me,

So huge, so hopeless to conceive
As these that twice befell.
Parting is all we know of Heaven,
And all we need of Hell.

Goodbye to the life I used to live,
And the world I used to know;
And kiss the hills for me, just once;
Now I am ready to go!"

THE COFFIN IS OPEN, AND AT EMILY'S THROAT ARE SOME VIOLETS. THEN VINNIE PLACES TWO HELIOTROPES IN EMILY'S HANDS

                                                    DISSOLVE TO

| 85 | EXT. HOMESTEAD. DAY | 85 |

EMILY'S COFFIN BEING CARRIED FROM THE HOUSE TO A HEARSE WITH GLASS BEING PULLED BY TWO HORSES - BOTH HORSES DRAPED IN BLACK WITH BLACK HEAD PLUMES

IT IS HIGH SUMMER AND THE WEATHER IS GLORIOUS

THE COFFIN IS LOADED INTO THE HEARSE AND THE FUNERAL PROCESSION MOVES SLOWLY OFF

S/TRAX

                    EMILY'S VO
"Because I could not stop for death

He kindly stopped for me -
                    (MORE)

>   EMILY'S VO (CONT'D)
>   The carriage held but just
>   ourselves -
>   And immortality."

DISSOLVE TO THE FUNERAL PROCESSION - ALL IN BLACK, THE WOMEN
ALL WEARING HEAVY BLACK VEILS - FOLLOWING THE HEARSE ON FOOT.
IT CONSISTS OF AUSTIN, VINNIE, SUSAN, AUSTIN'S TWO CHILDREN,
MR. AND MRS. TODD AND THE THREE DOMESTICS

TRACK (L TO R)

WONDERFUL WEATHER

>   EMILY'S VO (CONT'D)
>   "We slowly drove - he knew no haste
>   And I had put away
>   My labour and my leisure too,
>   For His civility.
>
>   We past the school where children
>   strove,
>   At recess - in the ring -
>   We past the fields of grazing grain
>   -
>   We past the setting sun - "

THE HIGH BRIGHT SUN - DAZZLING IN THE SKY

S/TRAX

>   EMILY'S VO (CONT'D)
>   "Or rather - he passed us -
>   The dews drew quivering and chill -
>   For only gossamer, my gown -
>   My tippet - only tulle -"

                                                            DISSOLVE

86   EXT. CEMETERY DAY - DAY   86

TRACK (L TO R)

THE COFFIN BEING CARRIED SHOULDER HIGH THROUGH THE CEMETERY -
THE MOURNERS FOLLOWING ON FOOT - A BLACK PROCESSION IN THE
OGLORIOUS MAY SUNSHINE

S/TRAX   RANDALL THOMPSON'S "ALLELUIA" IS BEING HEARD SOFTLY
INTONED BY A CHOIR AND RUNNING UNDER THE LAST TWO VERSES OF
THE EMILY DICKINSON POEM

>   EMILY'S VO
>   "We paused before a house that
>   seemed
>   A swelling of the ground -
>   (MORE)

                        EMILY'S VO (CONT'D)
                 The roof was scarcely visible -
                 The cornice - in the ground -

                  Since then - 'tis centuries - and
                                yet
                      Feels shorter than the day
                   I first surmised the horses heads
                        Were toward eternity -"

TRACK (L TO R) FROM THE FUNERAL PROCESSION THEN PRECEDE IT TO
THE GRAVE, A BLACK RECTANGLE

S/TRAX   THE POEM FINISHES BUT THE RANDALL THOMPSON "ALLELUIA"
IS SUSTAINED UNTIL ITS END

TRACK IN ON THE OPEN GRAVE UNTIL IT'S RECTANGULAR BLACKNESS
FILLS THE ENTIRE SCREEN

HOLD ON THE BLACKNESS

S/TRAX   THE RANDALL THOMPSON ENDS

HOLD ON THE BLACKNESS

THEN

                        EMILY'S VO (CONT'D)
                 "This is my letter to the world,
                     That never wrote to me -
                 The simple news that nature told,
                        With tender majesty.

                     Her message is committed
                       To hands I cannot see;
                 For love of her, sweet countrymen,
                        Judge tenderly of me!"

HOLD ON THE DARKNESS

THEN FADE UP THE OLDER EMILY. HOLD FOR A MOMENT

THEN DISSOLVE TO YOUNGER EMILY. HOLD FOR A MOMENT

THEN DISSOLVE TO THE PICTURE OF EMILY WHEN SHE WAS 17

HOLD THEN FADE UP TITLE

A QUIET PASSION

"EMILY DICKINSON

1830-1886

ONE OF THE WORLD'S GREATEST POETS"

HOLD

SLOW FADE

END CREDITS

THE END

A Quiet Passion (2016): Cynthia Nixon as Emily Dickinson.

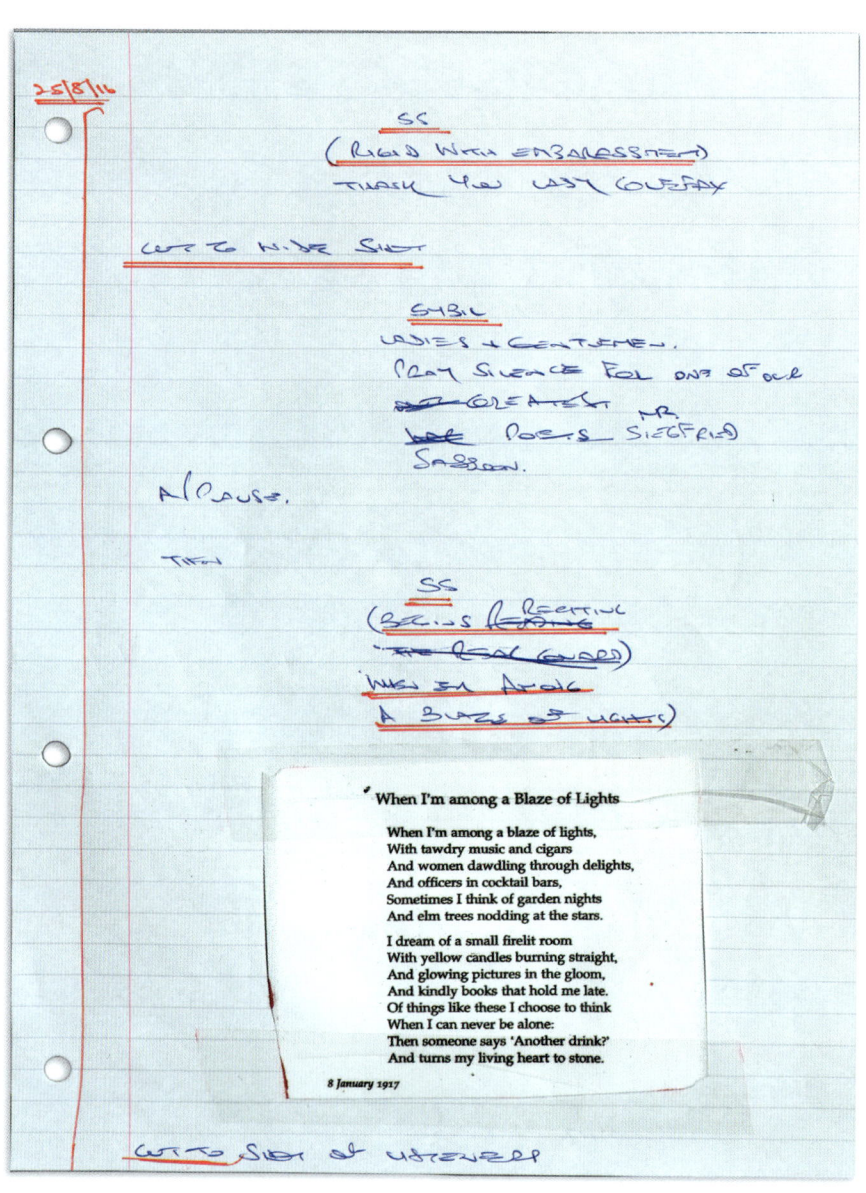

Benediction (2021): first draft, Scene 13 in shooting script. (© The Terence Davies Estate, held by the Terence Davies Archive at Edge Hill University)

BENEDICTION (2021)
(SIEGFRIED SASSOON)

Benediction (2021): Peter Capaldi as the older Siegfried Sassoon.

Benediction
SHOOTING SCRIPT – AUGUST 2020 (BLUE REVISIONS)

Cast and crew of *Benediction* include:

SIEGFRIED SASSOON (young)	Jack Lowden
SIEGFRIED SASSOON (older)	Peter Capaldi
ROBBIE ROSS	Simon Russell Beale
IVOR NOVELLO	Jeremy Irvine
STEPHEN TENNANT (young)	Calam Lynch
STEPHEN TENNANT (older)	Anton Lesser
WILFRED OWEN	Matthew Tennyson
HESTER GATTY (young)	Kate Phillips
HESTER GATTY (older)	Gemma Jones
GEORGE SASSOON	Richard Goulding
MOTHER	Geraldine James
DR RIVERS	Ben Daniels
LADY OTTOLINE MORRELL	Suzanne Bertish
GLEN BYAM SHAW	Tom Blyth
EDITH SITWELL	Lia Williams
LADY SYBIL COLEFAX	Joanna Bacon
CHIEF MEDICAL OFFICER	Julian Sands
Written and Directed by	Terence Davies
Producer	Michael Elliott
Director of Photography	Nicola Daley
Editor	Alex Mackie
Production Designer	Andy Harris
Art Director	Adam Tomlinson
Costume Designer	Annie Symons
Casting Director	Lucy Rands
Music Supervision	Ed Bailie and Abi Leland
Archive Producer	Jim Anderson

An EMU Films (2021) production with:
Reiver Pictures/BFI/BBC Films/Creative England/M.Y.R.A. Entertainment /Lipsync

FADE UP ON

THE OLD BBFC CERTIFICATE WITH THE RELEVANT DATE AND RATING.

FADE TO

TWO POSTERS FILLING THE SCREEN. SCREEN LEFT AND SCREEN RIGHT.

FIRST POSTER READS, "IGOR STRAVINSKY. THE RITE OF SPRING."

SECOND POSTER READS, "DIAGILEV'S RUSSIAN BALLET."

HOLD

THEN

THESE TWO POSTERS MOVE APART LIKE CURTAINS TO REVEAL

1   EXT. EVENING. THEATRE (1913)   1

CRANE DOWN to the entrance to the theatre.

A large crowd entering the front of theatre. Amongst them SIEGFRIED SASSOON and his brother HAMO.

TRACK BACK WITH THEM TO A WIDE SHOT OF THE THEATRE ENTRANCE, THEN TRACK IN WITH THEM AS THEY ENTER THE THEATRE.

SUPERIMPOSE CARD, "1913"   *

                                                          CUT TO:

SOUNDTRACK:

            SIEGFRIED SASSOON V/O
            "The audience pricks an
            intellectual ear...
            Stravinsky quite the concert of the
            year!"

2   INT. NIGHT. THEATRE. 1913   2

SHOT of the audience taking their seats in the stalls.

SOUNDTRACK:

            SIEGFRIED SASSOON V/O
            "Forgetting now that non so distant
            date..."

Balcony audience takes it's seats.

SOUNDTRACK:

>   SIEGFRIED SASSOON V/O (CONT'D)
> "When they (or folk facsimilar in
> state
> Of mind) first heard with hisses –
> hoots – guffaws
> This abstract symphony: (They booed
> because
> Stravinsky jumped their Wagner
> palisade
> With modes that seemed cacophonous
> and queer;)
> Forgetting now the hullabaloo they
> made,
> The audience pricks an intellectual
> ear."

SIEGFRIED SASSOON & his brother HAMO seated.

                                              CUT TO:

3   INT. NIGHT. THEATRE (1913)   3

SHOT OF CONDUCTOR COMING INTO THE PIT.

Audience applauds.

                                              CUT TO:

4   INT. NIGHT. THEATRE (1913)   4

TWO SHOT SIEGFRIED SASSOON AND HAMO

The lights go down. The audience becomes silent.

                                              CUT TO:

5   INT. NIGHT. THEATRE (1913)   5

BACK VIEW OF THE CONDUCTOR. He lifts his hands to start to conduct.

S/TRAX

>   SIEGFRIED SASSOON V/O
> "Bassoons begin...Sonority
> envelopes
> Our auditory innocence; and brings
> To me, I must admit, some drift of
> things
>   (MORE)

                    SIEGFRIED SASSOON V/O (CONT'D)
            Omnific, seminal, and
            adolescent..."

BEGIN TO FADE HIS V/O

Conductor beats time and we hear the bassoon.

The curtain rises.

CRANE UP TO CGI

As the curtain rises it reveals the following WW1 footage.

1) People in the park by a river

2) Toy boats on a pond

3) Henley Regatta

4) Oars in water

SOUNDTRACK OVER ALL OF THE ABOVE:

                    SIEGFRIED SASSON V/O
            In that long summer I hunted,
            played cricket but only watched
            tennis...
            ...men in boaters...far from
            Henley, girls in pink and blue
            taffeta...
            ...God was in His heaven and there
            were sausages for breakfast...

WW1 FOOTAGE CONTINUES:

1)   Kitchener's poster "Your Country Needs You!" (1914)

2)   INTERIOR RECRUITING OFFICE (1914)

SOUNDTRACK:

                    SIEGFRIED SASSON V/O (CONT'D)
            And in small Recruiting Offices
            dull young men wait to inscribe (in
            paper quires) the names of the
            living and the dead.

WW1 FOOTAGE CONTINUES:

1)   INTERIOR RECRUITING OFFICE (1914)

A soldier swearing on a bible.

2) EXTERIOR RECRUITING OFFICE (1914)

Soldiers coming towards the camera.

                CUT TO:

6 INT. MILITARY TAILORS SHOP. DAY. (1915)   6

TWO SHOT OF SIEGFRIED SASSOON AND HIS YOUNGER BROTHER HAMO

                CUT TO:

       TAILOR
   Mister Sassoon?

                CUT TO:

TWO SHOT

      SIEGFRIED SASSOON & HAMO
   Yes.

                CUT TO:

Tailor clearly flumoxed

                CUT TO:

TWO SHOT

      SIEGFRIED SASSOON
   I'm Siegfried.

      HAMO
   And I'm Hamo - younger brother.

      SIEGFRIED SASSOON
   We've both come for a fitting.

                CUT TO:

      TAILOR
   Just so sir. I think we should
   start with the shirts. You can't
   have your shirts too dark sir.

                CUT TO:

TWO SHOT

                HAMO
     Ah war! A la mode!

HAMO smiling

           SIEGFRIED SASSOON V/O
  I never said goodbye to him.

                              DISSOLVE TO:

7   EXT. NIGHT. VICTORIA STATION. (1915)   7

A shot of a locomotive engine hissing steam and getting ready to move off.

A swirl of steam.

HAMO (in uniform at the train window).

He's waving and smiling.

The train pulls out (R to L).

           SIEGFRIED SASSOON V/O
      (reading poem "To my
       brother")
 "Give me your hand, my brother,
 search my face;
 Look in these eyes lest I should
 think of shame;
 For we have made an end of all
 things base.
 We are returning by the road we
 came.

A swirl of steam blots out the train.

                              DISSOLVE TO:

SIEGFRIED SASSOON and MOTHER emerge from the steam.

They wave goodbye to HAMO.

                              DISSOLVE TO:

8   EXT. NIGHT. VICTORIA STATION. (1915)   8

A swirl of steam. A shot of a locomotive engine hissing steam and getting ready to move off.

SIEGFRIED SASSOON in uniform at the train window. He waves goodbye to his MOTHER.

The steam engine begins to move off, R to L, track with it.

          SIEGFRIED SASSON V/O
"Your lot is with the ghosts of
soldiers dead,
And I am in the field where men
must fight.
But in the gloom I see your
laurell'd head
And through your victory I shall
win the light."

                                            DISSOLVE TO:

MOTHER watching the train move out. She is in a swirl of steam.

                                                   CUT TO:

WW1 FOOTAGE, AND OVER ALL THE FOLLOWING WW1 FOOTAGE SOUNDTRACK OF SIEGFRIED SASSOON READING "A SHROPSHIRE LAD":

          SIEGFRIED SASSON V/O (CONT'D)
"On the idle hill of summer,
Sleepy with the flow of streams,
Far I hear the steady drummer
Drumming like a noise in dreams.

Far and near and low and louder
On the roads of earth go by,
Dear to friends and food for powder,
Soldiers marching, all to die.

East and west on fields forgotten
Bleach the bones of comrades slain,
Lovely lads and dead and rotten;
None that go return again.

Far the calling bugles hollo,
High the screaming fife replies,
Gay the files of scarlet follow:
Woman bore me, I will rise.

1)   Soldiers on station platform.

2)   Soldiers on train.

3)   Soldiers marching (Scots wearing kilts).

4)   Several explosions.

5)   Cavalry amidst explosions.

6) More explosions.

7) Soldiers moving through heavy cordite mist.

8) More explosions.

9) British troops, very weary, moving L to R.

10) More explosions.

11) Dead horses.

12) Dead bodies lining the road.

DISSOLVE TO:

9   EXT. DAY. GARSINGTON MANOR. (1916/17)   9

TWO SHOT SIEGFRIED SASSOON AND ROBBIE ROSS.

TRACK BACK WITH THEM.

ROBBIE ROSS & SIEGFRIED SASSOON walking towards the monastery studio where LADY OTTOLINE MORRELL is posing for her portrait painted by DOROTHY BRETT. OTTOLINE (in a very rigid pose) is wearing voluminous pale pink Turkish trousers, a purple hat, purple hair and an orange tunic.

CUT TO:

TWO SHOT ROBBIE ROSS & SIEGFRIED SASSOON

          ROBBIE ROSS
The woman posing - who appears to be wearing a spinnaker - is LADY OTTOLINE MORRELL. More hair than self restraint but <u>definitely</u> nobody's fool.

          SIEGFRIED SASSOON
She looks as though she hasn't heard a joke since the Boer War.

          ROBBIE ROSS
For Ottoline the Boer War <u>was</u> the joke.

ROBBIE ROSS walking out of shot.

                    ROBBIE ROSS (CONT'D)
                  (completely insincere)
               Ottoline!

                                                    CUT TO:

THREE SHOT OTTOLINE MORRELL, ROBBIE ROSS & DOROTHY BRETT

                    OTTOLINE MORRELL
                  (to DOROTHY BRETT)
               May we pause for a moment Dorothy
               before rigor mortis sets in?

                    DOROTHY BRETT
               Of course Ottoline.

                    OTTOLINE MORRELL
                  (to ROBBIE ROSS but
                   looking at SIEGFRIED
                   SASSOON)
               Who is this extremely beautiful
               young man, Robbie?

                                                    CUT TO:

SIEGFRIED SASSOON looking uncomfortable.

                    ROBBIE ROSS V/O
               Sassoon...Siegfried...

                                                    CUT TO:

THREE SHOT

                    OTTOLINE MORRELL
               It sounds Wagnerian.

                                                    CUT TO:

SIEGFRIED SASSOON

                    SIEGFRIED SASSOON
               Just Home Counties I'm afraid.

                                                    CUT TO:

OTTOLINE MORRELL

                    OTTOLINE MORRELL
          So you are not a keeper of the
          flame at Bayreuth?

                                                    CUT TO:

                    SIEGFRIED SASSOON
          I'm afraid not.

                                                    CUT TO:

                    OTTOLINE MORRELL
          What are your musical tastes then?

                                                    CUT TO:

                    SIEGFRIED SASSOON
          Ravel, Albeniz, Chausson...Scriabin
          if I must, Caesar Franck when I'm
          in the mood.

                                                    CUT TO:

                    OTTOLINE MORRELL
          And Bartok?

                                                    CUT TO:

                    SIEGFRIED SASSOON
          Never Bartok. His music always
          sounds to me like a lunatic playing
          the xylophone.

                                                    CUT TO:

                    OTTOLINE MORRELL
          Or vice versa.

                                                    CUT TO:

GROUP SHOT

Everyone laughs. The ice broken.

                    ROBBIE ROSS
          I once heard Paderewski play at
          Tunbridge Wells - but I found it
          rather disappointing.

                    OTTOLINE MORRELL
          Well what did you expect? It was
          Tunbridge Wells.
          Come into the main house and have
          tea.

                    DOROTHY BRETT
          May I join you Ottoline?

                    OTTOLINE MORRELL
          Of course, Dorothy. You are not a
          servant but an "Honourable".

They all walk towards the main house.

OTTOLINE with SIEGFRIED SASSOON slightly ahead. She slips her
arm through his.

                    OTTOLINE MORRELL (CONT'D)
          Now come along Mr. Bassoon and tell
          me what you really have against Mr.
          Bartok.

                    ROBBIE ROSS (V.O.)
          Oh, a word in your shell-like –
          she'll ask you to stay the
          night...she always asks attractive
          young men to stay the night. So
          lock your bedroom door or wear
          something very, very severe.

                                                  CUT TO:

10   INT. NIGHT. GARSINGTON MANOR. BEDROOM. (1916/17)   10

SIEGFRIED SASSOON in his comfortable bedroom, reading.

A knock on the door. OTTOLINE MORRELL opens the door and is
standing there in something diaphanous.

                    OTTOLINE MORRELL
          I thought that I might be more
          interesting than cocoa.

                                                  CUT TO:

                    SIEGFRIED SASSOON
               (shocked but composed)
          I'm afraid I prefer cocoa.

                    OTTOLINE MORRELL
          Sleep badly.

She exits.

SIEGFRIED SASSOON smiles and continues reading.

MID-WIDE SHOT

HOLD

THEN

SOUNDTRACK: We hear low moaning of someone in terrible pain.

TRACK IN on SIEGFRIED SASSOON in bed.

SOUNDTRACK: The moaning continues, delirium.

> SIEGFRIED SASSOON V/O
> (reading "Died of wounds")
> "His wet white face and miserable eyes
> Brought nurses to him more than groans and sighs:
> But hoarse and low and rapid rose and fell
> His troubled voice: he did the business well."

When in CLOSE UP, TRACK L to R, THEN

DISSOLVE TO:

11 INT. NIGHT. HOSPITAL WARD. (1916)

> SIEGFRIED SASSOON V/O
> "The ward grew dark; but he was still complaining
> And calling out for..."

Continue PANNING & TRACKING L to R

SOUNDTRACK:

> SOLDIERS V/O
> "...Dickie. Curse the Wood!
> It's time to go. O Christ, and what's the good?
> We'll never take it, and it's always raining."

The soldier's bed is surrounded by screens and the nurses come running up the ward to him.

Continue PANNING & TRACKING L to R

SOUNDTRACK:

>   SIEGFRIED SASSOON V/O
> "I wondered where he'd been; then
> heard him shout,"
>
>   SOLDIERS V/O
>   (delirious)
> They snipe like Hell! O Dickie,
> don't go out...

Continue PANNING & TRACKING L to R

To empty hospital bed

Continue PANNING & TRACKING L to R

SOUNDTRACK:

>   SIEGFRIED SASSOON V/O
> "I fell asleep...next morning he
> was dead;
> And some Slight Wound lay smiling
> on the bed."

                                DISSOLVE TO:

12   INT. DAY. SOMERVILLE COLLEGE. (1916)   12

The college has been turned into a hospital.

SIEGFRIED SASSOON descends the staircase to meet his MOTHER at the bottom.

>   MEDICAL OFFICER'S V/O
> Where the symptoms of diarrhoea are
> concerned he has not regained his
> strength. He has a cough and some
> breathing difficulty.

TWO SHOT MOTHER AND SIEGFRIED SASSOON.

TRACK BACK WITH THEM.

>   MOTHER
> I was anxious to know what you were
> suffering from.
>
>   SIEGFRIED SASSOON
> Only "trench fever". Nothing fatal.
> Just debilitating.

> MOTHER
> I dread everything now...the telephone...the telegram...

> SIEGFRIED SASSOON
> There's only one thing worse than remaining in the past mother, and that's begrudging the future.

> MOTHER
> The future, without either of my sons, is to be dreaded, not enjoyed. Robbie Ross rang me as soon as you were admitted.

> SIEGFRIED SASSOON
> He's a good man. And a loyal friend.

DISSOLVE TO:

13   INT. NIGHT. LADY SYBIL COLEFAX HOUSE/SALON. (1921)   13

ROBBIE ROSS & SIEGFRIED SASSOON coming into the room

> ROBBIE ROSS
> (indicating IVOR NOVELLO)
> Ivor Novello of "Keep the home fires burning" fame.

> SIEGFRIED SASSOON
> Yes. That loathsome little tune.

> ROBBIE ROSS
> He always writes at the top of his voice but we must _try_ to be charitable.

CUT TO:

Their POV of the piano being played by IVOR NOVELLO. Standing by the piano a young actor GLEN BYAM SHAW looking very lovingly at IVOR NOVELLO as he plays Scott Joplin.

CUT TO:

SIEGFRIED SASSOON & ROBBIE ROSS being joined by LADY SYBIL COLEFAX.

NOVELLO continues playing ragtime.

                    ROBBIE ROSS (CONT'D)
                (to SYBIL)
            Sybil, you ought to be ashamed of
            yourself...
                (indicating IVOR NOVELLO)
            ...ragtime indeed!

                    LADY SYBIL COLEFAX
            Yes, I know...but Mr. Novello plays
            it so well it's almost music.
            Besides, at the moment, he's
            appearing in the West End in a very
            successful play called "The Rat".

                    ROBBIE ROSS
            I know. Someone asked me was it
            autobiographical, but I said I
            wasn't sure.

                    LADY SYBIL COLEFAX
                (pleasantly)
            One day Robbie you will go too far.

                    ROBBIE ROSS
                (pleasantly)
            One day Sybil we will all go too
            far.

                    LADY SYBIL COLEFAX
            Thank you for coming Mr. Sassoon.
            We're all very eager to hear your
            recitation.

                    SIEGFRIED SASSOON
                (rigid with embarrassment)
            Thank you Lady Colefax.

                                                CUT TO:

WIDE SHOT

                    LADY SYBIL COLEFAX
            Ladies and Gentlemen, pray silence
            for one of our greatest poets, Mr.
            Siegfried Sassoon.

Applause

                    SIEGFRIED SASSOON
                (beginning reciting a poem
                 "When I'm among a blaze
                 of lights")
            "When I'm among a blaze of lights,
                    (MORE)

                    SIEGFRIED SASSOON (CONT'D)
               With tawdry music and cigars
               And women dawdling through
               delights,
               And officers in cocktail bars,
               Sometimes I think of garden nights
               And elm trees nodding at the stars.

               I dream of a small fire lit room
               With yellow candles burning
               straight,
               And glowing pictures in the gloom,
               And kindly books that hold me late.
               Of things like these I choose to
               think
               When I can never be alone:
               Then someone says,"Another drink?"
               And turns my living heart to stone.

                                                    CUT TO:

SHOT of listeners.

There is genuine but polite applause, but LADY COLEFAX isn't quite sure what to make of the poem.

                    LADY SYBIL COLEFAX
               Thank you Mr. Sassoon...that was
               very...touching.

                    ROBBIE ROSS
               We both thank you Sybil...now go
               and rejoin Lady Cunard before she
               starts launching something.

She moves away.

                                                    CUT TO:

MID LONG SHOT

ROBBIE ROSS & SIEGFRIED SASSOON POV

IVOR NOVELLO is joined by LADY COLEFAX and she clearly asks him to play some more. He sits back down at the piano and begins to play the introduction to his song, "And her mother came too".

                                                    CUT TO:

TWO SHOT ROBBIE ROSS & SIEGFRIED SASSOON

     ROBBIE ROSS (CONT'D)
 He's considered very beautiful.

     SIEGFRIED SASSOON
 Look at those shoulders!

     ROBBIE ROSS
 Yes - and look at his.

           CUT BACK TO:

Their POV of IVOR NOVELLO at the piano.

TRACK IN ON HIM.

As he begins to sing a ripple of laughter and applause.

     IVOR NOVELLO
   (singing)
 "I seem to be the victim of a cruel
 jest,
 It dogs my footsteps with the girl
 I love the best.
 She's just the sweetest thing I've
 ever known,
 But still we never get the chance
 to be alone.

 My car will meet her - and her
 mother comes too!
 It's a two seater - still her
 mother comes too!
 At Ciro's when I am free, at
 dinner, supper or tea,
 She loves to shimmy with me - and
 her mother does too!
 We buy her trousseau - and her
 mother comes too!
 Asked *not* to do so - still her
 mother comes too!
 She simply can't take a snub, I go
 and sulk at the club,
 Then have a bath and a rub - and
 her brother comes too!

 There may be times when couples
 need a chaperone,
 But mothers ought to learn to leave
 a chap alone.
    (MORE)

                    IVOR NOVELLO (CONT'D)
          I wish they'd have a heart and use
          their common sense
          For three's a crowd, and more, it's
          treble the expense.

          We lunch at Maxim's - and her
          mother comes too!
          How large a snack seems - when her
          mother comes too!
          And when they're visiting me, we
          finish afternoon tea,
          She loves to sit on my knee - and
          her mother does too!
          To golf we started - and her mother
          came too!
          Three bags I carted - when her
          mother came too!
          She fainted just off the tee, my
          darling whispered to me
          "Jack dear, at last we are free"
          but her mother came too!

TRACK ENDS ON HIM AND LADY COLEFAX.

He finishes the song. Then applause. He stands and bows with
LADY COLEFAX.

                                        CUT BACK TO:

TWO SHOT ROBBIE ROSS & SIEGFRIED SASSOON

                    ROBBIE ROSS
                (looking at IVOR NOVELLO)
          And to think he once played the
          triangle so beautifully.
                (shakes head)
          What a waste!

                                        CUT TO:

IVOR NOVELLO COMES TOWARD ROBBIE ROSS AND SIEGFRIED SASSOON
FOLLOWED BY GLEN BYAM SHAW

                    GLEN BYAM SHAW
          Are we leaving Ivor?

                    IVOR NOVELLO
          No precious. I'm anxious to meet
          our distinguished guest.

                                        CUT TO:

FOUR SHOT ROBBIE ROSS, SIEGFRIED SASSOON, IVOR NOVELLO AND GLEN BYAM SHAW

     IVOR NOVELLO (CONT'D)
   (very charming, ushering
   SIEGFRIED SASSOON further
   out of the room)
 Mr. Sassoon, I'm eager to have your
 advice about my next musical which
 I'm thinking of writing in terza
 rima.

     ROBBIE ROSS
 That's near Naples isn't it?

IVOR and SIEGFRIED SASSOON going out of the room, their backs to ROBBIE ROSS and GLEN BYAM SHAW

     IVOR NOVELLO
 Dear Robbie whose silences are
 always so much more eloquent than
 speech.
   (to GLEN BYAM SHAW)
 Robbie will give you a paw to guide
 you home Glen.

They walk off.

             CUT TO:

TWO SHOT ROBBIE ROSS & GLEN BYAM SHAW

     ROBBIE ROSS
 C'est la vie.

     GLEN BYAM SHAW
   (looking from IVOR NOVELLO
   and SIEGFRIED SASSOON to
   ROBBIE ROSS)
 C'est la guerre.

             CUT TO:

14 INT. NIGHT. IVOR NOVELLO'S BEDROOM. (1921) 14

SIEGFRIED SASSOON and IVOR NOVELLO in bed together.

IVOR NOVELLO leans across and completely covers SIEGFRIED SASSOON and starts to kiss and caress him.

Silence.

Then

CUT TO:

15 INT. NIGHT. IVOR NOVELLO'S BEDROOM. (1921) 15

The bedroom door opens and GLEN BYAM SHAW stands there looking at the bed.

                GLEN BYAM SHAW
  Oops!

CUT TO:

SIEGFRIED SASSOON AND IVOR NOVELLO IN BED.

SASSOON is terribly embarrassed but IVOR NOVELLO takes no notice at all of GLEN BYAM SHAW but keeps kissing SIEGFRIED SASSOON'S face and neck.

                IVOR NOVELLO
        (to GLEN BYAM SHAW but not
        looking at him - he
        delivers his dialogue as
        if he were making love)
  Just leave the keys on the
  dresser...you know how absent
  minded I am with them...

He continues to caress SIEGFRIED SASSOON who lays there motionless with embarrassment.

CUT TO:

GLEN BYAM SHAW at the bedroom door.

He takes the keys from a chain and drops them on the floor and exits.

CUT TO:

16 INT. DAY. IVOR NOVELLO'S BEDROOM. (1921) 16

IVOR NOVELLO is still in bed but SIEGFRIED SASSOON is fully dressed.

He walks towards the bedroom door, sees the keys on the floor and picks them up.

                    SIEGFRIED SASSOON
            I think he's still in love with
            you.

                                            CUT TO:

IVOR NOVELLO

                    IVOR NOVELLO
            The main drawback with love is that
            it descends, all to quickly, into
            possessiveness...and that really is
            a BORE!

                                            CUT TO:

SIEGFRIED SASSOON

                    SIEGFRIED SASSOON
                    (showing IVOR NOVELLO the
                    keys)
            What shall I do with these?

                                            CUT TO:

IVOR NOVELLO

                    IVOR NOVELLO
            Oh...they're for you...

                                            CUT TO:

SIEGFRIED SASSOON AT THE DOOR OF IVOR NOVELLLO'S FLAT (INTERIOR). (1921)

SOUNDTRACK: A man screaming and wailing.

SIEGFRIED SASSOON exits.

                                            CUT TO:

17   INT. DAY. CAMP BASE ROUEN. (1917)   17

      SIEGFRIED SASSOON comes through the door in full military uniform.

      SOUNDTRACK: Man screaming and crying continues.

PAN WITH SIEGFRIED SASSOON L to R. He stops in the middle of the room.

CONTINUE TRACKING L TO R TO A MAN ON THE FLOOR SCREAMING. THERE'S A SERGEANT NEAR HIM.

SOUNDTRACK:

>   SIEGFRIED SASSOON V/O
>   (reading the poems
>   "Lamentations")
>   "I found him in the Guardroom at
>   the base.
>   From the blind darkness I heard his
>   crying
>   And blundered in. With puzzled,
>   patient face
>   A sergeant watched him; it was no
>   good trying
>   To stop it; for he howled and beat
>   his chest.
>   And, all because his brother had
>   gone west,
>   Raved at the bleeding war; his
>   rampant grief
>   Moaned, shouted, sobbed, and
>   choked, while he was kneeling
>   Half-naked on the floor. In my
>   belief
>   Such men have lost all patriotic
>   feeling."

Underneath this a man shrieking.

                                              DISSOLVE TO:

18   INT. NIGHT. MOTHER'S LIVING ROOM. (1919)   18

SHOT OF A SWORD HANGING ON THE WALL. GLINTING IN THE FIRELIGHT.

CRANE DOWN L to R to MOTHER.

MOTHER and SIEGFRIED SASSOON sitting in the firelight. MOTHER reading. SIEGFRIED SASSOON looking at the fire.

Christmas and a tree.

Silence.

> MOTHER
> Hamo died so far away...while I have his sword I still have him.

> SIEGFRIED SASSOON
> We never grieved properly for him.

> MOTHER
> Before grief there's anger.

She continues reading.

SIEGFRIED SASSOON looks at her.

SOUNDTRACK:

> SIEGFRIED SASSOON V/O
> (reading "To my mother")
> "I watch you on your constant way,
> In selfless duty long grown grey;
> And to myself I say
> That I have lived my life to learn
> How lives like your unasking earn
> Aureoles that guide and burn
> In heart's remembrance when the proud
> Who snared the suffrage of the crowd
> Are dumb and dusty browed...
> For you live onward in my thought
> Because you have not sought
> Rewards that can be bought.
> And so when I remember you
> I think of all things rich and true
> That I have reaped and wrought."

CUT TO:

SIEGFRIED SASSOON THEN A WIDER SHOT

MOTHER gets up crosses to SIEGFRIED SASSOON kisses him then leaves.

> MOTHER
> Thank God you survived. Good night darling.

> SIEGFRIED SASSOON
> Good night mother.

HOLD on SIEGFRIED SASSOON

Silence.

Then start to TRACK AROUND from front of sofa on which SIEGFRIED SASSOON is sitting to see his POV of the fireplace but in it's place the whole wall is filled with WW1 archive footage of Christmas 1914.

TRACK STOPS when we get directly behind SIEGFRIED SASSOON.

A snowscape of WW1 Christmas.

THEN

DISSOLVE TO:

A series of still photographs of:

1) No Mans land in snow
2) Trenches in snow
3) British and German soldiers meeting
4) Snow covering all

Each photograph is linked by a dissolve.

SOUNDTRACK:

German soldiers singing the German version of "Silent night", then halfway through the dissolves on the still photographs CROSS FADE to English soldiers singing the English version of "Silent night".

DISSOLVE TO:

TRACK L TO R FROM WW1 SNOW SCENES.

CONTINUE TRACKING UNTIL WE ARE BACK WITH SIEGFRIED AT MOTHER'S HOUSE.

TRACK STOPS ON SIEGFRIED SASSOON STILL ON THE SOFA FRONT VIEW.

HE STANDS UP.

A SHOT RINGS OUT AND HE FALLS BACKWARDS BUT NOT ONTO THE SOFA.

DISSOLVE TO OR
MORPH TO:

19   INT. DAY. HOSPITAL. (1917)   19

SIEGFRIED SASSOON FRONT VIEW. He eases back onto the pillows.

20 INT. DAY. HOSPITAL IN ENGLAND. (1917) 20

SIEGFRIED SASSOON in bed recovering from his wound, ROBBIE ROSS at his bedside.

> ROBBIE ROSS
> 3,500 copies of "Counter-attack" sold - your fame is spreading Siegfried.

> SIEGFRIED SASSOON
> Like a virus.

> ROBBIE ROSS
> Don't be contrary.

> SIEGFRIED SASSOON
> So I wake up famous.

> ROBBIE ROSS
> Like Byron. And I believe you've been overwhelmed by visits from all the great and good...Massine, Lydia Lopokova, Keynes, Winston Churchill (and mother) even "boy actor" Noel Coward. Have I left anyone out?

> SIEGFRIED SASSOON
> The Pope.

> ROBBIE ROSS
> That's right Siegfried, think small. How did you find Mr. Churchill?

> SIEGFRIED SASSOON
> Imperial.

> ROBBIE ROSS
> And Mr. Coward?

> SIEGFRIED SASSOON
> Gushing.

> ROBBIE ROSS
> What would you have done if Royalty had paid a call?

> SIEGFRIED SASSOON
> I'd have tried to curtsey from a sitting position.

ROBBIE ROSS
Speaking of Royalty, I've come with a command from Her Majesty Edith Sitwell. You are to attend a performance (at Carlyle Square) of her "Entertainment - Facade".
Poetry - by Edith.
Music - Willie Walton
I've gone to a great deal of trouble to get this so don't let me down. If you don't attend La Sitwell has threatened to go to your flat at Half Moon Street and hum the whole of "Tannhauser" to you.
You have been warned.

SIEGFRIED SASSOON
Oh I forgot - Ottoline Morell popped in and wished to be remembered to you.

ROBBIE ROSS
How was she?

SIEGFRIED SASSOON
Let's just say I've always found lime green a very unforgiving colour.

ROBBIE ROSS
Poor Ottoline! She'll go to her grave overdressed.

(Goes out)

CUT TO:

21 INT. DAY. SIEGFRIED SASSOON'S FLAT AT HALF MOON STREET. 21
(1921/22)

SHOT of IVOR NOVELLO dressed in an overcoat sitting and waiting.

IVOR NOVELLO
I'm looking forward to meeting your mother.

SIEGFRIED SASSOON comes out of his bedroom finishing dressing.

SIEGFRIED SASSOON
What?

IVOR NOVELLO
I said I was looking forward to meeting you mother. Mothers - good or bad - are always fascinating. I once tried to set fire to mine - but she was all asbestos.
(getting up)
Come on! We'll never get down to Kent at this rate.
(handing SIEGFRIED SASSOON an envelope)
I found this on the floor when I came in.

SIEGFRIED SASSOON
(looking briefly at it)
Oh - it'll be from Robbie Ross...

IVOR NOVELLO pulls a face.

SIEGFRIED SASSOON (CONT'D)
Why are you so antipathetic towards him?

IVOR NOVELLO
I resent the way he speaks to me - as though he's always putting me in my place. And the only problem with knowing "one's place" is that other people never know theirs.

SIEGFRIED SASSOON laughs out loud.

SIEGFRIED SASSOON
He's acerbic, I grant you, but never malign and, as a friend, very steadfast. Robbie Ross took some considerable risk when he openly supported Oscar Wilde...he's been hounded ever since by Lord Alfred Douglas.

IVOR NOVELLO
Bosie was always vindictive...Robbie should have known that from the beginning...he's got no one to blame but himself.

SIEGFRIED SASSOON
That's really unfair! His loyalty to Wilde was exemplary.

                    IVOR NOVELLO
            Alright, alright - Robbie's a
            saint! Let's drop the subject!

IVOR NOVELLO and SIEGFRIED SASSOON exit. SIEGFRIED SASSOON
smiling.

                                              CUT TO:

22   EXT. DAY. WEIRLEIGH (MOTHER'S HOUSE). (1921/22)   22

        IVOR NOVELLO on a horse.

                    SIEGFRIED SASSOON
            What on earth are you doing up
            there?

                    IVOR NOVELLO
            Trying to be a gentleman.

                    SIEGFRIED SASSOON
            How does it feel?

                    IVOR NOVELLO
            Horrible! Any higher my nose will
            bleed.

SIEGFRIED SASSOON laughing.

                    IVOR NOVELLO (CONT'D)
            Will you please help me down - I
            refuse to look ridiculous!

                    SIEGFRIED SASSOON
            I'll get a hoist!

                    IVOR NOVELLO
            That was insensitive.

The horse suddenly bolts.

                    IVOR NOVELLO (CONT'D)
            AARRGGHH!!

                                              CUT TO:

23   INT. NIGHT. WEIRLEIGH. (1921/22)   23

        SIEGFRIED SASSOON and his MOTHER laughing - IVOR NOVELLO
        loving the attention.

> MOTHER
> How was your first experience on a horse?

> IVOR NOVELLO
> Bruising.

> MOTHER
> I take it then that you don't hunt.

> IVOR NOVELLO
> No...well not foxes anyway.
> (winks at SIEGFRIED
> SASSOON)

Silence.

> IVOR NOVELLO (CONT'D)
> (noticing HAMO'S sword)
> That's a very fine sword.

> SIEGFRIED SASSOON
> It was my brother's.

> MOTHER
> He was killed in Gallipoli.

Silence.

SIEGFRIED SASSOON, IVOR NOVELLO & MOTHER sitting in the firelight.

Silence.

Then suddenly.

> SIEGFRIED SASSOON
> (looking at his watch)
> Oh God!

> MOTHER
> What is it?

> SIEGFRIED SASSOON
> It's the first performance of "Facade" and I was supposed to go to it!

> IVOR NOVELLO
> Where is it being performed?

> SIEGFRIED SASSOON
> At a private performance in Carlyle Square.

					IVOR NOVELLO
				Chelsea -
					(looking at his watch)
				Well even if I drive like the wind, we'll never get back to town in time now.

					SIEGFRIED SASSOON
				Oh God. Robbie will be furious. And so will Edith Sitwell - it's being given to a very select audience.

					MOTHER
				I'm sure she'll understand once you've explained why you weren't able to attend.

					SIEGFRIED SASSOON
				I don't think so mother. Edith can be a very captious woman.

					IVOR NOVELLO
				She isn't a woman - she's an animated meringue. And those teeth!

					SIEGFRIED SASSOON
				Don't be horrible Ivor. She suffers, I believe, from a complaint known as "receding gums".

					IVOR NOVELLO
				She's so autocratic, I'm surprised she gave them permission to.

IVOR NOVELLO gets up.

					IVOR NOVELLO (CONT'D)
				Come on - we'll see if we can catch some of it.

He goes out.

					SIEGFRIED SASSOON
				I'm sorry to leave in such a rush mother.

					MOTHER
				It doesn't matter.

Silence.

					MOTHER (CONT'D)
				Is he just another one of your pretty boys?

SIEGFRIED SASSOON
No. It's deeper than that...Much deeper.

Silence.

SIEGFRIED SASSOON (CONT'D)
You don't like him do you mother?

MOTHER
He's amusing but unpleasant. It's the eyes, I think, they're cruel.

SIEGFRIED SASSOON doesn't know what to say.

Pause.

SIEGFRIED SASSOON
Good night mother.

MOTHER
Good night Siegfried.

CUT TO:

24 INT. DAY. EDITH SITWELL'S HOUSE. (1922) 24

EDITH SITWELL'S bedroom. The sun is coming through blinds and the air is stuffy and stale.

CLOSE UP EDITH SITWELL.

Silence.

She is lying in bed under a mosquito net. She is wearing an oversized turban and a large ring on one of her fingers.

EDITH SITWELL
You never came.

SIEGFRIED SASSOON
Please forgive me Edith.

EDITH SITWELL
I shall try.

SIEGFRIED SASSOON
I'm entirely to blame. We visited my mother in Kent and lost all sense of time.

EDITH SITWELL
We?

SIEGFRIED SASSOON
Me...and Ivor Novello...

EDITH SITWELL
A man at the cheaper end of poetry.

SIEGFRIED SASSOON
I do hope you can forgive me, for I am mortified by my thoughtlessness.

Silence.

SIEGFRIED SASSOON (CONT'D)
How was the work received?

EDITH SITWELL
They tittered.

SIEGFRIED SASSOON
Tittered?

EDITH SITWELL
Tittered. I overheard someone say (in the most odious manner), "It's this sort of thing that makes one glad to be semi-conscious." I was deeply wounded. My poetry has wonderful assonances and dissonances...I use words for their colour not merely for what they are supposed to mean.

SIEGFRIED SASSOON
Great art may sometimes be so ahead of it's time, Edith, that it's initial reception can sometimes be considered a Suces d'Estime...think of Stravinsky.

EDITH SITWELL
But I do not wish to think of Stravinsky.

Silence.

EDITH SITWELL (CONT'D)
We are performing "Facade" at the Aeolian Hall next week. I shall expect you there.

>   SIEGFRIED SASSOON
>   Of course Edith. I shall come with
>   the speed of a thousand gazelles.
>
>   EDITH SITWELL
>   There's no need for hyperbole
>   Siegfried...a taxi will do.

SOUNDTRACK: The introduction to "En Famille" is heard.

>   EDITH SITWELL'S V/O
>   "In the early springtime after
>   their tea,
>   Through the young fields of the
>   springing Bohea,"

TRACK BACK from her.

> DISSOLVE TO:

25   INT. NIGHT. AEOLIAN HALL. (1922)   25

CLOSE UP EDITH SITWELL. She is seated behind a gauze wearing another outrageous turban. She is reciting the end of "En Famille".

>   EDITH SITWELL
>   "...To scratch you, my dears, like
>   a mandoline."

CONTINUE TRACKING BACK.

> DISSOLVE TO:

26   INT. NIGHT. ENTRANCE TO THE AEOLIAN HALL. (1922)   26

TWO SHOT SIEGFRIED SASSOON & IVOR NOVELLO coming out of the auditorium.

CONTINUE TRACKING BACK WITH THEM.

>   IVOR NOVELLO
>   (saying one of the lines
>   from one of the poems)
>   "Gone the sweet swallow, gone
>   Philomel!"
>   Oh Christ!
>
>   SIEGFRIED SASSOON
>   I'll have to go backstage.

> IVOR NOVELLO
> Rather you than me.

DISSOLVE TO:

27   INT. NIGHT. AEOLIAN DRESSING ROOM. (1922)   27

TRACK BACK FROM EDITH SITWELL looking into her mirror. Next to her ROBBIE ROSS. She turns to look at the door.

> EDITH SITWELL
> Ah, The Prodigal!

CUT TO:

28   INT. NIGHT. AEOLIAN DRESSING ROOM. (1922)   28

TRACK TO DOOR.

It opens and SIEGFRIED SASSOON is standing there.

TRACK STOPS ON HIS CLOSE UP.

> SIEGFRIED SASSOON
> (beaming)
> Well Edith – you've done it again!

DISSOLVE TO:

WW1 FOOTAGE.

SOUNDTRACK OVER THE DISSOLVE:

> EDITH SITWELL'S V/O
> (From "En Famille")
> "For Hell is just as properly proper
> As Greenwich or as Bath or Joppa!"

DISSOLVE TO:

WW1 FOOTAGE: 1917

Over all this WW1 footage we will hear the letter and statement by SIEGFRIED SASSOON to his commanding officer.

                    SIEGFRIED SASSOON V/O
                (Letter)
            I am writing you this private
            letter with the greatest possible
            regret. I must inform you that it
            is my intention to refuse to
            perform any further military
            duties. I am doing this as a
            protest against the policy of the
            Government in prolonging the War by
            failing to state their conditions
            for peace.
            I have written a statement of my
            reasons, of which I enclose a copy.
            This statement is being circulated.
            I would have spared you this
            unpleasantness had it been
            possible.
            My only desire is to make things as
            easy as possible for you in dealing
            with my case. I will come to
            Litherland immediately I hear from
            you, if that is your wish.
            I am fully aware of what I am
            letting myself in for.

1)   British soldiers firing field guns.

2)   No mans land.

3)   British soldiers and cavalry marching towards us.

4)   Cheering crowds.

5)   More marching soldiers.

6)   Troops on train.

7)   Soldiers embarking on ship.

8)   More marching soldiers.

9)   British troops in waterlogged trenches.

10) More waterlogged trenches.

11) More explosions.

12) British soldiers moving through cordite mist.

SIEGFRIED SASSOON V/O (CONT'D)
(Statement)
I am making this statement as an act of willful defiance of military authority because I believe that the war is being deliberately prolonged by those who have the power to end it. I am a soldier, convinced that I am acting on behalf of soldiers. I believe that the war upon which I entered as a war of defence and liberation has now become a war of aggression and conquest. I believe that the purpose for which I and my fellow soldiers entered upon this war should and have been so clearly stated as to have made it impossible to change them and that had this been done the objects that actuated us would now be attainable by negotiation.
I have seen and endured the sufferings of the troops and I can no longer be a party to prolong these sufferings for ends which I believe to be evil and unjust. I am not protesting against the conduct of the war, but against the political errors and insincerities for which the fighting men are being sacrificed.
On behalf of those who are suffering now, I make this protest against the deception which is being practised upon them; also I believe it may help to destroy the callous complacency with which the majority of those at home regard the continuance of agonies which they do not share and which they have not enough imagination to realise.

ROBBIE ROSS V/O
(Disturbed)
Do you intend to send this?

SIEGFRIED SASSOON V/O
Yes.

> ROBBIE ROSS V/O
> I'd think this over very carefully if I were you.

DISSOLVE TO:

29 INT. EARLY EVENING. THE REFORM CLUB/LIBERAL CLUB. (1917) 29

SIEGFRIED SASSOON comes into one of the main reception rooms and is clearly furious.

TRACK BACK WITH HIM UNTIL HE SITS DOWN. As he does so he throws a copy of The Times to ROBBIE ROSS who is sitting opposite.

> SIEGFRIED SASSOON
> I suppose you had a hand in this?

> ROBBIE ROSS
> Yes, and Eddie Marsh.

> SIEGFRIED SASSOON
> I take this _very_ ill Robbie! Why did you involve Marsh?!

> ROBBIE ROSS
> Because he's Principal Private Secretary to Winston Churchill and he wanted to help. He was instrumental in getting you a Medical Board examination instead of a Court Martial.

A tense silence.

> ROBBIE ROSS (CONT'D)
> If you were found guilty at a Court Martial you could be shot.

> SIEGFRIED SASSOON
> That was a risk I was prepared to take.

> ROBBIE ROSS
> But there are those who care for you and who were not.

Silence.

> SIEGFRIED SASSOON
> A Court Martial would have been a platform to state my opposition to the conduct of the war.
> (MORE)

                    SIEGFRIED SASSOON (CONT'D)
          And you have prevented me from
          doing so not only for The Times
          article but for my statement read
          out on the floor of the House. You
          have rendered me impotent. You have
          robbed me of my dignity.

                    ROBBIE ROSS
          Better that than a firing squad.

                    SIEGFRIED SASSOON
          That is a matter of opinion.

                    ROBBIE ROSS
          Don't be angry with me Siegfried.
          My intentions were honourable.

PAN AWAY FROM THEM R TO L.

                                        DISSOLVE TO:

30   INT. TRAIN. EARLY EVENING. (1917)   30

     SIDE VIEW SHOT OF SASSOON AT THE WINDOW.

     He looks out of the window lost in thought.

                    ROBBIE ROSS V/O
          I'm quite appalled by what you've
          done. I can only hope that your
          C.O. in Liverpool will ignore your
          letter. I am terrified that you
          will be put under arrest.

                                        DISSOLVE TO:

31   INT. DAY. OFFICE AT ARMY HQ, LITHERLAND. (1917)   31

     C/U of MAJOR MCCARTNEY-FILGATE.

     He picks up a cup of tea from his desk.

                    MAJOR MCCARTNEY-FILGATE
               (Very amiable)
          Now then Lieutenant Sassoon...
               (He sips his tea)
          ...what seems to be the trouble?

                                        CUT TO:

32   INT. DAY. MEDICAL BOARD. (1917)   32

C/U OF SIEGFRIED SASSOON.

                    MAJOR MCCARTNEY-FILGATE'S V/O
          You may sit if you wish Lieutenant.

                    SIEGFRIED SASSOON
          Thank you Sir.

He sits.

                                                CUT TO:

WIDE SHOT of Medical Board consisting of 2 army doctors and MAJOR MCCARTNEY-FILGATE who is the President of the Board.

                    MAJOR MCCARTNEY-FILGATE
          We read your statement Lieutenant, with some alarm. Why did you make it?

                    SIEGFRIED SASSOON
          I wanted to state my position regarding the conduct of the war.

                    FIRST ARMY DOCTOR
          It is *not* your place to question how the war is being prosecuted. Your duty lies in obeying orders.

                    SIEGFRIED SASSOON
          Duty. That word covers a multitude of sins. In the face of such slaughter one cannot "order" ones conscience.

                    FIRST ARMY DOCTOR
          One can do better than that - one can ignore it.

                    SIEGFRIED SASSOON
          That reply was so disgraceful - you ought to be in politics.

                    MAJOR MCCARTNEY-FILGATE
          That was impertinent Lieutenant.

SIEGFRIED SASSOON does not reply or apologise.

Silence.

                    SECOND ARMY DOCTOR
          Are you pro-German?

SIEGFRIED SASSOON
No. I'm pro-human.

SECOND ARMY DOCTOR
We are not here to discuss humanity
- that is religion's sphere of
operations.

SIEGFRIED SASSOON
(Heated)
And what of morality?

SECOND ARMY DOCTOR
(Heated)
Morality is a luxury that we can
only afford during peacetime!

SIEGFRIED SASSOON
(Heated)
I would be grateful if you could
take that offensive tone out of
your voice. Voices raised in anger
only perpetuates war!

SECOND ARMY DOCTOR
And passive resistance only invites
defeat!

A tense silence.

SIEGFRIED SASSOON
(More controlled)
I simply cannot remain silent in
the face of such casualties -
someone should, _must_ be brought to
book.

FIRST ARMY DOCTOR
The casualties young man, are a
matter for the Imperial General
Staff and your statement, indeed
your entire attitude, is both
offensive and detrimental to
military discipline.

MAJOR MCCARTNEY-FILGATE
My colleague is quite right. It is
not your place to question your
superiors, much less to imply that
they are not honourable.

                SIEGFRIED SASSOON
          Perhaps, Sir, if any of you visit
          the front you might, at least,
          spare some thought for the many
          bereaved families and the pain they
          suffer.

                FIRST ARMY DOCTOR
             (Shouting)
          You are out of order sir!

                SIEGFRIED SASSOON
             (Calm)
          I thought that was the very reason
          for my being brought before you.

                MAJOR MCCARTNEY-FILGATE
          This has gone far enough.

The Major looks at his fellow officers and they confer sotto voce.

                MAJOR MCCARTNEY-FILGATE (CONT'D)
          Myself and my fellow officers feel
          that your mind is still in chaos
          and that you are unfit to be
          trusted with mens lives. It is
          therefore the Board's decision that
          you should be sent to a hospital
          for nervous diseases in Scotland.

The two army doctors nod in agreement.

                MAJOR MCCARTNEY-FILGATE (CONT'D)
          We therefore order you to report
          immediately to Craiglockhart, in
          Edinburgh.

SIEGFRIED SASSOON stands and salutes.

                                        DISSOLVE TO:

33   INT. TRAIN. DAY. (1917)   33

     SIDE VIEW OF SIEGFRIED SASSOON looking out of the window.

     HOLD

     SOUNDTRACK:

                    SIEGFRIED SASSOON V/O
          Thank you. They had, at least,
          spared me from having to sing,
          "Jerusalem".

                    MAJOR MCCARTNEY-FILGATE'S V/O
          His mental condition is abnormal.
          His conversation is disconnected
          and somewhat irrational. His manner
          nervous and excitable. In addition
          to this his family history is
          neuropathic. He is suffering from a
          nervous breakdown and we do not
          consider him responsible for his
          actions.

                                        DISSOLVE TO:

PANNING R TO L FROM TRAIN WINDOW TO THE ENTRANCE OF
CRAIGLOCKHART.

A doorbell is heard.

The doors open.

SASSOON is met by the Chief Medical Officer and the Matron.   *

                    CHIEF MEDICAL OFFICER
               (Curt)
          Good morning Lieutenant.

He is one of those officers who thinks that shell-shock is
just cowardice.

                                        DISSOLVE TO:

34   INT. DAY. CRAIGLOCKHART. (1917)   34

       TWO SHOT MATRON AND CHIEF MEDICAL OFFICER THEIR BACKS TO
       CAMERA; SIEGFRIED SASSOON'S POV; (invent a regiment for CMO
       at the rank of Captain).

       TRACK FORWARD WITH THEM

       During this track 2 or 3 men come towards the camera. They
       have prominent blue marks on their faces.

       SOUNDTRACK:

                    CHIEF MEDICAL OFFICER V/O
               Name?

                    SIEGFRIED SASSOON V/O
          Sassoon, Siegfried.

                    CHIEF MEDICAL OFFICER V/O
          Rank?

                    SIEGFRIED SASSOON V/O
          Second Lieutenant.

                    CHIEF MEDICAL OFFICER V/O
          Age?

                    SIEGFRIED SASSOON V/O
          30.

                    CHIEF MEDICAL OFFICER V/O
          Years of complete service?

                    SIEGFRIED SASSOON V/O
          2 years 11 months.

                                        CUT TO:

35   INT. DAY. CHIEF MEDICAL OFFICER'S OFFICE. (1917)   35

      TWO SHOT CMO AND MATRON BOTH SITTING.

      MATRON writing, CMO dictating. SASSOON standing.

                    CHIEF MEDICAL OFFICER
          Completed months with Field Force?

                    SIEGFRIED SASSOON
          13 months.

                    CHIEF MEDICAL OFFICER
          Disease?

                    SIEGFRIED SASSOON
          I've had some sort of breakdown.

                    CHIEF MEDICAL OFFICER
          Nervous debility?

                    SIEGFRIED SASSOON
          Yes, I believe that's what they
          called it.

                    CHIEF MEDICAL OFFICER
               (To Matron)
          Enter it as neurosthenia Matron.

      SASSOON lingers for a moment.

SIEGFRIED SASSOON
As we came in I noticed that several men had blue dots on their faces.

MATRON
Morphine.

SIEGFRIED SASSOON
Morphine?

MATRON
The dots denote that they've had their doses, so that they are given no more until the appropriate time.

CHIEF MEDICAL OFFICER
(To Matron)
Who will be treating this man?

MATRON
Dr. Rivers.

CHIEF MEDICAL OFFICER
(To Siegfried Sassoon)
Dr. Rivers' office is next door. I think it would be polite if you introduced yourself.

SIEGFRIED SASSOON
Yes sir.

SIEGFRIED SASSOON goes to leave then stops.

CHIEF MEDICAL OFFICER
(Sarcastic)
I nearly forgot to give you your armband. It must be worn at all times, especially outside the hospital grounds. It is to show that you are a serving soldier in hospital and not a conscientious objector. We wouldn't want you to be attacked in Princes Street now, would we?

SIEGFRIED SASSOON
Which arm should I wear it on sir?

CHIEF MEDICAL OFFICER
The pleasure of that choice, Lieutenant is entirely yours.

                              MATRON
                    Your room is on the upper floor at
                    the end of the corridor.

                                                    CUT TO:

36   INT. DAY. DOCTOR RIVER'S OFFICE. (1917)   36

        C/U DR. RIVERS.

                              SIEGFRIED SASSOON V/O
                    Sassoon...Siegfried...Lieutenant.

                              DR. RIVERS
                    Your burgeoning fame precedes you.
                    I enjoyed "The Old Huntsman" very
                    much. You may not know but we have
                    a house magazine, "Hydra". I'm sure
                    it would welcome a contribution
                    from you.

                              SIEGFRIED SASSOON
                    I'll try to write something light
                    and amusing.

                              DR. RIVERS
                    There's no need to go that far.
                    You have an appointment to see me -
                    10:30 - in the morning.

                                                    CUT TO:

37   INT. DAY. SIEGFRIED SASSOON'S ROOM AT CRAIGLOCKHART. (1917) 37

        He comes in, sits down and looks around. It's rather a dismal
        room.

                              SIEGFRIED SASSOON
                         (Rather downcast)
                    Dear Mother...have arrived in
                    Dottyville...wish you were here...

                                                    CUT TO:

38   INT. DAY. DOCTOR RIVER'S OFFICE. (1917)   38

        It has huge windows looking out over the grounds.

                              SIEGFRIED SASSOON
                    Good morning doctor.

> DR. RIVERS
> Good morning Sassoon. Please sit down, we are quite relaxed here.

Silence.

> DR. RIVERS (CONT'D)
> Although I must say, we do seem to go through rather too many Chief Medical Officers. Some are more flexible than others, then they are replaced by someone who wants everything to be as taut as Aldershot. Then they too are replaced.

> SIEGFRIED SASSOON
> And what is your persuasion?

> DR. RIVERS
> Oh, I prefer a certain measure of laxity...one can't be at attention forever...it plays havoc with the nerves.

Silence. Tense but not unpleasant.

> SIEGFRIED SASSOON
> From what little I know of your method of treatment here, I understand that from whatever I say you can deduce whether or not my grandmother was a dipsomaniac.

> DR. RIVERS
> Was she?

> SIEGFRIED SASSOON
> Alas, no. Just a sweet sherry at Christmas and on birthdays.

> DR. RIVERS
> Well done your grandmother! She didn't know what she wasn't missing.

Silence. This time very uncomfortable.

> SIEGFRIED SASSOON
> Just tell me what you want me to do and I will comply with your wishes.

DR. RIVERS
It isn't a question of what I want. It is a question of what you think you need.

SIEGFRIED SASSOON
Am I to start? Or will you?

DR. RIVERS
Is there anything you feel you wish to say?

SIEGFRIED SASSOON
What I feel cannot be talked away or soothed into silence.

DR. RIVERS
Why?

SIEGFRIED SASSOON
Too many have died, too much has been destroyed. The soul of the world has died.

DR. RIVERS
There can be an easement of pain, a move towards acceptance.

SIEGFRIED SASSOON
Pain is not the only terror...there are many more...

DR. RIVERS
Can you name them?

SIEGFRIED SASSOON
If I could name them they would cease to be terrors.

DR. RIVERS
That is a very elegant way of avoiding an answer.

SIEGFRIED SASSOON
All evasions are elegant - think of politics.

DR. RIVERS
I've always thought that politicians were too stupid to be subtle.

SIEGFRIED SASSOON
Or perhaps they are just too subtle to be inelegant.

Silence.

DR. RIVERS
Are you a good soldier?

SIEGFRIED SASSOON
Passable. But I was a poor marksman - I never knew which eye to shut.

DR. RIVERS
I understand that you were awarded the M.C..

SIEGFRIED SASSOON
Yes. It's supposed to signify gallantry - but bravery is only cowardice in extremis. At the root of bravery lies terror and the fear of fear.

DR. RIVERS
But you were conspicuous by your courage. Why did you discard the Military Cross.

SIEGFRIED SASSOON
Disgust at my own dwindling standards and the men I felt I had betrayed. It was nothing short of duplicity.

DR. RIVERS
And yet the men under your command held you in the highest esteem, I am told.

SIEGFRIED SASSOON
And I them. They seemed to me to be all that was good and true in the world.

DR. RIVERS
Are you searching for truth?

SIEGFRIED SASSOON
Isn't everyone?

DR. RIVERS
And if you find it - what then?

                    SIEGFRIED SASSOON
            Peace of mind. Contentment. No
            longer yearning for what has been
            lost.

Silence.

They sit there not saying anything. SIEGFRIED SASSOON very close to tears.

PAN UP TO WINDOWS R TO L. THE SUN FLOODING IN.

                    SIEGFRIED SASSOON V/O
                  (As we PAN to the windows)
            "How beautifully blue the sky
            The glass is rising very high,
            Continue fine I hope it may,
            And yet it rained but yesterday.

            Tomorrow it may pour again
            I hear the country needs some rain..."

                                        DISSOLVE TO:

39   EXT. DAY. CHERRY TREE IN FULL BLOSSOM FILLING THE SCREEN.   39
        (1917)

SOUNDTRACK:

"Loveliest of trees" being sung.

            "Loveliest of trees, the cherry now
            Is hung with bloom along the bough,
            And stands about the woodland ride
            Wearing white for Eastertide...

            Now, of my threescore years and ten,
            Twenty will not come again,
            And take from seventy springs a score,
            It only leaves me fifty more...

            And since to look at things in bloom
            Fifty springs are little room, About
            the woodlands I will go
            To see the cherry hung with snow."

                                        DISSOLVE TO:

WW1 FOOTAGE:

1) A shot of men coming towards the camera in a "V" shape.

2) A series of shots of soldiers in the sun waiting or marching but just before a battle commences digging trenches.

3) Coffins in grave.

4) Crowds in rain with umbrellas.

5) Soldiers in trenches smoking and playing cards.

6) No mans land. Soldiers coming through it.

DISSOLVE TO:

INT. DAY. SIEGFRIED SASSOON'S ROOM AT CRAIGLOCKHART. (1917)

He is seated at an open window - on a chair with his legs up on a window sill - the window is wide open. Lovely weather.

SOUNDTRACK:

"Loveliest of trees" ends.

He stops reading, then laying the book on his lap he closes his eyes and leans back savouring the sun.

HOLD

There's a knock on the door and SASSOON comes out of his reverie.

    SIEGFRIED SASSOON
 Come in.

    WILFRED OWEN V/O
 Lieutenant Sassoon?

    SIEGFRIED SASSOON
  (Turning round)
 Yes.

CUT TO SASSOON'S POV.

WILFRED OWEN standing at the half open door.

    WILFRED OWEN
  (A slight stammer)
 I'm W-ilfred Owen.

DISSOLVE TO:

41   INT.NIGHT.SIEGFRIED SASSOON'S ROOM AT CRAIGLOCKHART.(1917) 41

SIEGFRIED SASSOON in bed.

HOLD ON HIM.

SOUNDTRACK:

Terrible screaming, voices then the noise of footsteps.

SIEGFRIED SASSOON lying in the dark, awake but very disturbed.

SOUNDTRACK:

The sound of the screaming intensifies, then stops.

SASSOON lies in the dark afraid.

                                                    CUT TO:

42   INT. DAY. DOCTOR RIVER'S OFFICE. (1917)   42

                    SIEGFRIED SASSOON
               There was howling last night, like
               a wolf...

                    DR. RIVERS
               Strictly speaking, wolves
               "ululate", but howling will do.

                    SIEGFRIED SASSOON
               Don't make light of it like that
               doctor.

                    DR. RIVERS
               That is not what I am doing. I'm
               merely keeping it in perspective,
               but I'm sorry if I sounded
               uncaring.

                    SIEGFRIED SASSOON
               His screams were terrible! Worse
               than an animal. There was such
               anguish in his screaming.

Silence.

                    SIEGFRIED SASSOON (CONT'D)
               Why do all the worst terrors come
               at night?

                    DR. RIVERS
          The dark is, I think, like the
          unconscious...waiting all day so
          that it can steal over you in the
          dark.

                    SIEGFRIED SASSOON
          You make it sound almost benign.

                    DR. RIVERS
          Perhaps it is.

                                        DISSOLVE TO:

WW1 FOOTAGE:

1) Moving troops.

2) Trees on ridge.

3) Sky.

4) Troops moving L to R (dark sky ahead, explosions)

5) Field guns firing into the night.

6) Troops going over the top.

7) Empty ridge.

All this footage is in silhouette.

                                        DISSOLVE TO:

43   INT. DAY. DOCTOR RIVER'S OFFICE. (1917)   43

                    DR. RIVERS
          I believe Wilfred Owen introduced
          himself to you the other day.

                    SIEGFRIED SASSOON
          Yes. He seems so gentle...I feel
          rather protective of him...

                    DR. RIVERS
          Does that protectiveness hide
          something deeper?

SIEGFRIED SASSOON
Yes. All my friendships do, but I
have never allowed
my...emotions...to mar or spoil
them...I remain passive. It's how I
cope.

DR. RIVERS
You never act on impulse?

SIEGFRIED SASSOON
Never. I'm unable to take risks.
It's the "hero" in me.

DR. RIVERS
Why not?

SIEGFRIED SASSOON
Too afraid. Too inhibited. Shamed
by an inner corruption. Or perhaps
it's simply because of...what's the
phrase..."the love that dare not
speak it's name".

DR. RIVERS
You are not alone in that respect.

They both look at each other for a while.

SIEGFRIED SASSOON
Frankly doctor – I'm surprised.

DR. RIVERS
Why? The world is full of
anomalies.

SIEGFRIED SASSOON
Well speaking as one anomaly to
another – how do you cope with the
law?

DR. RIVERS
I adopt a less than honest respect
for it.

SIEGFRIED SASSOON
So evasion is not confined solely
to second lieutenants?

DR. RIVERS
No – it affects all ranks. I trust
that after this disclosure you will
be discreet.

                    SIEGFRIED SASSOON
               Discretion is my middle name.

                    DR. RIVERS
               Well, it's better than Ethel
               anyway.

They both smile.

                                                  CUT TO:

44   EXT. DAY. TENNIS COURT, CRAIGLOCKHART. (1917)   44

       WIDE SHOT FROM THE NET CHORD JUDGE POSITION.

       SIEGFRIED SASSOON AND WILFRED OWEN playing tennis.

       TRACK FORWARD along the net.

       They continue playing.

                    SIEGFRIED SASSOON V/O
               15, love.

                                               DISSOLVE TO:

45   EXT. DAY. SWIMMING POOL, CRAIGLOCKHART. (1917)   45

       SHOT UNDERWATER.

       The bodies of SIEGFRIED SASSOON and WILFRED OWEN plunge down
       into the water then, whilst still below the water, they
       circle each other.

                    SIEGFRIED SASSOON V/O
               30, love.

                                               DISSOLVE TO:

46   INT. DAY. THEATRE, CRAIGLOCKHART. (1917)   46

       TWO SHOT WILFRED OWEN & SIEGFRIED SASSOON doing the Tango and
       coming towards the camera.

                    SIEGFRIED SASSOON V/O
               40, love.

       They are rehearsing for a little show. Building scenery,
       etc..

At a piano a soldier is playing a tango and SIEGFRIED SASSOON and WILFRED OWEN are dancing it - and rather well too.

     SIEGFRIED SASSOON V/O (CONT'D)
Game... Set... and match.

TRACK BACK with them as they dance towards the camera and then stop abruptly. They come to attention and salute.

     CHIEF MEDICAL OFFICER
  (He carries a wooden
  swagger stick & tan
  leather gloves)
One assumes that these "theatricals" have some deeper purpose.

     SIEGFRIED SASSOON
I think, sir, they help to give some sort of ease away from the front line.

     CHIEF MEDICAL OFFICER
I doubt that. Should the enemy perceive that the British Army is always preparing for a Tango - the war is lost. Besides, the spectacle of men dancing with men is never palatable. I have always thought that such creatures went into the library with their service revolvers and did the decent thing.

Pause.

     CHIEF MEDICAL OFFICER (CONT'D)
And how is your "treatment" progressing Lieutenant?

     SIEGFRIED SASSOON
Oh, it has its unique moments, sir.

     CHIEF MEDICAL OFFICER
  (He puts the swagger stick
  under his arm & puts his
  leather gloves on)
Then let us hope that those unique moments coalesce enough to get you back to active service - fighting fit, as it were.

     SIEGFRIED SASSOON
Doesn't that rather depend on what is fit to fight for?
     (MORE)

SIEGFRIED SASSOON (CONT'D)
But perhaps I'm just being syndromatic – or is that a lapsus linguae?

CHIEF MEDICAL OFFICER
(Who's not paid any real attention)
I beg your pardon?

SIEGFRIED SASSOON
Lapsus linguae – a slip of the tongue.

CHIEF MEDICAL OFFICER
I know what it means Lieutenant! The rest of us may be unable to read "Beowulf" in the original but we're not all complete Philistines!

SIEGFRIED SASSOON
Of course not sir.

CHIEF MEDICAL OFFICER
Carry on!

SIEGFRIED SASSOON
(Towards Wilfred Owen)
Ready?

WILFRED OWEN
Yes.

SIEGFRIED SASSOON
One, two, three and...

The piano starts and they resume their Tango.

CUT TO:

47 INT. DAY. SIEGFRIED SASSOON'S ROOM AT CRAIGLOCKHART. (1917) 47

A shot of the hospital magazine, "Hydra", held aloft by WILFRED OWEN.

TILT DOWN WITH IT AS HE LOWERS IT AS HE GETS INTO THE ROOM.

WILFRED OWEN
Halitosis! Halitosis! Your first poem in "Hydra"!

SIEGFRIED SASSOON
Long live the editor!

WILFRED OWEN
I am the editor!

SIEGFRIED SASSOON
Hooray for nepotism!

The following exchanges are good humoured.

WILFRED OWEN
And what do you think of my verse Siegfried?

SIEGFRIED SASSOON
It seems to be a little too dependant on 19th century models.

WILFRED OWEN
You make it sound like, "The courtship of Miles Standish".

SIEGFRIED SASSOON
No. Nothing's as bad as that.

WILFRED OWEN
But you do find my work derivative?

SIEGFRIED SASSOON
While I was at Clare I wasted far too much time reading Swinburne - very bad for my adjectives. Speak directly. Not with another's voice.

Pause.

WILFRED OWEN clearly hurt.

SIEGFRIED SASSOON (CONT'D)
(Trying to make amends)
At first, everyone's work is derivative. We all have to start somewhere. At Cambridge - apart from Swinburne - I did nothing except read William Morris - in a punt! - and staggered through "Maud".

WILFRED OWEN looks a little downcast.

Short silence.

WILFRED OWEN
(He hands a poem to Siegfried Sassoon)
(MORE)

> WILFRED OWEN (CONT'D)
> Perhaps my latest effort will please you. It's called "Disabled".

STAY ON SIEGFRIED SASSOON AS HE SILENTLY READS THE POEM.

A long pause.

> SIEGFRIED SASSOON
> (With great emotion)
> It's magnificent. It pierces the heart.

WILFRED OWEN smiles.

> SIEGFRIED SASSOON (CONT'D)
> Oh what a gift you have!

A long pause, a difficult silence.

> WILFRED OWEN
> I have been passed by the Medical Board as fit for active service.

SIEGFRIED SASSOON clearly shaken.

> SIEGFRIED SASSOON
> When do you rejoin your regiment?

> WILFRED OWEN
> December. Just before Christmas.

> SIEGFRIED SASSOON
> Oh.

CUT TO:

48 INT. DAY. THEATRE, CRAIGLOCKHART. (1917) 48

TRACK and PAN R to L on singer as she moves across the stage.

> FEMALE SINGER & AUDIENCE
> ("Waiting at the church")
> "There was I waiting at the church
> Waiting at the church
> Waiting at the church.
> All day long he left me in the lurch
> Lord, how it did upset me
> All at once he sent around a note
> Here's the very note
> This is what he wrote
> 'Can't get away to marry you today,
> My wife won't let me.'"

TRACK and PAN in on the AUDIENCE DURING THE SINGING, UNTIL WE GET TO A TWO SHOT OF SIEGFRIED SASSOON AND WILFRED OWEN SITTING BY EACH OTHER.

THEN WE TRACK AROUND TO SIEGFRIED SASSOON. He stops singing and just looks at WILFRED OWEN.

CUT TO SIDE VIEW OF WILFRED OWEN. He is singing his heart out.

The song stops and everyone applauds.

    WILFRED OWEN
   (Looking at Siegfried
   Sassoon and smiling)
 What is it Siegfried?

CUT TO SIEGFRIED SASSOON.

    SIEGFRIED SASSOON
   (Snapping out of his
   reverie)
 Nothing.

              CUT TO:

49 INT. DAY. DOCTOR RIVER'S OFFICE. (1917) 49

SIEGFRIED SASSOON & DR. RIVERS sitting in silence.

They don't look at one another.

More silence.

    SIEGFRIED SASSOON
   (Without looking at Dr.
   Rivers)
 Wilfred is about to return to
 duty...

    DR. RIVERS
   (Not looking at Siegfried)
 I know.

A long silence.

 What will you do?

SIEGFRIED SASSOON
Nothing.

Another long silence.

I will not do anything that will make the parting even more painful.

Another long silence.

I would give all that I possess just to have him stay one more hour, one more minute.

(Smiles ruefully)

Quick to tears - slow to love. When I first met him he had a slight stammer and spoke, I thought, with a grammar school accent...how could I have been such a snob? He's a lovely man and I think, the greater poet.

Silence.

DR. RIVERS
And what about your poetry?

SIEGFRIED SASSOON
Egotism really.

DR. RIVERS
That seems a little harsh.

SIEGFRIED SASSOON
The truth often is.

Silence.

SIEGFRIED SASSOON (CONT'D)
I have no idea why I come here - it has done no good at all.

Pause.

DR. RIVERS
Think of it as a cleansing of the soul.

                    SIEGFRIED SASSOON
               (Nearly crying)
          Why did you have to put it so
          beautifully?

                                                  CUT TO:

50   EXT. DAY. MAIN ENTRANCE/STAIRS CRAIGLOCKHART. (1917)   50

       TOP OF THE STAIRS. WILFRED OWEN comes down one side of the
       stairs, helped with his luggage by the TAXI DRIVER. SIEGFRIED
       SASSOON down the other.

       They both look wretched.

       They stand for a moment in silence by the taxi.

       A long pause.

                    SIEGFRIED SASSOON
               (Barely controlling
                himself)
          Will you stay? Please...for just a
          few more moments...

       WILFRED OWEN nods - as deeply moved as SIEGFRIED SASSOON.

       Throughout scene suppressed tears.

       The driver stands with the doors open.

                    TAXI DRIVER
          Whenever you're ready sir.

       Silence.

       TWO SHOT WILFRED OWEN & SIEGFRIED SASSOON. Very reluctantly
       they shake hands.

       PAN L TO R.

       Without looking back WILFRED OWEN gets into the taxi.

       Taxi drives off and dissolves into a military vehicle at
       Fricourt driving away surrounded by troops.

       WW1 FOOTAGE: Over this footage "Anthem for Doomed Youth" read
       by SIEGFRIED SASSOON.

                    SIEGFRIED SASSOON V/O
          "What passing-bells for these who
          die as cattle?
                    (MORE)

BENEDICTION

                                                              61.

                    SIEGFRIED SASSOON V/O (CONT'D)
          Only the monstrous anger of the
          guns.
          Only the stuttering rifles' rapid
          rattle
          Can patter out their hasty orisons.
          No mockeries for them from prayers
          or bells,
          Nor any voice of mourning save the
          choirs,-
          The shrill, demented choirs of
          wailing shells;
          And bugles calling for them from
          sad shires.

          What candles may be held to speed
          them all?
          Not in the hand of boys, but in
          their eyes
          Shall shine the holy glimmers of
          good-byes.
          The pallor of girls' brows shall be
          their pall;
          Their flowers the tenderness of
          silent minds,
          And each slow dusk a drawing-down
          of blinds."

1) A still photograph of a young soldier looking straight into camera.

2) Explosions.

3) Montage of British soldiers.

4) Footage of the dead.

5) Persian head carving.

6) Dhows on the River Nile moving L to R.

SOUNDTRACK:

                    SIEGFRIED SASSOON V/O (CONT'D)
          People die here too...in the land
          of the Pharaohs...

                                        DISSOLVE TO:

51   EXT. LATE AFTERNOON. EGYPTIAN BASECAMP. (1918)   51

      SIEGFRIED SASSOON sitting at the front of his tent reading.
      He stops reading and looks up.

SOUNDTRACK:

> SIEGFRIED SASSOON V/O
> (Reading "Concert Party")
> "They are gathering round...
> Out of the twilight; over the grey-blue sand,
> Shoals of low jargoning men drift inward to the sound –
> The jangle and throb of a piano...tum-ti-tum...
> Drawn by a lamp, they come
> Out of the glimmering lines of their tents, over the shuffling sand.
>
> O sing us the songs, the songs of our own land,
> You warbling ladies in white
> Dimness conceals the hunger in our faces,
> This wall of faces risen out of the night,
> These eyes that keep their memories of the places
> So long beyond their sight.
>
> Jaded and gay, the ladies sing; and the chap in brown
> Tilts his grey hat; jaunty and lean and pale,
> He rattles the keys...some actor-bloke from town...
> "God send you home"; and then "A long, long trail";
> "I hear you calling me"; and "Dixieland"...
> Sung slowly...now the chorus...one by one
> We hear them, drink then; 'til the concerts done
> Silent, I watch the shadowy mass of soldiers stand.
> Silent, they drift away, over the glimmering sand."

A young soldier carrying a football pauses by the tent as he notices SASSOON.

BENEDICTION

Blue Revisions 11/08/2020　　　　　　　　63.

      YOUNG SOLDIER
  What are you reading sir?

      SIEGFRIED SASSOON
  "War and Peace".

      YOUNG SOLDIER
  Any jokes?

      SIEGFRIED SASSOON
    (Smiling)
  Nothing but!

The soldier smiles and moves away.

HOLD on soldier.

He turns for a moment then smiles again them ambles away over the sands.

HOLD ON HIM.

          DISSOLVE TO:

52 EXT. DAY. A SPA. (EARLY 1920'S)   52

A young elegant man sporting a tennis outfit moves towards camera.

The sun blazing down.

HOLD

          DISSOLVE TO:

53 EXT. DAY. A SPA. (EARLY 1920'S)   53

SIEGFRIED SASSOON & IVOR NOVELLO sunbathing.

IVOR NOVELLO looking towards young man. Then IVOR NOVELLO closes his eyes.

Silence.

      IVOR NOVELLO V/O
  How still it is today.

                    SIEGFRIED SASSOON V/O
               How beautiful you are.

                                             DISSOLVE TO:

54   INT. EVENING. SPA BALLROOM. (EARLY 1920'S)   54

         Everyone in evening dress. A slow dance is being played.

         IVOR NOVELLO & SIEGFRIED SASSOON come in with their drinks
         and sit down.

         IVOR NOVELLO eyeing all the men.

                    IVOR NOVELLO
               All the fine young cannibals.

                    SIEGFRIED SASSOON
               You make it sound like a raiding
               party.

                    IVOR NOVELLO
               Isn't it?

         He waves to someone.

         SIEGFRIED SASSOON looks at him.

                    IVOR NOVELLO (CONT'D)
               Stephen Tennant.

         CUT TO IVOR NOVELLO'S POV.

         STEPHEN TENNANT waves and comes over with a young woman.

                    STEPHEN TENNANT
                 (To Siegfried Sassoon)
               I am...

                    IVOR NOVELLO
               We already know who you are
               Stephen...but who is this absolute
               dream in oyster grey silk?

                    HESTER GATTY
               Hester Gatty.

                    SIEGFRIED SASSOON
               Lady Gatty's daughter?

> HESTER GATTY
> Yes. She once invited you to Carlton House Terrace but you hardly noticed me.
>
> SIEGFRIED SASSOON
> Then I apologise for my lack of taste.
>
> STEPHEN TENNANT
> We're great admirers of your poetry Siegfried.
> (To Ivor Novello)
> Before you take offence Ivor - we like your work too.
>
> IVOR NOVELLO
> Careful Stephen - that was almost enthusiasm.
>
> HESTER GATTY
> Perhaps they could play one of your charming songs Mr. Novello. Then we could dance to it. I can't tempt Stephen though.
>
> IVOR NOVELLO
> Why not?
>
> STEPHEN TENNANT
> Because I only do the Valeta and only when pressed.

CUT TO:

C/U HESTER GATTY.

She is in focus but the background is out of focus. She sways to the slow soft rhythm.

CUT TO:

C/U SIEGFRIED SASSOON.

He is in focus but the background is out of focus. He looks at HESTER.

CUT TO:

> HESTER GATTY
> I do *love* dancing.

                    SIEGFRIED SASSOON
          So do I.

                    HESTER GATTY
          Come on then!

They go - hand in hand - to the dance floor.

They're playing "The Charleston" and they both start dancing and they are very good at it.

Dance finishes, both smiling and a little out of breath.

                    HESTER GATTY (CONT'D)
          I didn't know great poets did "The
          Charleston".

                    SIEGFRIED SASSOON
          I didn't know "The Charleston" did
          that to gay young things.

                    HESTER GATTY
          I think everyone should be gay,
          don't you?

                    SIEGFRIED SASSOON
          Only in the wider sense.

They walk towards IVOR NOVELLO & STEPHEN TENNANT.

SIEGFRIED SASSOON's POV OF IVOR NOVELLO.

IVOR NOVELLO is still with STEPHEN TENNANT. The young elegant man from before has joined them and IVOR NOVELLO is clearly interested in him.

                    IVOR NOVELLO
          This young man is...?

                    ALEXANDER FENTON
          Alexander Fenton.

                    IVOR NOVELLO
          Doesn't it sound as if it should
          have a title in front of it?

                    STEPHEN TENNANT
          Sir Alexander Fenton...for his
          services to the theatre...

                    IVOR NOVELLO
               (riled)
          That hasn't happened yet.

STEPHEN TENNANT
It will Ivor...it will...

CUT TO:

55   INT. EARLY EVENING. LONDON RESTAURANT. (1922)   55

SHOT OF SIEGFRIED SASSOON & IVOR NOVELLO reading their menus.

SHOT OF GLEN BYAM SHAW walking past their table and stopping.

GLEN BYAM SHAW
I hardly see you these days Ivor. How are you? Horizontally speaking.

IVOR NOVELLO
Busy, old thing, very, very busy.

GLEN BYAM SHAW
Still gathering lilacs?

IVOR NOVELLO
You _could_ say that.

GLEN BYAM SHAW
Well when you've exhausted botany, you might consider moving into the field of blood sports...I'm told that the men who indulge in them are very, very rugged...isn't that so Mr. Sassoon?

SIEGFRIED SASSOON is too embarrassed to speak.

IVOR NOVELLO
I think that's what I'll miss most about you Glen – your quaint sense of humour.

Pause.

And how have you been passing your time?

GLEN BYAM SHAW
Seeing lots of musical theatre.

IVOR NOVELLO
Such as?

GLEN BYAM SHAW
"Rose Marie" – very enjoyable.

                    IVOR NOVELLO
            But so Rudolph Frimilly.

                    SIEGFRIED SASSOON
                      (Quite innocently)
            But it is by Rudolph Friml.

                    IVOR NOVELLO
            That was a joke Siegfried.
                      (to Glen Byam Shore)
            And tonight?

                    GLEN BYAM SHAW
            "Lady be good". Gershwin - an
            unsurpassed genius.

                    IVOR NOVELLO
                      (Riled)
            We really mustn't keep you Glen.

GLEN BYAM SHAW exits.

                    SIEGFRIED SASSOON
            You have to admit it...Gershwin is
            an exceptional talent.

                    IVOR NOVELLO
            I don't have to admit anything!

He bangs his glass down on the table.

                    SIEGFRIED SASSOON
            What's wrong?

                    IVOR NOVELLO
            We're going!

                    SIEGFRIED SASSOON
            I thought you wanted supper?

                    IVOR NOVELLO
            I'm no longer hungry!

                                          CUT TO:

56   INT. NIGHT. THEATRE. (1925)   56

SIEGFRIED SASSOON comes in through the stage door.

SOUNDTRACK:

Audience applause is heard.

STAGE DOORMAN
Name sir?

SIEGFRIED SASSOON
Mr. Sassoon.

STAGE DOORMAN
Sassoon you say?

SIEGFRIED SASSOON
Yes!

STAGE DOORMAN
(Checking list)
Would you mind spelling it for me sir?

SIEGFRIED SASSOON
S..A..S..S..O..O..N.

STAGE DOORMAN
I'm afraid you're not on the list sir.

SIEGFRIED SASSOON
(Angry)
I'm going up anyway!

CUT TO:

57 INT. NIGHT. THEATRE. (1925)   57

SIEGFRIED SASSOON goes into the dressing room. As he comes in he sees IVOR NOVELLO and ALEXANDER FENTON break from a loose embrace.

IVOR NOVELLO
(To Alexander Fenton)
Telephone me in a couple of days.

As ALEXANDER FENTON leaves he and SIEGFRIED SASSOON exchange hostile looks.

SIEGFRIED SASSOON at the door.

Silence.

                SIEGFRIED SASSOON
        I had to practically force my way
        in - past the stage doorman.

                IVOR NOVELLO
        You were fortunate - he's been told
        to shoot anyone not on my list.

Silence.

                SIEGFRIED SASSOON
        But why wasn't I on the list?

                IVOR NOVELLO
        Oh for Christ's sake!

Silence.

                IVOR NOVELLO (CONT'D)
            (trying to stay calm)
        I'm tired Siegfried. It's been a
        long run - and I'm exhausted.

He looks into his dressing room mirror. His stage make-up still on.

A tense silence.

IVOR NOVELLO starts to take off his stage make-up.

                SIEGFRIED SASSOON
        Do you still want supper?

                IVOR NOVELLO
            (Angry)
        Yes!

An angry silence.

                SIEGFRIED SASSOON
        I was surprised to see Fenton here.

                IVOR NOVELLO
        Why? I know lots of people. Fenton
        is just another...

                    SIEGFRIED SASSOON
          Admirer?

                    IVOR NOVELLO
          ...Fan.

Silence.

                    SIEGFRIED SASSOON
          You both seemed to me to be very
          friendly after so short an
          acquaintance.

                    IVOR NOVELLO
          I get the distinct impression that
          I am being grilled. And that a
          storm in an egg cup is brewing.

Silence.

                    SIEGFRIED SASSOON
          I'm sorry, I didn't mean to be
          petty but I am <u>very</u> jealous of you.

                    IVOR NOVELLO
          Affairs are always messy – who can
          know the secrets of the human
          heart?

                    SIEGFRIED SASSOON
          Usually the people who don't have
          one.

                    IVOR NOVELLO
          My,my hasn't it gone chilly in
          here.

                    SIEGFRIED SASSOON
          But I love you.

                    IVOR NOVELLO
          Yes. You've said.

                                             CUT TO:

58   INT. DAY. FLAT, HALF MOON STREET. (1925)   58

     SIEGFRIED SASSOON picks up the receiver and dials.

     HOLD

     Then the receiver is picked up at the other end but no one
     speaks.

SIEGFRIED SASSOON
Ivor?...Ivor!

The receiver is put down and we hear just the dialling tone.

SIEGFRIED SASSOON replaces his receiver.

CUT TO

59   INT. DAY. STAGE DOOR, THEATRE. (1925)   59

SIEGFRIED SASSOON comes in and attempts to go to IVOR NOVELLO's dressing room.

But the Stage Doorman literally bars his way.

SIEGFRIED SASSOON
(Angry)
Let me pass!

STAGE DOORMAN
I'm sorry sir, but I can't let you go up.

SIEGFRIED SASSOON
(Angry)
Why!?

STAGE DOORMAN
Mr. Novello never sees anyone after a matinee.

SIEGFRIED SASSOON tries to push past the STAGE DOORMAN but is prevented.

SIEGFRIED SASSOON
(Angry)
Will you inform Mr. Novello that I've booked a table for 8pm. I'll be expecting him for dinner.

STAGE DOORMAN
Yes sir.

CUT TO:

60   INT. NIGHT. LONDON RESTAURANT. (1925)   60

SIEGFRIED SASSOON
Is there someone else?

IVOR NOVELLO
There's always someone else.

SIEGFRIED SASSOON
How do you justify your behaviour?

IVOR NOVELLO
By asking myself questions to which I already know the answers. And when all is said and done, my career comes before anything and anyone. And my work is as popular as I am.

SIEGFRIED SASSOON
There is a school of thought that regards musical theatre as a second rate means of expression.

IVOR NOVELLO
Before you judge other people's work Siegfried, make sure your own is above criticism.

SIEGFRIED SASSOON
What do you mean?!

IVOR NOVELLO
Just this - that since 1918 your poetry has gone from the sublime to the meticulous.

SIEGFRIED SASSOON
(Angry)
And tell me Mr. Novello, what did you do during the war?

IVOR NOVELLO
(Angry)
I gave my talent to my country. I boosted morale by playing *every* theatre in the land!

SIEGFRIED SASSOON
(Very angry)
Weren't you the lucky one! We had the Somme - you had Rhyl!

A tense silence.

IVOR NOVELLO
I see no point in prolonging this unpleasant conversation.

He hails the waiter, who comes with the bill and puts it on the table.

IVOR NOVELLO goes to get it but SIEGFRIED SASSOON stops him.

>   SIEGFRIED SASSOON
> After what's been said I don't expect you to foot the bill as well.
>
>   IVOR NOVELLO
> Always the gentleman eh, Siegfried?
>
>   SIEGFRIED SASSOON
> It's better than being a cad.
>
>   IVOR NOVELLO
> I suspect that this is goodbye then?
>
>   SIEGFRIED SASSOON
> Au revoir might have been kinder.
>
>   IVOR NOVELLO
> Don't undermine yourself Siegfried, that's what friends are for.
>
>   SIEGFRIED SASSOON
> If you wish to see me again I'll be at my flat at Half Moon Street.
>
>   IVOR NOVELLO
> At least that's more original than going home to mother.

IVOR NOVELLO leaves.

GLEN BYAM SHAW emerges from the back of the restaurant and stops at the table.

>   GLEN BYAM SHAW
> Snap!
>
>   SIEGFRIED SASSOON
>   (He shrugs, then laughs)
>
>   GLEN BYAM SHAW
> May I sit down?
>
>   SIEGFRIED SASSOON
> Of course.
> Do you still dine here?

GLEN BYAM SHAW
Of course.

SIEGFRIED SASSOON
Why?

GLEN BYAM SHAW
Let's just say I like the trips down memory lane.
    (Pause)
What now?

SIEGFRIED SASSOON
I suppose in bad melodrama I'd kill myself.

GLEN BYAM SHAW
And in really bad melodrama you kill Ivor.
    (Pause)
Seriously, are you alright?

SIEGFRIED SASSOON
The moment passes but the hurt remains.

Silence.

SIEGFRIED SASSOON (CONT'D)
    (Looking at his watch)
And I was supposed to go and visit my mother and now I've missed the train.

GLEN BYAM SHAW
Drive down, why don't you?

SIEGFRIED SASSOON
No car. Can't drive.

GLEN BYAM SHAW
I was going to motor down to the coast - why don't I give you a lift?

SIEGFRIED SASSOON
Oh, that is kind of you.

GLEN BYAM SHAW
Where does she live?

SIEGFRIED SASSOON
Kent.

                    GLEN BYAM SHAW
                Then let's get going.

                                                    CUT TO:

61   OMITTED   61

62   EXT. NIGHT. COUNTRY ROAD. (1925)   62

     Fog.

                    SIEGFRIED SASSOON V/O
                Why do the cars look so sad in the
                early evening rain?

     Then the car driven by GLEN BYAM SHAW comes through the dense
     fog.

     The car stops.

     They are in dense fog.

                    GLEN BYAM SHAW
                I have absolutely no idea where we
                are.

     Silence.

     SIEGFRIED SASSOON looking at GLEN BYAM SHAW. GLEN BYAM SHAW
     goes to speak, but doesn't. He returns SIEGFRIED SASSOON's
     gaze.

                    SIEGFRIED SASSOON
                Although I don't possess the wit to
                woo – may I see you again?

                    GLEN BYAM SHAW
                I live in Margate.

                    SIEGFRIED SASSOON
                Pity Margate is so far away.

                    GLEN BYAM SHAW
                 It's not at the moment.

They smile at one another.

                    SIEGFRIED SASSOON
                 What about Ivor?

                    GLEN BYAM SHAW
                 Oh, he's already been to Margate.

They both laugh.

THEN TRACK AND PAN AWAY INTO THE FOG.

SOUNDTRACK:

The rumble of field guns.

Tanks and soldiers coming out of the fog.

WW1 FOOTAGE:

1) A tank - huge and black comes over a hill and descends.

2) A tank and a field gun move L to R with a small group of soldiers.

3) Servicing of the tanks.

SOUNDTRACK:

                    SIEGFRIED SASSOON V/O
                 (Reading "Attack")
              "At dawn the ridge emerges massed
              and dun
              In wild purple of the glow'ring
              sun,
              Smouldering through spouts of
              drifting smoke that shroud
              The menacing scarred slope; and,
              one by one,
              Tanks creep and topple forward to
              the wire.
              The barrage roars and lifts. Then,
              clumsily bowed
              With bombs and guns and shovels and
              battle-gear,
              Men jostle and climb to meet the
              bristling fire.
              Lines of grey, muttering faces,
              masked with fear,
              They leave their trenches, going
              over the top,
                          (MORE)

                    SIEGFRIED SASSOON V/O (CONT'D)
                While time ticks blank and busy on
                their wrists,
                And hope, with furtive eyes and
                grappling fists,
                Flounders in mud. O Jesus, make it
                stop!"

WW1 FOOTAGE:

1) Burial of British soldiers and numbering the dead.

2) Dead in trenches.

3) Cavalry/soldiers in mud.

4) Cavalry on ridge - waterlogged trench in foreground.

                                        DISSOLVE TO:

63   INT. NIGHT. IVOR NOVELLO'S FLAT. (1925)   63

SIEGFRIED SASSOON comes into the living room and he is shocked by what he sees.

CUT TO HIS POV.

IVOR NOVELLO & BOBBY ANDREWS in an embrace and exchanging light kisses.

                    BOBBY ANDREWS
                We have a guest.

                    IVOR NOVELLO
                He isn't a guest. He's an
                afterthought.
                This is my life partner Bobby
                Andrews.
                Siegfried - Bobby, Bobby -
                Siegfried.
                Don't look so shocked Siegfried,
                love has nothing to do with
                monogamy. Or are you the faithful
                type?

                    SIEGFRIED SASSOON
                I suppose I must be.

                    IVOR NOVELLO
                If you want fidelity, Siegfried,
                buy a pet.

                    SIEGFRIED SASSOON
                You kept very quiet about this.

>   IVOR NOVELLO
>   That's because I didn't want anyone
>   else to shake him down from the
>   tree.
>
>   SIEGFRIED SASSOON
>   You really are a bastard, aren't
>   you?
>
>   IVOR NOVELLO
>   I do my best. Now you'll have to
>   excuse us - we have a casserole
>   waiting.

SIEGFRIED SASSOON is deeply hurt. He stands looking at them for a moment then turns to go.

He puts his hand in his pocket and takes out the keys to IVOR NOVELLO's flat.

>   SIEGFRIED SASSOON
>   Where shall I put these?
>
>   IVOR NOVELLO
>   Back on floor.

SIEGFRIED SASSOON drops the keys but in slow motion.

PAN/CRANE DOWN WITH THEM.

THEN

MORPH INTO MILITARY CROSS being dropped into the Mersey at Litherland (1917).

CRANE DOWN WITH IT

The medal and the ribbon float for a moment then sink.

CRANE DOWN WITH IT

The waters of the Mersey swirl then MORPH INTO a cloudy turbulent sky.

THE ABOVE THREE MORPHING SHOTS MUST GIVE THE IMPRESSION THAT IT IS A SINGLE CONTINUOUS SHOT.

Boiling clouds - huge and bubbling, grey and dark like the sea. They fume and snake.

SOUNDTRACK: SONG "GHOST RIDERS IN THE SKY" (1949).

GHOST RIDERS IN THE SKY
"An old cowboy went ridin' one dark and windy day
Upon a ridge he rested as he went along his way
When all at once a mighty herd of red-eyed cows he saw
Flowin' through the ragged skies, and up a cloudy draw
Yipee-i-oh, yipee-i-ay
Ghost riders in the sky."

"Their brands were still on fire and their hooves were made of steel
Their horns were black and shiny and their hot breath he could feel
A bolt of fear went through him as they thundered through the sky
For he saw the riders comin' hard, and he heard their mournful cry
Yipee-i-oh, yipee-i-ay
Ghost riders in the sky."

DISSOLVE TO:

CATTLE STAMPEDING THROUGH DUST R TO L.

DISSOLVE TO:

Soldiers moving through a mist of cordite R to L.

SOUNDTRACK: Song continues

"Their faces gaunt, their eyes were blurred, their shirts all soaked with sweat
They're ridin' hard to catch that herd, but they 'ain't caught 'em yet
'cause they've got to ride for ever on that range up in the sky
On horses snorting fire, as they ride on, hear their cry
Yipee-i-oh, yipee-i-ay
Ghost riders in the sky."

HOLD ON SKY

More soldiers moving through the grey bubbling sky. The clouds fume and snake, then the procession of soldiers fills the sky.

SOUNDTRACK: song continues

"As the riders loped on by him, he
heard one call his name
"If you want to save your soul from
Hell a riding on our range
Then cowboy change your ways today,
or with us you will ride
Tryin' to catch the devils herd,
across these endless skies"
Yipee-i-oh, yipee-i-ay
Ghost riders in the sky.
Yipee-i-oh, yipee-i-ay
Ghost riders in the sky.
Yipee-i-oh, yipee-i-ay
Ghost riders in the sky."

DISSOLVE TO:

64 INT. DAY. DOWNSIDE ABBEY, THE NAVE. (1918/19) 64

SIEGFRIED SASSOON sitting in a pew with his back to camera.

Instead of seeing the altar we stay on the turbulent sky and just before we begin to TRACK the sky becomes the high altar.

C/U OF SIEGFRIED SASSOON SITTING IN A PEW SEEN FROM BEHIND (1918/19)

TRACK L TO R AROUND HIM TO A FRONT VIEW OF HIS OLDER SELF. DURING THIS TRACK AROUND SIEGFRIED SASSOON MORPHS FROM HIS YOUNGER TO HIS OLDER SELF (1957/60).

BEHIND HIM SITS HIS SON GEORGE.

Silence.

> GEORGE SASSOON
> I'm intrinsically against <u>any</u> kind of conversion. It's too much like wishful thinking. Besides, in a poet, it seems to imply that he has nothing interesting left to say.

> SIEGFRIED SASSOON
> I said I was only thinking about it.

> GEORGE SASSOON
> Surely you're not looking for God?

                    SIEGFRIED SASSOON
          That's one way of putting it.

                    GEORGE SASSOON
          Well, speaking as one of the
          spiritually undernourished, if you
          find him make sure he's still an
          Englishman and doesn't live on the
          wrong side of the park.

                    SIEGFRIED SASSOON
          I assume that was supposed to be
          amusing.

Silence.

                    GEORGE SASSOON
          But why Catholicism, father?

                    SIEGFRIED SASSOON
          Something permanent, unchanging.

                    GEORGE SASSOON
          You can get that from dressage but
          without the guilt.

                    SIEGFRIED SASSOON
          There's no need to be snide. And if
          all you can do is ridicule it would
          be better if you remained silent or
          better still go outside and wait in
          the car.

Silence.

                    GEORGE SASSOON
          It's a long drive to London, so the
          sooner we get started the better.

SIEGFRIED SASSOON doesn't answer.

GEORGE SASSOON leaves.

SIEGFRIED SASSOON just sits there.

HOLD ON HIM

                                                  DISSOLVE TO:

SOUNDTRACK OVER THE DISSOLVE:

          PRIEST'S V/O
Siegfried quid petis ab Ecclesia Dei?

          SIEGFRIED SASSOON V/O
Fidem.

          PRIEST'S V/O
Fides, quid tibi praestal?

          SIEGFRIED SASSOON V/O
Vitam aeternam.

          PRIEST'S V/O
Si igitur vis ad vitam ingredi serva mandata. Diligis dominum deum tuum ex toto corde tuo, et ex tota anima tua, et ex tota mente tua, et proximum tuum sicut teipsum.

CROSS FADE TO ENGLISH

          PRIEST'S V/O (CONT'D)
Siegfried, what do you ask of the Church of God?

          SIEGFRIED SASSOON V/O
Faith.

          PRIEST'S V/O
What does Faith offer you?

          SIEGFRIED SASSOON V/O
Life everlasting.

          PRIEST'S V/O
If you then desire to enter into life, keep the commandments. "Thou shalt love the Lord thy God with thy whole heart and with thy whole soul and with thy whole mind and thy neighbour as thyself".

                                        DISSOLVE TO:

65   INT. DAY. NAVE, DOWNSIDE ABBEY. (1957/60)   65

TRACK IN ON THE PRIEST.

                    PRIEST'S V/O
                (Making the Sign of the
                Cross)
            Receive the Sign of the Cross upon
            your forehead and also upon your
            heart. Take to you the Faith of the
            heavenly precepts and so order your
            life as to be, from henceforth, the
            temple of God.

                                        DISSOLVE TO:

66   INT. DAY. NAVE, DOWNSIDE ABBEY. (1957/60)   66

        TRACK IN ON THE PRIEST

        The priest places his outstretched hand on the candidate's
        head but we do not see SIEGFRIED SASSOON.

                    THE PRIEST
            Let us pray: Almighty, everlasting
            God, Father of our Lord Jesus
            Christ, look graciously down upon
            this thy servant, Siegfried, whom
            thou hast graciously called unto
            the beginnings of the Faith; drive
            out from him all blindness of
            heart; break all the toils of Satan
            where with he was held; open unto
            him, O Lord, the gate of thy loving
            kindness, that, being impressed
            with the sign of thy wisdom, he may
            be free from the foulness of all
            wicked desires, and in the sweet
            odour of thy precepts may joyfully
            serve thee in thy church, and grow
            in grace from day to day. Through
            the same Christ Our Lord, Amen.

                    SIEGFRIED SASSOON V/O
            Amen.

                                        DISSOLVE TO:

67   INT. DAY. NAVE, DOWNSIDE ABBEY. (1957/60)   67

        TRACK IN ON PRIEST

        He carries a small receptacle of salt. He wears a violet
        coloured stole.

He takes a pinch of salt and offers it to SIEGFRIED SASSOON whom we still do not see.

> THE PRIEST
> Siegfried, receive the salt of wisdom; let it be to thee a token of mercy unto everlasting life. May it make your way easy to eternal life.

> SIEGFRIED SASSOON V/O
> Amen.

> THE PRIEST
> Peace be with you.

> SIEGFRIED SASSOON V/O
> And with your spirit.

> THE PRIEST
> Let us pray: O God of our fathers, O God the author of all truth, vouch safe, we humbly beseech thee, to look graciously down upon thy servant Siegfried, and as he tastes this first nutriment of salt, suffer him no longer to hunger for want of heavenly food, to the end that he may always be fervent in spirit, rejoicing in hope, always serving thy name.

DISSOLVE TO:

68   INT. DAY. NAVE, DOWNSIDE ABBEY. (1957/60)   68

HIGH SHOT OF SIEGFRIED SASSOON PROSTRATE IN FRONT OF THE HIGH ALTAR.

> PRIEST'S V/O
> I exorcise thee, unclean spirit, in the name of the Father and of the Son and of the Holy Spirit, that thou goest out and depart from this servant of God, Siegfried, for he commands thee, accursed one, who walked upon the sea, and stretched out his right hand to Peter about to sink.
> (MORE)

                        PRIEST'S V/O (CONT'D)
              Therefore, accursed devil,
              acknowledge thy sentence, and give
              honour to the living and true God:
              give honour to Jesus Christ, His
              son, and to the Holy Spirit, and
              depart from this servant of God,
              Siegfried, because God and our Lord
              Jesus Christ hath vouchsafed to
              call him to his holy grace and
              benediction unto the font of
              baptism.
              And this sign of the Holy Cross,
              upon his forehead, do thou,
              accursed devil, never dare to
              violate. Through the same Christ
              Our Lord.

                        SIEGFRIED SASSOON V/O
              Amen.

                                                DISSOLVE TO:

69   INT. DAY. NAVE, DOWNSIDE ABBEY. (1957/60)   69

        TRACK IN ON PRIEST.

        PRIEST (now wearing a white stole) his hands spread ready to
        make the Sign of the Cross.

                        THE PRIEST
              Siegfried, do you renounce Satan?

                        SIEGFRIED SASSOON V/O
              I do renounce him.

                        THE PRIEST
              And all his works?

                        SIEGFRIED SASSOON V/O
              I do renounce him.

                        THE PRIEST
              And all his pomps?

                        SIEGFRIED SASSOON V/O
              I do renounce him.

        PRIEST makes the Sign of the Cross.

                                                DISSOLVE TO:

70   INT. DAY. NAVE, DOWNSIDE ABBEY. (1957/60)   70

TRACK IN ON PRIEST

His hands and arms splayed.

          THE PRIEST
I annoint you with the oil of salvation in Christ Jesus our Lord, that you may have everlasting life.

          SIEGFRIED SASSOON V/O
Amen.

          THE PRIEST
Siegfried, do you believe in God, the Father Almighty, creator of heaven and earth?

          SIEGFRIED SASSOON V/O
I do believe.

          THE PRIEST
Do you believe in Jesus Christ, His only son Our Lord, who was born and who suffered?

          SIEGFRIED SASSOON V/O
I do believe.

          THE PRIEST
Do you believe in the Holy Ghost, the Holy Catholic Church, the communion of Saints, the forgiveness of sins, the resurrection of the body and life everlasting?

          SIEGFRIED SASSOON V/O
I do believe.

                                  DISSOLVE TO:

71   INT. DAY. NAVE, DOWNSIDE ABBEY. (1957/60)   71

TRACK IN ON PRIEST

He holds a white linen cloth.

                    THE PRIEST
          Receive this white garment, which
          mayest thou carry without stain
          before the judgement seat of Our
          Lord Jesus Christ, that thou mayest
          have life everlasting.

                                        DISSOLVE TO:

72   INT. DAY. NAVE, DOWNSIDE ABBEY. (1957/60)   72

     TRACK IN ON PRIEST. He carries a candle.

                    THE PRIEST
          Receive this burning light, and
          keep thy baptism so as to be
          without blame; keep the
          commandments of God, that when the
          Lord shall come to the nuptials,
          thou mayest meet Him together with
          all the Saints in the heavenly
          court, and mayest thou have eternal
          life for ever and ever.
          Siegfried, go in peace and the Lord
          be with you.

     CROSS FADE TO LATIN

                    THE PRIEST (CONT'D)
          Accipe lampadem ardentem et
          irreprehensibilis costodi baptismum
          tuum: serva Dei mandata ut cum
          dominus venerit ad nuptias, possis
          occurrere ei una cum omnibus
          sanctis in aula caelesti, habeasque
          vitam aeternam, et vivas in saecula
          saeculorum.
          Siegfried, vade in pace et dominus
          sit tecum. Amen.

                                        DISSOLVE TO:

73   INT. DAY. NAVE, DOWNSIDE ABBEY. (1960)   73

     The priest (back to camera and wearing a cope) turns around
     to face camera holding the monstrance in front of his face
     which it completely hides. He is in clouds of incense.

     SOUNDTRACK:

> SIEGFRIED SASSOON V/O
> Give me peace, O give me peace.

DISSOLVE TO:

74 INT. DUSK. DOWNSIDE ABBEY, LADY CHAPEL. (1957/60) 74

TRACK FORWARD to iron gates looking towards the Nave.

SOUNDTRACK: PRIEST'S V/O.

> PRIEST'S V/O
> "You will be drawn up in your feelings above understanding to the radiance of divine darkness that transcends all being."

DISSOLVE TO:

75 INT. DUSK. DOWNSIDE ABBEY, LADY CHAPEL. (1957/60) 75

TRACK FORWARD TO GATES.

DISSOLVE TO:

76 INT. DUSK. DOWNSIDE ABBEY. (1957/60) 76

A flight of stairs.

TRACK FORWARD TO THEM.

A door at the end of them is closed.

SOUNDTRACK:

> PRIEST'S V/O
> "The fool hath said in his heart...there is no God."

> SIEGFRIED SASSOON V/O
> Christ receive my soul and release me from the imprisonment of doubt. And grant me peace.

HOLD

DISSOLVE TO:

77   INT. EARLY EVENING. HALF MOON STREET FLAT. (1932/33)   77

STEPHEN TENNANT comes into the bedroom. He is just wearing underpants. He carries a cup of tea. He comes in and sits on the side of the bed next to SIEGFRIED SASSOON who is still in bed.

> SIEGFRIED SASSOON
> I can't face tea until at least 11am.

> STEPHEN TENNANT
> Drink it you misery. I don't do this for everyone you know. I'm the invalid remember - like Chekhov...
> (gives a theatrically weak cough)

Pause

> (running his hand through his hair)
> Oh what should I do about my hair?

> SIEGFRIED SASSOON
> Have you considered topiary?

STEPHEN TENNANT makes a face.

> STEPHEN TENNANT
> I think I might dye it...or I could leave it in its natural colour - when I'm sunburnt it looks like spun gold...

Then a car horn is heard from outside loud and insistent.

SIEGFRIED SASSOON gets out of bed and exits bedroom.

CUT TO:

78   EXT. EARLY EVENING. HALF MOON STREET FLAT. (1932/33)   78

SIEGFRIED SASSOON comes to the window and looks out.

> SIEGFRIED SASSOON
> (Seeing someone he shouts down)
> I'll be with you in a moment.
> (to STEPHEN TENNANT inside)
> It's Glen Byam Shaw.

He exits the window and is replaced by STEPHEN TENNANT.

                    STEPHEN TENNANT
            Isn't that good news?
                (to the person honking on
                 the horn)
            Siggy will be down in a trice -
            he's just finishing getting
            dressed.
            We've just been talking about you -
            so I hope your ears were burning -
            all three of them.

                                        CUT TO:

79   EXT. EARLY EVENING. HALF MOON STREET FLAT. (1932/33)   79

      SIEGFRIED SASSOON comes to the car outside.

      GLEN BYAM SHAW is standing by it. SIEGFRIED SASSOON very
      embarrassed.

                    GLEN BYAM SHAW
                (to SIEGFRIED SASSOON)
            Is Stephen naturally unpleasant or
            does he take private tuition?

                    STEPHEN TENNANT
            I heard that!

                    GLEN BYAM SHAW
            You were supposed to.

      STEPHEN TENNANT goes back inside the flat.

      An awkward pause.

                    SIEGFRIED SASSOON
            I'm sorry...what can I say?

                    GLEN BYAM SHAW
            There's nothing to say. It's one of
            the "inconveniences" of the shadow
            life we lead. Friends may come,
            friends may go but enemies are
            always faithful. How is Ivor?

                    SIEGFRIED SASSOON
            I've no idea. I don't see him
            anymore.

      Pause
            Did you know about Bobby?

                    GLEN BYAM SHAW
          Yes.

                    SIEGFRIED SASSOON
          You might have warned me.

                    GLEN BYAM SHAW
          I didn't want to seem vindictive.
          Sour grapes and all that.

Silence

          I wanted to tell you personally
          that I'm planning to marry...she's
          an actress and a good sort I think
          and we're very fond of each other.

                    SIEGFRIED SASSOON
          When did you decide?

                    GLEN BYAM SHAW
          Some months ago.
               (pause)
          You should give some thought to it
          too.

                    SIEGFRIED SASSOON
          If the intention wasn't pure I
          don't think I could go through with
          it.

                    GLEN BYAM SHAW
          Purity is like virginity. As soon
          as you touch it, it becomes
          corrupt.

                    SIEGFRIED SASSOON
          I hope that both of you will be
          very happy.

                    GLEN BYAM SHAW
          Thank you Siegfried. I shall do my
          best.

                    STEPHEN TENNANT
          Siggy! Siggy!

GLEN BYAM SHAW & SIEGFRIED SASSOON shake hands and GLEN BYAM
SHAW drives off.

SIEGFRIED SASSOON looks up at the window.

                    STEPHEN TENNANT (CONT'D)
          "Hey ho - sing hey ho unto the
          green holly.
               (MORE)

                    STEPHEN TENNANT (CONT'D)
          Most friendship is feigning,
          Most loving mere folly."

He starts to cough.

                                                  CUT TO:

80   INT. EARLY EVENING. HALF MOON STREET FLAT. (1932/33)   80

STEPHEN TENNANT coughing uncontrollably and spitting blood.

STEPHEN TENNANT lying on the bed. SIEGFRIED SASSOON sitting beside him. STEPHEN TENNANT has stopped coughing.

Pause

                    SIEGFRIED SASSOON
          What's the matter?

                    STEPHEN TENNANT
          T.B..

                    SIEGFRIED SASSOON
          You should have told me.

                    STEPHEN TENNANT
          Why? There's nothing you can do
          about it.

                    SIEGFRIED SASSOON
          I could've taken you to a dryer,
          warmer climate.

                    STEPHEN TENNANT
          That rules out Frinton then.

                    SIEGFRIED SASSOON
          Is there somewhere we can go to
          help you?

                    STEPHEN TENNANT
          Yes. I've gone there before. In
          Germany - Haus Hirth in Bavaria -
          all cow bells, lederhosen and very,
          very thick thighs - it's so idyllic
          you'll want to scream! But the
          German men are _gorgeous_! I wonder
          what the collective noun for them
          is?

SIEGFRIED SASSOON clearly hurt.

                    STEPHEN TENNANT (CONT'D)
          Don't look so glum Siggy - I'm not
          about to join the Hitler Youth.

The phone rings and SIEGFRIED SASSOON picks it up.

                    SIEGFRIED SASSOON
          Yes? Who is it?
               (to STEPHEN TENNANT very
                angry)
          Don't ring here again!
               (he puts the phone down)
          It was Fenton! I don't like this at
          all!

                    STEPHEN TENNANT
          We bumped into each other on
          Piccadilly the other day. We had a
          harmless drink and I gave him your
          number.

                    SIEGFRIED SASSOON
          Don't do it again!

                    STEPHEN TENNANT
               (Now equally angry)
          If that were a request I might
          consider it. If it's an order I'll
          make a point of disobeying it.

Tense silence
          What did Glen want?

                    SIEGFRIED SASSOON
          He's getting married.

                    STEPHEN TENNANT
          Ah, the ultimate capitulation. I'm
          sure they'll be very happy. She's
          probably as mediocre as he is.
          You'll be doing it next.

                                              CUT TO:

81   EXT. DAY. CHURCHYARD NEAR FITZ HOUSE. (1932/33)   81

SIEGFRIED SASSOON comes out of the house and stops as he sees
HESTER GATTY painting/drawing in her sketch book. He crosses   *
the road and goes to her. He looks at her working.

HESTER GATTY
I thought I'd try my hand at some water colours...landscapes and things...it's the Magritte in me...
(she shows him the painting)
This is not a pipe.

SIEGFRIED SASSOON
Rene will be pleased. How would you describe your style?

HESTER GATTY
Erratic. But I'm giving this to a friend whom I really detest.

Pause

HESTER GATTY (CONT'D)
You don't remember me at all, do you?

SIEGFRIED SASSOON very embarrassed.

The spa...Ivor Novello...Stephen Tennant...

SIEGFRIED SASSOON
(Dawning)
Oh of course! The oyster grey silk!

HESTER GATTY
(Good humoured)
Your supposed to remember _me_ not the dress.

They both laugh.

Before I met you for the first time I'd always thought you'd be either mercurial or dark.

SIEGFRIED SASSOON
And what am I - dark or mercurial?

HESTER GATTY
Neither...you're more "opaque" I think.

SIEGFRIED SASSOON looks down and away from her - the remark having inadvertently hit home.

> SIEGFRIED SASSOON
> What brings you down here?

> HESTER GATTY
> I should like to say "the picturesque" but it wouldn't be true.
>   (pause)
> I came down in the hope of seeing you again - I used the painting as a ploy.

> SIEGFRIED SASSOON
> Oh I'm touched, really touched! No one has ever used subterfuge before in order to see me.

> HESTER GATTY
> It's the modern thing...liberated woman and all that.

They both laugh.

> HESTER GATTY (CONT'D)
> It would be very pleasant if you invited me to lunch.

> SIEGFRIED SASSOON
> It would be very pleasant if you accepted.

82   INT. DUSK. FITZ HOUSE. (1932/33)   82

Both SIEGFRIED SASSOON & HESTER GATTY are dancing alone to "Our Love is Here to Stay" on a wind-up gramophone.

They sit together. Hester silently mouths the lyric to the song.

PAUSE

> SIEGFRIED SASSOON
> You are _very_ lovely. May I kiss you?

> HESTER GATTY
> You don't have to ask.

They kiss and it is delicate in its passion.

SILENCE

SIEGFRIED SASSOON
I have never had an affair with a woman...only men...

HESTER GATTY
Stephen told me all I need to know.

LONG PAUSE

SIEGFRIED SASSOON
All my life I feel as though I've been waiting for a catastrophe to happen.

HESTER GATTY
Well - that's optimism for you.

SIEGFRIED SASSOON
My whole future could depend on you. Oh Hester, you must redeem my life for me!

HESTER GATTY
That sounds like some sort of proposal.

SIEGFRIED SASSOON
If I were selfish enough I'd ask you to marry me.

HESTER GATTY
If I were foolish enough I'd accept.

CUT TO:

83 INT. DAY. FLAT, HALF MOON STREET. (1932/33) 83

BEDROOM.

C/U STEPHEN TENNANT sitting at a dressing table.

STEPHEN TENNANT
Oh, I look five hundred years old.

STEPHAN TENNANT looking at himself in the mirror. He is practising various looks and is holding various pieces of clothing against his skin.

STEPHEN TENNANT (CONT'D)
Some say I am beautiful and, as an aesthete, I feel beauty is eternal.
(MORE)

                    STEPHEN TENNANT (CONT'D)
          We see it in the eyes of those who
          love us...although my mother thinks
          that my eyes are like cold sea
          water...my buttocks and my
          shoulders are very well shaped...
                    (then running his hand
                     down the length of his
                     throat)

TRACK IN ON STEPHEN TENNANT.

DISSOLVE TO 4 photographs of very facially disfigured WW1 soldiers. These photographs are linked by dissolves.

After the final photograph.

                                        DISSOLVE TO:

84   INT. DAY. FLAT, HALF MOON STREET. (1932/33)   84

        C/U STEPHAN TENNANT

                    STEPHEN TENNANT
          My neck is very long and
          graceful...but my best feature is
          the beauty of my hands...almond
          milk and lemon creams are perfect
          for them...and one should never
          laugh too much, it coarsens ones
          face, especially if the laughter is
          gleeful...

TRACK IN ON SIEGFRIED SASSOON.

                    SIEGFRIED SASSOON
                (almost speechless)
          Stephen, how can you be so
          narcissistic?

                    STEPHEN TENNANT
          It is my defence against nihilism
          and the vulgar.

                    SIEGFRIED SASSOON
          You cannot conduct a life in that
          way.

                    STEPHEN TENNANT
          Of course one can. My life is my
          art.

SIEGFRIED SASSOON
Yours isn't a life – it's barely a hobby.

STEPHEN TENNANT
That was an ugly thing to say.

SIEGFRIED SASSOON
I know that sometimes it's better to be kind than honest – but you're frittering your life away...in pomades and powder. If you don't believe me ask someone with more sense and less love.

STEPHEN TENNANT
You've made your antipathy to me <u>very</u> obvious. I don't need a second opinion.

Pause.

SIEGFRIED SASSOON
I'm going down to Salisbury for the weekend...Edith Oliver has found me a cottage to rent in Teffont Magna...I thought we could spend weekends there...will you come?

STEPHEN TENNANT
I too have had an invitation.

SIEGFRIED SASSOON
From whom?

STEPHEN TENNANT
A German Prince whom I think you more than know...

SIEGFRIED SASSOON
Phillipp of Hesse...Yes...

STEPHEN TENNANT
And one of Edith Sitwell's protege's ... a concert pianist called Tchelitchew ... very cyrillic, <u>very</u> Russian and <u>very</u> <u>divine</u>!

SIEGFRIED SASSOON
And where are you going to?

                    STEPHEN TENNANT
          Paris first. Then we'll motor down
          to Bavaria...so I can recuperate –
          from life...after Bavaria they're
          going to go on to Venice...Phillipp
          told me that he once tried
          to make love in a gondola but there wasn't
          enough privacy...

                    SIEGFRIED SASSOON
                (correcting him)
          Stability.

                    STEPHEN TENNANT
          Oh, so it was with you, was it? You
          sly old thing.

                    SIEGFRIED SASSOON
          This all seems very sudden.

                    STEPHEN TENNANT
          Yes. It does, doesn't it? But then
          that's my life – all go...

STEPHEN TENNANT looks into the mirror and begins to pluck his eyebrows.

He stops.

                    STEPHEN TENNANT (CONT'D)
                (Over the morphing shot)
          Older than God but without any of
          the influence.

HOLD on his image in the mirror.

He morphs into his older self – he's not aged well.

TRACK AWAY from him (R to L) and PAN into living room.

                                             DISSOLVE TO:

85   INT. DAY. FLAT, HALF MOON STREET. (1932/33)   85

        Continue TRACKING and PANNING R to L.

        SIEGFRIED SASSOON & HESTER GATTY seated at window.

        TRACK to them.

        SIEGFRIED SASSOON & HESTER GATTY are sitting by one another
        by the window which is open. Pleasant weather.

A long intimate silence.

> HESTER GATTY
> Will you come to dinner tonight at mother's?

> SIEGFRIED SASSOON
> At Carlton House Terrace?

> HESTER GATTY
> Yes.

> SIEGFRIED SASSOON
> Oh *must* I?

> HESTER GATTY
> Yes! You *must*! She's invited a whole galaxy of stars to impress you... Hardy, Wells, Lady Colefax, Graves, Virginia Woolf... she'd have invited God if she thought He'd come.

> SIEGFRIED SASSOON
> I'm uncomfortable with all that distinction... I'm not at all intellectual, I have a very cumbersome mind.

> HESTER GATTY
> Oh please come! Max Beerbohm said he might drop in for a drink.

> SIEGFRIED SASSOON
> Then I *shall* come! Just to hear Max's delectable gossip... he once described T.S. Elliot as "Poor old Tom who sits there ironically analysing an empty sardine tin".

SIEGFRIED SASSOON kissing HESTER on the top of her head.

> SIEGFRIED SASSOON (CONT'D)
> Come on! You'll have to get your skates on and I'll have to get my glad rags out of mothballs.

She exits.

Stay on SIEGFRIED SASSOON at the window.

He waves to HESTER GATTY.

CUT TO:

86	EXT. DAY. FLAT, HALF MOON STREET. (1932/33)	86

SIEGFRIED SASSOON'S POV of HESTER GATTY coming out of the building. She waves to SIEGFRIED SASSOON and then goes out of the courtyard.

STAY on the courtyard.

As HESTER GATTY disappears a car pulls into the courtyard.

It holds four young men - including STEPHEN TENNANT - they all make a great deal of noise.

STEPHEN TENNANT gets out of the car.

    STEPHEN TENNANT
  Goodbye darlings!

The car drives off and STEPHEN TENNANT comes into the building.

            CUT TO:

87	INT. DAY. FLAT, HALF MOON STREET. (1932/33)	87

STEPHEN TENNANT comes in with two suitcases, drops them on the floor then sinks into a chair.

Silence.

    STEPHEN TENNANT
  No welcome? No bunting? Not even
  "You're looking <u>frightfully</u> well
  Stephen?"

SIEGFRIED doesn't respond.

    STEPHEN TENNANT (CONT'D)
  Am I going to get the silent
  treatment or are we going to
  conduct the rest of this
  conversation entirely in braille?

    SIEGFRIED SASSOON
  Beware the wrath of a patient man.

    STEPHEN TENNANT
  Who said that?

    SIEGFRIED SASSOON
  Confucius, I think - on one of his
  better days.

                    STEPHEN TENNANT
          Well, if you're going to go all
          profound on me perhaps you could
          throw in "Old Man River" as a
          bonus.

Silence.

                    SIEGFRIED SASSOON
          How was Bavaria?

                    STEPHEN TENNANT
          Bavarian.

                    SIEGFRIED SASSOON
          Did your companions stay long?

                    STEPHEN TENNANT
          Long enough.

                    SIEGFRIED SASSOON
          What did you do - apart from cough?

                    STEPHEN TENNANT
          I... oh, what's the phrase... "I
          lived life to the full".

                    SIEGFRIED SASSOON
          All three of you?

                    STEPHEN TENNANT
          Yes... it's called triolism I
          believe.

                    SIEGFRIED SASSOON
          Or an orgy.

                    STEPHEN TENNANT
          Yes that's probably more accurate.
          But I won't go into details... you
          know how discreet I am in these
          matters.

Silence.

                    STEPHEN TENNANT (CONT'D)
          My spies tell me that you've been
          seeing a lot of Hester Gatty.

                    SIEGFRIED SASSOON
          And Hester Gatty has been seeing a
          lot of me.

> STEPHEN TENNANT
> I'm beginning to see the light - a new secretive you.

> SIEGFRIED SASSOON
> Surely you're not jealous?

> STEPHEN TENNANT
> Of course not. Now we can be all girls together - like Roedean.

Silence.

> STEPHEN TENNANT (CONT'D)
> Have you slept with her?

> SIEGFRIED SASSOON
> No. Our relationship is as deep as it is decorous. I've even bought myself some passion-killing pyjamas.

> STEPHEN TENNANT
> Are you going to marry her?

> SIEGFRIED SASSOON
> Yes. I think I probably shall.

> STEPHEN TENNANT
> You'll make a vile partner, Siggy.

> SIEGFRIED SASSOON
> Perhaps - but then I have been taught by a master.

Silence.

> STEPHEN TENNANT
> You'll be taking a great risk.

> SIEGFRIED SASSOON
> I'm taking the same risk I took with you... it can't be much worse, it may even be better.

> STEPHEN TENNANT
> I can see years ahead for both of you filled with passionless silences and compulsory cocoa at bedtime.

Silence.

SIEGFRIED SASSOON
Oh, by the way – as we intend to be living in the country I'm giving up the lease on this flat. I didn't want to keep you in the dark unnecessarily – so once we've found a house you'll have to move out.

STEPHEN TENNANT
That sounds almost like a threat.

SIEGFRIED SASSOON
It almost is.

STEPHEN TENNANT
So you're going to throw baby's little body out into the cold, cold snow.

SIEGFRIED SASSOON
Not immediately. We'll wait for warmer weather.

DISSOLVE TO:

88 INT. DAY. CHRISTCHURCH PRIORY. (1933) 88

A small subdued wedding party consisting of SIEGFRIED SASSOON, GLEN BYAM SHAW, ROBERT GRAVES, GEOFFREY KEYNES, REX WHISTLER, EDITH OLIVER and T.E. LAWRENCE.

SIEGFRIED SASSOON
(Very happy)
I have given you all a surprise haven't I?

ROBERT GRAVES
Remember – marry in haste, repent at leisure.

SIEGFRIED SASSOON
I was shocked when you got married and for exactly the same reason.

ROBERT GRAVES
Now it's my turn to be shocked.

REX WHISTLER
Who's officiating?

SIEGFRIED SASSOON
Canon Gay.

> REX WHISTLER
> Ask a silly question.

> SIEGFRIED SASSOON
> Lawrence, this is Glen Byam Shaw...
> Glen this is T.E. Lawrence.

> GLEN BYAM SHAW
> Of Arabia?

> T.E. LAWRENCE
> Not recently.

> EDITH OLIVER
> (Quietly to Siegfried
> Sassoon)
> Don't betray her Siegfried, she
> doesn't deserve that.

> GEOFFREY KEYNES
> (To Siegfried Sassoon)
> Are you sure you know what you're
> doing?

> SIEGFRIED SASSOON
> I think so.

> ROBERT GRAVES
> In the end, "We few, we happy few"
> are always exogamus.

> T.E. LAWRENCE
> Christ, what does that mean?

> ROBERT GRAVES
> To marry outside of one's tribe or
> group...

> T.E. LAWRENCE
> Do you specialise in using words
> that no one understands?

> ROBERT GRAVES
> Yes. It's my revenge on people who
> don't know what exogamus means.

An uneasy silence.

> ROBERT GRAVES (CONT'D)
> Have you chosen any music?

> SIEGFRIED SASSOON
> No.

>   ROBERT GRAVES
>   Oh, I'm disappointed. I thought
>   we'd get something English and
>   dismal.

At the last minute STEPHEN TENNANT joins them.

>   SIEGFRIED SASSOON
>   What are you doing here?

>   STEPHEN TENNANT
>   Hester invited me. I'm her Maid-of-
>   Honour.

                                                    CUT TO:

89   INT. DAY. CHRISTCHURCH PRIORY. (1933)   89

TWO SHOT HESTER GATTY & SIEGFRIED SASSOON exchanging vows in front of the VICAR at the altar.

>   SIEGFRIED SASSOON
>   I will.

>   HESTER GATTY
>   I will.

CUT TO EXT. CHURCH where they pose for the wedding photograph.

They are looking straight at us.

HOLD

THEN

FREEZE FRAME

THEN MORPH from wedding photograph to INT. DAY/EVENING. HOUSE (1936)

TRACK BACK from the wedding photograph on a side cupboard.

WE CONTINUE TO TRACK AND PAN R TO L TO A TWO SHOT.

HESTER in bed.

SIEGFRIED SASSOON sitting on the end of the bed.

HESTER lying in bed after the birth of their child.

She looks exhausted and very weak.

Silence

>   SIEGFRIED SASSOON
> How are you?

>   HESTER SASSOON
> Just <u>very</u> tired.

>   SIEGFRIED SASSOON
> Is there anything I can get you?

HESTER just shakes her head.

Silence

>   HESTER SASSOON
> Have you thought of a name?

SIEGFRIED SASSOON just shakes his head.

> I thought we might call him
> "George".

>   SIEGFRIED SASSOON
>   (A rueful smile)
> Yes.
>   (pause)
> My whole future depends on him.

>   HESTER SASSOON
> You once said that about me.

Silence

> Would you like to hold him?

>   SIEGFRIED SASSOON
> No.

DISSOLVE TO:

90   INT. DAY. HOTEL RECEPTION ROOM. (1936)   90

A christening party. A small gathering – same guests as in the wedding.

>   SIEGFRIED SASSOON
>   (Holding his baby son)
> I'm very happy!
>   (MORE)

BENEDICTION

Blue Revisions 11/08/2020

                    SIEGFRIED SASSOON (CONT'D)
                (Showing his son to
                everyone)
            And this is the reason!

Smiles and applause. A nurse takes the baby.

Soundtrack:

Someone has put a record on. It is "Tea for two" (1925).

Couples come into the middle of the floor and dance. *

The rhythm is slow.

SIEGFRIED & HESTER come together and dance. *

TRACK IN on SIEGFRIED & HESTER dancing. *

TRACK STOPS when we are immediately behind them. As they *
dance their reflection stays in the mirror on the wall but *
becomes large enough to fill the entire screen. *

Their reflection is sharp but all the other dancers are *
blurred. *

HOLD. *

Then as SIEGFRIED looks directly into the mirror TRACK IN on *
HESTER & SIEGFRIED (and so they do not have to part) ZOOM *
past them. *

Then we see: *

1. SIEGFRIED dancing with ROBBIE ROSS. *

TRACK into & ZOOM past them. *

Then. *

DISSOLVE TO *

2. SIEGFRIED dancing with WILFRED OWEN. *

TRACK into & ZOOM past them. *

Then. *

DISSOLVE TO *

3. SIEGFRIED dancing with IVOR NOVELLO. *

TRACK into & ZOOM past them. *

Then. *

Blue Revisions 11/08/2020   109A.

DISSOLVE TO

4. SIEGFRIED dancing with STEPHEN TENNANT.

TRACK into & ZOOM past them.

Then.

DISSOLVE TO

5. OLDER SIEGFRIED dancing with OLDER HESTER.

TRACK STOPS on them.

They stop dancing.

SIEGFRIED looks away from her and HESTER looks directly at us.

                                                                        DISSOLVE TO:

91   INT. DAY. SIEGFRIED SASSOON'S HOUSE. (1951/52)   91

C/U of the door.

HESTER SASSOON opens the front door.

                    STEPHEN TENNANT
                  (now older and looking
                   very seedy)
              Am I welcome?

                    HESTER SASSOON
              Come in and see.

STEPHEN TENNANT comes in.

                                                    CUT TO:

92   INT. DAY. SIEGFRIED SASSOON'S HOUSE. (1951/52)   92

LIVING ROOM, HESTER SASSOON & STEPHEN TENNANT sit down.
SIEGFRIED SASSOON already sitting.

A hostile atmosphere.

Silence.

                    STEPHEN TENNANT
              Siegfried.

                    SIEGFRIED SASSOON
              Stephen.

Silence.

                    STEPHEN TENNANT
              How dreadful we all look.

Silence.
              But I still have beautiful hands I
              think.

Silence.

                    HESTER SASSOON
              I'll make some tea.

She goes out.

Silence.

                    STEPHEN TENNANT
              I suppose you've heard of Ivor's
              death.

                    SIEGFRIED SASSOON
              Yes. They say that the funeral
              attracted a thousand people.

                    STEPHEN TENNANT
          Probably made up mostly by all the
          people he slept with.

Silence.

          I still have a soft spot for Ivor's
          work though - all those tortured
          princesses and lovers who have no
          money but plenty of sex appeal.

                    SIEGFRIED SASSOON
          His work was always sentimental
          nonsense. He cheapened everything
          he touched.

                    STEPHEN TENNANT
          I've always thought that his
          particular brand of mawkishness was
          a kind of catharsis for the dimmer
          members among us.

                    SIEGFRIED SASSOON
          That's because you've never known
          the difference between the two.

                    STEPHEN TENNANT
          We can't all possess your purity of
          thought.

                    SIEGFRIED SASSOON
          It isn't a question of purity but
          of discernment - and you were never
          very good at discernment.

                    STEPHEN TENNANT
               (A little taken aback)
          That was rather _too_ acerbic.

                    SIEGFRIED SASSOON
          Mordant would be the more accurate
          word.

Silence.

                    STEPHEN TENNANT
          Are you still _very_ angry?

                    SIEGFRIED SASSOON
          What do you expect? You ended our
          relationship with a letter from
          your _doctor_! How was I supposed to
          feel?

>STEPHEN TENNANT
>And still clearly very hurt. I had hoped that you might have been a little more forgiving.

>SIEGFRIED SASSOON
>If I had treated you the way in which you treated me - how forgiving would you be? Besides, when the parade's gone by you have to have enough sense to realise that you are no longer part of it.

>STEPHEN TENNANT
>I'm trying to apologise.

>SIEGFRIED SASSOON
>You're thirty years too late.

Silence.

>STEPHEN TENNANT
>Can't we still be friends?

>SIEGFRIED SASSOON
>No. You once meant so much and now you mean so little...

STEPHEN TENNANT goes to speak.

>SIEGFRIED SASSOON (CONT'D)
>... and don't trivialise it by saying something glib.

>STEPHEN TENNANT
>May I see you again? In London perhaps?

>SIEGFRIED SASSOON
>No. I rarely go to London now.

Silence.

HESTER comes in with the tea, sits down and pours. She hands them their tea.

They all sit in silence and drink.

A very awkward silence.

>STEPHEN TENNANT
>And how is George?

                    HESTER SASSOON
               Young... thriving...

                    SIEGFRIED SASSOON
               He's like all children. He has the
               worst aspects of both his parents.

                    STEPHEN TENNANT
               How about his parents' virtues?

                    SIEGFRIED SASSOON
               He's cursed with those as well.

Silence.

                    STEPHEN TENNANT
                  (for the first time a
                   genuine emotion)
               I'm very lonely Siggy.

                    SIEGFRIED SASSOON
               Is it agony? One does hope so.

                    HESTER SASSOON
               George has an independent mind
               which sometimes shocks Siegfried.

                    SIEGFRIED SASSOON
               It isn't independence - it's
               wilfulness.

George comes in smoking a pipe and sensing the atmosphere sits down.

                    GEORGE SASSOON
               Who's died?

                    SIEGFRIED SASSOON
               All of us. And George, the pipe was
               not a good idea - it looks as if
               it's smoking you.

                    GEORGE SASSOON
                  (Smiling)
               Old silver tongue!

                    SIEGFRIED SASSOON
               And we can do without the smirk.

                    HESTER SASSOON
                  (To George)
               Tea?

GEORGE just shakes his head.

Silence.

> **STEPHEN TENNANT**
> Thank you for the tea.

> **SIEGFRIED SASSOON**
> George will see you out.

GEORGE & STEPHEN TENNANT leave.

> **STEPHEN TENNANT**
> Goodbye.

> **HESTER SASSOON**
> Goodbye.

Silence.

> **SIEGFRIED SASSOON**
> As charming as ever but there was still malice at the edge of his voice... as there always was.

> **HESTER SASSOON**
> Sometimes Siegfried it's more humane to be kind than to be honest.

> **SIEGFRIED SASSOON**
> He constantly goaded my jealousy. It was like being killed by degrees.

Silence.

> **HESTER SASSOON**
> He once told me he thought you were matchless.

> **SIEGFRIED SASSOON**
> We are unique only to the people who really loathe us.

DISSOLVE TO:

93   INT. DAY. HOUSE. (1950/60)   93

C/U of older HESTER.

C/U of SIEGFRIED. He turns on the radio.

SOUNDTRACK:

"The Third Programme" on the radio.

                    HESTER SASSOON
                 (to SIEGFRIED)
            Is there anything I can get you
            before I leave?

                    SIEGFRIED SASSOON
            No.

Just the sound of the radio.

                    HESTER SASSOON
            I'll write once I've got to
            Scotland.

SIEGFRIED SASSOON doesn't answer.

            I said...

                    SIEGFRIED SASSOON
            I heard you! I am trying to listen
            to the radio.

HESTER just stands there.

Silence

                    HESTER SASSOON
            Shall I phone?

                    SIEGFRIED SASSOON
            NO!

SOUNDTRACK:

A car hooting from outside then GEORGE comes in.

                    GEORGE SASSOON
            What time is your train mother?

                    HESTER SASSOON
            Not for another hour - we've plenty
            of time to get to the station.

                    GEORGE SASSOON
                 (to SIEGFRIED)
            I'll come back for you later.

They leave.

                                        DISSOLVE TO:

94 INT. DAY. SIEGFRIED SASSOON'S HOUSE. (1960)   94

WINDOWS. Outside pouring with rain.

HOLD.

SIEGFRIED SASSOON reflected in one of the window panes.

SOUNDTRACK:

                   SIEGFRIED SASSOON YOUNGER V/O
        I stood with the dead...

The poem "INVOCATION" runs over the next five shots.

                 SIEGFRIED SASSOON YOUNGER V/O (CONT'D)
    "Come down from Heaven to meet me when my breath
    Chokes, and through drumming shafts of stifling death
    I stumble towards escape, to find the door
    Opening on morn where I may breath once more
    Clear cock-crow airs across some valley dim
    With whispering trees. While dawn along the rim
    Of night's horizon flows in lakes of fire,
    Come down from Heaven's bright hill, my songs desire

    Belov'd and faithful, teach my soul to wake
    In glades deep-ranked with flowers that gleam and shake
    And flock your paths with wonder. In your gaze
    Show me the vanquished vigil of my days.
    Mute in that golden silence hung with green,
    Come down from Heaven and bring me in your eyes
    Remembrance of all beauty that has been,
    And stillness from the pools of Paradise."

A series of shots with DISSOLVES between them.

SHOT 1: Mother smiling at Victoria Station.

SHOT 2:   ROBBIE ROSS sitting in a chair and smiling.

SHOT 3:   IVOR NOVELLO smoking and then smiling.

SHOT 4:   Dr. Rivers at his desk smiling.

SHOT 5:   WILFRED OWEN at the door of SIEGFRIED SASSOON'S room at Craiglockhart. He smiles.

>   SIEGFRIED SASSOON YOUNGER V/O (CONT'D)
> Rising, rising the voices of the
> muffled dead.

HOLD on the window, heavy rain.

>   DISSOLVE TO:

95   INT. DAY. GEORGE'S HOUSE. (1960)   95

Windows. Glorious sunshine.

TRACK BACK from windows to a TWO SHOT of GEORGE (frame left) and older SIEGFRIED SASSOON (frame right) sitting at the lunch table opposite one another. The remains of a lunch.

An angry silence.

>   GEORGE SASSOON
> Are you going to keep this silence
> up for the rest of the day?

Silence

>   GEORGE SASSOON (CONT'D)
>   (becoming angrier)
> I brought you down to London
> because I was worried about you.

>   SIEGFRIED SASSOON
>   (angry)
> I'm fine!

>   GEORGE SASSOON
>   (angry)
> No you're not! There was no food in
> the house, no heating and you were
> sitting in the dark like a
> protestant bishop!

>   SIEGFRIED SASSOON
> I can manage!

                    GEORGE SASSOON
                No you can't!

An even more intense silence.

                    GEORGE SASSOON (CONT'D)
                If you're going to sulk I'm going
                upstairs.

SIEGFRIED SASSOON gives no response.

GEORGE gets up and goes upstairs.

HOLD ON SIEGFRIED SASSOON.

Silence. Then he hears GEORGE playing pop music very loudly (Helen Shapiro singing, "Walking back to happiness" (1961)).

SIEGFRIED SASSOON in a fury goes to the bottom of the stairs.

                    SIEGFRIED SASSOON
                  (shouting)
                Turn that rubbish off!

                    GEORGE SASSOON V/O
                  (shouting)
                I'll do as I like! It's my house,
                it's my music!

                    SIEGFRIED SASSOON
                It isn't music! It's commercially
                grotesque noise made by stupid
                people for stupid people!

                    GEORGE SASSOON V/O
                Oh don't be so bigoted!

SIEGFRIED SASSOON storms from the house.

                                                    CUT TO:

96   EXT. DAY. GEORGE'S HOUSE. (1960)   96

SIEGFRIED SASSOON sitting in the garden.

SIEGFRIED SASSOON in chair left of screen.

THEN

To camera right we see (whilst holding onto SIEGFRIED SASSOON all the time).

WW1 FOOTAGE:

1) Shot of cavalry on a ridge, and tattered netting.

2) Soldiers against the light.

3) Troops by a river.

4) Inside Westminster Abbey, the burial of the Unknown Soldier

SOUNDTRACK: (The statistics of the numbers of soldiers killed)

          SIEGFRIED SASSOON V/O
    These are the statistics of catastrophe... yet from Prime to Compline life goes slowly on.

The visions fade and SIEGFRIED SASSOON just sits there.

GEORGE comes out and goes to SIEGFRIED SASSOON.

          GEORGE SASSOON
    Are you thinking great thoughts?

          SIEGFRIED SASSOON
    No. I'm just sitting here being petty and trying to understand the enigma of other people.

Long silence.

          SIEGFRIED SASSOON (CONT'D)
    So many have died...too many...

          GEORGE SASSOON
    Most people live for the moment – you live for eternity.

          SIEGFRIED SASSOON
    Oh don't say that!

          GEORGE SASSOON
    Why not?

          SIEGFRIED SASSOON
    Because I'm afraid I might believe it.

Silence

    I would have liked to have been recognised though – in some significant way – for my work.

Silence

BENEDICTION

>   Eliot got the Order of Merit <u>and</u>
>   the Nobel Prize - I've had to make
>   do with the Queen's Award for
>   Poetry.
>
> Silence
>
>   But Sir Siegfried Sassoon would
>   have been nice - despite all the
>   sibilants.
>
>   GEORGE SASSOON
>   Oh father, how can you be seduced
>   by all that Ruritanian nonsense?
>   The greatest argument against
>   Damehoods and Knighthoods is - just
>   look at the people who've got them.
>
> Pause
>
>   (With tact)
>   Why do you hate the modern world
>   father?
>
>   SIEGFRIED SASSOON
>   (Without rancour)
>   Because it's younger than I am.
>
>   GEORGE SASSOON
>   Well you've got to bathe and
>   change...we're going to the theatre
>   remember.
>
>   SIEGFRIED SASSOON
>   Do I have too?
>
>   GEORGE SASSOON
>   Yes. You promised. Besides it's a
>   witty and elegant score...even you
>   might enjoy it.
>
> Silence
>
>   GEORGE SASSOON (CONT'D)
>   I'm sorry I shouted.
>
>   SIEGFRIED SASSOON
>   So am I.
>
>   GEORGE SASSOON
>   Peace?
>
>   SIEGFRIED SASSOON
>   Peace.

They shake hands.

                                                    CUT TO:

97   EXT. EARLY EVENING. THEATRE. (1960)   97

      WIDE SHOT OF THE FRONT OF THE THEATRE. "STOP THE WORLD - I
      WANT TO GET OFF" on the marquee.

      SOUNDTRACK Applause and laughter then the musical
      introduction to "Typically English" sung by a woman.

      TRACK IN ON THEATRE.

      SOUNDTRACK: Song starts.

                "My mother said I never should
                 Play with the young men in the
                 wood"

                                                    DISSOLVE TO:

98   INT. NIGHT. THEATRE. (1960)   98

      TWO SHOT OF SIEGFRIED SASSOON AND GEORGE WATCHING THE SHOW.

      Song continues:

                "If I did she would say
                 Naughty little girl to disobey"

      SIEGFRIED SASSOON AND GEORGE SMILE ENJOYING IT.

                                                    CUT TO:

      THE STAGE.

      SHOT OF GIRL SINGING. She moves across the stage bathed in
      the softest pastel coloured spots.

      SOUNDTRACK: "Typically English" continues:

                "I'm a typically English rosebud
                 Born of typically English stock
                 With a typically Anglo-Saxon family
                 tree.

> I received my education in a
> typically English way
> At a typically English girls
> academy.
>
> I play typically English tennis
> At a typically English club.
> With my typically English feelings
> for fair play.
>
> I eat typically English crumpets
> With my typically English tea
> At the end of every typically
> English day."

                                                    CUT TO:

SIEGFRIED SASSOON AND GEORGE.

SOUNDTRACK: song continues:

> "Father is a typically English
> Colonel
> Living in a typical county town.
> Mum and I play typically English
> Patience
> While the typically English rain is
> pouring down."

                                                    CUT TO:

Singer on stage.

SOUNDTRACK: song continues:

> "We've a typically English spaniel
> Who likes typically English walks
> Past those typically English trees
> upon the heath.
>
> And if anyone should ask me how I
> like this typically English life.
> I am fed up to my typically English
> teeth.

"I've a typically English suitor
In a typically English suit
Calls to take me out to typically English tea.
There's a typically English table
Set for typically English two
But my typically English mother makes it three."

CUT TO:

SIEGFRIED SASSOON AND GEORGE.

SOUNDTRACK: song continues:

"When I go to typically English dances
Mother gives me typically sound advice
How to cope with typically coarse advances
But I'm bound to confess I find them rather nice.
Stay there."

CUT TO:

SHOT OF THE STAGE

SOUNDTRACK: song continues:

"In a typically English summer
We take typically English hols.
At a typically English place with Auntie Maude."

DISSOLVE TO:

99   EXT. NIGHT. THEATRE. (1960)   99

Audience streams out.

SOUNDTRACK: song continues:
"And if anyone should ask me
How I like this typically English life
I have never been so typically English bored."

Song ends.

Lots of applause.

The crowd thins out until only SIEGFRIED SASSOON AND GEORGE are alone in the front of the theatre.

The lights from the theatre are switched off.

> GEORGE SASSOON
> Shall we take a cab?

> SIEGFRIED SASSOON
> No. I'll walk home - it's such a lovely evening.

> GEORGE SASSOON
> Will you be alright?

> SIEGFRIED SASSOON
> Of course.

They part. GEORGE EXITS FRAME LEFT. SIEGFRIED SASSOON FRAME RIGHT.

DISSOLVE TO:

100   EXT. NIGHT. PARK. (1960)   100

It is night in the park and the lamps are lit.

PAN AND TRACK R TO L TO SIDE VIEW OF SIEGFRIED SASSOON. TRACK CONTINUES FOR A MOMENT THEN TRACK L TO R TO A FRONT VIEW OF HIM. TRACK CONTINUES FOR A TIME THEN AS WE TRACK BACK WITH HIM HE MORPHS INTO HIS YOUNGER SELF. HE IS WEARING HIS ARMY UNIFORM AND GREATCOAT.

THE YEAR IS 1918 AS ARE ALL THE SUBSEQUENT SCENES TO THE END OF THE FILM.

HE SITS DOWN ON A BENCH AND TRACK STOPS.

HOLD

Light reverts to twilight.

CUT TO:

SIEGFRIED SASSOON'S POV. (1918) TWILIGHT

Young lads playing football in the early dark.

Watching them is a young disabled man in a wheelchair.

He has had both legs amputated.

SOUNDTRACK:

              SIEGFRIED SASSOON V/O
        (reading Wilfred Owen's
        poem "Disabled")

"He sat in a wheeled chair, waiting for dark,
And shivered in his ghastly suit of grey,
Legless, sewn short at elbow.
Through the park
Voices of boys rang saddening like a hymn,
Voices of play and pleasure after day,
Till gathering sleep had mothered them from him.

                                      CUT TO:

Some young girls walking through the park laughing and talking.

              SIEGFRIED SASSOON V/O
"About this time Town used to swing so gay
When glow-lamps budded in the light-blue trees,
And girls glanced lovelier as the air grew dim, –
In the old times, before he threw away his knees.
Now he will never feel again how slim
Girls waists are, or how warm their subtle hands,
All of them touch him like some queer disease.

                                      CUT TO:

SHOT OF SIEGFRIED SASSOON.

              SIEGFRIED SASSOON V/O
"There was an artist silly for his face,
For it was younger than his youth, last year.
Now, he is old; his back will never brace;
He's lost his colour very far from here,
                (MORE)

                    SIEGFRIED SASSOON V/O (CONT'D)
            Poured it down shell-holes 'til the
            veins ran dry,
            And half his lifetime lapsed in the
            hot race
            And leap of purple spurted from his
            thigh.

                                            CUT TO:

Young men wearing tight white shorts playing football.

                    SIEGFRIED SASSOON V/O
            "One time he liked a blood-smear
            down his leg,
            After the matches carried shoulder-
            high.
            It was after football, when he'd
            drunk a peg,
            He thought he'd better join. He
            wonders why.
            Someone had said he'd look a god in
            kilts.
            That's why; and maybe, too, to
            please his Meg,
            Aye, that was it, to please the
            giddy jilts,
            He'd asked to join. He didn't have
            to beg;
            Smiling they wrote his lie: aged 19
            years.
            Germans he scarcely thought of, all
            their guilt,
            And Austria's, did not move him.
            And no fears
            Of Fear came yet. He thought of
            jeweled hilts
            For daggers in plaid socks; of
            smart salutes;
            And care of arms; and leave; and
            pay arrears;
            Esprit de corps; and hints for
            young recruits.
            And soon, he was drafted out with
            drums and cheers.

                                            CUT TO:

SHOT of amputee still watching the football.

                    SIEGFRIED SASSOON V/O
            "Some cheered him home, but not as
            crowds cheer Goal.
            Only a solemn man who brought him
            fruits
                        (MORE)

                SIEGFRIED SASSOON V/O (CONT'D)
            Thanked him; and then inquired
            about his soul.

            Now, he will spend a few sick years
            in Institutes,
            And do what things the rules
            consider wise,
            And take whatever pity they may
            dole.
            Tonight he noticed how the women's
            eyes
            Passed from him to the strong men
            who are whole.

                                            CUT TO:

SHOT OF SIEGFRIED SASSOON SITTING ON THE BENCH. (1918)

                SIEGFRIED SASSOON V/O
            How cold and late it is! Why don't
            they come
            And put him into bed? Why don't
            they come?

SIEGFRIED SASSOON on the bench. Now he starts to cry, sobs for all the suffering and pain. He sobs and sobs and cannot stop sobbing.

SOUNDTRACK:

We hear the beginning of "The Fantasia on a theme by Thomas Tallis" by Ralph Vaughen Williams. This runs under everything that follows including the closing credits.

                                            DISSOLVE TO:

TRACK IN AND OVER the machine gun memorial opposite Apsley House.

                                            DISSOLVE TO:

TRACK IN AND UP on the names on the Menin Gate.

                                            DISSOLVE TO:

TRACK IN AND OVER a sea of endless crosses in the war graves.

END CREDITS.